Range of Philosophy

The Range of Philosophy

Introductory Readings Third Edition

HAROLD H. TITUS
Denison University

MAYLON H. HEPP
Denison University

MARILYN S. SMITH
Quinnipiac College

D. VAN NOSTRAND COMPANY
New York Cincinnati Toronto London Melbourne

D. Van Nostrand Company Regional Offices:
New York Cincinnati

D. Van Nostrand Company International Offices:
London Toronto Melbourne

Library of Congress Catalog Card Number: 74-17625
ISBN: 0-442-25821-6

Published by Van Nostrand Reinhold Company
135 West 50th Street, New York, N.Y. 10020

10 9 8 7 6

Preface

The Third Edition of *The Range of Philosophy: Introductory Readings* has been extensively revised from the earlier editions. Departing from a rigid arrangement of parts and chapters, the book begins with a series of topics that concentrate on subjects of lasting concern and importance to philosophy and then moves on to more inclusive questions that deal with current philosophical outlooks and a comprehensive vision of life and the world. The selections under each topic number from two to seven. The topics may be taken up in any order that the instructor considers appropriate.

We envision two principal uses for the book: as supplementary readings in conjunction with an expository text or as a basic source book to be used with other original writings by selected philosophers.

Over thirty new selections have been included in the Third Edition. The introductory paragraphs to each selection have been expanded to give the student a fuller background to the author and selection. While many selections, especially those from the classical philosophers, have been retained, some of them appear in different form.

The editors have wished to emphasize both the broad scope and the immediacy of philosophic thinking. To convey range and relevance has been a primary objective. We have tried to select material that is clear and readable and stated in language that is not too technical. Our aim has been to introduce the student to the living issues in philosophy and to deal with questions that have a close relation to life and are, therefore, of general human interest.

We have included selections from the philosophical "greats" of the past —Plato, Aristotle, Descartes, Berkeley, Hume, Kant, and Mill—as well as from more recent representatives of the main philosophical outlooks. Selections are included from such movements as philosophical analysis and existentialism. On the whole, emphasis is on present-day thinkers and issues. Multiple selections under a given topic present contrasting views on controversial issues.

The extent of our editing varies with the nature of the material; throughout we have tried to keep the interests and needs of the student in mind. When selections were cut or points omitted, an effort was made to preserve the main argument or point of view and to eliminate less relevant or repetitious material or points not essential or appropriate in an introductory book of readings. Adaptability for classroom use was also a factor.

Harold H. Titus
Maylon H. Hepp
Marilyn S. Smith

Contents

THE MIND OF MAN

THE ISSUE OF FREEDOM

THE SEARCH FOR VALUES

ETHICAL THEORIES

LIBERTY, LAW, AND CIVIL DISOBEDIENCE

AESTHETICS AND ART

WHAT IS HISTORY?

THE AIMS OF EDUCATION

THE WAYS OF KNOWING

THE STRUCTURE OF SCIENCE

THE RELIGIOUS TRADITIONS OF THE WEST

IS A COMPREHENSIVE VISION POSSIBLE?

What Is Philosophy?

MORTIMER J. ADLER

*Philosophy Is Everybody's Business**

Mortimer J. Adler (b. 1902) has taught at Columbia University (1923–1929) and at the University of Chicago (1930–1942). More recently he has been Director of the Institute for Philosophical Research; a member of the Board of Editors of the *Encyclopedia Britannica;* editor of the twenty-volume set, *The Annals of America;* and editor of *The Great Ideas, A Synopticon of the Great Books of the Western World.* He is author of more than a dozen books, including *What Man Has Made of Man, How to Read a Book, A Dialectic of Morals, The Difference of Man and the Difference It Makes,* and *The Time of Our Lives: The Ethics of Common Sense.*

In the selection that follows, Adler tells how he came to select philosophy as a life career and why he believes it is the business of every man and should be a part of everyone's liberal education. He is critical of much academic philosophy, for it has lost touch with the thinking and questioning of the ordinary man. Note his distinction between "first-order" and "second-order" questions of knowledge, and his contention that philosophy must be constructive or synthetic.

When I was a very young man, barely fifteen, the first philosophical book that I read was *Pragmatism,* based on the lectures William James delivered to popular audiences at the Lowell Institute in Boston in 1906 and at Columbia University in New York in 1907. The opening pages of that book made a lasting impression on me; they did more than that, I should add, for together with my reading of a dialogue by Plato at about the same time, they determined my choice of a career. That, however, is not my reason for referring to them here; it is rather that they eloquently state the striking fact that philosophy is the business of every man, as other intellectual callings are not—at least not in a comparable sense.

*Excerpted from *The Conditions of Philosophy* by Mortimer J. Adler. Copyright © 1965 by Mortimer J. Adler. Reprinted by permission of Atheneum Publishers.

William James begins by quoting from an essay by Chesterton, who had written: "There are some people—and I am one of them—who think that the most practical and important thing about a man is still his view of the universe. We think that for a landlady considering a lodger it is important to know his income, but still more important to know his philosophy. We think that for a general about to fight an enemy it is important to know the enemy's numbers, but still more important to know the enemy's philosophy." Saying that he agreed with Mr. Chesterton in this matter, James then addressed his lecture audience as follows:

> I know that you, ladies and gentlemen, have a philosophy, each and all of you, and that the most interesting and important thing about you is the way in which it determines the perspective in your several worlds. You know the same of me. And yet I confess to a certain tremor at the audacity of the enterprise which I am about to begin. For the philosophy which is so important in each of us is not a technical matter; it is our more or less dumb sense of what life honestly and deeply means. It is only partly got from books; it is our individual way of just seeing and feeling the total push and pressure of the cosmos. I have no right to assume that many of you are students of the cosmos in the classroom sense, yet here I stand desirous of interesting you in a philosophy which to no small extent has to be technically treated. I wish to fill you with sympathy with a contemporaneous tendency in which I profoundly believe, and yet I have to talk like a professor to you who are not students....
>
> Philosophy is at once the most sublime and the most trivial of human pursuits. It works in the minutest crannies and it opens out the widest vistas. It "bakes no bread," as has been said, but it can inspire our souls with courage; and repugnant as its manners, its doubting and challenging, its quibbling and dialectics, often are to common people, no one of us can get along without the far-flashing beams of light it sends over the world's perspectives. These illuminations at least, and the contrast-effects of darkness and mystery that accompany them, give to what it says an interest that is much more than professional.

But for one point that needs elucidation, I would gladly let the foregoing statement stand without comment, passing it on to the nonprofessional philosophers who have read thus far as their motivation for reading further. The point which I think needs comment is the distinction, adverted to by William James, between the philosophizing done by the man in the street and the philosophizing that is done in classrooms or in books by men who regard themselves and are regarded as engaged in a special professional task for which they have a special technical competence. Since it is my feeling, as it was William James's when he introduced his lectures on pragmatism, that what follows should be of concern to the layman as well as to the professional, I think it may be useful to say how I see the interests of the one in relation to the interests of the other.

There is a continuum, as I see it, between the novice in any sport and the champion player of the game. They are both engaged in playing tennis, golf, or baseball, though the one does it with little and the other with consummate skill. The vast difference in degree of competence which separates them does not prevent us from acknowledging that both are playing the same game. On the contrary, precisely because it is the same game, we also recognize that the inexpert at it can learn from the more expert, acquiring through imitation and practice higher degrees of skill and satisfaction. The same holds true of every art. The child who begins to draw pictures or the man who begins to paint stands at one end of a continuum which has Leonardo or Michelangelo at the other....

Thus it is with the philosophizing done by the layman and the professional. Both are engaged in the same intellectual activity. The difference between Socrates and the ordinary man, each thinking about the nature of things, the choices that life presents, and the values which bear on them, is one of degree, not of kind, as is the difference between the champion at a particular sport and the tyro, or the difference between Leonardo or Escoffier in their particular arts and the novice. But there is one very important distinction to be made between these others and Socrates (here taken as the symbol of a high degree of skill in philosophical inquiry).

To realize their humanity, all men need not—and, in fact, they do not—engage in every particular sport, nor try to acquire skill in every art, just as they need not try to acquire the techniques of law, medicine, or engineering, or the technical knowledge of a physicist or a biologist. Hence, while Leonardo may represent the acme for those who want to draw or paint, and Escoffier for those who want to cook, they do not represent a competence or expertness which all men should try to approach to whatever degree their native capacities make possible. Not so Socrates: as the symbol of consummate skill in philosophizing, he does represent an ideal which every man should try to approximate in the highest degree possible; precisely because philosophizing, as William James declared, is everybody's business, or because, as Socrates before him said, "the unexamined life is not worth living" (and, might one add, the unexamined world and the unquestioned society or culture are not worth living in).

It may, nevertheless, be the case that most men, as regards philosophizing, are like children in kindergarten drawing their first pictures rather than like those who take up tennis or golf with the serious intention of learning how to play the game as well as possible. The latter are inclined to read books about the game, take coaching lessons, go to exhibition matches, and study, as well as admire, the technique of the champions at their particular game. The champion for them is the master from whom they can learn—not directly, of course, but through intermediary lesser lights. They usually know his name and regard themselves as starting at the bottom of a ladder to the top of which he has risen. This is not true of kindergarten children beginning to draw; they are not conscious that they are engaged in the practice of an art which has superior practitioners or, for that matter, that they have anything to learn. They draw almost in the same way that their elders doodle—without premeditation, plan, or purpose. In the same sense in which it can be said that they draw without knowing that they are doing it or what is involved in doing it, so it can be said that most men philosophize.

Since philosophizing is everybody's business, as drawing is not, this common defect should be remedied by schooling. Everyone should receive training in philosophy in the course of his education. Everyone should be made conscious of the fact that he, if he is going to be fully human, cannot avoid thinking about certain types of problems; he should come to understand the special character of these problems, which have traditionally been called "philosophical"; he should recognize that he is a novice at thinking about them and that other men have displayed great skill or expertness in doing so; he should try to improve his own skill within the limits of his capacity, getting what help he can from books or teachers more proximate to his station than the very great; yet he should be inspired by those sources of his tutelage to study and to imitate the masters; in short, he should see himself at the bottom of a ladder which has Socrates at the top.

To say that some training in philosophy and some study of philosophy should be an essential part of everyone's liberal education can be defended only if what I am now going to call academic or technical philosophy—the philosophy that is taught and studied in courses or read in books which bear the official label—has a certain character. The essential requirement here is that it should be, both in its problems and in its techniques, continuous with the philosophizing of the man in the street or the child, as was and is the philosophizing of Socrates (and a relatively small number of others). With few exceptions, academic philosophy, as it is now taught and studied or written in books, does not meet this requirement. Since the seventeenth century, it has progressively lost the character it should have in order to justify its playing an essential part in everyone's liberal education. It has more and more lost touch with the thinking of the ordinary man....

In our universities and in our culture, oriented as they are toward science and technology, philosophy is more and more needed, not just to bolster up the humanities, but to shed a light on science and technology that would enable them to be viewed in their proper perspective as parts of the whole human enterprise. Understanding the human enterprise as a whole—in which science and technology, as well as history, religion, the various arts, and the institutions of the state and of the church are component parts—is a task that calls for philosophizing of a high order, yet philosophizing of a kind that everyone engages in to some degree. It is a task that no other discipline, no other part of our culture, is able to discharge. It is a task that academic philosophy, as currently constituted and practiced, either turns away from or fails to measure up to.

The importance of reconstituting philosophy for the performance of this task, as well as the importance of making academic philosophy serve, as it should, to guide and perfect everyone's natural human tendency to philosophize, may overshadow the importance of philosophy's becoming as respectable as science or other intellectual disciplines that are now accorded more respect than philosophy, certainly in learned or academic circles and by the public generally, or at least by the well-informed public. Nevertheless, it is the third of these three points of importance which seems to me basic; for, in my judgment, unless philosophy as an intellectual enterprise can and does become as worthy of respect as science and other disciplines, it cannot discharge the cultural and educational functions for which it, and it alone, is specially suited....

...Try to imagine a world in which everything else is exactly the same, but from which philosophy is totally absent. I do not mean just academic philosophy; I mean philosophizing in every degree—that done almost unconsciously by ordinary men or inexpertly by scientists, historians, poets, and novelists, as well as that done with technical competence by professional philosophers.

Since philosophizing is an ingrained and inveterate human tendency, I know that it is hard to imagine a world without philosophy in which everything else is the same, including human nature; yet it is certainly no harder than imagining a world without sex as one in which everything else is the same. In each case, of course, we are required to excise one element from human nature and leave the rest unaffected by the surgery. That can be done. It has been done before, for example, when we imagine men, who are by nature social, living anarchically in a state of nature, totally bereft of civil society and government—a useful hypothesis, as Rousseau pointed out, even though it involves a supposition contrary to fact.

In the world I have asked you to imagine, all the other arts and sciences remain continuing enterprises; history and science are taught in colleges and universities; and it is assumed without question that everyone's education should include some acquaintance with them. But philosophy is completely expunged. No one asks any philosophical questions; no one philosophizes; no one has any philosophical knowledge, insight, or understanding; philosophy is not taught or learned; and no philosophical books exist.

Would this make any difference to you? Would you be completely satisfied to live in such a world? Or would you come to the conclusion that it lacked something of importance?

You would realize—would you not?—that even though education involved acquiring historical and scientific knowledge, it could not include any understanding of either science or history, since questions about history and science (other than questions of fact) are not historical or scientific but philosophical questions. You would also realize that a great many of your opinions or beliefs, shared with most of your fellow men, would have to go unquestioned, because to question them would be to philosophize; they would remain unenlightened opinions or beliefs, because any enlightenment on these matters would have to come from philosophizing about them. You would be debarred from asking questions about yourself and your life, questions about the shape of the world and your place in it, questions about what you should be doing and what you should be seeking—all questions which, in one form or another, you do in fact often ask and would find it difficult to desist from asking.

There may be some whose only response to all this is a shrug of indifference. To them I have nothing more to say. The rest, I am sure, would find a world devoid of philosophy and philosophizing sorely lacking an important ingredient, one they would feel deprived of if they did not have it as part of their education and their intellectual life....

[Let us consider] those questions which are purely philosophical—that is, which belong to philosophy, and to philosophy alone, as a special field of learning or mode of inquiry. Such questions ... must be primarily questions about that which is and happens in the world or about what men should do and seek, and only secondarily questions about how we know, think, or speak about that which is and happens or about what men do and seek.

Philosophical questions about that which is and happens in the world deal, for example, with such matters as: the nature of being and existence; the properties of anything which is; the modes of being and the types of existence; change and permanence in being or mutability and immutability; the existence of that which changes; change itself and the types of change; causation and the types of causes; necessity and contingency; the material and the immaterial; the physical and the non-physical; freedom and indeterminacy; the powers of the human mind; the nature and extent of human knowledge; the freedom of the will. (In addition to such purely philosophical questions, there is a host of mixed questions—questions about the nature of man, about society, and about history—the answers to which depend in part upon scientific and historical knowledge.)

Questions about what men should do and seek are concerned with human conduct and the organization of society. They deal, for example, with such matters as: good and evil; right and wrong; the order of goods; duties and obligations; virtues and vices; happiness, life's purpose or goal; justice and rights in the sphere of human relations and social interaction; the state and its relation to the individual; the good society, the just polity, and the just economy; war and peace.

For brevity of reference in all that follows, I propose to call questions about that which is and happens or about what men should do and seek "first-order questions" and the knowledge that is contained in tenable answers to such questions, "first-order philosophical knowledge." In contrast, "second-order questions" are questions about our first-order knowledge, questions about the content of our thinking when we try to answer first-order questions, or questions about the ways in which we express such thought in language. The tenable answers to such questions constitute "second-order philosophical knowledge."

As second-order knowledge, philosophy may be reflexive; that is, it may be analytical and critical of its own concepts or of its own language; it may examine its own knowledge and try to give an account of it. But it may also deal with other branches of knowledge or other modes of inquiry; and, by doing so, provide us with an account of scientific knowledge, historical knowledge, mathematical knowledge, or the kind of knowledge that is to be found in the deposit of common-sense beliefs. Furthermore, on the plane of its second-order questions, philosophy may achieve clarification of concepts and language, not only in its own field of discourse, but in that of any other special discipline; and it may also perform what has come to be called the therapeutic function of curing the intellectual defects that arise from conceptual unclarity or the misuse of language, on the part of philosophers or any other specialists.

If we use the words "critical" or "analytic" for all these aspects of philosophy as second-order knowledge or as a mode of inquiry on the plane of second-order questions, then what [this] condition stipulates is that philosophy *must be more than critical or analytic.* And if we use the words "constructive" or "synthetic" for philosophy as first-order knowledge or as a mode of inquiry on the plane of first-order questions, then the other face of this same stipulation is that philosophy *must be constructive or synthetic.*

C. D. BROAD

*The Main Tasks of Philosophy**

C. D. Broad (1887–1971) was a distinguished British philosopher. Born in London and educated at Cambridge University, he was a lecturer on logic, moral philosophy, the philosophy of science, and psychical research. Among his various

*C. D. Broad, from "Introduction," in *Scientific Thought* (New Jersey: Humanities Press, Inc., 1952), pp. 16–22. Used by permission of the publisher.

books are *Five Types of Ethical Theory, Mind and Its Place in Nature,* and *Scientific Thought,* from which we quote.

In the selection below, the author views the fundamental task of philosophy as two-fold: that of clearing up meanings and defining concepts and that of attacking and exposing our unquestioned beliefs. These tasks are not adequately performed by any other discipline. The author goes on to discuss two kinds of philosophy, which should be clearly distinguished by the reader.

Now the most fundamental task of Philosophy is to take the concepts that we daily use in common life and science, to analyse them, and thus to determine their precise meanings and their mutual relations. Evidently this is an important duty. In the first place, clear and accurate knowledge of anything is an advance on a mere hazy general familiarity with it. Moreover, in the absence of clear knowledge of the meanings and relations of the concepts that we use, we are certain sooner or later to apply them wrongly or to meet with exceptional cases where we are puzzled as to how to apply them at all. For instance, we all agree pretty well as to the place of a certain pin which we are looking at. But suppose we go on to ask: "Where is the image of that pin in a certain mirror; and is it in this place (whatever it may be) in precisely the sense in which the pin itself is in *its* place?" We shall find the question a very puzzling one, and there will be no hope of answering it until we have carefully analysed what we mean by *being in a place.*

Again, this task of clearing up the meanings and determining the relations of fundamental concepts is not performed to any extent by any other science. Chemistry *uses* the notion of substance, geometry that of space, and mechanics that of motion. But they assume that you already know what is meant by *substance* and *space* and *motion.* So you do in a vague way; and it is not their business to enter, more than is necessary for their own special purposes, into the meaning and relations of these concepts as such. Of course the special sciences do in some measure clear up the meanings of the concepts that they use. A chemist, with his distinction between elements and compounds and his laws of combination, has a clearer idea of substance than an ordinary layman. But the special sciences only discuss the meanings of their concepts so far as this is needful for their own special purposes. Such discussion is incidental to them, whilst it is of the essence of Philosophy, which deals with such questions for their own sake. Whenever a scientist begins to discuss the concepts of his science in this thorough and disinterested way we begin to say that he is studying, not so much Chemistry or Physics, as the *Philosophy* of Chemistry or Physics. It will therefore perhaps be agreed that, in the above sense of Philosophy, there is both room and need for such a study, and that there is no special reason to fear that it will be beyond the compass of human faculties.

At this point a criticism may be made which had better be met at once. It may be said: "By your own admission the task of Philosophy is purely verbal; it consists entirely of discussions about the meanings of words." This criticism is of course absolutely wide of the mark. When we say that Philosophy tries to clear up the meanings of concepts we do not mean that it is simply concerned to substitute some long phrase for some familiar word. Any analysis, when once it has been made, is naturally *expressed* in words; but so too is any other discovery. When Cantor gave his definition of Continuity, the final result of his work was expressed by saying that you can substitute for the word "continuous" such and such a verbal phrase. But the essential part of the work was to find out exactly what properties are present in objects when we predicate continuity of them, and what properties are absent when we refuse to predicate continuity. This was evidently not a question of words but of things and their properties.

Philosophy has another and closely connected task. We not only make continual use of vague and unanalysed concepts. We have also a number of uncriticised beliefs, which we constantly assume in ordinary life and in the sciences. We constantly assume, *e.g.* that every event has a cause, that nature obeys uniform laws, that we live in a world of objects whose existence and behaviour are independent of our knowledge of them, and so on. Now science takes over these beliefs without criticism from common-sense, and simply works with them. We know by experience, however, that beliefs which are very strongly held may be mere prejudices.... Is it not possible that we believe that nature as a whole will always act uniformly simply because the part of nature in which the human race has lived has happened to act so up to the present? All such beliefs then, however deeply rooted, call for criticism. The first duty of Philosophy is to state them clearly; and this can only be done when we have analysed and defined the concepts that they involve. Until you know exactly what you mean by *change* and *cause* you cannot know what is meant by the statement that *every change has a cause*. And not much weight can be attached to a person's most passionate beliefs if he does not know what precisely he is passionately believing. The next duty of Philosophy is to test such beliefs; and this can only be done by resolutely and honestly exposing them to every objection that one can think of oneself or find in the writings of others. We ought only to go on believing a proposition if, at the end of this process, we still find it impossible to doubt it. Even then of course it may not be true, but we have at least done our best.

These two branches of Philosophy—the analysis and definition of our fundamental concepts, and the clear statement and resolute criticism of our fundamental beliefs—I call *Critical Philosophy*. It is obviously a necessary and a possible task, and it is not performed by any other science. The other sciences *use* the concepts and *assume* the beliefs; Critical Philosophy tries to analyse the former and to criticise the latter. Thus, so long as science and Critical Philosophy keep to their own spheres, there is no possibility of conflict between them, since their subject-matter is quite different. Philosophy claims to analyse the general concepts of substance and cause, *e.g.;* it does not claim to tell us about particular substances, like gold, or about particular laws of causation, as that *aqua regia* dissolves gold. Chemistry, on the other hand, tells us a great deal about the various kinds of substances in the world, and how changes in one cause changes in another. But it does not profess to analyse the general concepts of substance or causation, or to consider what right we have to assume that every event has a cause.

It should now be clear why the method of Philosophy is so different from that of the natural sciences. Experiments are not made, because they would be utterly useless. If you want to find out how one substance behaves in presence of another you naturally put the two together, vary the conditions, and note the results. But no experiment will clear up your ideas as to the meaning of *cause* in general or of *substance* in general. Again, all conclusions from experiments rest on some of those very assumptions which it is the business of Philosophy to state clearly and to criticise. The experimenter assumes that nature obeys uniform laws, and that similar results will follow always and everywhere from sufficiently similar conditions. This is one of the assumptions that Philosophy wants to consider critically. The method of Philosophy thus resembles that of pure mathematics, at least in the respect that neither has any use for experiment.

There is, however, a very important difference. In pure mathematics we start either from axioms which no one questions, or from premises which are quite explicitly assumed merely as hypotheses; and our main interest is to deduce remote consequences. Now most of the tacit assumptions of ordinary life and of natural science claim to be true and not merely to be hypotheses, and at the same time they are found to be neither clear nor self-evident when critically reflected upon. Most mathematical axioms are very simple and clear, whilst most other propositions which men strongly believe are highly complex and confused. Philosophy is mainly concerned, not with remote conclusions, but with the analysis and appraisement of the original premises. For this purpose analytical power and a certain kind of insight are necessary, and the mathematical method is not of much use.

Now there is another kind of Philosophy; and, as this is more exciting, it is what laymen generally understand by the name. This is what I call *Speculative Philosophy*. It has a different object, is pursued by a different method, and leads to results of a different degree of certainty from Critical Philosophy. Its object is to take over the results of the various sciences, to add to them the results of the religious and ethical experiences of mankind, and then to reflect upon the whole. The hope is that, by this means, we may be able to reach some general conclusions as to the nature of the Universe, and as to our position and prospects in it.

There are several points to be noted about Speculative Philosophy. (i) If it is to be of the slightest use it must presuppose Critical Philosophy. It is useless to take over masses of uncriticised detail from the sciences and from the ethical and religious experiences of men. We do not know what they mean, or what degree of certainty they possess till they have been clarified and appraised by Critical Philosophy. It is thus quite possible that the time for Speculative Philosophy has not yet come; for Critical Philosophy may not have advanced far enough to supply it with a firm basis. In the past people have tended to rush on to Speculative Philosophy, because of its greater practical interest. The result has been the production of elaborate systems which may quite fairly be described as moonshine. The discredit which the general public quite rightly attaches to these hasty attempts at Speculative Philosophy is reflected back on Critical Philosophy, and Philosophy as a whole thus falls into undeserved disrepute.

(ii) At the best Speculative Philosophy can only consist of more or less happy guesses, made on a very slender basis. There is no hope of its reaching the certainty which some parts of Critical Philosophy might quite well attain. Now speculative philosophers as a class have been the most dogmatic of men. They have been more certain of everything than they had a right to be of anything.

(iii) A man's final view of the Universe as a whole, and of the position and prospects of himself and his fellows, is peculiarly liable to be biased by his hopes and fears, his likes and dislikes, and his judgments of value. One's Speculative Philosophy tends to be influenced to an altogether undue extent by the state of one's liver and the amount of one's bank-balance. No doubt livers and bank-balances have their place in the Universe, and no view of it which fails to give them their due weight is ultimately satisfactory. But their due weight is considerably less than their influence on Speculative Philosophy might lead one to suspect. But, if we bear this in mind and try our hardest to be "ethically neutral," we are rather liable to go to the other extreme and entertain a theory of the Universe which renders the existence of our judgments of value unintelligible.

A large part of Critical Philosophy is almost exempt from this source of error. Our analysis of truth and falsehood, or of the nature of judgment, is not very likely to be influenced by our hopes and fears. Yet even here there is a slight danger of intellectual dishonesty. We sometimes do our Critical Philosophy, with half an eye on our Speculative Philosophy, and accept or reject beliefs, or analyse concepts in a certain way, because we feel that this will fit in better than any alternative with the view of Reality as a whole that we happen to like.

(iv) Nevertheless, if Speculative Philosophy remembers its limitations, it is of value to scientists, in its methods, if not in its results. The reason is this. In all the sciences except Psychology we deal with objects and their changes, and leave out of account as far as possible the mind which observes them. In Psychology, on the other hand, we deal with minds and their processes, and leave out of account as far as possible the objects that we get to know by means of them. A man who confines himself to either of these subjects is likely therefore to get a very one-sided view of the world. The pure natural scientist is liable to forget that minds exist, and that if it were not for them he could neither know nor act on physical objects. The pure psychologist is inclined to forget that the main business of minds is to know and act upon objects; that they are most intimately connected with certain portions of matter; and that they have apparently arisen gradually in a world which at one time contained nothing but matter. Materialism is the characteristic Speculative Philosophy of the pure natural scientist, and subjective idealism that of the pure psychologist. To the scientist subjective idealism seems a fairy tale, and to the psychologist materialism seems sheer lunacy. Both are right in their criticisms, but neither sees the weakness of his own position. The truth is that both these doctrines commit the fallacy of over-simplification; and we can hardly avoid falling into some form of this unless at some time we make a resolute attempt to think *synoptically* of all the facts. Our *results* may be trivial; but the *process* will at least remind us of the extreme complexity of the world, and teach us to reject any cheap and easy philosophical theory, such as popular materialism or popular theology.

SIDNEY HOOK

*The Uses of Philosophy**

Sidney Hook (b. 1902) has been a professor and chairman of philosophy at New York University for many years. He has been active in many educational and social movements and is a defender of human freedom. His writings include *Education for Modern Man; Heresy, Yes—Conspiracy, No; Political Power and Personal Freedom; The Quest for Being;* and *Academic Freedom and Academic Anarchy.*

Hook believes we can best arrive at a notion of what philosophy is by examining its uses. He gives some examples to clarify his points, and he raises some important questions about our values and the ends we seek as we face alternatives in the concrete situations of life.

*Sidney Hook, from "Does Philosophy Have a Future?", *Saturday Review,* 50 (November 11, 1967) pp. 21–23, 62. Used by permission of the author and the publisher.

In periods of world and national crisis, such as we are passing through, many individuals are wont to turn to philosophy and philosophers in hope of finding a faith to sustain them in time of troubles.... Those who ask questions find that the answer which the philosopher gives them is an invitation to inquiry, not a conclusion or credo. Philosophy, they are sometimes told, is not so much an activity that offers definite answers to questions as one that questions answers. But surely philosophy does not question answers to anything or everything.

This failure to get a specific answer sometimes leads to frustration and to a series of other questions. What is philosophical inquiry as distinct from other forms? What is philosophy, after all? What has it to say? Why study it?

I propose to discuss briefly some of the uses of philosophy without offering a formal definition of it, because any definition presupposes some conception not likely to be shared by all philosophers. Further, it seems possible to convey a notion of what philosophy is by describing its common uses.

The first and most obvious use of the study of philosophy is that it helps us to understand the nature and history of our civilization. We cannot grasp the pattern of its events and the character of its institutions without some knowledge of the ideas of Plato, Aristotle, Plotinus, Aquinas, Kant, Hegel, and Marx. We cannot understand the political history of the United States without some appreciation of the philosophy of Locke. We cannot appreciate the recent history of Europe and Asia without a grasp of the social philosophy of Marx. I am not saying that the philosophical ideas of these thinkers alone are the forces which entered into the determination of history. Obviously, economic and national interests as well as outstanding personalities played a large role, too; but I am saying that philosophical conceptions of the nature of man, of the nature of justice, of social welfare, of human personality, of freedom, had some influence upon events, and that without reference to them we cannot explain the shape of the past.

Ideas—philosophical ideas—also have a direct relevance to present-day religious, social, and political movements. They are not merely a part of the heritage of the West. They are the means by which we seek to preserve and defend the West. That is why ideas are among the most practical things in the world. Whoever wants to understand our world, and the world of the past out of which it grew, must therefore pay some attention to philosophical ideas. The study of philosophy, in other words, gives us a perspective upon our human history and our present-day experience. It reveals, in John Dewey's words, "the predicaments, the prospects, and aspirations of men."

But philosophy has an even more important use. It has a bearing not only on the shape of the past, but on the shape of things to come. To the extent that fundamental ideas determine our actions, they flow from our basic commitments. Philosophy is a mode of thought which analyzes our presuppositions and assumptions in every field of action and thought. It enables us to make explicit our allegiances to the ideals in behalf of which we are prepared to live, to fight, sometimes even to die. Its primary concern here is with meaning, not truth, and it aims to produce an awareness of what we are about. This awareness or self-consciousness is not easy to achieve. The fruit of ancient wisdom was expressed in the Greek injunction, "Know thyself," but this is a difficult task. Very few of us can answer the questions: "What do we really want?"; "What do we really mean by the large terms which play a role in human discourse?" We inherit a large mass—usually a mess—of traditional beliefs. Some of these we call first principles. Others, who do not share them, dub them prejudices. How do we sort them out?

This suggests the third use of philosophy. Awareness and self-consciousness do not come about by revelation. For the revelations—"the moments of truth," as the phrase goes—which overtake us are themselves in need of understanding. This can be reliably achieved only by the activity of logical analysis. A person may utter statements that are true or false and yet not be clear about their meaning or their justification or relevance. Whatever else philosophy is, it is an activity of logical analysis which seeks to locate issues in dispute and to help clarify them. When properly pursued, philosophy gives a methodological sophistication that can be achieved by no other discipline. It is not a mere matter of reasoning from premises to conclusion, as in mathematics or chess, because it scrutinizes the premises and basic terms which all subjects take for granted. It enables us to distinguish between statements of fact and disguised definitions, between hypotheses which may be true or false and resolutions which are adequate or inadequate. It is always prepared to consider alternatives to the familiar. William James actually defines philosophy as a quest for alternatives and their investigation. In summary, then, philosophy consists of an analysis of concepts and ideas in an attempt to cut through slogans to genuine issues and problems....

[A simple illustration of this] is the belief that the equality or inequality of races necessarily has a bearing on the question of segregation or integration in housing, transportation, schooling. The view which condemns discrimination against human beings on the basis of religion or race is primarily a moral view. It flows from our belief in the validity of the democratic ideal which rests upon an equality of concern for all human beings to develop their personality to their highest potential. Some facts may have a bearing on this policy, but not the discovery that there is a greater distribution of natural capacity in one race or group than another. Whatever be the facts about the distribution of capacity in group A or B, each member of that group is morally entitled to the rights and privileges which flow from the obligation of a democratic community to all its citizens....

...There is a further use of philosophy. It concerns itself with the place of man in the universe from the point of view of certain large and perennial questions which all reflective men at some time or another ask. These questions are not raised or answered in any of the special sciences, but to answer them intelligently one must be familiar with the best science and theology of the day, and approach them in a rational spirit. These are questions such as: In what sense, if any, does the universe show a design? Does this design imply a designer or a God or a Friend behind the phenomena? Is man a tenement of clay inhabited by an immortal soul or a handful of wonderful salts in a solution of water? Are human beings responsible for their actions? If they are, does this mean that they have free wills? If the will is free, does this mean that the will is uncaused? If the will is uncaused, does this mean that actions are a matter of chance, and if so, in what sense are men morally responsible for their conduct?

This leads on to all sorts of exacting and intricate questions. What do we mean by a cause? Can there be a first cause? Are these questions answerable? What is a genuine question anyhow? Does every sentence which has the form of a question possess the sense of one? Concerning these questions there is dogmatic belief and often dogmatic disbelief. Philosophy is the discipline which considers the fundamental questions in such a way that no matter what answers one makes to them, one can give reasons or grounds for belief or disbelief.

...Finally, I come to what I regard as the most important use of philosophy, to which all the other uses of philosophy are ancillary—philosophy as the quest for wisdom. Everyone knows that there is a difference between knowledge and wisdom, but not everyone can tell in what this difference consists. We are aware that a man can have a great deal of knowledge about many things and still be a learned fool. We sometimes say he has been educated beyond his capacities. We also know there are wise men who are not encyclopedias of learning, and that wise men of the past often lacked the knowledge of present-day schoolboys. This has led some thinkers to contrast knowledge and wisdom as if they belonged to entirely different orders or dimensions of insight. But if we speak of a wise man, we are entitled to ask: "What is he wise about?" If he were ignorant of everything, he couldn't be wise.

Consequently, we must conclude that wisdom is a species of knowledge —it is knowledge of the origin, careers, interrelations, and reliabilities of human values in our experience. Wisdom is an affair of values, and of value judgments. It is intelligent conduct of human affairs. It is knowledge of what is of most worth in our experience, of the ends which we can justifiably pursue, of the good, the better, and the best, the bad, the worse, and the worst in those concrete situations in which, confronted by alternatives of policy or action, we ask: "What shall I do?"

This raises a very large question. How can we be wise or even rational about our values or our ends? What does it mean to be rational or reasonable about them? The term "rational," or "reasonable," has many meanings, but some eminent thinkers claim that they can all be reduced to variations of one meaning, viz., the appropriate or economical use of means to achieve ends. They assert that once we have an end we can be rational about the means of realizing it, but that it makes no sense to speak of ends being rational or reasonable. This suggests that ultimately all ends are on the same plane and that no good reason or rational ground can be given for accepting one or rejecting others. If one accepts Gandhi's ends, one can be rational about achieving them. If one accepts Hitler's ends, one can be rational about achieving them. But we cannot be rational in choosing between Gandhi's and Hitler's ends.

This is the position of Bertrand Russell, who says, "There is no such thing as an irrational end except one impossible of realization." Now, this is false on its face because in one sense there are many ends which are impossible of realization, but are not irrational to pursue because of the desirable consequences of our pursuit of them. Suppose I take all knowledge as my province. It is impossible to achieve literal mastery of the whole of knowledge, but it may not be irrational to pursue it as a goal, because I may thereby acquire more knowledge in this fashion than if I had taken a more restricted end. Or, suppose I take as my end kindness in all circumstances to everyone. This, too, given men as we know them, is impossible, but the world would be a far better place if I try to be invariably kind than if I take as my ideal a more restricted sort of kindness or an ideal of indifference.

One might retort that what Russell means is still valid, for in these cases what I am really taking as my end are those consequences which are realizable. The problem then is: How can you rationally decide concerning alternative ends, all of which are equally realizable?

The answer, it seems to me, is suggested by analyzing how we proceed in any concrete situation in which we must make a choice between ends. If we have only one end, we have no moral problem. It is only a question of means. But the obvious truth is that we always have more than one end—usually a cluster of ends or values—to which we are committed. Our problem is, which end should we commit ourselves to? Now, the answer I suggest is that we always proceed by checking the alternative possible ends in terms of the consequences of the means used to achieve them and in the light of all the other ends which, on the basis of past experience, we have accepted as having prima facie validity. Of course, every one of these other ends may itself be questioned. Every end in human experience is also a means to some other end. How do we test them? By the same process. But does this not set up an infinite regress? No, not if we take our problems one at a time.

Consider a simple example. A student comes to me in distress and wants to know whether he should remain in school or exploit some opportunity for remunerative employment. I point out the relative advantages and disadvantages of both, stressing the fact that in the modern world he is more likely to find a creative vocation through continuing his schooling. Now, this assumes that a creative vocation is a good thing to have. How do we know that? Suppose it is denied. Again, we point to the alternative uses of the concrete goals or possibilities of living. A creative vocation is a center around which to organize experience; it is a source of satisfaction and delight; it also provides occasions for companionship and friendship. But are *these* worthwhile? To which I reply that they enrich living. Yes, comes the rejoinder, but is life worthwhile? Now, at this point we can very well question the validity of the process. A student who wants to know whether to continue his schooling or discontinue it is not interested in knowing whether life is worth living. That is a legitimate question, too, in its context. But it is out of context here.

What I have been trying to illustrate is the general method by which we do, in fact, seek to answer specific moral questions. They are much more complicated, of course, when they concern other human beings. (I am not giving any answers here or claiming to be wise. A philosopher in his own life need be no more wise than a physician need be healthy.) I am particularly concerned to challenge the view that all our values are ultimate values that are inarbitrable. Indeed, I question whether it is true that any value in a specific context is an ultimate value rather than a penultimate one which is tested by its successive consequences. At any rate, I believe I have shown that we can be wise or foolish about the ends of action, that it makes good sense to undertake rational criticism of our ends, and that the originally desired end may sometimes appear in the light of our reflective analysis as undesirable.

Although the philosopher does not himself have to be a wise man, at his best he knows more than the methods and techniques by which the process of reflection is carried out. He has vision of possibilities. He is not only a critic but a seer. His vision is often expressed as a glimpse into what can make our society better for our time, into what can most enrich our life and give it abiding worth, an insight into human possibilities and how to realize them. When the philosopher is a man of vision, he leaves his mark upon the experience of others, whose ordinary life acquires new dimensions of significance.

Of such philosophers, Santayana says: "It is not easy for him to shout or to address a crowd; he must be silent for long periods; for he is watching stars that move slowly and in courses that it is possible though difficult to see; and he is crushing all things in his heart as in a winepress, until his life and their secret flow out together."

What is Man?

PAUL WEISS

*Man as a Human Being**

Paul Weiss (b. 1901) is a philosopher and educator who has taught at a number of colleges and universities in the United States and given many series of lectures. He taught philosophy at Yale University from 1945 to 1969, when he retired. He was a founding member and first president of the Metaphysical Society and edited the *Review of Metaphysics,* 1947–1963. His many writings include *Reality, Modes of Being, Nine Basic Arts,* and *Philosophy and Process.*

In the selection below, Weiss points out that while man has an animal ancestry, he is a distinct type of being. Some of man's special characteristics, bodily and nonbodily, are discussed. Man is both a constant and a changing being: he has a constant essence, since all change presupposes something constant, that is expressed in and through the body which changes. The selection concludes with the author's view of the task of man.

It does not seem worth while to dispute that man has an animal ancestry and came to be in the course of history. The view is supported by the independent investigations of geologists, archeologists and anthropologists. It is opposed only by the theory that man has always existed in his present form or that he is a special creation inserted within the frame of nature. It would be a mistake, however, to suppose that if it be granted that man had an animal origin it is also granted that he is nothing but an animal. Just as it is possible for a child to surpass its parents, so it is possible for an animal to pass beyond the limits within which its ancestors dwelt, and to arrive at the stage where it becomes a radically distinct type of being. It would then attain and exercise powers which it did not have before and which have no

*Paul Weiss, from *Nature and Man* (Carbondale and Edwardsville: Southern Illinois U. Press, 1965. Copyright 1947 by Paul Weiss), pp. 124–267 with omissions. Used by permission of the author and the publisher.

animal mode of expression. In short, it is possible for an animal to become a man, though a man is not and cannot become an animal.

DARWIN'S THESIS

To show that man is an animal, one must show that every trait of man, bodily or nonbodily in nature, is a developed, complex or variant form of some animal character, differing from it in degree and not in kind. An attempt to do this has been made a number of times in the course of history, notably by Montaigne, La Mettrie and Condillac. The most persuasive presentation of the thesis, however, is I think to be found in Darwin's *Descent of Man*.

Darwin maintained that man's capacity for happiness and sorrow, love and hate, his sense of beauty and of right and wrong, as well as his ability to remember, imagine and reason, were either duplicated in other animals or were present in them in a rudimentary form. Dogs impressed Darwin as not only having intelligence, but self-consciousness; he thought birds had a sense of beauty, monkeys an ability to make tools, and dogs, birds and monkeys some form of speech and moral sense. He could find nothing in man which was not duplicated, at least in embryonic form, elsewhere in the animal kingdom. As he quaintly put it, "If man had not been his own classifier, he would never have thought of founding a separate order for his reception."

Darwin erred, however, in supposing that every human characteristic is duplicated somewhere and to some degree in the animal kingdom.

Man is sometimes religious. No animal ever is. It is not to the point to say, as Darwin does, that there are men who have no religion, for one kind of being is not to be distinguished from another by virtue of an *activity* in which all the members of one group engage and all the members of the other do not. One type of being differs from another by virtue of a *capacity* which all its members and no other beings have. What Darwin should have shown is that there are types of men who *cannot* be religious or that there are animals which are or can be religious, if only in a minor way. But this he fails to do.

Animals decorate and occasionally show sensitivity in color and design. But an artist reproduces in his art the meaning of another thing, and this no mere manipulation of color or design begins to approach. The sense of beauty of an animal, and the art of which it is capable, differ not in degree but in kind from that open to a man.

Man, too, alone has science, philosophy and history—speculative inquiries into the nature of realities he never directly encounters through the senses. What animals know is what they learn from sense experience. No multiplication of such experiences could ever sum up to a knowledge of that which lies outside the reach of any sense.

And then there is man's speech, his use of symbols, his ability to pledge himself to do something in the future, his ability to cook and his ability to engage in sexual acts for pleasure rather than for the sake of reproduction....

THE HUMAN CONSTANT

A man is not a body. He has a body, and that body is necessary and desirable. This conclusion is so obvious and inevitable that it would be hard to find anyone who consistently and explicitly denies it. Even those who underscore other interpretations of the nature of man, constantly shift their emphases and assert this last as well....

The problem of the nature of man is one of our most neglected problems. One clue is to be found in the fact that he is, in some sense, the self-same being from birth to death. He is not, of course, self-identical as a body. He grows vertically and horizontally in the course of his career. As an adult his appearance often differs so greatly from the appearance he presented as a child that it would be hazardous to assert that anyone could see a similarity. Even more important is the physiologically substantiated fact that his body contains hardly any of the cells that were present a dozen years or so before. So far as size, shape, skill, strength and appearance are concerned, a man becomes considerably transformed over the years, while so far as the constituent cells of his body are in question, he is almost entirely changed. Yet there is a deep and undeniable sense in which it is the same man who is adult and who was embryo or child. Unless a man is to be designated as a new being every time he loses or adds a cell, changes in strength, skill or appearance, it is necessary to affirm that there is something in him which is of his essence and which remains constant throughout his days. Despite the fact that he changes, he remains self-same, a being with a single essence and career....

There are men; the men change. But to be that which changes, a man must also be that which is constant. Otherwise what was before and what was later would not characterize *him*. But if he is constant he cannot be a new substance at each moment....

A man is guilty of a crime he committed a year ago. His guilt is not decreased but in fact increased if he changes his face and fingerprints in the meantime. He is guilty all the while, and this whether or not he is conscious of the fact. We want him to be conscious of his guilt before we punish him so that the full meaning of the punishment will be clear. We await his awakening, not his recovery of identity. He does not lose his identity by forgetting who he is; he does not become a renewed man by remembering who he was. He is self-same all the while, in sleep and waking, but the latter alone is the appropriate time to let him know the nature of the crimes he committed. If he changes his face and fingerprints he is different in appearance from what he was. But throughout he is the self-same being. The differences characterize him; they are changes *of* him, not changes *to* and *from* or *in* him.

A man has a single, constant essence. It is tempting to suppose that this essence is the life which quickens his body. The embryo does not have a life which passes away as soon as the embryo assumes the shape of a child. The child does not die in order to become a youth. It is the same life which vitalizes the embryo and the developed body. Only one life is allotted to a man. That life relates, permeates and vitalizes every part of the body; it is sensitive to the adventures these parts undergo. One life suffuses the whole and suffuses it from birth to death.

The life of a being, however, varies in intensity, force, mode of expression and bent from the beginning to the end of his days. The vitality of an embryo is different in nature and stress from that of a man. The life in the body is a continuous rather than a constant thing. There is more to a man, too, than the life that happens to be exhibited in his body. He is equally himself when he is passive as when he is active, when asleep as when awake, though the degree of life exhibited in the body varies considerably at these different times. Only part of him is immersed in the form of a life in the body, and this seems to ebb and flow in the course of the day. A part of man's nature might be said to be expressed as the life of his body but there must be a part existing outside his bodily frame....

All changes presuppose something constant. Either, then, men are but passing shadows across the face of some more constant thing, or there is within them a constant factor which is expressed as a fluctuating life in a changing body. But men act on their own and are self-same throughout their careers. There must be something in them which is neither body, the life which animates it, nor the changing composite of the two. We must look elsewhere for the secret of man's identity.

Were men merely unified bodies, everything they did would be a function of those bodies. Yet all seem to have a reason of their own. Though that reason expresses, responds and reports the things the body does and undergoes, it frequently concerns itself with other things as well. While the body feeds and grows, it thinks of mathematical truths or the scent of the rose. Though it does not operate until the brain is developed, and though it often reflects the state of the glands and the general health of the body, it is often vigorous though the body is weak, and feeble though the body is strong. The greatest intellects do not necessarily have the largest or most convoluted brains, the best physiques or the most stable and perfect bodily health.

One could then make out a strong case for the identification of oneself with one's reason. Despite the fact that the body constantly changes in shape, size and accomplishment, the reason seems to have a rather constant cast. Men seem to retain the same mental qualities and intellectual bents throughout their lives. No matter how they vary the nature of their bodies they do not seem to be able to change themselves from engineers into poets, or from poets into mathematicians. The body also distorts and limits their intentions, but the reason seems to allow them full play.

Yet the reason cannot be what we seek. The reason is a late achievement, not present in the embryo. It has a different cargo and a different destination at different times. The statement that a man is a rational being expresses the character of a hope rather than the nature of a fact, unless experience deceives us most grievously.

Nor is it the memory, as Locke suggests, which is at the end of our search. The memory splits into multiple unrelated fragments as one develops, embraces only part of what one is, does not encompass the present moment, and has little, if any, existence at the moment of birth. But what is constant in man is unitary and all-embracing, exists at the very beginning of his life, and encompasses the present moment.

The human constant might more reasonably be identified with the will than with the memory or the reason. One can will to act, to think or to remember, and so far as this is true the will must be more fundamental than these others. The will, too, seems to remain constant for quite a while. Future deliberations run along the same course as past ones, and men hold themselves responsible for those past promises and acts they willingly performed. Yet despite all this, the will cannot be that of which we are in search. The will waxes and wanes in strength and direction from time to time. It is not a constant. It is not possessed by all human beings, nor by any all the time. Infants and those asleep and unconscious seem to be without a will of any kind. A will exists only when one is willing; the rest of the time it disappears into the recesses of one's being, appearing once again with somewhat the same, though not necessarily the identical, bent it had before.

The constant factor characteristic of a man lies beneath his life, memory, mind and will. It is not the whole of him, for the life and the body, the memory, mind and will are part of him as well. Nor is it separated off from these, for he is one being and not many. A man is both a constant and a changing being. He can be both and still be a unity because his changes are determinations, because they are the possessions of a single undetermined factor which is unchanged throughout his days. That constant, undetermined unit is his *self*.

To know oneself it is necessary to know something of one's self. That self is what a psyche becomes when it is concerned with realizing not only its own good or that of its kind but also a good pertinent to others. Baby or idiot, immature or ill, a human, by virtue of his self, is concerned with some goods that do good neither to him nor even to mankind. This of course must be shown, but for the time being it will perhaps suffice to remark that the self is partly expressed from the very beginning as a life in the body and soon becomes expressed as well in the form of a will and a mind, to make man an embodied self which may eventually will and think.

The self is a constant, enabling a man to be self-same throughout his career. But because that self, from the very beginning, is expressed in and through his body, a man can change in acts, structure and powers in the course of time.

MAN'S FOURFOLD BOND

Like the rest of the beings in nature all of us are held captive by our pasts, our bodies, our fellows and the world about. These form a fourfold barrier, standing perpetually in our way. They limit what we could possibly and actually be, have and do....

Our bodies have requirements, drives and modes of acting which can be controlled at times, but never entirely defied. Possessing their own structures and habits, those bodies have rhythms and make demands to which we must submit whether we will or no. Those who have often exhibited fear by running, find it hard to avoid a frightened run even when they would prefer to be at rest. Before a timid man has a chance to say what he would like to do, his legs are on the move, precipitately carrying him from the scene. Anyone else, in the same circumstances, might also have been frightened. But some would have had their bodies so well keyed that it would be hard to discern a move. If we demand of the brave that they do not budge when startled—a common, though not easily satisfied demand—only those can be brave whose bodies have been properly trained. Whatever praise they deserve is earned then and there by their bodies alone, though credit is also due them, as distinct from their bodies, for past practice and control. Whether trained or untrained, the body leaves its mark on whatever we do.

All of us have been shaped by our societies. We act as social beings even in solitude. The lives of other human beings constantly interplay with and intersect our own.... Our attempts and our achievements bear unmistakable signs of the pressure exerted by our fellow men....

There is no real escape from our fourfold bond, struggle as we may. If a man could free himself from his past, his body, his fellows or the world, he would be without roots, a language or a home: in the world and yet not part of it. He would be alone and ignorant, untaught and untrained.

Something can be said, in fact, for those who recommend that we passively submit to all our bonds. The more a man yields to the conditions which hem him in, the more secure and stable he often is, the more definite is his future, the more routine and easy is his life. Those who persist in battering their heads against a wall are caught as surely as are those who passively yield. And in addition they lose the peace that comes from the acceptance of the conditions that prevail. They also soon batter according to a pattern, thereby revealing how much they are under the influence of habit, the demands of the body, the pressure of their fellows and the character of the wall. Professional rebels are conservatives in disguise, breaking the fixtures of thought and existence in a somewhat steady and tedious way. They are trapped as surely as others are; their judgments and acts are no less dated and are no less predictable than are those of the quietest conservative. The heresies of today are the prelude to the dogmas of tomorrow. Rebellion at bondage is but a preparation for being bound again, sometimes even more firmly than before.

Yet each man does and must avoid being a creature of any one of these four bonds. Otherwise he would be dead in spirit and in body. He would do nothing, but would have everything done to and for him. Those who pride themselves on being stable steadily recede into the background. The defenders of the *status quo* are now in the process of becoming part of the *status ante*. "I am a man of my times," is the birthcry of an antiquarian. To be alive is to master the fourfold ring of conditions in a manner all one's own. And this every man does to some degree. None is wholly passive. All subject their bonds to some control. We differ from one another primarily in the extent to which we master our bonds while we submit to them....

All four barriers are forever in our way. We are always trying to subject them to some control. As a result of our efforts they take on the contours of our intentions and we, though still trapped, often do what we want. We are in fact free beings, for we can and do initiate acts, and can and do assert ourselves—sometimes with considerable success—while firmly bound....

THE TASK OF MAN

No matter how insignificant, servile, impotent or vicious a man, he has a unique value, unduplicatable, unrepeatable and irreplaceable. He may look like, behave like and think like others, his power may be weak and his productions trivial. His character may be contemptible. He may be less good than he ought to be; yet he has a value that cannot be reproduced or replaced and which is greater than that possessed by any other type of being.

The birth of a human being ought always to be an occasion for rejoicing, for nothing so deserves celebration as the coming to be of a new value. One may, to be sure, pay a high price for it. It may prove to be the occasion, then or later, of the loss of other equal values. There are times when joy must be restrained; there are other times when it can be nothing more than a tinge to a sorrow deep and lasting. It is tragic that there should be infants crippled in mind and body, orphaned, starved and diseased, or that they should be born in times of famine and pestilence. These are poignant occurrences because they produce new, fresh and precious values in such a way as to subtract from the totality of the good that could have been. Looked at in their setting, as having distorted or inadequate bodies and minds in environments which tend to make them worse, their presence may sometimes be so regrettable that it might be thought wise and charitable to destroy them; taken by themselves, as human beings infinitely rich in value and in potency, they are to be appreciated as new, infinitely precious goods which never were before and never can be again....

No man is a mere creature of circumstances. He molds them in a characteristic way. Changes in his cells or organs, or the conditions which hem him in from without, make possible new acts and enterprises otherwise beyond his reach, enabling him to develop and exercise new talents, and prompting him occasionally to undergo a radical reform. Yet everything he does bears the self-same signature, written though it is on different things, at different times and in different ways. Each makes and mars in his own individual way.

Given equal health, fortune and opportunity, each man, it would seem, should be able to achieve what every other can. Men begin to diverge, however, from the very start, for as embryos they already live in different environments, are fed by different foods, and inevitably lay the ground for patterns of expression and activity which cannot readily be dislodged or radically changed. Not all can be professional athletes, mathematicians, or political leaders, for as embryos they have already set individual limits to what they can attain as mature technicians of mind and body. No change in health, opportunity or determination will suffice to turn one into a violinist of distinction if his gifts do not lie in that direction. Free and unlimited though a man's promise is and always remains, it is yet bound irrevocably at the beginning of his life, for the individual works in new contexts from the standpoint and with the equipment of the old. Though there is nothing which is not in principle open to everyone equally, from the first much that a man might do is excluded beyond recall, and as he grows, more and more is outside his possible reach.

Each man can, to some degree, control the activities of most of his organs, individually and together, for the good of his body. He can also interrelate them for an end beyond. His problem is to move from the state of living in and through his body to the state of living by means of it in order to benefit others as well as himself. It is his task to remake the world, to realize to a maximum the good with which he is concerned. Only so far as he succeeds, does he fulfill his duty. Only then does he exhibit himself as one not bound by things as they are. Only then does he do what he ought—improve the world by making it the embodiment of the absolute good.

Man is a natural being with a fixed core, directed towards a good which is pertinent to all that exists. And he has a responsibility from which he can never escape. It is the primary function of his body, mind and will to help him live up to this responsibility. Trapped though he is by the bonds of past, body, society and the world, he is free to act and thus is accountable for his every failure to realize the good fully in fact. Even if he could not possibly master those bonds, he would still be responsible. He has infinite value because he has an infinite responsibility, and conversely. To deny him the one is to deny him the other.

ERICH FROMM

*The Human Situation**

Erich Fromm (b. 1900), psychoanalyst and educator, was born in Germany and received his early education there. He has taught at various institutes and universities in Germany and the United States and at the National University of Mexico. His many books include *Psychoanalysis and Religion, Psychology and Culture, The Heart of Man,* and *The Crisis in Psychoanalysis.*

In the selection below, Fromm discusses man's physiological relation to the animal kingdom and the biological laws of nature. Yet, Fromm maintains, man is a unique creature who transcends his past and who can create and destroy. He is endowed with reason, imagination, and a sense of identity.

Man, in respect to his body and his physiological functions, belongs to the animal kingdom. The functioning of the animal is determined by instincts, by specific action patterns which are in turn determined by inherited neurological structures. The higher an animal is in the scale of development, the more flexibility of action pattern and the less completeness of structural adjustment do we find at birth. In the higher primates we even find considerable intelligence; that is, use of thought for the accomplishment of

*From *The Sane Society* by Erich Fromm. Copyright © 1955 by Erich Fromm. Reprinted by permission of Holt, Rinehart and Winston, Inc.

desired goals, thus enabling the animal to go far beyond the instinctively prescribed action pattern. But great as the development within the animal kingdom is, certain basic elements of existence remain the same.

The animal "is lived" through biological laws of nature; it is part of nature and never transcends it. It has no conscience of a moral nature, and no awareness of itself and of its existence; it has no reason, if by reason we mean the ability to penetrate the surface grasped by the senses and to understand the essence behind that surface; therefore the animal has no concept of the truth, even though it may have an idea of what is useful.

Animal existence is one of harmony between the animal and nature; not, of course, in the sense that the natural conditions do not often threaten the animal and force it to a bitter fight for survival, but in the sense that the animal is equipped by nature to cope with the very conditions it is to meet, just as the seed of a plant is equipped by nature to make use of the conditions of soil, climate, etcetera, to which it has become adapted in the evolutionary process.

At a certain point of animal evolution, there occurred a unique break, comparable to the first emergence of matter, to the first emergence of life, and to the first emergence of animal existence. This new event happens when in the evolutionary process, action ceases to be essentially determined by instinct; when the adaptation of nature loses its coercive character; when action is no longer fixed by hereditarily given mechanisms. When the animal transcends nature, when it transcends the purely passive role of the creature, when it becomes, biologically speaking, the most helpless animal, *man is born*. At this point, the animal has emancipated itself from nature by erect posture, the brain has grown far beyond what it was in the highest animal. This birth of man may have lasted for hundreds of thousands of years, but what matters is that a new species arose, transcending nature, that *life became aware of itself*.

Self-awareness, reason and imagination disrupt the "harmony" which characterizes animal existence. Their emergence has made man into an anomaly, into the freak of the universe. He is part of nature, subject to her physical laws and unable to change them, yet he transcends the rest of nature. He is set apart while being a part; he is homeless, yet chained to the home he shares with all creatures. Cast into this world at an accidental place and time, he is forced out of it, again accidentally. Being aware of himself, he realizes his powerlessness and the limitations of his existence. He visualizes his own end: death. Never is he free from the dichotomy of his existence: he cannot rid himself of his mind, even if he should want to; he cannot rid himself of his body as long as he is alive—and his body makes him want to be alive.

Reason, man's blessing, is also his curse; it forces him to cope everlastingly with the task of solving an insoluble dichotomy. Human existence is different in this respect from that of all other organisms; it is in a state of constant and unavoidable disequilibrium. Man's life cannot "be lived" by repeating the pattern of his species; *he* must live. Man is the only animal that can be *bored,* that can feel evicted from paradise. Man is the only animal who finds his own existence a problem which he has to solve and from which he cannot escape. He cannot go back to the prehuman state of harmony with nature; he must proceed to develop his reason until he becomes the master of nature, and of himself.

...He lacks the instinctive adaptation to nature, he lacks physical strength, he is the most helpless of all animals at birth, and in need of protection for a much longer period of time than any of them. While he has lost the unity with nature, he has not been given the means to lead a new existence outside of nature. His reason is most rudimentary, he has no knowledge of nature's processes, nor tools to replace the lost instincts; he lives divided into small groups, with no knowledge of himself or of others; indeed, the biblical Paradise myth expresses the situation with perfect clarity. Man, who lives in the Garden of Eden, in complete harmony with nature but without awareness of himself, begins his history by the first act of freedom, disobedience to a command. Concomitantly, he becomes aware of himself, of his separateness, of his helplessness; he is expelled from Paradise, and two angels with fiery swords prevent his return.

Man's evolution is based on the fact that he has lost his original home, nature—and that he can never return to it, can never become an animal again. There is only one way he can take: to emerge fully from his natural home, to find a new home—one which he creates, by making the world a human one and by becoming truly human himself.

When man is born, the human race as well as the individual, he is thrown out of a situation which was definite, as definite as the instincts, into a situation which is indefinite, uncertain and open. There is certainty only about the past, and about the future as far as it is death—which actually is return to the past, the inorganic state of matter.

The problem of man's existence, then, is unique in the whole of nature; he has fallen out of nature, as it were, and is still in it; he is partly divine, partly animal; partly infinite, partly finite. *The necessity to find ever-new solutions for the contradictions in his existence, to find ever-higher forms of unity with nature, his fellowmen and himself, is the source of all psychic forces which motivate man, of all his passions, affects and anxieties.*

The animal is content if its physiological needs—its hunger, its thirst and its sexual needs—are satisfied. Inasmuch as man is *also* animal, these needs are likewise imperative and must be satisfied. *But inasmuch as man is human, the satisfaction of these instinctual needs is not sufficient to make him happy; they are not even sufficient to make him sane. The archimedic point of the specifically human dynamism lies in this uniqueness of the human situation; the understanding of man's psyche must be based on the analysis of man's needs stemming from the conditions of his existence.*

The problem, then, which the human race as well as each individual has to solve is that of being born. Physical birth, if we think of the individual, is by no means as decisive and singular an act as it appears to be. It is, indeed, an important change from intrauterine into extrauterine life; but in many respects the infant after birth is not different from the infant before birth; it cannot perceive things outside, cannot feed itself; it is completely dependent on the mother, and would perish without her help. Actually, the process of birth continues. The child begins to recognize outside objects, to react affectively, to grasp things and to co-ordinate his movements, to walk. But birth continues. The child learns to speak, it learns to know the use and function of things, it learns to relate itself to others, to avoid punishment and gain praise and liking. Slowly, the growing person learns to love, to develop reason, to look at the world objectively. He begins to develop his powers; to acquire a sense of identity, to overcome the seduction of his senses for the sake of an integrated life. Birth then, in the conventional meaning of the word, is only the beginning of birth in the broader sense. The whole life of the individual is nothing but the process of giving birth to himself; indeed, we should be fully born, when we die—although it is the tragic fate of most individuals to die before they are born.

From all we know about the evolution of the human race, the birth of man is to be understood in the same sense as the birth of the individual. When man had transcended a certain threshold of minimum instinctive adaptation, he ceased to be an animal; but he was as helpless and unequipped for human existence as the individual infant is at birth. The birth of man began with the first members of the species homo sapiens, and human history is nothing but the whole process of this birth. It has taken man hundreds of thousands of years to take the first steps into human life; he went through a narcissistic phase of magic omnipotent orientation, through totemism, nature worship, until he arrived at the beginnings of the formation of conscience, objectivity, brotherly love. In the last four thousand years of his history, he has developed visions of the fully born and fully awakened man, visions expressed in not too different ways by the great teachers of man in Egypt, China, India, Palestine, Greece and Mexico....

Another aspect of the human situation, closely connected with the need for relatedness, is man's situation as a *creature,* and his need to transcend this very state of the passive creature. Man is thrown into this world without his knowledge, consent or will, and he is removed from it again without his consent or will. In this respect he is not different from the animal, from the plants, or from inorganic matter. But being endowed with reason and imagination, he cannot be content with the passive role of the creature, with the role of dice cast out of a cup. He is driven by the urge to transcend the role of the creature, the accidentalness and passivity of his existence, by becoming a "creator."

Man can create life. This is the miraculous quality which he indeed shares with all living beings, but with the difference that he alone is aware of being created and of being a creator. Man can create life, or rather, woman can create life, by giving birth to a child, and by caring for the child until it is sufficiently grown to take care of his own needs. Man—man and woman—can create by planting seeds, by producing material objects, by creating art, by creating ideas, by loving one another. In the act of creation man transcends himself as a creature, raises himself beyond the passivity and accidentalness of his existence into the realm of purposefulness and freedom. In man's need for transcendence lies one of the roots for love, as well as for art, religion and material production.

To create presupposes activity and care. It presupposes love for that which one creates. How then does man solve the problem of transcending himself, if he is not capable of creating, if he cannot love? *There is another answer to this need for transcendence: if I cannot create life, I can destroy it. To destroy life makes me also transcend it.* Indeed, that man can destroy life is just as miraculous a feat as that he can create it, for life is *the* miracle, the inexplicable. In the act of destruction, man sets himself above life; he transcends himself as a creature. Thus, the ultimate choice for man, inasmuch as he is driven to transcend himself, is to create or to destroy, to love or to hate. The enormous power of the will for destruction which we see in the history of man, and which we have witnessed so frightfully in our own time, is rooted in the nature of man, just as the drive to create is rooted in it. To say that man is capable of developing his primary potentiality for love and reason does not imply the naive belief in man's goodness. Destructiveness is a secondary potentiality, rooted in the very existence of man, and having the same intensity and power as any passion can have. But—and this is the essential point of my argument—it is only the *alternative* to creativeness. Creation and destruction, love and hate, are not two instincts which exist independently. They are both answers to the same need for transcendence, and the will to destroy must rise when the will to create cannot be satisfied. However, the satisfaction of the need to create leads to happiness; destructiveness to suffering, most of all, for the destroyer himself....

Man may be defined as the animal that can say "I," that can be aware of himself as a separate entity. The animal being within nature, and not transcending it, has no awareness of himself, has no need for a sense of identity. Man, being torn away from nature, being endowed with reason and imagination, needs to form a concept of himself, needs to say and to feel: "I am I." Because he is not *lived,* but *lives,* because he has lost the original unity with nature, has to make decisions, is aware of himself and of his neighbor as different persons, he must be able to sense himself as the subject of his actions. As with the need for relatedness, rootedness, and transcendence, this need for a sense of identity is so vital and imperative that man could not remain sane if he did not find some way of satisfying it. Man's sense of identity develops in the process of emerging from the "primary bonds" which tie him to mother and nature. The infant, still feeling one with mother, cannot yet say "I," nor has he any need for it. Only after he has conceived of the outer world as being separate and different from himself does he come to the awareness of himself as a distinct being, and one of the last words he learns to use is "I," in reference to himself.

In the development of *the human race* the degree to which man is aware of himself as a separate self depends on the extent to which he has emerged from the clan and the extent to which the process of individuation has developed. The member of a primitive clan might express his sense of identity in the formula "I am we"; he cannot yet conceive of himself as an "individual," existing apart from his group. In the medieval world, the individual was identified with his social role in the feudal hierarchy. The peasant was not a man who happened to be a peasant, the feudal lord not a man who happened to be a feudal lord. *He was* a peasant or a lord, and this sense of his unalterable station was an essential part of his sense of identity. When the feudal system broke down, this sense of identity was shaken and the acute question "who am I?" arose—or more precisely, "How do I know that I am I?" This is the question which was raised, in a philosophical form, by Descartes. He answered the quest for identity by saying, "I doubt—hence I think, I think—hence I am." This answer put all the emphasis on the experience of "I" as the subject of any *thinking* activity, and failed to see that the "I" is experienced also in the process of feeling and creative action.

The development of Western culture went in the direction of creating the basis for the full experience of individuality. By making the individual free politically and economically, by teaching him to think for himself and freeing him from an authoritarian pressure, one hoped to enable him to feel "I" in the sense that he was the center and active subject of his powers and experienced himself as such. But only a minority achieved the new experience of "I." For the majority, individualism was not much more than a façade behind which was hidden the failure to acquire an individual sense of identity.

Many substitutes for a truly individual sense of identity were sought for, and found. Nation, religion, class and occupation serve to furnish a sense of identity. "I am an American," "I am a Protestant," "I am a businessman," are the formulae which help a man experience a sense of identity after the original clan identity has disappeared and before a truly individual sense of identity has been acquired. These different identifications are, in contemporary society, usually employed together. They are in a broad sense status identifications, and they are more efficient if blended with older feudal remnants, as in European countries. In the United States, in which so little is left of feudal relics, and in which there is so much social mobility, these status identifications are naturally less efficient, and the sense of identity is shifted more and more to the experience of conformity.

Inasmuch as I am not different, inasmuch as I am like the others, and recognized by them as "a regular fellow," I can sense myself as "I." I am—"as you desire me"—as Pirandello put it in the title of one of his plays. Instead of the pre-individualistic clan identity, a new herd identity develops, in which the sense of identity rests on the sense of an unquestionable belonging to the crowd. That this uniformity and conformity are often not recognized as such, and are covered by the illusion of individuality, does not alter the facts.

The problem of the sense of identity is not, as it is usually understood, merely a philosophical problem, or a problem only concerning our mind and thought. The need to feel a sense of identity stems from the very condition of human existence, and it is the source of the most intense strivings. Since I cannot remain sane without the sense of "I," I am driven to do almost anything to acquire this sense. Behind the intense passion for status and conformity is this very need, and it is sometimes even stronger than the need for physical survival. What could be more obvious than the fact that people are willing to risk their lives, to give up their love, to surrender their freedom, to sacrifice their own thoughts, for the sake of being one of the herd, of conforming, and thus of acquiring a sense of identity, even though it is an illusory one.

The Nature of the Self

DAVID HUME

*The Self as a Bundle of Perceptions**

David Hume (1711–1776), a Scottish philosopher and man of letters, lived at a time when thinkers were engaged in controversy about the nature of morals and religion. He influenced the development of skepticism in philosophy, for he distrusted philosophical speculation and asserted that all knowledge comes from experience. In religion he was an agnostic who held that the existence of God could not be proven or disproven. After applying unsuccessfully for positions in philosophy at Edinburgh and Glasgow, he decided to spend most of his life writing. His best-known philosophical works are *A Treatise of Human Nature, Philosophical Essays Concerning Human Understanding,* and *An Inquiry Concerning the Principles of Morals.*

In the following selection, Hume struggles with the problem of personal identity and the existence of what some philosophers call the self. Note the steps in his argument and the fact that he comes to deny the existence of any permanent self.

OF THE ORIGIN OF OUR IDEAS

All the perceptions of the human mind resolve themselves into two distinct kinds, which I shall call *impressions* and *ideas.* The difference betwixt these consists in the degrees of force and liveliness, with which they strike upon the mind, and make their way into our thought or consciousness. Those perceptions which enter with most force and violence, we may name *impressions;* and under this name I comprehend all our sensations, passions, and emotions, as they make their first appearance in the soul. By *ideas* I mean the faint images of these in thinking and reasoning; such as, for instance,

*David Hume, from *A Treatise of Human Nature* (1738), Book I, Part 1, Secs. 1, 6, and Appendix.

are all the perceptions excited by the present discourse, excepting only those which arise from the sight and touch, and excepting the immediate pleasure or uneasiness it may occasion. I believe it will not be very necessary to employ many words in explaining this distinction....

...We shall here content ourselves with establishing one general proposition, *That all our simple ideas in their first appearance are derived from simple impressions, which are correspondent to them, and which they exactly represent....*

OF PERSONAL IDENTITY

There are some philosophers who imagine we are every moment intimately conscious of what we call our *self;* that we feel its existence and its continuance in existence; and are certain, beyond the evidence of a demonstration, both of its perfect identity and simplicity. The strongest sensation, the most violent passion, say they, instead of distracting us from this view, only fix it the more intensely and make us consider their influence on *self* either by their pain or pleasure. To attempt a further proof of this were to weaken its evidence; since no proof can be derived from any fact of which we are so intimately conscious; nor is there anything of which we can be certain if we doubt of this.

Unluckily all these positive assertions are contrary to that very experience which is pleaded for them; nor have we any idea of *self,* after the manner it is here explained. For from what impression could this idea be derived? This question it is impossible to answer without a manifest contradiction and absurdity; and yet it is a question which must necessarily be answered, if we would have the idea of self pass for clear and intelligible. It must be some one impression that gives rise to every real idea. But self or person is not any one impression, but that to which our several impressions and ideas are supposed to have a reference. If any impression gives rise to the idea of self, that impression must continue invariably the same, through the whole course of our lives; since self is supposed to exist after that manner. But there is no impression constant and invariable. Pain and pleasure, grief and joy, passions and sensations succeed each other, and never all exist at the same time. It cannot therefore be from any of these impressions, or from any other, that the idea of self is derived; and consequently there is no such idea.

But further, what must become of all our particular perceptions upon this hypothesis? All these are different, and distinguishable, and separable from each other, and may be separately considered, and may exist separately, and have no need of anything to support their existence. After what manner therefore do they belong to self, and how are they connected with it? For my part, when I enter most intimately into what I call *myself,* I always stumble on some particular perception or other, of heat or cold, light or shade, love or hatred, pain or pleasure. I never can catch *myself* at any time without a perception, and never can observe anything but the perception. When my perceptions are removed for any time, as by sound sleep, so long am I insensible of *myself,* and may truly be said not to exist. And were all my perceptions removed by death, and could I neither think, nor feel, nor see, nor love, nor hate, after the dissolution of my body, I should be entirely annihilated, nor do I conceive what is further requisite to make me a perfect nonentity. If any one, upon serious and unprejudiced reflection, thinks he has a different notion of *himself,* I must confess I can reason no longer with him. All I can allow him is, that he may be in the right as well as I, and that we are essentially different in this particular. He may, perhaps, perceive something simple and continued, which he calls *himself;* though I am certain there is no such principle in me.

But setting aside some metaphysicians of this kind, I may venture to affirm of the rest of mankind, that they are nothing but a bundle or collection of different perceptions, which succeed each other with an inconceivable rapidity, and are in a perpetual flux and movement. Our eyes cannot turn in their sockets without varying our perceptions. Our thought is still more variable than our sight; and all our other senses and faculties contribute to this change; nor is there any single power of the soul, which remains unalterably the same, perhaps for one moment. The mind is a kind of theatre, where several perceptions successively make their appearance; pass, repass, glide away, and mingle in an infinite variety of postures and situations. There is properly no *simplicity* in it at one time, nor *identity* in different, whatever natural propension we may have to imagine that simplicity and identity. The comparison of the theatre must not mislead us. They are the successive perceptions only, that constitute the mind; nor have we the most distant notion of the place where these scenes are represented, or of the materials of which it is composed....

We now proceed to explain the nature of *personal identity,* which has become so great a question in philosophy, especially of late years in England, where all the abstruser sciences are studied with a peculiar ardour and application. And here it is evident the same method of reasoning must be continued which has so successfully explained the identity of plants, and animals, and ships, and houses, and of all compounded and changeable productions either of art or nature. The identity which we ascribe to the mind of man is only a fictitious one, and of a like kind with that which we ascribe to vegetable and animal bodies. It cannot therefore have a different origin, but must proceed from a like operation of the imagination upon like objects.

But lest this argument should not convince the reader, though in my opinion perfectly decisive, let him weigh the following reasoning, which is still closer and more immediate. It is evident, that the identity which we attribute to the human mind, however perfect we may imagine it to be, is not able to run the several different perceptions into one, and make them lose their characters of distinction and difference, which are essential to them. It is still true that every distinct perception which enters into the composition of the mind, is a distinct existence, and is different, and distinguishable, and separable from every other perception, either contemporary or successive. But as, notwithstanding this distinction and separability, we suppose the whole train of perceptions to be united by identity, a question naturally arises concerning this relation of identity, whether it be something that really binds our several perceptions together, or only associates their ideas in the imagination; that is, in other words, whether in pronouncing concerning the identity of a person, we observe some real bond among his perceptions, or only feel one among the ideas we form of them. This question we might easily decide, if we would recollect what has been already proved at large, that the understanding never observes any real connection among objects, and that even the union of cause and effect, when strictly examined, resolves itself into a customary association of ideas. For from thence it evidently follows, that identity is nothing really belonging to these different perceptions, and uniting them together, but is merely a quality which we attribute to them, because of the union of their ideas in the imagination when we reflect upon them. Now, the only qualities which can give ideas a union in the imagination, are the three relations below mentioned. These are the uniting principles in the ideal world, and without them every distinct object is separable by the mind, and may be separately considered, and appears not to have any more connection with any other object than if disjointed by the greatest difference and remoteness. It is therefore on some of these three relations of resemblance, contiguity, and causation, that identity depends; and as the very essence of these relations consists in their producing an easy transition of ideas, it follows that our notions of personal identity proceed entirely from the smooth and uninterrupted progress of the thought along a train of connected ideas, according to the principles above explained....

I had entertained some hopes, that however deficient our theory of the intellectual world might be, it would be free from those contradictions and absurdities which seem to attend every explication that human reason can give of the material world. But upon a more strict review of the section concerning *personal identity,* I find myself involved in such a labyrinth that, I must confess, I neither know how to correct my former opinions, nor how to render them consistent. If this be not a good *general* reason for scepticism, it is at least a sufficient one (if I were not already abundantly supplied) for me to entertain a diffidence and modesty in all my decisions.

When we talk of *self* or *substance,* we must have an idea annexed to these terms, otherwise they are altogether unintelligible. Every idea is derived from preceding impressions; and we have no impression of self or substance, as something simple and individual. We have, therefore, no idea of them in that sense....

APPENDIX

Whatever is distinct is distinguishable, and whatever is distinguishable is separable by the thought or imagination. All perceptions are distinct. They are, therefore, distinguishable, and separable, and may be conceived as separately existent, and may exist separately, without any contradiction or absurdity.

When I view this table and that chimney, nothing is present to me but particular perceptions, which are of a like nature with all the other perceptions. This is the doctrine of philosophers. But this table, which is present to me, and that chimney, may, and do exist separately. This is the doctrine of the vulgar, and implies no contradiction. There is no contradiction, therefore, in extending the same doctrine to all the perceptions.

In general, the following reasoning seems satisfactory. All ideas are borrowed from preceding perceptions. Our ideas of objects, therefore, are derived from that source. Consequently no proposition can be intelligible or consistent with regard to objects, which is not so with regard to perceptions. But it is intelligible and consistent to say, that objects exist distinct and independent, without any common *simple* substance or subject of inhesion. This proposition, therefore, can never be absurd with regard to perceptions.

When I turn my reflection on *myself,* I never can perceive this *self* without some one or more perceptions; nor can I ever perceive anything but the perceptions. It is the composition of these, therefore, which forms the self.

We can conceive a thinking being to have either many or few perceptions. Suppose the mind to be reduced even below the life of an oyster. Suppose it to have only one perception, as of thirst or hunger. Consider it in that situation. Do you conceive anything but merely that perception? Have you any notion of *self* or *substance?* If not, the addition of other perceptions can never give you that notion.

The annihilation which some people suppose to follow upon death, and which entirely destroys this self, is nothing but an extinction of all particular perceptions; love and hatred, pain and pleasure, thought and sensation. These, therefore, must be the same with self, since the one cannot survive the other.

Is *self* the same with *substance?* If it be, how can that question have place, concerning the subsistence of self, under a change of substance? If they be distinct, what is the difference betwixt them? For my part, I have a notion of neither, when conceived distinct from particular perceptions.

Philosophers begin to be reconciled to the principle, *that we have no idea of external substance, distinct from the ideas of particular qualities.* This must pave the way for a like principle with regard to the mind, *that we have no notion of it, distinct from the particular perception.*

So far I seem to be attended with sufficient evidence. But having thus loosened all our particular perceptions, when I proceed to explain the principle of connection, which binds them together, and makes us attribute to them a real simplicity and identity, I am sensible that my account is very defective, and that nothing but the seeming evidence of the precedent reasonings could have induced me to receive it. If perceptions are distinct existences, they form a whole only by being connected together. But no connections among distinct existences are ever discoverable by human understanding. We only *feel* a connection or determination of the thought to pass from one object to another. It follows, therefore, that the thought alone feels personal identity, when reflecting on the train of past perceptions that compose a mind, the ideas of them are felt to be connected together, and naturally introduce each other. However extraordinary this conclusion may seem, it need not surprise us. Most philosophers seem inclined to think that personal identity *arises* from consciousness, and consciousness is nothing but a reflected thought or perception. The present philosophy, therefore, has so far a promising aspect. But all my hopes vanish when I come to explain the principles that unite our successive perceptions in our thought or consciousness. I cannot discover any theory which gives me satisfaction on this head.

In short, there are two principles which I cannot render consistent, nor is it in my power to renounce either of them, viz. *that all our distinct perceptions are distinct existences,* and *that the mind never perceives any real connection among distinct existences.* Did our perceptions either inhere in something simple and individual, or did the mind perceive some real connection among them, there would be no difficulty in the case. For my part, I must plead the privilege of a sceptic, and confess that this difficulty is too hard for my understanding. I pretend not, however, to pronounce it absolutely insuperable. Others, perhaps, or myself, upon more mature reflections, may discover some hypothesis that will reconcile those contradictions.

JAMES BISSETT PRATT

*The Self as Substance**

James Bissett Pratt (1875–1944) was professor of philosophy at Williams College for many years. He was a member of the group known as critical realists, but preferred the name *personal realism* for his own philosophy. He had wide interests in the psychology and philosophy of religion, as well as in epistemology and metaphysics. His many books include *Matter and Spirit, Adventures in Philosophy, The Religious Consciousness,* and *Can We Keep the Faith?*

In the selection below, Pratt discusses the nature of the human self and why it is so frequently misunderstood. The self, he says, is a unique substance possessing distinctive qualities. Note especially the kind of knowledge we have of the self; for Pratt, the fact that the self cannot be directly discovered, as Hume maintained, is irrelevant.

From the beginning I have maintained that the self is a substance; and that means an existent being possessing qualities. But there are many grades and many kinds of substance and a self is a substance of its own kind. It is *sui generis*. I cannot make this too emphatic. One of the chief reasons why the self is so persistently misunderstood, so very hard to understand, is because we naturally seek to form an image of it, even to visualize it, and naturally construct our image on the outline of the spatial things we see and handle. This is a costly mistake, but it is a natural one. Both in the individual and in the race, theory or understanding follows action, and is in all men first produced, and in many men only produced, for the sake of action. Now action, the vital needs of life, the necessities that dominate our activities as living beings in a spatial world of dangerous and useful, tangible and visible things, force us to center most of our attention on the spatial, tangible, and visible. Hence it has come about that the very notion of an entity or real being is associated in our minds with spatial characters, and even when we come to realize that there are, or may be, real beings which are not spatial, our inveterate tendency is still to think of them by means of visual images and to interpret them in spatial terms.... And so it has come about that every word one can discover when used to express

*Reprinted with permission of Macmillan Publishing Co., Inc. from *Personal Realism* by James Bissett Pratt. Copyright 1937 by Macmillan Publishing Co., Inc. renewed 1965 by Catherine Pratt. From "The Nature of the Self," pp. 301–306, 311–317.

the meaning of the self tends to betray one, and to lead the hearer, and often the speaker, into materialistic pictures the very reverse of what one really wishes to convey.

Hence, let me repeat, the necessity of realizing that by the self one means something essentially unique and *sui generis*. It is a substance, but this does not mean that it is either tangible or visible. And since it is not visible, all efforts to visualize it must be misleading. We must, therefore, not expect that the self will be a substance of the same sort as material things....

...We must remember that by substance one does not mean an abstract core of being taken by itself, but an entity with characters. There is no substance without attributes and no characterless self without qualities or acts. As well ask for an existent form completely divorced from matter. The self is therefore full of variety. In it variety and unity are harmonized. That this can be is no miracle, except as all existence is miraculous....

Of course questions may be asked about the self which it will be hard to answer. If the self is more than a stream of consciousness, more than a collection, it may well be asked, what is this *more?* A partial answer, and one which at least points in a hopeful direction, will be that the self is the doer of certain acts. It is the sort of being that does the acts we find it doing. This may not be a complete answer, but it is at least as much of an answer as we can give concerning other things. Things are known by what they do: so is the self. If, then, the question be raised: What is the self aside from all its attributes and all its acts? the answer is that the self is never without attributes and that if it were it would be just nothing at all. It is *that which* has certain characters and acts in certain ways....

THE UNITY OF THE SELF

The self is *sui generis* in possessing a unity of an inherent sort which no other substance possesses. Non-living material things have, indeed, relations, but no inherent unity. Many of them possess only so much unity as we read into them. The Great Bear, or Dipper, is a unity because we choose to regard it as such. My watch is a unity because of its relation to my purposes. But without relation to conscious purpose or thought it would have no unity. The unities of the physical and nonliving world depend upon living and conscious beings. Living organisms have a certain degree of inherent unity. But in so far as this unity is unconscious, unrealized, it is of a potential sort. It is true that the root and the leaves of the rose plant co-operate, and that we justly find in them together a unity in variety. But it is just as true that they are *two* as that they are one. The only being that is *essentially* one is a self.

The unity-in-variety which uniquely characterizes a self is seen in each of its three most noticeable characters or functions. The first of these is its role as subject in feeling and cognition. The second is its agency as the actor, the doer of deeds, the one who wills in volition, the efficient cause in its achievements. Finally the self is not only the unity that lies behind each mental state and the grasper that unites and compares: it is also the unity and the unifier in successive states, the identical being that endures in the midst of its changing acts and states. As Professor Wilson has admirably put it, the self is "that which maintains itself through its experiences."

CAN THE SELF BE KNOWN?

...Knowledge is a notoriously ambiguous word. To know *about* an object is one thing: to be directly aware of it, to have it as one's immediate experience, is another. Plainly it is only this second and direct kind of knowledge of the self, "knowledge of acquaintance," which is denied by both Yajnavalkya and Hume. It is conceivable that though we lack this, it still may be possible for us to have knowledge about the self. How, one may ask, do we know *physical* things? I do not mean, How do we know our own sensations and percepts, but how do we know the physical things all men except idealistic philosophers in their few official moments believe in? The answer to this question given by the form of Realism I have advocated in this volume is the following: We do not perceive or know physical things "directly," *i.e.,* not in the direct fashion in which we know our own sensations. But we have a strong and native impulsion to believe there are physical things corresponding to and causing our percepts, and our reflective thought discovers that we can make sense of our experience only by supposing that this native impulsion is justified. Our knowledge of the physical world is indirect: it is *knowledge about,* not *acquaintance with.* We have at least this same kind of knowledge of the self. We do not find it as we do its feelings and percepts; but everyone has a natural impulsion to believe in it, and our experience is such that no theory is satisfactory which fails to recognize self as the actor and knower, the inner unity and the inner unifier of our multiform lives. We know *that* the self is, and we know *what* it is by observing what it does. And this we know because every theory of the inner life which fails to recognize a knower and actor does violence to the facts of experience. If this is the case, and I believe I have shown that it is the case, the fact that the self cannot be directly found is irrelevant: in fact it is exactly what, upon our theory, we should expect to be true. "How couldst thou know the knower?"

But it would be only a partial presentation of the truth should we stop here. I think we do have the same kind of evidence for the existence of the self that we have for the existence of physical things; but I think we have also a kind of knowledge concerning the self that we do not have concerning any physical thing.... The self is not part of the conscious content found directly as feelings and sensa are. But in every case of knowledge we are directly aware of the "datum" not merely as a thing but *as a datum, i.e.,* as something given. The givenness is given. The datum is something given to us, it is an object of our awareness or of our thought. *All experience contains the implications of a subject.* The subject-object relation is one of the characters which we find or feel whenever we are aware of anything. It is like the stick illustration—the stick which, no matter how often one cuts it, has two ends. The self, indeed, cannot be found in the way Hume sought to find it, but the reason is that it is too near to be seen. It is, of course, the very finder, and we can never get away from it. "When me thy fly, I am the wings."...

CHARACTERISTICS OF THE SELF

...The self is a substance. We have considerable knowledge about it, and a certain immediate realization of it. It is not a blank and abstract substance nor a blank unity, but a substance with qualities, a unity that possesses rich variety. These qualities or characters and this variety are seen in the conscious states of the self and in its activities. It is characterized by its passing sensa—a relatively unimportant matter—by its memories, its tendencies, its activities, its powers or potentialities for action, its efforts of attention and will, its reasoning power, its sentiments, its purposes. From the point of view of the social and ethical life, the purposes of the self are perhaps its most important characteristic....

The self is to be discerned in every act and moment of our conscious living. But it is probably in the free act of will that it makes itself most vividly plain. In attention with effort, in sticking to the distasteful mental task in spite of monotony, in spite of weariness, in spite of pain, we are often most obvious to ourselves. And in those crises in which the will acts against instinctive tendency, even against the biological interests of the organism, the self shines with its own light, in its essential superiority to the merely physical and physiological and psychological. Asceticism has often been carried to utterly irrational limits, but the fact that asceticism is possible, that the soul can so triumph over the flesh as the great ascetics East and West have shown us that it can, throws a new light upon human nature. The martyrs of all time, the Irish and Indian patriots of a few years ago refusing to allow their hungry bodies to taste of food until they die of starvation for the sake of an ideal—things like these make almost ludicrous any attempt to explain human nature out of stimuli and reflexes and associations. Nor need we turn to martyrs for striking cases of the self in unmistakable action. The steady drive of the will against the choice of the weary body *most* of us have known. And in many a case where we outsiders see no sign of effort, the self may be struggling with and dominating the great mass of native psycho-physical tendencies, and its victory be all the greater, all the surer token of its own reality, because quite hidden....

B. F. SKINNER

*The Self as an Organized System of Responses**

B. F. Skinner, (b. 1901), psychologist and educator, taught at the universities of Michigan and of Indiana and at Harvard University. During World War II he conducted research on training pigeons and developed the "Skinner Box" in which animal behavior was studied and controlled. He has received many awards and distinctions. His books include *Behavior of Organisms, Walden Two, Science and Human Behavior, The Technology of Teaching,* and *Beyond Freedom and Dignity.*

In his approach to the traditional concept of the self, Skinner adopts a skeptical attitude reminiscent of Hume. In contrast to Pratt, he denies that there is a substantial self seen as the cause of actions. Hume and Skinner have often been viewed as asserting that there is no self. Their remarks may be viewed, however, as giving us an analysis which they think is more accurate. In this light, "the self" for Skinner is "an organized system of responses."

What is meant by the "self" in self-control or self-knowledge? When a man jams his hands into his pockets to keep himself from biting his nails, *who* is controlling *whom?* When he discovers that a sudden mood must be due to a glimpse of an unpleasant person, *who* discovers *whose* mood to be due to *whose* visual response? Is the self which works to facilitate the recall of a name the same as the self which recalls it? When a thinker teases out an idea, is it the teaser who also eventually has the idea?

The self is most commonly used as a hypothetical cause of action. So long as external variables go unnoticed or are ignored, their function is

*Reprinted with permission of Macmillan Publishing Co., Inc. from *Science and Human Behavior* by B. F. Skinner. Copyright 1953 by Macmillan Publishing Co., Inc. Pages 283–288.

assigned to an originating agent within the organism. If we cannot show what is responsible for a man's behavior, we say that he himself is responsible for it. The precursors of physical science once followed the same practice, but the wind is no longer blown by Aeolus, nor is the rain cast down by Jupiter Pluvius. Perhaps it is because the notion of personification is so close to a conception of a behaving individual that it has been difficult to dispense with similar explanations of behavior. The practice resolves our anxiety with respect to unexplained phenomena and is perpetuated because it does so.

Whatever the self may be, it is apparently not identical with the physical organism. The organism behaves, while the self initiates or directs behavior. Moreover, more than one self is needed to explain the behavior of one organism. A mere inconsistency in conduct from one moment to the next is perhaps no problem, for a single self could dictate different kinds of behavior from time to time. But there appear to be two selves acting simultaneously and in different ways when one self controls another or is aware of the activity of another.

The same facts are commonly expressed in terms of "personalities." The personality, like the self, is said to be responsible for features of behavior. For example, delinquent behavior is sometimes attributed to a psychopathic personality. Personalities may also be multiple. Two or more personalities may appear in alternation or concurrently. They are often in conflict with each other, and one may or may not be aware of what the other is doing.

Multiple selves or personalities are often said to be systematically related to each other. Freud conceived of the ego, superego, and id as distinguishable agents within the organism. The id was responsible for behavior which was ultimately reinforced with food, water, sexual contact, and other primary biological reinforcers. It was not unlike the selfish, aggressive "Old Adam" of Judeo-Christian theology, preoccupied with the basic deprivations and untouched by similar requirements on the parts of others. The superego—the "conscience" of Judeo-Christian theology—was responsible for the behavior which controlled the id. It used techniques of self-control acquired from the group. When these were verbal, they constituted "the still small voice of conscience." The superego and the id were inevitably opposed to each other, and Freud conceived of them as often in violent conflict. He appealed to a third agent—the ego—which, besides attempting to reach a compromise between the id and the superego, also dealt with the practical exigencies of the environment.

We may quarrel with any analysis which appeals to a self or personality as an inner determiner of action, but the facts which have been represented with such devices cannot be ignored. The three selves or personalities in the Freudian scheme represent important characteristics of behavior in a social milieu. Multiple personalities which are less systematically related to each other serve a similar function. A concept of self is not essential in an analysis of behavior, but what is the alternative way of treating the data?

The best way to dispose of any explanatory fiction is to examine the facts upon which it is based. These usually prove to be, or suggest, variables which are acceptable from the point of view of scientific method. In the present case it appears that a self is simply a device for representing *a functionally unified system of responses.* In dealing with the data, we have to explain the functional unity of such systems and the various relationships which exist among them.

The Unity of a Self. A self may refer to a common *mode of action.* Such expressions as "The scholar is Man Thinking" or "He was a better talker than plumber" suggest personalities identified with *topographical subdivisions* of behavior. In a single skin we find the man of action and the dreamer, the solitary and the social spirit.

On the other hand, a personality may be tied to a particular type of occasion—when a system of responses is organized around a given *discriminative stimulus.* Types of behavior which are effective in achieving reinforcement upon occasion *A* are held together and distinguished from those effective upon occasion *B*. Thus one's personality in the bosom of one's family may be quite different from that in the presence of intimate friends.

Responses which lead to a common reinforcement, regardless of the situation, may also comprise a functional system. Here the principal variable is *deprivation.* A motion to adjourn a meeting which has run through the lunch hour may show "the hungry man speaking." One's personality may be very different before and after a satisfying meal. The libertine is very different from the ascetic who achieves his reinforcement from the ethical group, but the two may exist side by side in the same organism.

Emotional variables also establish personalities. Under the proper circumstances the timid soul may give way to the aggressive man. The hero may struggle to conceal the coward who inhabits the same skin.

The effects of *drugs* upon personality are well known. The euphoria of the morphine addict represents a special repertoire of responses the strength of which is attributable to an obvious variable. The alcoholic wakes on the morrow a sadder and wiser man.

It is easy to overestimate the unity of a group of responses, and unfortunately personification encourages us to do so. The concept of a self may have an early advantage in representing a relatively coherent response system, but it may lead us to expect consistencies and functional integrities which do not exist. The alternative to the use of the concept is simply to deal with demonstrated covariations in the strength of responses.

Relations Among Selves. Organized systems of responses may be related to each other in the same way as are single responses and for the same reasons.... For example, two response systems may be incompatible. If the relevant variables are never present at the same time, the incompatibility is unimportant. If the environment of which behavior is a function is not consistent from moment to moment, there is no reason to expect consistency in behavior. The pious churchgoer on Sunday may become an aggressive, unscrupulous businessman on Monday. He possesses two response systems appropriate to different sets of circumstances, and his inconsistency is no greater than that of the environment which takes him to church on Sunday and to work on Monday. But the controlling variables may come together; during a sermon, the churchgoer may be asked to examine his business practices, or the businessman may engage in commercial transactions with his clergyman or his church. Trouble may then arise. Similarly, if an individual has developed different repertoires with family and friends, the two personalities come into conflict when he is with both at the same time. Many of the dramatic struggles which flood the literature on multiple personalities can be accounted for in the same way.

More systematic relations among personalities arise from ... controlling relations.... In self-control, for example, the responses to be controlled are organized around certain immediate primary reinforcements. To the extent that competition for reinforcement makes this behavior aversive to others—and to this extent only—we may refer to an anti-social personality, the id or Old Adam. On the other hand, the controlling behavior engendered by the community consists of a selected group of practices evolved in the history of a particular culture because of their effect upon anti-social behavior. To the extent that this behavior works to the advantage of the community—and again to this extent only—we may speak of a unitary conscience, social conscience, or superego. These two sets of variables account, not only for the membership of each group of responses, but for the relation between them which we describe when we say that one personality is engaged in controlling the other. Other kinds of relations between personalities are evident in the processes of making a decision, solving a problem, or creating a work of art.

An important relation between selves is ... self-knowledge.... The behavior which we call knowing is due to a particular kind of differential reinforcement. In even the most rudimentary community such questions as "What did you do?" or "What are you doing?" compel the individual to respond to his own overt behavior. Probably no one is completely unselfconscious in this sense. At the other extreme an advanced and relatively nonpractical society produces the highly introspective or introverted individual, whose repertoire of self-knowledge extends to his covert behavior—a repertoire which in some cultures may be almost nonexistent. An extensive development of self-knowledge is common in certain Eastern cultures and is emphasized from time to time in those of the West—for example, in the *culte du moi* of French literature. An efficient repertoire of this sort is sometimes set up in the individual for purposes of therapy. The patient under psychoanalysis may become highly skilled in observing his own covert behavior.

When an occasion arises upon which a report of the organism's own behavior, particularly at the covert level, is likely to be reinforced, the personality which makes the report is a specialist trained by a special set of contingencies. The self which is concerned with self-knowing functions concurrently with the behavioral system which it describes. But it is sometimes important to ask whether the selves generated by other contingencies "know about each other." The literature on multiple personalities raises the question as one of "continuity of memory." It is also an important consideration in the Freudian scheme: to what extent, for example, is the superego aware of the behavior of the id? The contingencies which set up the superego as a controlling system involve stimulation from the behavior of the id, but they do not necessarily establish responses of knowing about the behavior of the id. It is perhaps even less likely that the id will know about the superego. The ego can scarcely deal with conflicts between the other selves without responding to the behavior attributed to them, but this does not mean that the ego possesses a repertoire of knowing about such behavior in any other sense.

GERALD E. MYERS

*Self and Self-Knowledge**

Gerald E. Myers (b. 1923) is professor of philosophy at Queens College and Graduate Center, City University of New York. In addition to the book from which our selection is taken and articles in professional journals, he has written *Self, Religion, and Metaphysics* and *The Spirit of American Philosophy*.

In the following selection, Myers examines the traditional philosophical view of the self as something neither physical nor mental—a *nonbodily* something. He then discusses some of the puzzles that such a view generates, and offers some

*From *Self, An Introduction to Philosophical Psychology* by Gerald E. Myers, Chapters 1 and 10 with omissions.

suggestions for the solution of these puzzles. He concludes by exploring the role of self-knowledge, especially in its relation to self-evaluation.

> His causes were air, and ether, and water, and many other strange things. I thought he was exactly like a man who should begin by saying that Socrates does all that he does by Mind, and who, when he tried to give a reason for each of my actions, should say, first, that I am sitting here now, because my body is composed of bones and muscles, and that the bones are hard and separated by joints, while the muscles can be tightened and loosened, and, together with the flesh and the skin which holds them together, cover the bones; and that therefore, when the bones are raised in their sockets, the relaxation and contraction of the muscles make it possible for me now to bend my limbs, and that is the cause of my sitting here with my legs bent. And in the same way he would go on to explain why I am talking to you: he would assign voice, and air, and hearing, and a thousand other things as causes; but he would quite forget to mention the real cause, which is that since the Athenians thought it right to condemn me, I have thought it right and just to sit here and to submit to whatever sentence they may think fit to impose. For, by the dog of Egypt, I think that these muscles and bones would long ago have been in Megara or Boeotia, prompted by their opinion of what is best, if I had not thought it better and more honorable to submit to whatever penalty the state inflicts, rather than escape by flight.
>
> Plato's *Phaedo*

1. THE PHILOSOPHICAL CONCEPT OF THE SELF

Socrates' point in the above epigraph may be put like this: It would be grotesque to say that his body decided to remain in prison and accept the death penalty; obviously, it was *he,* Socrates, who decided and was responsible for his sitting in the jail awaiting his end. Socrates' body was simply executing the orders of Socrates, the person or self housed in or somehow connected with that body. A person or self is certainly not identical with the body in which it lives, according to Socrates, since our bodies obviously do not ponder alternatives and make decisions; on the contrary, it is *we,* conceived as persons or selves somehow *more* or *other* than our bodies, who weigh and pick from among alternatives, manifesting our decisions in the way *we* move our bodies. Traditionally, that aspect or part of a person which ponders, decides, and initiates changes in that person's body has been known as "the self." What we mean by a "person" or "human being" must therefore include more than a human body; a human body is not a human being until a "self" has been added.

Another way of introducing the traditional concept of the self is to offer it as the claim that, for each of us, it is "oneself" rather than one's body which is referred to by the first-person pronoun; "I" refers only incidentally to my body, but it refers primarily and essentially to that other aspect of me which is "myself." It would be grotesque, on the traditional account, for you to tap some part of your body and insist that your use of "I" referred to *that;* it would be almost as absurd to suggest that "I" refers to the entire body rather than any part of it. If we were merely bodies, personal pronouns would be linguistic superfluities, but clearly they are not, since they refer to selves while *impersonal* pronouns in most languages refer to whatever is not a self or person. Thus, the problem of explicating the concept of the self is the problem of explaining what, for each of us, is the referent of the first-person pronoun.

A contemporary Socrates might cite recent experimental achievements on behalf of the claim that "I" must refer to something other than one's body, that other being *oneself.* The pertinent scientific achievement concerns amputees. An amputee, who had manipulated the conventional harness-operated arm for twenty-six years, has recently succeeded in using a new device, substituting for his amputated arm, for lifting things—in the language of the public announcement of the feat—"merely by thinking the lifting process." The new artificial limb has not been attached directly to the man but is connected to him via electrodes; these, attached to the stump of his upper arm, are also connected to a large computer which translates the signals with the flexing movements and stress control of the artificial limb. The novelty here is not the translation of electric signals into mechanical force but the translation into stress control. Former clamp-like devices required the same force, whether lifting a feather or a brick. The signals that tell the arm when to use the biceps and triceps muscles and when to exert stress were sorted out after several years of experimenting, and a mechanical arm was then built that translated the signal–information from the computer into flexing movements with a stress that can be controlled merely by "thinking it." The amputee, intending to grasp a feather rather than a brick, sends the appropriate electric signals as a result of his deliberate intention from the stump of his arm to the computer which conveys this information to the artificial limb, which then exerts only the force required to lift a feather. The amputee may say of the electric signals themselves, as Socrates said of the movements of his limbs, that they are what "*I* cause to happen." It is *oneself* who initiates the changes in the brain resulting in the electric signals sent to the muscular system; it is another case of the body responding to orders from the self whose body it is.

The self, then, is initially conceived as what is referred to by "I" when it is true to say "*I* caused such-and-such changes in my body." Given the beliefs that my body is not what is primarily or essentially meant by "I," and that I and not my body often cause changes in my body, and that the expression "my body" includes reference to all the physico-chemical events constituting my body, it is indeed natural to conclude, as many distinguished thinkers have concluded, that the *self* is a nonphysical, nonchemical *something*. It is natural, upon such assumptions, to infer that what is essentially referred to by "I" is a *nonbodily something*. This conclusion is often expressed by saying that oneself is a mental, psychic, or spiritual thing or being. Certain philosophies and religions owe their appeal to the fact that this conclusion really does seem to their adherents to fit the facts.

It should be remarked that, according to some philosophers, the self is not only not identical with one's body, it is also not identical with one's mind. It can be argued that, just as specific changes in my bodily condition are caused by me rather than by my body, so particular changes in my mind or mental condition originate with me rather than in my mind. My mind is often as responsive as my body to what *I* decide to do, decide to think about, and so on. As my body is mine, so my mind is mine, leaving *me* in some sense the "possessor" of my mind and my body and not identical with either or both. It appears that Descartes (1596–1650) accepted this account. In considering what he should or should not believe in certain difficult cases, Descartes said that "it seems to me that it is the business of the mind alone, and not of the being composed of mind and body, to decide the truth of such matters." This indicates that Descartes distinguished himself, conceived of as somehow composed of his mind and body, from both his mind and body. Descartes appears to have believed that, just as it was better for *him* to leave his respiratory system to breathe for itself, so it was sometimes expedient for *him* to abdicate and permit his mind to think for itself. If so, then the human being consists of a body, a mind, and a self. The self is, in some sense, the *possessor* of a mind and a body, and is what is referred to, by each of us, by the first-person pronoun. In particular, the self is what can initiate changes in the mind and body which it possesses. We may call this the "philosophical" concept of the self, to distinguish it from other concepts found in the literature of psychoanalysis, personality theory, and empirical psychology. The "philosophical self" has also been referred to in traditional philosophy as the pure ego, the unity of consciousness, the personal subject, and the soul. Whatever label used, the notion of the self is of something neither physical nor mental; rather, it "owns" a mind and a body and can set off changes in both possessions. To simplify the following discussion, and because it probably represents the philosophical problem most vividly, we shall focus on the self considered as a *nonbodily* something....

Children are taught to substitute "I" for their names when talking about themselves. If a very young child is asked, after learning to use the first-person pronoun in appropriate contexts, whether his use of "I" refers just to his body or to something else, he will express bewilderment. For he did not learn, in acquiring the use of "I," that the pronoun does or does not refer to his body. Somewhat older, he draws a distinction between himself as owner and his body as owned; he calls his body, like his tricycle, *mine*. If he is then asked whether "I" refers to just his body or something else, he will probably express a more sophisticated bewilderment, characteristic of the burgeoning as well as the burgeoned philosopher, since he appreciates the logical fact that owner and owned can hardly be identical, yet also appreciates the realistic fact that there is only his body to point to as the referent of "I." The bewilderment thickens when he subsequently refers the responsibility for his actions to himself rather than to his body. He has learned to speculate like Socrates, like many of us. He is ripe for Hume's bewilderment.

The conclusion that one's self is a nonbodily something is drawn from the premisses that I am not identical with my body and that I can cause changes in my body. But part of the problem has its source in how we understand the word "body," and if we appreciated that fact we might then see how we can sensibly deny the premiss that I am not identical with my body; or, if not quite that, at least how we might deny the premiss that I am not identical with a bodily something. Most of us probably associate "the body" primarily with something publicly perceptible and only capable on its own of reflex behavior. Whether this is to be ungenerous toward our own bodies was a consideration of Spinoza (1632–1677) when he remarked, while noting the already-known "marvels" of the human body, "No one has so far determined what the body is capable of...."

Substituting "organism" for "body" *can* work philosophical wonders. We are less resistant, if at all, to thinking of ourselves as physiological "organisms" than as "bodies," and for good reasons. The word "organism" was invented to refer to a physiological entity that is alive, self-moving, develops, evolves, is capable of feelings, thoughts, etc. which are not publicly perceptible, capable of a psychological dynamic, and so on. The word "body" does not connote so richly. For common-sense reasons we may not boggle, therefore, at identifying ourselves as organisms, at understanding the referent of "I" to be identical with the referent of "this organism." Indeed, just this simply, the puzzlement attending "*What* am I?" may be dissipated. Of course, I am not merely a body; *I* am this complex organism sitting here. And notice: Though we speak of "my body" and "your body," we don't speak of "my organism" and "your organism." In the vocabulary of bodies, owner and owned get distinguished, but not so in the vocabulary of organisms. The human organism has no landlord, being its own proprietor.

Certainly, some thinkers may object to our suggestion that the referent of "I" is not a nonbodily (and nonmental) something, that it is rather identical with "this organism sitting here, writing these words," etc. They may argue that this suggestion is theologically or scientifically incomplete, citing possible evidence, ranging from sacred scriptures to psychical research, for the conclusion that I am somehow "more" than a human organism. But many people are perplexed, like Hume, by and into the philosophical concept of the self, not because of very special or unusual evidence, but simply because of what routine experience seems to indicate. This suggestion is only intended for those who thought, on the basis of everyday experience, they could not identify *themselves* with their bodies, but consequently could not locate anything else with which to identify. It may suffice for those whose problem was, it turns out, a certain opinion about the human body.

But citing the advantages of regarding persons as organisms rather than as bodies merely shows how "What am I?" can be answered, how a referent for the first-person pronoun, consistent with the way the pronoun was originally learned, is easily located. We must, in addition, suggest why this does not really conflict with anything revealed to our subjective experiences. For a person sharing Hume's perplexity may say, "*Objectively,* I know it makes sense to conclude that what *I* am is a certain type of organism. But, *subjectively,* I can't help returning to the feeling that what "I" refers to is more mysterious and elusive. I can't explain this feeling, but something in my experience must provoke it."

An explanation of this "returning feeling" is this: I slide into Hume's perplexity by thinking of myself as a *momentary cause,* as the cause of my writing these words at this moment. By accepting uncritically the premiss that I am not identical with my body, and given my knowledge that I am responsible for my writing these words at this very moment, I infer that "I" refers to the cause at this moment of my writing these words. I feel that this momentary cause, myself, ought to be discoverable, but it is not. The philosophical concept of the self is the concept of an elusive momentary causal agent.

The mistake here is to forget that the organism that I am *is* self-moving, capable of causing its own actions; it does not require another I to make it move. The source of this mistake is perhaps our inability to see, on the basis of what is revealed to subjective awareness, how we, as human organisms, move ourselves. Physiologists can explain how my muscles work when I write, but neither they nor I can apparently explain *how I originate* the action. I feel that I ought to be able to detect myself causing my own actions, ought to see how I originate my own movements. The absence of a supposed causal connection in the activity of the organism that I am leads me to fill the absence with a *nonbodily I as momentary cause* of a momentary action. In looking for the nonbodily I, I am looking for the missing cause in the organism's activity, but the nonbodily I turns out to be equally missing. But that frustrating fact does not prevent the "returning feeling," on the occasion when I say truly "*I* am the origin of this action," that the elusive cause in myself as an organism must therefore be "outside" myself as an organism, i.e., must be a nonbodily self or cause.

But in wondering *how* I originate my own actions, I have already committed the mistake of thinking that initiating an action is a causal process. Originating one's own action, however, is just *doing* it on one's own. Of course, the neurophysiological details of how I move my arm in writing these words are complex; they reveal, for example, the now familiar fact that, in writing, I originate changes in the brain and the nervous system that precede my arm movements. But there is no causal mechanism whereby I originate the initial item in the causal series leading to my arm movements, which is what I mistakenly assume in wondering "how" I initiate it. Of course, unlike lower forms of life, humans often plan, ponder, and deliberate before acting, and we sometimes mean to refer to that preparatory mental activity in speaking of "how" the act was done. But when, after the pondering and deliberating, I originate an action, there is no process whereby the organism that I am originates the action; originating the action is simply doing it on one's own. There is no more a special problem of "how" humans originate their actions than there is of how animals move themselves. Once I realize that there is no basis for "How do I originate my own actions?" and consequently am not tempted to think that "I" refers to an origin (other than the organism that I am) of my actions, the "returning feeling" that "I" *must* refer to a nonbodily and nonmental self may never return again.

...The concept of self is prominent in psychological and psychiatric literature. Sometimes the philosophical concept of self seems to be defended, when, for example, it is said that effective therapy requires one's "experiencing" one's real self. It is sometimes suggested that mental health and self-knowledge depend upon literally experiencing one's self as one experiences, say, a feeling of hope or a sense of despair. However, clinical psychology, like experimental or behavioral psychology, generally avoids the metaphysical "I." What is rather intended by "self" is either the whole human organism, or the attitudes which a person has toward himself (his "image" of himself), or a set of distinctive processes (for instance, defense mechanisms) invoked by psychoanalytic theory to explain certain kinds of behavior.

When clinical psychology stresses the importance of "the self," it means to emphasize how our ability to function depends upon our attitudes toward ourselves, and how such attitudes result from distinctive psychological as well as physiological processes. Understanding what are our attitudes toward ourselves (and others) and what produced them is a complex process which, if successful, constitutes self-knowledge. In this process we may experience "sudden insights" concerning our attitudes and their origins, but this does not imply that self-knowledge is ever the result of experiencing the sort of thing Hume vainly sought. Further, from a psychoanalytic perspective, it may be deleterious to suppose that self-knowledge can be acquired through a sudden, illuminating experience of one's elusive "real self" rather than through the complex process of understanding how the organism that one is has developed from infancy as it did.

In fact, it is startling to learn how complex are the conditions to be fulfilled if a child is to acquire, or retain, or acknowledge a sense of self. Studies of autistic children, withdrawn into their fantasy worlds, reveal that being able to use "I" in a normal way is hardly automatic. Examples of eight- and nine-year-old youngsters who don't refer to themselves at all, or refer to themselves by a mathematical formula and avoid pronouns altogether, or refer to themselves as machines or animals, point to many lessons. But two of these deserve mention here. First, recent investigations greatly reinforce the picture of the infant as a striving and demanding organism. How it fares in those first days, how its first movements get responded to, may figure significantly in shaping the subsequent psychology of that infant. The *psychological* demands, as it were, of the infantile organism are there long before it can become aware of them. Autistic children, who were rejected or ill treated as infants, are often found to be full of hatred and longing, hatred of a rejecting environment and longing for an accepting one. The infant's responses to rejection or acceptance may be such as to be describable as a young organism's refusal or inability to develop a sense of self.

Secondly, there is some evidence for the hypothesis that, if a child is to learn the normal uses of "I," he must experience more than love, affection, and warmth. Included also must be the realization that he *causally* operates upon his environment, that his wishes and volitions create changes in his world. People respond and objects move at his bidding. Deprived of this realization, the infantile organism may "give up" and withdraw autistically. And, at eight or nine years, a long, agonizing process of rehabilitation of that same organism may be required (if at all possible) before it can become a person, before it can handle personal pronouns in a normal way. Put in this light, the story of the human self is really a story of how the human organism acquires and modifies crucial attitudes toward itself. Becoming philosophically accurate about the origin and nature of the philosophical concept of the self is itself probably an important modification in attitude for many in securing a more accurate knowledge of who and what they are. . . .

[2.] SELF-KNOWLEDGE

Many thinkers, who are on the side of reason, may find themselves, because remembering the sad facts of life, curbing an instinctive urge to embrace Plato's confidence in what knowledge can do. You are moved by what you know, Plato believed, and if you know what is good, you will then try to do it, and if you know what is bad, you will try to avoid it. Plato's kind of faith in the moving power of knowledge is probably what underlies the appeal of the injunction to "know thyself."

The trouble of course is that we all have met people possessing keen insight into themselves but who are powerless to employ such insight for their own benefit. Their drives overpower, but without obliterating, their reason. Yet it would clearly be a mistake not to see these as exceptional cases and to appreciate Plato's statement of what knowledge can do. Everything being equal, self-knowledge can only be applauded. In obvious ways it is indispensable for preparedness, self-security, and self-control. You would only recommend in abnormal cases that people ought to live in ignorance of themselves.

Self-knowledge is clearly relevant also to self-evaluation. Knowing one's own perversities makes preserving self-esteem difficult. But, as the preceding chapters have recognized, coming to know oneself is also difficult. Introspection plays an important part, but it is fallible and often frustrating. Self-knowledge is nowadays constantly in doubt, because we have learned from psychoanalysis how deceptive the techniques of self-deception are. Hyperbolic concern for the possibility of self-deception leads some thinkers to the curious conclusion that knowledge of others is actually easier to come by than knowledge of ourselves, and that, accordingly, we ought to try to learn about ourselves just as we learn about others. But this is plausible if we attend only to a person's behavior and forget the relevance of his *experiences.* The mistake of supposing that knowledge of others is more assured than knowledge of ourselves, on the grounds that we allow only their behavior to count and thus avoid the subjective traps of self-delusion, is apparent once we recall that our knowledge of others certainly depends in part upon their testimony about what they experience. We necessarily consider their testimony about the nature of their experiences before deciding what it is that they intend, hope, desire, believe, suspect, regret, and so on. We must therefore rely upon the accuracy of their testimony as a piece of introspective self-diagnosis. It is simpler to know oneself. Admittedly, to achieve this you have to worry about the possibility of self-deception. But, in knowing the character of another, you have to worry about the possibility of his self-deception as well as yours. Insofar as knowledge is relevant to evaluation, it really is easier, in this respect, to pass judgment upon oneself than upon someone else.

Some evaluations, it should be noted, are more exclusively tested in terms of behavior than others. A person's performances are what determine you to judge him to be generous, brave, ambitious. But we should need to know the true nature of his experiences, besides his behavior, to know whether, in the full sense of the words, he is a person "of character," possesses "fortitude," is sensitive, sympathetic, and so on. In general, it is certainly not the case that we find it easier to be confident about such evaluations when we make them about others than about ourselves. For, again, we must worry both about the other person's susceptibility to self-deception in diagnosing his own experiences and about our own susceptibility to self-deception in accepting his testimony.

However, an individual can make the process of self-evaluation more difficult by adopting for himself more severe standards than he sets for others, and not necessarily because he is masochistic or guilt-ridden. His relation to himself, after all, is more complex and extensive than his relationship to any other person. Suppose I am trying to decide whether I am more courageous than cowardly, more sensitive than callous, more thoughtful than impulsive, and so on. I may find myself hesitating a long time before responding confidently to my own questions here, because I not only review my behavior and experience in the past but also try to anticipate how I might act and feel in a remarkable variety of hypothetical situations that come to mind. I may feel reasonably certain about how I would respond in some but not in all of the imagined circumstances. And the presence of any such uncertainty is naturally experienced as a hiatus in self-knowledge. If I were not troubled by such uncertainty, I might then be open to the charge of only taking a casual, irresponsible interest in myself. But I might, and justifiably so, relax my standards in judging whether you are more courageous than cowardly, etc. If, knowing how you behaved and felt in a few specific situations, I feel confident about how you would behave and feel in a few other critical situations, I make my judgment. I decide about you with reference to a comparatively restricted set of situations, whereas I decide about myself with reference to a comparatively unrestricted set of circumstances. It can be argued that this is as it should be. If I were to insist upon the same standards for others as for myself, that would be tantamount to trying to treat everyone met as if he were myself. The consequences of doing that would be disastrous in the extreme.

Another factor complicating self-evaluation is the wealth of subjective detail to be considered. I constantly live in my feelings, sensations, images, impulses, tendencies, conflicts, hopes, worries, intentions, resolutions, etc. Yours I only occasionally encounter. Insofar as these are relevant to the assessment of personality, I am content, in judging you, to allow the small sample of subjective detail known to me from your life to determine the verdict. But, in judging myself, the task of sorting and diagnosing is much more complex. And, again, if I did not make it such, I might be open to the accusation that the interest I take in myself is irresponsible. That I do not consult, to the same extent, the subjective details of your experiences is demanded by the fact that, to try to do so, I should be trying to treat you as myself. I can take a profound interest in you and treat you in some respects as I do myself. In doing so, I must allow you to make for yourself the task of self-evaluation as difficult as I make it for myself. I must allow you to do it in the way that only you can do it. We are forced, to keep life moving, to pass our quicker judgments upon each other. But the spirit in which we do this may be more considerate and tentative, if we remember, despite the advantage of his own information, how each person finds it slow going in arriving at a deserved judgment about himself.

The Mind of Man

RENÉ DESCARTES

*A Thinking Thing**

René Descartes (1596–1650), French philosopher, mathematician, and scientist, is often called the "Father of Modern Philosophy" because of his criticism of earlier thought and his advocacy of methodical doubt as a first step in the discovery of truth. As a young man he became disillusioned with the formal education he had been receiving, but was greatly impressed by the elegance and certainty of mathematics. Inspired by this model, he sought to introduce into our thinking in other areas the same rigorous use of reason. His most important works are *Discourse on Method, Meditations,* and *Principles of Philosophy.*

In the following selection, Descartes applies his method of doubt in order to discover what kind of being he is. At this stage of his inquiry, he finds it more certain that he is a mind, a thinking thing, than even that he has a body. In his further explorations, beyond the scope of our selection, he becomes convinced of the reality of bodies also. His insistence that both minds and bodies are real and irreducible leads him to the position called metaphysical dualism.

The meditation of yesterday has filled my mind with so many doubts, that it is no longer in my power to forget them. Nor do I see, meanwhile, any principle on which they can be resolved; and, just as if I had fallen all of a sudden into very deep water, I am so greatly disconcerted as to be unable either to plant my feet firmly on the bottom or sustain myself by swimming on the surface. I will, nevertheless, make an effort, and try anew the same path on which I had entered yesterday, that is, proceed by casting aside all that admits of the slightest doubt, not less than if I had discovered it to be absolutely false; and I will continue always in this track until I shall find something that is certain, or at least, if I can do nothing more, until I

*René Descartes, from "Meditations," in *The Method, Meditations and Philosophy,* trans. John Veitch (Washington: Dunne, 1901), Meditation II, pp. 224–229, 232–233.

shall know with certainty that there is nothing certain. Archimedes, that he might transport the entire globe from the place it occupied to another, demanded only a point that was firm and immovable; so, also, I shall be entitled to entertain the highest expectations, if I am fortunate enough to discover only one thing that is certain and indubitable.

I suppose, accordingly, that all the things which I see are false (fictitious); I believe that none of those objects which my fallacious memory represents ever existed; I suppose that I possess no senses; I believe that body, figure, extension, motion, and place are merely fictions of my mind. What is there, then, that can be esteemed true? Perhaps this only, that there is absolutely nothing certain.

But how do I know that there is not something different altogether from the objects I have now enumerated, of which it is impossible to entertain the slightest doubt? Is there not a God, or some being, by whatever name I may designate him, who causes these thoughts to arise in my mind? But why suppose such a being, for it may be I myself am capable of producing them? Am I, then, at least not something? But I before denied that I possessed senses or a body; I hesitate, however, for what follows from that? Am I so dependent on the body and the senses that without these I cannot exist? But I had the persuasion that there was absolutely nothing in the world, that there was no sky and no earth, neither minds nor bodies; was I not, therefore, at the same time, persuaded that I did not exist? Far from it; I assuredly existed, since I was persuaded. But there is I know not what being, who is possessed at once of the highest power and the deepest cunning, who is constantly employing all his ingenuity in deceiving me. Doubtless, then, I exist, since I am deceived; and, let him deceive me as he may, he can never bring it about that I am nothing, so long as I shall be conscious that I am something. So that it must, in fine, be maintained, all things being maturely and carefully considered, that this proposition (*pronunciatum*) I am, I exist, is necessarily true each time it is expressed by me, or conceived in my mind.

But I do not yet know with sufficient clearness what I am, though assured that I am; and hence, in the next place, I must take care, lest perchance I inconsiderately substitute some other object in place of what is properly myself, and thus wander from truth, even in that knowledge (cognition) which I hold to be of all others the most certain and evident. For this reason, I will now consider anew what I formerly believed myself to be, before I entered on the present train of thought; and of my previous opinion I will retrench all that can in the least be invalidated by the grounds of doubt I have adduced, in order that there may at length remain nothing but what is certain and indubitable. What then did I formerly think I was? Undoubtedly I judged that I was a man. But what is a man? Shall I say a rational animal? Assuredly not; for it would be necessary forthwith to inquire into what is meant by animal, and what by rational, and thus, from a single question, I should insensibly glide into others, and these more difficult than the first; nor do I now possess enough of leisure to warrant me in wasting my time amid subtleties of this sort. I prefer here to attend to the thoughts that sprung up of themselves in my mind, and were inspired by my own nature alone, when I applied myself to the consideration of what I was. In the first place, then, I thought that I possessed a countenance, hands, arms, and all the fabric of members that appears in a corpse, and which I called by the name of body. It further occurred to me that I was nourished, that I walked, perceived, and thought, and all those actions I referred to the soul; but what the soul itself was I either did not stay to consider, or, if I did, I imagined that it was something extremely rare and subtile, like wind, or flame, or ether, spread through my grosser parts. As regarded the body, I did not even doubt of its nature, but thought I distinctly knew it, and if I had wished to describe it according to the notions I then entertained, I should have explained myself in this manner: By body I understand all that can be terminated by a certain figure; that can be comprised in a certain place, and so fill a certain space as therefrom to exclude every other body; that can be perceived either by touch, sight, hearing, taste, or smell; that can be moved in different ways, not indeed of itself, but by something foreign to it by which it is touched [and from which it receives the impression]; for the power of self-motion, as likewise that of perceiving and thinking, I held as by no means pertaining to the nature of body; on the contrary, I was somewhat astonished to find such faculties existing in some bodies.

But [as to myself, what can I now say that I am], since I suppose there exists an extremely powerful, and, if I may so speak, malignant being, whose whole endeavors are directed toward deceiving me? Can I affirm that I possess any one of all those attributes of which I have lately spoken as belonging to the nature of body? After attentively considering them in my own mind, I find none of them that can properly be said to belong to myself. To recount them were idle and tedious. Let us pass, then, to the attributes of the soul. The first mentioned were the powers of nutrition and walking; but, if it be true that I have no body, it is true likewise that I am capable neither of walking nor of being nourished. Perception is another attribute of the soul; but perception too is impossible without the body; besides, I have frequently, during sleep, believed that I perceived objects which I afterward observed I did not in reality perceive. Thinking is another attribute of the soul; and here I discover what properly belongs to myself. This alone is inseparable from me. I am—I exist: this is certain; but how often? As often as I think; for perhaps it would even happen, if I should wholly cease to think, that I should at the same time altogether cease to be. I now admit nothing that is not necessarily true. I am therefore, precisely speaking, only a thinking thing, that is, a mind (*mens sive animus*), understanding, or reason, terms whose signification was before unknown to me. I am, however, a real thing, and really existent; but what thing? The answer was, a thinking thing. The question now arises, am I aught besides? I will stimulate my imagination with a view to discover whether I am not still something more than a thinking being. Now it is plain I am not the assemblage of members called the human body; I am not a thin and penetrating air diffused through all these members, or wind, or flame, or vapor, or breath, or any of all the things I can imagine; for I supposed that all these were not, and, without changing the supposition, I find that I still feel assured of my existence.

But it is true, perhaps, that those very things which I suppose to be nonexistent, because they are unknown to me, are not in truth different from myself whom I know. This is a point I cannot determine, and do not now enter into any dispute regarding it. I can only judge of things that are known to me: I am conscious that I exist, and I who know that I exist inquire into what I am. It is, however, perfectly certain that the knowledge of my existence, thus precisely taken, is not dependent on things, the existence of which is as yet unknown to me: and consequently it is not dependent on any of the things I can feign in imagination. Moreover, the phrase itself, I frame an image (*effingo*), reminds me of my error; for I should in truth frame one if I were to imagine myself to be anything, since to imagine is nothing more than to contemplate the figure or image of a corporeal thing; but I already know that I exist, and that it is possible at the same time that all those images, and in general all that relates to the nature of body, are merely dreams [or chimeras]. From this I discover that it is not more reasonable to say, I will excite my imagination that I may know more distinctly what I am, than to express myself as follows: I am now awake, and perceive something real; but because my perception is not sufficiently clear, I will of express purpose go to sleep that my dreams may represent to me the object of my perception with more truth and clearness. And, therefore, I know that nothing of all that I can embrace in imagination belongs to the knowledge which I have of myself, and that there is need to recall with the utmost care the mind from this mode of thinking, that it may be able to know its own nature with perfect distinctness.

But what, then, am I? A thinking thing, it has been said. But what is a thinking thing? It is a thing that doubts, understands [conceives], affirms, denies, wills, refuses; that imagines also, and perceives. Assuredly it is not little, if all these properties belong to my nature. But why should they not belong to it? Am I not that very being who now doubts of almost everything; who, for all that, understands and conceives certain things; who affirms one alone as true, and denies the others; who desires to know more of them, and does not wish to be deceived; who imagines many things, sometimes even despite his will; and is likewise percipient of many, as if through the medium of the senses. Is there nothing of all this as true as that I am, even although I should be always dreaming, and although he who gave me being employed all his ingenuity to deceive me? Is there also any one of these attributes that can be properly distinguished from my thought, or that can be said to be separate from myself? For it is of itself so evident that it is I who doubt, I who understand, and I who desire, that it is here unnecessary to add anything by way of rendering it more clear. And I am as certainly the same being who imagines; for although it may be (as I before supposed) that nothing I imagine is true, still the power of imagination does not cease really to exist in me and to form part of my thought. In fine, I am the same being who perceives, that is, who apprehends certain objects as by the organs of sense, since, in truth, I see light, hear a noise, and feel heat. But it will be said that these presentations are false, and that I am dreaming. Let it be so. At all events it is certain that I seem to see light, hear a noise, and feel heat; this cannot be false, and this is what in me is properly called perceiving (*sentire*), which is nothing else than thinking. From this I begin to know what I am with somewhat greater clearness and distinctness than heretofore.

But, nevertheless, it still seems to me, and I cannot help believing, that corporeal things, whose images are formed by thought [which fall under the senses], and are examined by the same, are known with much greater distinctness than that I know not what part of myself which is not imaginable; although, in truth, it may seem strange to say that I know and comprehend with greater distinctness things whose existence appears to me doubtful, that are unknown, and do not belong to me, than others of whose reality I am persuaded, that are known to me, and appertain to my proper nature; in a word, than myself. But I see clearly what is the state of the case. My mind is apt to wander, and will not yet submit to be restrained within the limits of truth. Let us therefore leave the mind to itself once more, and, according to it every kind of liberty [permit it to consider the objects that appear to it from without], in order that, having afterward withdrawn it from these gently and opportunely [and fixed it on the consideration of its being and the properties it finds in itself], it may then be the more easily controlled.

Let us now accordingly consider the objects that are commonly thought to be [the most easily, and likewise] the most distinctly known, viz, the bodies we touch and see; not, indeed, bodies in general, for these general notions are usually somewhat more confused, but one body in particular. Take, for example, this piece of wax; it is quite fresh, having been but recently taken from the beehive; it has not yet lost the sweetness of the honey it contained; it still retains somewhat of the odor of the flowers from which it was gathered; its color, figure, size, are apparent (to the sight); it is hard, cold, easily handled; and sounds when struck upon with the finger. In fine, all that contributes to make a body as distinctly known as possible, is found in the one before us. But, while I am speaking, let it be placed near the fire—what remained of the taste exhales, the smell evaporates, the color changes, its figure is destroyed, its size increases, it becomes liquid, it grows hot, it can hardly be handled, and, although struck upon, it emits no sound. Does the same wax still remain after this change? It must be admitted that it does remain; no one doubts it, or judges otherwise. What, then, was it I knew with so much distinctness in the piece of wax? Assuredly, it could be nothing of all that I observed by means of the senses, since all the things that fell under taste, smell, sight, touch, and hearing are changed, and yet the same wax remains.... There certainly remains nothing, except something extended, flexible, and movable.... But (and this it is of moment to observe) the perception of it is neither an act of sight, of touch, nor of imagination, and never was either of these, though it might formerly seem so, but is simply an intuition (*inspectio*) of the mind, which may be imperfect and confused, as it formerly was, or very clear and distinct, as it is at present, according as the attention is more or less directed to the elements which it contains, and of which it is composed....

...But when I distinguish the wax from its exterior forms, and when, as if I had stripped it of its vestments, I consider it quite naked, it is certain, although some error may still be found in my judgment, that I cannot, nevertheless, thus apprehend it without possessing a human mind.

But, finally, what shall I say of the mind itself, that is, of myself? for as yet I do not admit that I am anything but mind. What, then! I who seem to possess so distinct an apprehension of the piece of wax, do I not know myself, both with greater truth and certitude, and also much more distinctly and clearly? For if I judge that the wax exists because I see it, it assuredly follows, much more evidently, that I myself am or exist, for the same reason: for it is possible that what I see may not in truth be wax, and that I do not even possess eyes with which to see anything; but it cannot be that when I see, or, which comes to the same thing, when I think I see, I myself who think am nothing. So likewise, if I judge that the wax exists because I touch it, it will still also follow that I am; and if I determine that my imagination, or any other cause, whatever it be, persuades me of the existence of the wax, I will still draw the same conclusion. And what is here remarked of the piece of wax, is applicable to all the other things that are external to me. And further, if the [notion or] perception of wax appeared to me more precise and distinct, after ... not only sight and touch, but many other causes besides, rendered it manifest to my apprehension, with how much greater distinctness must I now know myself, since all the reasons that contribute to the knowledge of the nature of wax, or of any body whatever, manifest still better the nature of my mind? And there are besides so many other things in the mind itself that contribute to the illustration of its nature, that those dependent on the body, to which I have here referred, scarcely merit to be taken into account.

But, in conclusion, I find I have insensibly reverted to the point I desired; for, since it is now manifest to me that bodies themselves are not properly perceived by the senses nor by the faculty of imagination, but by the intellect alone; and since they are not perceived because they are seen and touched, but only because they are understood [or rightly comprehended by thought], I readily discover that there is nothing more easily or clearly apprehended than my own mind. But because it is difficult to rid one's self so promptly of an opinion to which one has been long accustomed, it will be desirable to tarry for some time at this stage, that, by long continued meditation, I may more deeply impress upon my memory this new knowledge.

GILBERT RYLE

*Descartes' Myth**

Gilbert Ryle (b. 1900) has been a leading member of the Oxford University school of analysis which emphasizes the analysis of ordinary language as a clue to the solution of philosophical puzzles. Ryle's work, *The Concept of Mind,* has stimulated widespread controversy, and its impact continues.

In the following selection from this book, Ryle attacks what he views as the "nonsense" of Descartes' famous analysis of mind and argues that Descartes has created a "myth" through committing a "category-mistake." Ryle's simple example of the confused visitor to a university illustrates this kind of mistake. Myth, in Ryle's special use of the term, results from presenting facts of a given kind or class in language appropriate only for facts of a different kind.

(1) THE OFFICIAL DOCTRINE

There is a doctrine about the nature and place of minds which is so prevalent among theorists and even among laymen that it deserves to be described as the official theory. Most philosophers, psychologists and religious teachers subscribe, with minor reservations, to its main articles and, although

*Gilbert Ryle, from "Descartes' Myth," in *The Concept of Mind* (London: Hutchinson, 1949; New York: Harper and Row), pp. 11–18, 22–23. Used by permission of the publishers.

they admit certain theoretical difficulties in it, they tend to assume that these can be overcome without serious modifications being made to the architecture of the theory. It will be argued here that the central principles of the doctrine are unsound and conflict with the whole body of what we know about minds when we are not speculating about them.

The official doctrine, which hails chiefly from Descartes, is something like this. With the doubtful exceptions of idiots and infants in arms every human being has both a body and a mind. Some would prefer to say that every human being is both a body and a mind. His body and his mind are ordinarily harnessed together, but after the death of the body his mind may continue to exist and function.

Human bodies are in space and are subject to the mechanical laws which govern all other bodies in space. Bodily processes and states can be inspected by external observers. So a man's bodily life is as much a public affair as are the lives of animals and reptiles and even as the careers of trees, crystals and planets.

But minds are not in space, nor are their operations subject to mechanical laws. The workings of one mind are not witnessable by other observers; its career is private. Only I can take direct cognisance of the states and processes of my own mind. A person therefore lives through two collateral histories, one consisting of what happens in and to his body, the other consisting of what happens in and to his mind. The first is public, the second private. The events in the first history are events in the physical world, those in the second are events in the mental world.

It has been disputed whether a person does or can directly monitor all or only some of the episodes of his own private history; but, according to the official doctrine, of at least some of these episodes he has direct and unchallengeable cognisance. In consciousness, self-consciousness and introspection he is directly and authentically apprised of the present states and operations of his mind. He may have great or small uncertainties about concurrent and adjacent episodes in the physical world, but he can have none about at least part of what is momentarily occupying his mind.

It is customary to express this bifurcation of his two lives and of his two worlds by saying that the things and events which belong to the physical world, including his own body, are external, while the workings of his own mind are internal. This antithesis of outer and inner is of course meant to be construed as a metaphor, since minds, not being in space, could not be described as being spatially inside anything else, or as having things going on spatially inside themselves. But relapses from this good intention are common and theorists are found speculating how stimuli, the physical sources of which are yards or miles outside a person's skin, can generate mental responses inside his skull, or how decisions framed inside his cranium can set going movements of his extremities.

Even when "inner" and "outer" are construed as metaphors, the problem how a person's mind and body influence one another is notoriously charged with theoretical difficulties. What the mind wills, the legs, arms and the tongue execute; what affects the ear and the eye has something to do with what the mind perceives; grimaces and smiles betray the mind's moods and bodily castigations lead, it is hoped, to moral improvement. But the actual transactions between the episodes of the private history and those of the public history remain mysterious, since by definition they can belong to neither series. They could not be reported among the happenings described in a person's autobiography of his inner life, but nor could they be reported among those described in some one else's biography of that person's overt career. They can be inspected neither by introspection nor by laboratory experiment. They are theoretical shuttlecocks which are forever being bandied from the physiologist back to the psychologist and from the psychologist back to the physiologist.

Underlying this partly metaphorical representation of the bifurcation of a person's two lives there is a seemingly more profound and philosophical assumption. It is assumed that there are two different kinds of existence or status. What exists or happens may have the status of physical existence, or it may have the status of mental existence. Somewhat as the faces of coins are either heads or tails, or somewhat as living creatures are either male or female, so, it is supposed, some existing is physical existing, other existing is mental existing. It is a necessary feature of what has physical existence that it is in space and time; it is a necessary feature of what has mental existence that it is in time but not in space. What has physical existence is composed of matter, or else is a function of matter; what has mental existence consists of consciousness, or else is a function of consciousness.

There is thus a polar opposition between mind and matter, an opposition which is often brought out as follows. Material objects are situated in a common field, known as "space," and what happens to one body in one part of space is mechanically connected with what happens to other bodies in other parts of space. But mental happenings occur in insulated fields, known as "minds," and there is, apart maybe from telepathy, no direct causal connection between what happens in one mind and what happens in another. Only through the medium of the public physical world can the mind of one person make a difference to the mind of another. The mind is its own place and in his inner life each of us lives the life of a ghostly Robinson Crusoe. People can see, hear and jolt one another's bodies, but they are irremediably blind and deaf to the workings of one another's minds and inoperative upon them.

What sort of knowledge can be secured of the workings of a mind? On the one side, according to the official theory, a person has direct knowledge of the best imaginable kind of the workings of his own mind. Mental states and processes are (or are normally) conscious states and processes, and the consciousness which irradiates them can engender no illusions and leaves the door open for no doubts. A person's present thinkings, feelings and willings, his perceivings, rememberings and imaginings are intrinsically "phosphorescent"; their existence and their nature are inevitably betrayed to their owner. The inner life is a stream of consciousness of such a sort that it would be absurd to suggest that the mind whose life is that stream might be unaware of what is passing down it.

True, the evidence adduced recently by Freud seems to show that there exist channels tributary to this stream, which run hidden from their owner. People are actuated by impulses the existence of which they vigorously disavow; some of their thoughts differ from the thoughts which they acknowledge; and some of the actions which they think they will to perform they do not really will. They are thoroughly gulled by some of their own hypocrisies and they successfully ignore facts about their mental lives which on the official theory ought to be patent to them. Holders of the official theory tend, however, to maintain that anyhow in normal circumstances a person must be directly and authentically seized of the present state and workings of his own mind.

Besides being currently supplied with these alleged immediate data of consciousness, a person is also generally supposed to be able to exercise from time to time a special kind of perception, namely inner perception, or introspection. He can take a (non-optical) "look" at what is passing in his mind. Not only can he view and scrutinize a flower through his sense of sight and listen to and discriminate the notes of a bell through his sense of hearing; he can also reflectively or introspectively watch, without any bodily organ of sense, the current episodes of his inner life. This self-observation is also commonly supposed to be immune from illusion, confusion or doubt. A mind's reports of its own affairs have a certainty superior to the best that is possessed by its reports of matters in the physical world. Sense-perceptions can, but consciousness and introspection cannot, be mistaken or confused.

On the other side, one person has no direct access of any sort to the events of the inner life of another. He cannot do better than make problematic inferences from the observed behaviour of the other person's body to the states of mind which, by analogy from his own conduct, he supposes to be signalised by that behaviour. Direct access to the workings of a mind is the privilege of that mind itself; in default of such privileged access, the workings of one mind are inevitably occult to everyone else. For the supposed arguments from bodily movements similar to their own to mental workings similar to their own would lack any possibility of observational corroboration. Not unnaturally, therefore, an adherent of the official theory finds it difficult to resist this consequence of his premises, that he has no good reason to believe that there do exist minds other than his own. Even if he prefers to believe that to other human bodies there are harnessed minds not unlike his own, he cannot claim to be able to discover their individual characteristics, or the particular things that they undergo and do. Absolute solitude is on this showing the ineluctable destiny of the soul. Only our bodies can meet.

As a necessary corollary of this general scheme there is implicitly prescribed a special way of construing our ordinary concepts of mental powers and operations. The verbs, nouns and adjectives, with which in ordinary life we describe the wits, characters and higher-grade performances of the people with whom we have to do, are required to be construed as signifying special episodes in their secret histories, or else as signifying tendencies for such episodes to occur. When someone is described as knowing, believing or guessing something, as hoping, dreading, intending or shirking something, as designing this or being amused at that, these verbs are supposed to denote the occurrence of specific modifications in his (to us) occult stream of consciousness. Only his own privileged access to this stream in direct awareness and introspection could provide authentic testimony that these mental-conduct verbs were correctly or incorrectly applied. The onlooker, be he teacher, critic, biographer or friend, can never assure himself that his comments have any vestige of truth. Yet it was just because we do in fact all know how to make such comments, make them with general correctness and correct them when they turn out to be confused or mistaken, that philosophers found it necessary to construct their theories of the nature and place of minds. Finding mental-conduct concepts being regularly and effectively used, they properly sought to fix their logical geography. But the logical geography officially recommended would entail that there could be no regular or effective use of these mental-conduct concepts in our descriptions of, and prescriptions for, other people's minds.

(2) THE ABSURDITY OF THE OFFICIAL DOCTRINE

Such in outline is the official theory. I shall often speak of it, with deliberate abusiveness, as "the dogma of the Ghost in the Machine." I hope to prove that it is entirely false, and false not in detail but in principle. It is not merely an assemblage of particular mistakes. It is one big mistake and a mistake of a special kind. It is, namely, a category-mistake. It represents the facts of mental life as if they belonged to one logical type or category (or range of types or categories), when they actually belong to another. The dogma is therefore a philosopher's myth. In attempting to explode the myth I shall probably be taken to be denying well-known facts about the mental life of human beings, and my plea that I aim at concepts will probably be disallowed as mere subterfuge.

I must first indicate what is meant by the phrase "Category-mistake." This I do in a series of illustrations.

A foreigner visiting Oxford or Cambridge for the first time is shown a number of colleges, libraries, playing fields, museums, scientific departments and administrative offices. He then asks "But where is the University? I have seen where the members of the Colleges live, where the Registrar works, where the scientists experiment and the rest. But I have not yet seen the University in which reside and work the members of your University." It has then to be explained to him that the University is not another collateral institution, some ulterior counterpart to the colleges, laboratories and offices which he has seen. The University is just the way in which all that he has already seen is organized. When they are seen and when their co-ordination is understood, the University has been seen. His mistake lay in his innocent assumption that it was correct to speak of Christ Church, the Bodleian Library, the Ashmolean Museum *and* the University, to speak, that is, as if "the University" stood for an extra member of the class of which these other units are members. He was mistakenly allocating the University to the same category as that to which the other institutions belong.

The same mistake would be made by a child witnessing the march-past of a division, who, having had pointed out to him such and such battalions, batteries, squadrons, etc., asked when the division was going to appear. He would be supposing that a division was a counterpart to the units already seen, partly similar to them and partly unlike them. He would be shown his mistake by being told that in watching the battalions, batteries and squadrons marching past he had been watching the division marching past. The march-past was not a parade of battalions, batteries, squadrons *and* a division; it was a parade of the battalions, batteries and squadrons *of* a division.

One more illustration. A foreigner watching his first game of cricket learns what are the functions of the bowlers, the batsmen, the fielders, the umpires and the scorers. He then says "But there is no one left on the field to contribute the famous element of team-spirit. I see who does the bowling, the batting and the wicket-keeping; but I do not see whose role it is to exercise *esprit de corps*." Once more, it would have to be explained that he was looking for the wrong type of thing. Team-spirit is not another cricketing-operation supplementary to all of the other special tasks. It is, roughly, the keenness with which each of the special tasks is performed, and performing a task keenly is not performing two tasks. Certainly exhibiting team-spirit is not the same thing as bowling or catching, but nor is it a third thing such that we can say that the bowler first bowls *and* then exhibits team-spirit or that a fielder is at a given moment *either* catching *or* displaying *esprit de corps*.

These illustrations of category-mistakes have a common feature which must be noticed. The mistakes were made by people who did not know how to wield the concepts *University, division* and *team-spirit*. Their puzzles arose from inability to use certain items in the English vocabulary.

The theoretically interesting category-mistakes are those made by people who are perfectly competent to apply concepts, at least in the situations with which they are familiar, but are still liable in their abstract thinking to allocate those concepts to logical types to which they do not belong. An instance of a mistake of this sort would be the following story. A student of politics has learned the main differences between the British, the French and the American Constitutions, and has learned also the differences and connections between the Cabinet, Parliament, the various Ministries, the Judicature and the Church of England. But he still becomes embarrassed when asked questions about the connections between the Church of England, the Home Office and the British Constitution. For while the Church and the Home Office are institutions, the British Constitution is not another institution in the same sense of that noun. So inter-institutional relations which can be asserted or denied to hold between the Church and the Home Office cannot be asserted or denied to hold between either of them and the British Constitution. "The British Constitution" is not a term of the same logical type as "the Home Office" and "the Church of England." In a partially similar way, John Doe may be a relative, a friend, an enemy or a stranger to Richard Roe; but he cannot be any of these things to the Average Taxpayer. He knows how to talk sense in certain sorts of discussions about the Average Taxpayer, but he is baffled to say why he could not come across him in the street as he can come across Richard Roe.

It is pertinent to our main subject to notice that, so long as the student of politics continues to think of the British Constitution as a counterpart to the other institutions, he will tend to describe it as a mysteriously occult institution; and so long as John Doe continues to think of the Average Taxpayer as a fellow-citizen, he will tend to think of him as an elusive insubstantial man, a ghost who is everywhere yet nowhere.

My destructive purpose is to show that a family of radical category-mistakes is the source of the double-life theory. The representation of a person as a ghost mysteriously ensconced in a machine derives from this argument. Because, as is true, a person's thinking, feeling and purposive doing cannot be described solely in the idioms of physics, chemistry and physiology, therefore they must be described in counterpart idioms. As the human body is a complex organised unit, so the human mind must be another complex organised unit, though one made of a different sort of stuff and with a different sort of structure. Or, again, as the human body, like any other parcel of matter, is a field of causes and effects, so the mind must be another field of causes and effects, though not (Heaven be praised) mechanical causes and effects....

(3) THE ORIGIN OF THE CATEGORY MISTAKE

When two terms belong to the same category, it is proper to construct conjunctive propositions embodying them. Thus a purchaser may say that he bought a left-hand glove and a right-hand glove, but not that he bought a left-hand glove, a right-hand glove and a pair of gloves. "She came home in a flood of tears and a sedan-chair" is a well-known joke based on the absurdity of conjoining terms of different types. It would have been equally ridiculous to construct the disjunction "She came home either in a flood of tears or else in a sedan-chair." Now the dogma of the Ghost in the Machine does just this. It maintains that there exist both bodies and minds; that there occur physical processes and mental processes; that there are mechanical causes of corporeal movements and mental causes of corporeal movements. I shall argue that these and other analogous conjunctions are absurd; but, it must be noticed, the argument will not show that either of the illegitimately conjoined propositions is absurd in itself. I am not, for example, denying that there occur mental processes. Doing long division is a mental process and so is making a joke. But I am saying that the phrase "there occur mental processes" does not mean the same sort of thing as "there occur physical processes," and, therefore, that it makes no sense to conjoin or disjoin the two.

If my argument is successful, there will follow some interesting consequences. First, the hallowed contrast between Mind and Matter will be dissipated, but dissipated not by either of the equally hallowed absorptions of Mind by Matter or of Matter by Mind, but in quite a different way. For the seeming contrast of the two will be shown to be as illegitimate as would be the contrast of "she came home in a flood of tears" and "she came home in a sedan-chair." The belief that there is a polar opposition between Mind and Matter is the belief that they are terms of the same logical type.

It will also follow that both Idealism and Materialism are answers to an improper question. The "reduction" of the material world to mental states and processes, as well as the "reduction" of mental states and processes to physical states and processes, presuppose the legitimacy of the disjunction "either there exist minds or there exist bodies (but not both)." It would be like saying, "Either she bought a left-hand and a right-hand glove or she bought a pair of gloves (but not both)."

It is perfectly proper to say, in one logical tone of voice, that there exist minds and to say, in another logical tone of voice, that there exist bodies. But these expressions do not indicate two different species of existence, for "existence" is not a generic word like "coloured" or "sexed." They indicate two different senses of "exist," somewhat as "rising" has different senses in "the tide is rising," "hopes are rising," and "the average age of death is rising." A man would be thought to be making a poor joke who said that three things are now rising, namely the tide, hopes and the average age of death. It would be just as good or bad a joke to say that there exist prime numbers and Wednesdays and public opinions and navies; or that there exist both minds and bodies....

C. J. DUCASSE

*In Defense of Dualism**

C. J. Ducasse (1881–1969) came to America from his native France as a young man interested in the business world. He "discovered" philosophy at the age of twenty-four through reading a chapter in an otherwise unnotable work on some views of Berkeley, Hume, and Kant. His new interest took him first to the University of Washington and then to Harvard, where he was a student of Josiah Royce. His own independent views were set forth in more than thirty years of teaching at Brown University and in such books as *Philosophy as a Science, The Philosophy of Art, A Philosophical Scrutiny of Religion,* and *Nature, Mind and Death* (The Carus Lectures).

In the selection that follows, the author defends the dualist-interactionist view of the relation between mind and brain. He points out that there is a fundamental difference between what we call "physical" or "material" and what we call "psychical" or "mental." Note the various positions that could be held and how Ducasse defends his position.

Neither in the section of this symposium on "The Mind-Body Problem" nor in that on "The Brain and the Machine" is much, if any, attention given

*Reprinted by permission of New York University Press from *Dimensions of Mind* by Sidney Hook, ed. © 1960 by New York University. From "In Defense of Dualism," pp. 85–89.

to the dualist-interactionist conception of the relation between mind and brain. A summary presentation of the case for it and against its rivals may therefore be appropriate here.

The first point to which attention must be called is that, beyond question, there are things—events, substances, processes, relations, etc.—denominated "material," or "physical," that there are also certain others denominated instead "mental," or "psychical," and that no thing is denominated both "physical" and "psychical," or both "material" and "mental." Rocks, trees, water, air, animal and human bodies, and the processes occurring among them or within them, are examples of the things called "material" or "physical"; emotions, desires, moods, sensations, cravings, images, thoughts, etc., are examples of the things called "mental" or "psychical."

To question whether the first *really* are physical or the second *really* are psychical would be absurd, as it would be absurd to question whether a certain boy whom his parents named "George" really was George. For just as "George" is a name, so "physical" or "material," and "psychical" or "mental," are names; and a name is essentially a *pointer,* which does point at—designates, indicates, denotes, directs attention to—whatever it actually is employed to point at.

It is necessary, however, to ask what characteristic shared by all the things called "physical" or "material" determined their being all designated by one and the same name; and the same question arises with regard to those denominated instead "psychical" or "mental." Evidently, the characteristic concerned had to be an obvious, not a recondite one, since investigation of the recondite characteristics respectively of physical and of psychical things could begin only *after* one knew which things were the physical and which the psychical ones.

In the case of the things called "physical," the patent characteristic common to and peculiar to them, which determined their being all denoted by one and the same name, was simply that all of them were, or were capable of being, *perceptually public*—the same tree, the same thunderclap, the same wind, the same dog, the same man, etc., can be perceived by every member of a human public suitably located in space and in time. To be material or physical, then, *basically* means to be, or to be capable of being, perceptually public. And the unperceivable, recondite things physicists discover—electrons, protons, etc., and the processes that occur among them—only have title at all to be also called physical *derivatively*—in virtue, namely, (and *only* in virtue) of their being *constituents* of the things that are perceptually public.

On the other hand, the patent characteristic which functioned as a basis for the application of one identical name to all the things called "psychical" or "mental" was their *inherently private* character, attention *to them,* as distinguished from attention to what they may signify, being accordingly termed "introspection," not "perception."

The events called "psychical," it must be emphasized, are private in a sense radically different from that in which the events occurring inside the body are private. The latter are private only in the sense that visual, tactual, or other exteroceptive perception of them is *difficult*—indeed, even more difficult for the person whose body is concerned than for other persons —such perception of those events being possible, perhaps, only by means of special instruments, or perhaps only by anatomical "introspection"(!), i.e., by opening up the body surgically and looking at the processes going on inside it. The "privacy" of intra-somatic stimuli, including so-called "covert" behavior, is thus purely adventitious. The privacy of psychical events, on the other hand, is *inherent and ultimate.*

It is sometimes alleged, of course, that their privacy too is only adventitious. But this allegation rests only on failure to distinguish between being *public* and being *published.* Psychical events can be more or less adequately published. That is, perceptually public forms of behavior correlated with occurrence of them can function as *signs* that they are occurring —but *only* as signs, for correlation is not identity. Indeed, correlation presupposes non-identity.

Psychical events *themselves* are never *public* and never can be made so. That, for example, I *now remember* having dreamed of a Siamese cat last night is something which I can *publish* by means of perceptually public words, spoken or written. Other persons are then *informed of it.* But to be informed *that I remember* having so dreamed is one thing, and to *remember* having so dreamed is altogether another thing, and one *inherently private.* The dreaming itself was not, and the remembering itself is not, a *public* event at all and cannot possibly be made so in the way in which my *statement* that I remember that I so dreamed is or can be made public.

How then does it happen that we have names understood by all for events of inherently private kinds? The answer is, of course, that we heard those names—e.g., "anger," "desire," "remembering," etc.,—uttered by other persons when they perceived us behaving in certain more or less stereotyped manners. But the point crucial here is that although each of us acquires his vocabulary for mental events in this way, the words of it, at the times when they are applied by others to *his* behavior, denote *for him* not primarily or perhaps at all his behavior, but the particular kind of inherently private event, i.e., of psychical state, which *he* is experiencing at the time. It is only in "behaviorese," i.e., in the language of dogmatic behaviorism, that for example the word "anger," and the words "anger-behavior," both denote the same event, to wit, the event which ordinary language terms "behaving angrily."

There are several varieties of behaviorism, but they agree in that they attempt to account for the behavior of organisms wholly without invoking a psychical cause for any behavior—that is, wholly by reference to physical, perceptually public causes, present and/or past.

Dogmatic behaviorism is the pious belief that the causes of the behavior of organisms, including human organisms, *are never other than physical.* Nothing but this dogma dictates that even when no physical occurrences are actually found that would account for a given behavior, physical occurrences nevertheless *must* be assumed to have taken place.

Empirical or methodological behaviorism, on the other hand, is not thus fideistic. It is simply *a research program,* perfectly legitimate and often fruitful—the program, namely, of *seeking,* for all behavior, causes consisting of physical, i.e., of perceptually public stimulus events, present and past. Evidently, the fact that one undertakes to search for causes of this kind for all behavior leaves entirely open the possibility that, in many of the innumerable cases where no physical causes adequate to account for the given behavior can in fact be observed, the behavior had a psychical not a physical cause.

For, contrary to what is sometimes alleged, causation of a physical by a psychical event, or a psychical event by stimulation of a physical sense organ, is not in the least paradoxical. The causality relation—whether defined in the terms of regularity of succession, or (preferably) in terms of single antecedent difference—does not presuppose at all that its cause-term and its effect-term both belong to the same ontological category, but only that both of them be *events.*

Moreover, the objection that we cannot understand how a psychical event could cause a physical one (or vice versa) has no basis other than blindness to the fact that the "how" of causation is capable at all of being either mysterious or understood only in cases of *remote* causation, never in cases of *proximate* causation. For the question as to the "how" of causation of a given event by a given other event never has any other sense than *through what intermediary causal steps* does the one cause the other. Hence, to ask it in a case of proximate causation is to be guilty of what Professor Ryle has called a "category mistake"—a mistake, incidentally, of which he is himself guilty when he alleges that the "how" of psycho-physical causation would be mysterious.

Again, the objection to interactionism that causation, in either direction, as between psychical and physical events is precluded by the principle of the conservation of energy (or of energy-matter) is invalid for several reasons.

(A) One reason is that the conservation which that principle asserts is not something known to be true without exception, but is, as M. T. Keeton has pointed out, only a defining-postulate of the notion of a *wholly closed* physical world, so that the question whether psycho-physical or physico-psychical causation ever occurs is (but in different words) the question whether the physical world *is* wholly closed. And that question is not answered by dignifying as a "principle" the assumption that the physical world is wholly closed.

(B) Anyway, as C. D. Broad has pointed out, it might be the case that whenever a given amount of energy vanishes from, or emerges in, the physical world at one place, then an equal amount of energy respectively emerges in, or vanishes from, that world at another place.

(C) And thirdly, if "energy" is meant to designate something experimentally measurable, then "energy" is defined in terms of causality, *not* "causality" in terms of transfer of energy. That is, it is not known that *all* causation, or, in particular, causation as between psychical and physical events, involves transfer of energy.

Interactionism, then, as presented in what precedes, though not as presented by Descartes, is a perfectly tenable conception of the relation between some mental events and some brain events, allowing as it does also that some brain events have bodily causes, and that some mental events directly cause some other mental events. It conceives minds as consisting, like material substances, of sets of systematically interrelated dispositions, i.e., of capacities, abilities, powers, and susceptibilities, each of which can be analyzed as a causal connection, more or less enduring, between any event of some particular kind—C, occurring in a state of affairs of some particular kind—S, and a sequent event in it, of some particular kind—E. The series of *exercises* of the different dispositions (which together define the *nature* of a given mind) constitutes the *history* of that particular mind, i.e., its *existence* as distinguished from only its *description.*

The Issue of Freedom

BRAND BLANSHARD

*The Case for Determinism**

Brand Blanshard (b. 1892) has taught philosophy at a number of schools, including Swarthmore College (1925–1945) and Yale University (1945–1961). He has received many honors and given many series of lectures, including the Gifford Lectures at St. Andrews University in Scotland and the Carus Lectures for the American Philosophical Association. He has written many articles and books, including *The Nature of Thought* (2 volumes), *Reason and Goodness,* and *Reason and Analysis.*

Blanshard in the selection below says he is a determinist—that is, he believes that all events are caused—but he is a special kind of determinist. He examines indeterminism, or the view that there are some events whose antecedents do not make them necessary, and tells us why he does not think the grounds for that position are conclusive. Action on the highest causal level is compatible with freedom. Rational determinism, or control by an ideal or sense of duty, is control by the self and is the best kind of freedom.

I am a determinist. None of the arguments offered on the other side seem of much weight except one form of the moral argument, and that itself is far from decisive. Perhaps the most useful thing I can do in this paper is explain why the commoner arguments for indeterminism do not, to my mind, carry conviction. In the course of this explanation the brand of determinism to which I am inclined should become gradually apparent.

But first a definition or two. Determinism is easier to define than indeterminism, and at first glance there seems to be no difficulty in saying what one means by it. It is the view that all events are caused. But unless one also says what one means by "event" and "caused," there is likely to be

*Reprinted by permission of New York University Press from *Determinism and Freedom* by Sidney Hook, ed. © 1958 by New York University. From "The Case for Determinism," pp. 3–7, 10–15.

trouble later. Do I include among events not only changes but the lack of change, not only the fall of the water over the cataract's edge, but the persistence of ice in the frozen river? The answer is "Yes." By an event I mean any change or persistence of state or position. And what is meant by saying that an event is caused? The natural answer is that the event is so connected with some preceding event that unless the latter had occurred the former would not have occurred. Indeterminism means the denial of this. And the denial of this is the statement that there is at least one event to which no preceding event is necessary. But that gets us into trouble at once, for it is doubtful if any indeterminist would want to make such an assertion. What he wants to say is that his decision to tell the truth is undetermined, not that there is no preceding event necessary to it. He would not contend, for example, that he could tell the truth if he had never been born. No, the causal statement to which the indeterminist takes exception is a different one. He is not saying that there is any event to which some namable antecedents are not necessary; he is saying that there are some events whose antecedents do not make them necessary. He is not denying that all consequents have necessary antecedents; he is denying that all antecedents have necessary consequents. He is saying that the state of things just before he decided to tell the truth might have been exactly what it was and yet he might have decided to tell a lie.

By determinism, then, I mean the view that every event *A* is so connected with a later event *B* that, given *A, B* must occur. By indeterminism I mean the view that there is some event *B* that is not so connected with any previous event *A* that, given *A,* it must occur. Now, what is meant here by "must"? We cannot in the end evade that question, but I hope you will not take it as an evasion if at this point I am content to let you fill in the blank in any way you wish. Make it a logical "must," if you care to, or a physical or metaphysical "must," or even the watered-down "must" that means "*A* is always in fact followed by *B*." We can discuss the issue usefully though we leave ourselves some latitude on this point.

With these definitions in mind, let us ask what are the most important grounds for indeterminism. This is not the same as asking what commonly moves people to be indeterminists; the answer to that seems to me all too easy. Everyone vaguely knows that to be undetermined is to be free, and everyone wants to be free. My question is rather, When reflective people accept the indeterminist view nowadays, what considerations seem most cogent to them? It seems to me that there are three: first, the stubborn feeling of freedom, which seems to resist all dialectical solvents; second, the conviction that natural science itself has now gone over to the indeterminist side; and, third, that determinism would make nonsense of moral responsibility. The third of these seems to me the most important, but I must try to explain why none of them seem to me conclusive.

One of the clearest heads that ever devoted itself to this old issue was Henry Sidgwick. Sidgwick noted that, if at any given moment we stop to think about it, we always feel as if more than one course were open to us, that we could speak or be silent, lift our hand or not lift it. If the determinist is right, this must be an illusion, of course, for whatever we might have done, there must have been a cause, given which we had to do what we did. Now, a mere intuitive assurance about ourselves may be a very weak ground for belief; Freud has shown us that we may be profoundly deceived about how we really feel or why we act as we do. But the curious point is that, though a man who hates his father without knowing it can usually be shown that he does and can often be cured of his feeling, no amount of dialectic seems to shake our feeling of being free to perform either of two proposed acts. By this feeling of being free I do not mean merely the freedom to do what we choose. No one on either side questions that we have that sort of freedom, but it is obviously not the sort of freedom that the indeterminist wants, since it is consistent with determinism of the most rigid sort. The real issue, so far as the will is concerned, is not whether we can do what we choose to do, but whether we can choose our own choice, whether the choice itself issues in accordance with law from some antecedent. And the feeling of freedom that is relevant as evidence is the feeling of an open future as regards the choice itself. After the noise of argument has died down, a sort of intuition stubbornly remains that we can not only lift our hand if we choose, but that the choice itself is open to us. Is this not an impressive fact?

No, I do not think it is. The first reason is that when we are making a choice our faces are always turned toward the future, toward the consequences that one act or the other will bring us, never toward the past with its possible sources of constraint. Hence these sources are not noticed. Hence we remain unaware that we are under constraint at all. Hence we feel free from such constraint. The case is almost as simple as that. When you consider buying a new typewriter your thought is fixed on the pleasure and advantage you would gain from it, or the drain it would make on your budget. You are not delving into the causes that led to your taking pleasure in the prospect of owning a typewriter or to your having a complex about expenditure. You are too much preoccupied with the ends to which the choice would be a means to give any attention to the causes of which your choice may be an effect. But that is no reason for thinking that if you did preoccupy yourself with these causes you would not find them at work. You may remember that Sir Francis Galton was so much impressed with this possibility that for some time he kept account in a notebook of the occasions on which he made important choices with a full measure of this feeling of freedom; then shortly after each choice he turned his eye backward in search of constraints that might have been acting on him stealthily.

He found it so easy to bring such constraining factors to light that he surrendered to the determinist view.

But this, you may say, is not enough. Our preoccupation with the future may show why we are not aware of the constraints acting on us, and hence why we do not feel bound by them; it does not explain why our sense of freedom persists after the constraints are disclosed to us. By disclosing the causes of some fear, for example, psychoanalytic therapy can remove the fear, and when these causes are brought to light, the fear commonly does go. How is it, then, that when the causes of our volition are brought to light volition continues to feel as free as before? Does this not show that it is really independent of those causes?

No again. The two cases are not parallel. The man with the panic fear of dogs is investing all dogs with the qualities remembered, though in disguised form—of the monster that frightened him as a child. When this monster and his relation to it are brought to light, so that they can be dissociated from the Fidos and Towsers around him, the fear goes, because its appropriate object has gone. It is quite different with our feeling of freedom. We feel free, it was suggested, because we are not aware of the forces acting on us. Now, in spite of the determinist's conviction that when a choice is made there are always causal influences at work, he does not pretend to reveal the influences at work in our present choice. The chooser's face is always turned forward; his present choice is always unique; and no matter how much he knows about the will and the laws, his present choice always emerges out of deep shadow. The determinist who buys a typewriter is as little interested at the moment in the strings that may be pulling at him from his physiological or subconscious cellars as his indeterminist colleague, and hence feels just as free. Thus, whereas the new knowledge gained through psychoanalysis does remove the grounds of fear, the knowledge gained by the determinist is not at all of the sort that would remove the grounds for the feeling of freedom. To make the persistence of this feeling in the determinist an argument against his case is therefore a confusion.

The second reason, I suggested, why so many thoughtful persons remain indeterminists is that they are convinced that science has gone indeterminist. Well, has it? If you follow Heisenberg, Eddington, and Born, it has. If you follow Russell, Planck, and Einstein, it has not. When such experts disagree it is no doubt folly for the layman to rush in. But since I am discussing the main reasons why people stick to indeterminism, and have admitted that the new physics is one of them, I cannot afford to be quite prudent. Let me say, then, with much hesitation that, as far as I can follow the argument, it provides no good evidence for indeterminism even in the physical world, and that, if it did, it would provide no good evidence for indeterminism in the realm of will....

We come now to the third of the reasons commonly advanced in support of indeterminism. This is that determinism makes a mess of morality. The charge has taken many forms. We are told that determinism makes praise and blame meaningless, punishment brutal, remorse pointless, amendment hopeless, duty a deceit. All these allegations have been effectively answered except that one about duty, where I admit I am not quite satisfied. But none of them are in the form in which determinism most troubles the plain man. What most affronts him, I think, is the suggestion that he is only a machine, a big foolish clock that seems to itself to be acting freely but whose movements are controlled completely by the wheels and weights inside, a Punch-and-Judy show whose appearance of doing things because they are right or reasonable is a sham because everything is mechanically regulated by wires from below. He has no objections to determinism as applied by physicists to atoms, by himself to machines, or by his doctor to his body. He has an emphatic objection to determinism as applied by anyone to his reflection and his will, for this seems to make him a gigantic mechanical toy, or worse, a sort of Frankenstein monster.

In this objection I think we must agree with the plain man. If anyone were to show me that determinism involved either materialism or mechanism, I would renounce it at once, for that would be equivalent, in my opinion, to reducing it to absurdity. The "physicalism" once proposed by Neurath and Carnap as a basis for the scientific study of behavior I could not accept for a moment, because it is so dogmatically anti-empirical. To use empirical methods means, for me, not to approach nature with a preconceived notion as to what facts must be like, but to be ready to consider all kinds of alleged facts on their merits. Among these the introspectively observable fact of reflective choice, and the inference to its existence in others, are particularly plain, however different from anything that occurs in the realm of the material or the publicly observable or the mechanically controlled.

Now, what can be meant by saying that such choice, though not determined mechanically, is still determined? Are you suggesting, it will be asked, that in the realm of reflection and choice there operates a different kind of causality from any we know in the realm of bodies? My answer is: Yes, just that. To put it more particularly, I am suggesting (1) that even within the psychical realm there are different causal levels, (2) that a causality of higher level may supervene on one of lower level, and (3) that when causality of the highest level is at work, we have precisely what the indeterminists, without knowing it, want.

1. First, then, as to causal levels. I am assuming that even the indeterminist would admit that most mental events are causally governed. No one would want to deny that his stepping on a tack had something to do with his feeling pain, or that his touching a flame had something to do with his

getting burned, or that his later thought of the flame had something to do with his experience of its hotness. A law of association is a causal law of mental events. In one respect it is like a law of physical events: in neither case have we any light as to *why* the consequent follows on the antecedent. Hume was right about the billiard balls. He was right about the flame and the heat; we do not see why something bright and yellow should also be hot. He was right about association; we do not understand how one idea calls up another; we only know that it does. Causality in all such cases means to us little if anything more than a routine of regular sequence.

Is all mental causation like that? Surely not. Consider a musician composing a piece or a logician making a deduction. Let us make our musician a philosopher also, who after adding a bar pauses to ask himself, "Why did I add just that?" Can we believe he would answer, "Because whenever in the past I have had the preceding bars in mind, they have always been followed by this bar"? What makes this suggestion so inept is partly that he may never have thought of the preceding bars before, partly that, if he had, the repetition of an old sequence would be precisely what he would avoid. No, his answer, I think, would be something like this: "I wrote what I did because it seemed the right thing to do. I developed my theme in the manner demanded to carry it through in an aesthetically satisfactory way." In other words, the constraint that was really at work in him was not that of association; it was something that worked distinctly against association; it was the constraint of an aesthetic ideal. And, if so, there is a causality of a different level. It is idle to say that the musician is wholly in the dark about it. He can see not only *that B* succeeded *A;* as he looks back, he can see in large measure *why* it did.

It is the same with logical inference, only more clearly so. The thinker starts, let us say, with the idea of a regular solid whose faces are squares, and proceeds to develop in thought the further characteristics that such a solid must possess. He constructs it in imagination and then sees that it must have six faces, eight vertices, and twelve edges. Is this association merely? It may be. It is, for example, if he merely does in imagination what a child does when it counts the edges on a lump of sugar. This is not inference and does not feel like it. When a person, starting with the thought of a solid with square faces, deduces that it must have eight vertices, and then asks why he should have thought of that, the natural answer is, Because the first property entails the second. Of course this is not the only condition, but it seems to me contrary to introspectively plain fact to say that it had nothing to do with the movement of thought. It is easy to put this in such a way as to invite attack. If we say that the condition of our thinking of *B* is the observed necessity between *A* and *B,* we are assuming that *B* is already thought of as a means of explaining how it comes to be thought of.

But that is not what I am saying. I am saying that in thinking at its best thought comes under the constraint of necessities in its object, so that the objective fact that *A* necessitates *B* partially determines our passing in thought from *A* to *B*. Even when the explanation is put in this form, the objection has been raised that necessity is a timeless link between concepts, while causality is a temporal bond between events, and that the two must be kept sharply apart. To which the answer is: Distinct, yes; but always apart, no. A timeless relation may serve perfectly well as the condition of a temporal passage. I hold that in the course of our thinking we can easily verify this fact, and, because I do, I am not put off by pronouncements about what we should and should not be able to see.

2. My second point about the causal levels is that our mental processes seldom move on one level alone. The higher is always supervening on the lower and taking over partial control. Though brokenly and imperfectly rational, rational creatures we still are. It must be admitted that most of our so-called thinking moves by association, and is hardly thinking at all. But even in the dullest of us "bright shoots of everlastingness," strands of necessity, aesthetic or logical, from time to time appear. "The quarto and folio editions of mankind" can follow the argument with fewer lapses than most of us; in the texts of the greatest of all dramas, we are told, there was seldom a blot or erasure; but Ben Jonson added, and no doubt rightly, that there ought to have been a thousand. The effort of both thought and art is to escape the arbitrary, the merely personal, everything that, causal and capricious, is irrelevant, and to keep to lines appointed by the whole that one is constructing. I do not suggest that logical and aesthetic necessity are the same. I do say that they are both to be distinguished from association or habit as representing a different level of control. That control is never complete; all creation in thought or art is successful in degree only. It is successful in the degree to which it ceases to be an expression of merely personal impulses and becomes the instrument of a necessity lying in its own subject matter.

3. This brings us to our last point. Since moral choice, like thought and art, moves on different causal levels, it achieves freedom, just as they do, only when it is determined by its own appropriate necessity. Most of our so-called choices are so clearly brought about by association, impulse, and feeling that the judicious indeterminist will raise no issue about them. When we decide to get a drink of water, to take another nibble of chocolate, to go to bed at the usual hour, the forces at work are too plain to be denied. It is not acts like these on which the indeterminist takes his stand. It is rather on those where, with habit, impulse, and association prompting us powerfully to do *X*, we see that we ought to do *Y* and therefore do it. To suppose that in such cases we are still the puppets of habit and impulse seems to the indeterminist palpably false.

So it does to us. Surely about this the indeterminist is right. Action impelled by the sense of duty, as Kant perceived, is action on a different level from anything mechanical or associative. But Kant was mistaken in supposing that when we were determined by reason we were not determined at all. This supposition seems to me wholly unwarranted. The determination is still there, but, since it is a determination by the moral necessities of the case, it is just what the moral man wants and thus is the equivalent of freedom. For the moral man, like the logician and the artist, is really seeking self-surrender. Through him as through the others an impersonal ideal is working, and to the extent that this ideal takes possession of him and molds him according to its pattern, he feels free and is free.

The logician is most fully himself when the wind gets into his sails and carries him effortlessly along the line of his calculations. Many an artist and musician have left it on record that their best work was done when the whole they were creating took the brush or pen away from them and completed the work itself. It determined them, but they were free, because to be determined by this whole was at once the secret of their craft and the end of their desire. This is the condition of the moral man also. He has caught a vision, dimmer perhaps than that of the logician or the artist, but equally objective and compelling. It is a vision of the good. This good necessitates certain things, not as means to ends merely, for that is not usually a necessary link, but as integral parts of itself. It requires that he should put love above hate, that he should regard his neighbor's good as of like value with his own, that he should repair injuries, and express gratitude, and respect promises, and revere truth. Of course it does not guide him infallibly. On the values of a particular case he may easily be mistaken. But that no more shows that there are no values present to be estimated, and no ideal demanding a special mode of action, than the fact that we make a mistake in adding figures shows that there are no figures to be added, or no right way of adding them. In both instances what we want is control by the objective requirements of the case. The saint, like the thinker and the artist, has often said this in so many words. I feel most free, said St. Paul, precisely when I am most a slave.

We have now dealt, as best we can in a restricted space, with the three commonest objections to determinism. They all seem to admit of answers. To the objection that we always feel free, we answer that it is natural to feel so, even if we are determined, since our faces are set toward results and not toward causes, and the causes of present action always elude us. To the objection that science has gone indeterminist, we answer that that is only one interpretation of recent discoveries, and not the most plausible one, and that, even if it were true, it would not carry with it indeterminism for human choice. To the objection that determinism would reduce us to the level of mechanical puppets, we answer that though we are puppets in part we live, as Aristotle said, on various levels. And so far as causality in reflection, art, and moral choice involves control by immanent ideal, mechanism has passed over into the rational determinism that is the best kind of freedom.

WILLIAM JAMES

*The Dilemma of Determinism**

William James (1842–1910) was born in New York and had early contact with intellectual leaders. From 1855 to 1860 he studied in England, France, Switzerland, and Germany. His interests shifted from art (painting) to natural science. After receiving an M.D. and teaching physiology, he turned to psychology, then to philosophy. From 1872 until his death he taught at Harvard University. He gave public lectures and became a leader in the movement known as pragmatism. His writings, which are classics in American philosophy, include *The Will to Believe, The Varieties of Religious Experience, Pragmatism, The Meaning of Truth,* and *A Pluralistic Universe.* After his death, *Some Problems in Philosophy* and *Essays in Radical Empiricism* were published.

In the following essay, James states the case for what has traditionally been called "freedom of the will" or moral freedom, or what philosophers have often called indeterminism. He also gives the case against ("the dilemma of") determinism. For James, the first act of freedom, if indeed we are free, must be to affirm that we are free. This is his starting point.

A common opinion prevails that the juice has ages ago been pressed out of the free-will controversy, and that no new champion can do more than warm up stale arguments which every one has heard. This is a radical mistake. I know of no subject less worn out, or in which inventive genius has a better chance of breaking open new ground,—not, perhaps, of forcing a conclusion or of coercing assent, but of deepening our sense of what the issue between the two parties really is, of what the ideas of fate and of free-will imply.... [O]ur first act of freedom, if we are free, ought in all inward propriety to be to affirm that we are free....

With this much understood at the outset, we can advance. But not

*William James, from *The Will to Believe and Other Essays in Popular Philosophy* (New York: Longmans, Green, 1897), pp. 145–183 with omissions.

without one more point understood as well. The arguments I am about to urge all proceed on two suppositions: first, when we make theories about the world and discuss them with one another, we do so in order to attain a conception of things which shall give us subjective satisfaction; and, second, if there be two conceptions, and the one seems to us, on the whole, more rational than the other, we are entitled to suppose that the more rational one is the truer of the two....

To begin, then, I must suppose you acquainted with all the usual arguments on the subject. I cannot stop to take up the old proofs from causation, from statistics, from the certainty with which we can foretell one another's conduct, from the fixity of character, and all the rest.... Old-fashioned determinism was what we may call *hard* determinism. It did not shrink from such words as fatality, bondage of the will, necessitation, and the like. Nowadays, we have a *soft* determinism which abhors harsh words, and, repudiating fatality, necessity, and even predetermination, says that its real name is freedom; for freedom is only necessity understood, and bondage to the highest is identical with true freedom....

[Determinism] professes that those parts of the universe already laid down absolutely appoint and decree what the other parts shall be. The future has no ambiguous possibilities hidden in its womb: the part we call the present is compatible with only one totality. Any other future complement than the one fixed from eternity is impossible. The whole is in each and every part, and welds it with the rest into an absolute unity, an iron block, in which there can be no equivocation or shadow of turning.

> With earth's first clay they did the last man knead,
> And there of the last harvest sowed the seed.
> And the first morning of creation wrote
> What the last dawn of reckoning shall read.

Indeterminism, on the contrary, says that the parts have a certain amount of loose play on one another, so that the laying down of one of them does not necessarily determine what the others shall be. It admits that possibilities may be in excess of actualities, and that things not yet revealed to our knowledge may really in themselves be ambiguous. Of two alternative futures which we conceive, both may now be really possible; and the one become impossible only at the very moment when the other excludes it by becoming real itself. Indeterminism thus denies the world to be one unbending unit of fact. It says there is a certain ultimate pluralism in it; and, so saying, it corroborates our ordinary unsophisticated view of things. To that view, actualities seem to float in a wider sea of possibilities from out of which they are chosen; and, *somewhere,* indeterminism says, such possibilities exist, and form a part of truth.

Determinism, on the contrary, says they exist *nowhere,* and that necessity on the one hand and impossibility on the other are the sole categories of the real. Possibilities that fail to get realized are, for determinism, pure illusions: they never were possibilities at all. There is nothing inchoate, it says, about this universe of ours, all that was or is or shall be actual in it having been from eternity virtually there. The cloud of alternatives our minds escort this mass of actuality withal is a cloud of sheer deceptions, to which "impossibilities" is the only name that rightfully belongs.

The issue, it will be seen, is a perfectly sharp one, which no eulogistic terminology can smear over or wipe out. The truth *must* lie with one side or the other, and its lying with one side makes the other false.

The question relates solely to the existence of possibilities, in the strict sense of the term, as things that may, but need not, be. Both sides admit that a volition, for instance, has occurred. The indeterminists say another volition might have occurred in its place: the determinists swear that nothing could possibly have occurred in its place. Now, can science be called in to tell us which of these two point-blank contradicters of each other is right? Science professes to draw no conclusions but such as are based on matters of fact, things that have actually happened; but how can any amount of assurance that something actually happened give us the least grain of information as to whether another thing might or might not have happened in its place? Only facts can be proved by other facts. With things that are possibilities and not facts, facts have no concern. If we have no other evidence than the evidence of existing facts, the possibility-question must remain a mystery never to be cleared up.

And the truth is that facts practically have hardly anything to do with making us either determinists or indeterminists. Sure enough, we make a flourish of quoting facts this way or that; and if we are determinists, we talk about the infallibility with which we can predict one another's conduct; while if we are indeterminists, we lay great stress on the fact that it is just because we cannot foretell one another's conduct, either in war or statecraft or in any of the great and small intrigues and businesses of men, that life is so intensely anxious and hazardous a game. But who does not see the wretched insufficiency of this so-called objective testimony on both sides? What fills up the gaps in our minds is something not objective, not external. What divides us into possibility men and anti-possibility men is different faiths or postulates,—postulates of rationality. To this man the world seems more rational with possibilities in it,—to that man more rational with possibilities excluded; and talk as we will about having to yield to evidence, what makes us monists or pluralists, determinists or indeterminists, is at bottom always some sentiment like this. . . .

Nevertheless, many persons talk as if the minutest dose of disconnectedness of one part with another, the smallest modicum of independence, the faintest tremor of ambiguity about the future, for example, would ruin everything, and turn this goodly universe into a sort of insane sand-heap or nulliverse, no universe at all. Since future human volitions are as a matter of fact the only ambiguous things we are tempted to believe in, let us stop for a moment to make ourselves sure whether their independent and accidental character need be fraught with such direful consequences to the universe as these.

What is meant by saying that my choice of which way to walk home after the lecture is ambiguous and matter of chance as far as the present moment is concerned? It means that both Divinity Avenue and Oxford Street are called; but that only one, and that one *either* one, shall be chosen. Now, I ask you seriously to suppose that this ambiguity of my choice is real; and then to make the impossible hypothesis that the choice is made twice over, and each time falls on a different street. In other words, imagine that I first walk through Divinity Avenue, and then imagine that the powers governing the universe annihilate ten minutes of time with all that it contained, and set me back at the door of this hall just as I was before the choice was made. Imagine then that, everything else being the same, I now make a different choice and traverse Oxford Street. You, as passive spectators, look on and see the two alternative universes,—one of them with me walking through Divinity Avenue in it, the other with the same me walking through Oxford Street. Now, if you are determinists you believe one of these universes to have been from eternity impossible: you believe it to have been impossible because of the intrinsic irrationality or accidentality somewhere involved in it. But looking outwardly at these universes, can you say which is the impossible and accidental one, and which the rational and necessary one? I doubt if the most ironclad determinist among you could have the slightest glimmer of light on this point. In other words, either universe *after the fact* and once there would, to our means of observation and understanding, appear just as rational as the other. There would be absolutely no criterion by which we might judge one necessary and the other matter of chance. Suppose now we relieve the gods of their hypothetical task and assume my choice, once made, to be made forever. I go through Divinity Avenue for good and all. If, as good determinists, you now begin to affirm, what all good determinists punctually do affirm, that in the nature of things I *couldn't* have gone through Oxford Street,—had I done so it would have been chance, irrationality, insanity, a horrid gap in nature,—I simply call your attention to this, that your affirmation is what the Germans call a *Machtspruch,* a mere conception fulminated as a dogma and based on no insight into details. Before my choice, either street seemed as natural to you as to me. Had I happened to take Oxford Street, Divinity Avenue would have figured in your philosophy as the gap in nature; and you would have so proclaimed it with the best deterministic conscience in the world....

And this at last brings us within sight of our subject. We have seen what determinism means: we have seen that indeterminism is rightly described as meaning chance; and we have seen that chance, the very name of which we are urged to shrink from as from a metaphysical pestilence, means only the negative fact that no part of the world, however big, can claim to control absolutely the destinies of the whole. But although, in discussing the word "chance," I may at moments have seemed to be arguing for its real existence, I have not meant to do so yet. We have not yet ascertained whether this be a world of chance or no; at most, we have agreed that it seems so. And I now repeat what I said at the outset, that, from any strict theoretical point of view, the question is insoluble. To deepen our theoretic sense of the *difference* between a world with chances in it and a deterministic world is the most I can hope to do; and this I may now at last begin upon, after all our tedious clearing of the way.

I wish first of all to show you just what the notion that this is a deterministic world implies. The implications I call your attention to are all bound up with the fact that it is a world in which we constantly have to make what I shall, with your permission, call judgments of regret. Hardly an hour passes in which we do not wish that something might be otherwise; and happy indeed are those of us whose hearts have never echoed the wish of Omar Khayam—

> That we might clasp, ere closed, the book of fate,
> And make the writer on a fairer leaf
> Inscribe our names, or quite obliterate.
>
> Ah! Love, could you and I with fate conspire
> To mend this sorry scheme of things entire,
> Would we not shatter it to bits, and then
> Remould it nearer to the heart's desire?

Now, it is undeniable that most of these regrets are foolish, and quite on a par in point of philosophic value with the criticisms on the universe of that friend of our infancy, the hero of the fable The Atheist and the Acorn,—

> Fool! had that bough a pumpkin bore,
> Thy whimsies would have worked no more, etc.

Even from the point of view of our own ends, we should probably make a botch of remodelling the universe. How much more then from the point of view of ends we cannot see! Wise men therefore regret as little as they can. But still some regrets are pretty obstinate and hard to stifle,—regrets for acts of wanton cruelty or treachery, for example, whether performed by others or by ourselves. Hardly any one can remain *entirely* optimistic after reading the confession of the murderer at Brockton the other day: how, to get rid of the wife whose continued existence bored him, he inveigled her into a desert spot, shot her four times, and then, as she lay on the ground and said to him, "You didn't do it on purpose, did you, dear?" replied, "No, I didn't do it on purpose," as he raised a rock and smashed her skull. Such an occurrence, with the mild sentence and self-satisfaction of the prisoner, is a field for a crop of regrets, which one need not take up in detail. We feel that, although a perfect mechanical fit to the rest of the universe, it is a bad moral fit, and that something else would really have been better in its place.

But for the deterministic philosophy the murder, the sentence, and the prisoner's optimism were all necessary from eternity; and nothing else for a moment had a ghost of a chance of being put into their place. To admit such a chance, the determinists tell us, would be to make a suicide of reason; so we must steel our hearts against the thought. And here our plot thickens, for we see the first of those difficult implications of determinism and monism which it is my purpose to make you feel. If this Brockton murder was called for by the rest of the universe, if it had to come at its preappointed hour, and if nothing else would have been consistent with the sense of the whole, what are we to think of the universe? Are we stubbornly to stick to our judgment of regret, and say, though it *couldn't* be, yet it *would* have been a better universe with something different from this Brockton murder in it? That, of course, seems the natural and spontaneous thing for us to do; and yet it is nothing short of deliberately espousing a kind of pessimism. The judgment of regret calls the murder bad. Calling a thing bad means, if it mean anything at all, that the thing ought not to be, that something else ought to be in its stead. Determinism, in denying that anything else can be in its stead, virtually defines the universe as a place in which what ought to be is impossible,—in other words, as an organism whose constitution is afflicted with an incurable taint, an irremediable flaw. The pessimism of a Schopenhauer says no more than this,—that the murder is a symptom; and that it is a vicious symptom because it belongs to a vicious whole, which can express its nature no otherwise than by bringing forth just such a symptom as that at this particular spot. Regret for the murder must transform itself, if we are determinists and wise, into a larger regret. It is absurd to regret the murder alone. Other things being what they are, *it* could not be different. What we should regret is that whole frame of things of which the murder is one member. I see no escape whatever from this pessimistic conclusion, if, being determinists, our judgment of regret is to be allowed to stand at all.

The only deterministic escape from pessimism is everywhere to abandon the judgment of regret. That this can be done, history shows to be not impossible. The devil, *quoad existentiam,* may be good. That is, although he be a *principle* of evil, yet the universe, with such a principle in it, may practically be a better universe than it could have been without. On every hand, in a small way, we find that a certain amount of evil is a condition by which a higher form of good is bought. There is nothing to prevent anybody from generalizing this view, and trusting that if we could but see things in the largest of all ways, even such matters as this Brockton murder would appear to be paid for by the uses that follow in their train. An optimism *quand même,* a systematic and infatuated optimism like that ridiculed by Voltaire in his Candide, is one of the possible ideal ways in which a man may train himself to look on life. Bereft of dogmatic hardness and lit up with the expression of a tender and pathetic hope, such an optimism has been the grace of some of the most religious characters that ever lived.

> Throb thine with Nature's throbbing breast,
> And all is clear from east to west.

Even cruelty and treachery may be among the absolutely blessed fruits of time, and to quarrel with any of their details may be blasphemy. The only real blasphemy, in short, may be that pessimistic temper of the soul which lets it give way to such things as regrets, remorse, and grief.

Thus, our deterministic pessimism may become a deterministic optimism at the price of extinguishing our judgments of regret.

But does not this immediately bring us into a curious logical predicament? Our determinism leads us to call our judgments of regret wrong, because they are pessimistic in implying that what is impossible yet ought to be. But how then about the judgments of regret themselves? If they are wrong, other judgments, judgments of approval presumably, ought to be in their place. But as they are necessitated, nothing else *can* be in their place; and the universe is just what it was before,—namely, a place in which what ought to be appears impossible. We have got one foot out of the pessimistic bog, but the other one sinks all the deeper. We have rescued our actions from the bonds of evil, but our judgments are now held fast. When murders and treacheries cease to be sins, regrets are theoretic absurdities and errors. The theoretic and the active life thus play a kind of seesaw with each other on the ground of evil. The rise of either sends the other down. Murder and treachery cannot be good without regret being bad: regret cannot be good without treachery and murder being bad. Both, however, are supposed to have been foredoomed: so something must be fatally unreasonable, absurd, and wrong in the world. It must be a place of which either sin or error forms a necessary part. From this dilemma there seems at first sight no escape. . . .

The Search for Values

ARISTOTLE

*Good and the Highest Good**

Aristotle (384–322 B.C.), philosopher, scientist, and educator, has been one of the most influential thinkers in the Western world. Born in Stagira in northern Greece, he entered Plato's Academy in Athens at age eighteen and remained there until the death of Plato nearly two decades later. After a period of travel, he returned to Athens about 334 B.C. and founded his own school, the Lyceum. His interests and research embraced all the then-known fields of knowledge. His writings, between thirty and forty, include science, society, the state (politics), the arts, metaphysics, logic, and ethics. His *Nicomachean Ethics,* from which we draw the following selection, was the first systematic treatise in the field and is still read today.

Aristotle maintains that, while there are many things that are considered good, if there is something that is good for its own sake and not just as a means for attaining something else, that is the highest good or at least an element in it. Is this good happiness, honor, the life of contemplation, activity in accordance with reason, excellence, or the unity of moral virtue and wisdom? Is the highest good some combination of these? To describe it, Aristotle used the Greek term *eudaemonia,* variously translated as "happiness," "well-being," or activity in harmony with virtue. It does not come from wealth or pleasure. It includes the development of the functions that make a man a human being and a member of a good society; it appears to be the living of a "complete life."

Every art and every inquiry, and similarly every action and pursuit, is thought to aim at some good; and for this reason the good has rightly been declared to be that at which all things aim. But a certain difference is found among ends; some are activities, others are products apart from the activities

*Aristotle, from "Ethica Nicomachea," from *The Works of Aristotle* (1925), trans. W. D. Ross. Books 1, 2, and 10 with omissions. Used by permission of The Clarendon Press, Oxford.

that produce them. Where there are ends apart from the actions, it is the nature of the products to be better than the activities. Now, as there are many actions, arts, and sciences, their ends also are many; the end of the medical art is health, that of shipbuilding a vessel, that of strategy victory, that of economics wealth. But where such arts fall under a single capacity—as bridle-making and the other arts concerned with the equipment of horses fall under the art of riding, and this and every military action under strategy, in the same way other arts fall under yet others—in all of these the ends of the master arts are to be preferred to all the subordinate ends; for it is for the sake of the former that the latter are pursued. It makes no difference whether the activities themselves are the ends of the actions, or something else apart from the activities, as in the case of the sciences just mentioned.

If, then, there is some end of the things we do, which we desire for its own sake (everything else being desired for the sake of this), and if we do not choose everything for the sake of something else (for at that rate the process would go on to infinity, so that our desire would be empty and vain), clearly this must be the good and the chief good. Will not the knowledge of it, then, have a great influence on life? Shall we not, like archers who have a mark to aim at, be more likely to hit upon what is right? If so, we must try, in outline at least, to determine what it is, and of which of the sciences or capacities it is the object. It would seem to belong to the most authoritative art and that which is most truly the master art. And politics appears to be of this nature; for it is this that ordains which of the sciences should be studied in a state, and which each class of citizens should learn and up to what point they should learn them; and we see even the most highly esteemed of capacities to fall under this, e.g. strategy, economics, rhetoric; now, since politics uses the rest of the sciences, and since, again, it legislates as to what we are to do and what we are to abstain from, the end of this science must include those of the others, so that this end must be the good for man. For even if the end is the same for a single man and for a state, that of the state seems at all events something greater and more complete whether to attain or to preserve; though it is worth while to attain the end merely for one man, it is finer and more godlike to attain it for a nation or for city-states. These, then, are the ends at which our inquiry aims, since it is political science, in one sense of that term....

Now each man judges well the things he knows, and of these he is a good judge. And so the man who has been educated in a subject is a good judge of that subject, and the man who has received an all-round education is a good judge in general....

Let us resume our inquiry and state, in view of the fact that all knowledge and every pursuit aims at some good, what it is that we say political science aims at and what is the highest of all goods achievable by action. Verbally there is very general agreement; for both the general run of men and people of superior refinement say that it is happiness, and identify living well and doing well with being happy; but with regard to what happiness is they differ, and the many do not give the same account as the wise. For the former think it is some plain and obvious thing, like pleasure, wealth, or honour; they differ, however, from one another—and often even the same man identifies it with different things, with health when he is ill, with wealth when he is poor; but, conscious of their ignorance, they admire those who proclaim some great ideal that is above their comprehension. Now some thought that apart from these many goods there is another which is self-subsistent and causes the goodness of all these as well. To examine all the opinions that have been held were perhaps somewhat fruitless; enough to examine those that are most prevalent or that seem to be arguable....

But what then do we mean by the good? It is surely not like the things that only chance to have the same name. Are goods one, then, by being derived from one good or by all contributing to one good, or are they rather one by analogy? Certainly as sight is in the body, so is reason in the soul, and so on in other cases. But perhaps these subjects had better be dismissed for the present; for perfect precision about them would be more appropriate to another branch of philosophy. And similarly with regard to the Idea; even if there is some one good which is universally predicable of goods or is capable of separate and independent existence, clearly it could not be achieved or attained by man; but we are now seeking something attainable. Perhaps, however, some one might think it worth while to recognize this with a view to the goods that *are* attainable and achievable; for having this as a sort of pattern we shall know better the goods that are good for us, and if we know them shall attain them. This argument has some plausibility, but seems to clash with the procedure of the sciences; for all of these, though they aim at some good and seek to supply the deficiency of it, leave on one side the knowledge of *the* good. Yet that all the exponents of the arts should be ignorant of, and should not even seek, so great an aid is not probable. It is hard, too, to see how a weaver or a carpenter will be benefited in regard to his own craft by knowing this "good itself," or how the man who has viewed the Idea itself will be a better doctor or general thereby. For a doctor seems not even to study health in this way, but the health of man, or perhaps rather the health of a particular man; it is individuals that he is healing. But enough of these topics.

Let us again return to the good we are seeking, and ask what it can be. It seems different in different actions and arts; it is different in medicine, in strategy, and in the other arts likewise. What then is the good of each? Surely that for whose sake everything else is done. In medicine this is health, in strategy victory, in architecture a house, in any other sphere something else, and in every action and pursuit the end; for it is for the sake of this that all men do whatever else they do. Therefore, if there is an end for all that we do, this will be the good achievable by action, and if there are more than one, these will be the goods achievable by action.

So the argument has by a different course reached the same point; but we must try to state this even more clearly. Since there are evidently more than one end, and we choose some of these (e.g. wealth, flutes, and in general instruments) for the sake of something else, clearly not all ends are final ends; but the chief good is evidently something final. Therefore, if there is only one final end, this will be what we are seeking, and if there are more than one, the most final of these will be what we are seeking. Now we call that which is in itself worthy of pursuit more final than that which is worthy of pursuit for the sake of something else, and that which is never desirable for the sake of something else more final than the things that are desirable both in themselves and for the sake of that other thing, and therefore we call final without qualification that which is always desirable in itself and never for the sake of something else.

Now such a thing happiness, above all else, is held to be; for this we choose always for itself and never for the sake of something else, but honour, pleasure, reason, and every virtue we choose indeed for themselves (for if nothing resulted from them we should still choose each of them), but we choose them also for the sake of happiness, judging that by means of them we shall be happy. Happiness, on the other hand, no one chooses for the sake of these, nor, in general, for anything other than itself.

From the point of view of self-sufficiency the same result seems to follow; for the final good is thought to be self-sufficient. Now by self-sufficient we do not mean that which is sufficient for a man by himself, for one who lives a solitary life, but also for parents, children, wife, and in general for his friends and fellow citizens, since man is born for citizenship. But some limit must be set to this; for if we extend our requirement to ancestors and descendants and friends' friends we are in for an infinite series. Let us examine this question, however, on another occasion; the self-sufficient we now define as that which when isolated makes life desirable and lacking in nothing; and such we think happiness to be; and further we think it most desirable of all things, without being counted as one good thing among others—if it were so counted it would clearly be made more desirable by the addition of even the least of goods; for that which is added becomes an excess of goods, and of goods the greater is always more desirable. Happiness, then, is something final and self-sufficient, and is the end of action.

Presumably, however, to say that happiness is the chief good seems a platitude, and a clearer account of what it is is still desired. This might perhaps be given, if we could first ascertain the function of man. For just as for a flute-player, a sculptor, or any artist, and, in general, for all things that have a function or activity, the good and the "well" is thought to reside in the function, so would it seem to be for man, if he has a function. Have the carpenter, then, and the tanner certain functions or activities, and has man none? Is he born without a function? Or as eye, hand, foot, and in general each of the parts evidently has a function, may one lay it down that man similarly has a function apart from all these? What then can this be? Life seems to be common even to plants, but we are seeking what is peculiar to man. Let us exclude, therefore, the life of nutrition and growth. Next there would be a life of perception, but *it* also seems to be common even to the horse, the ox, and every animal. There remains, then, an active life of the element that has a rational principle; of this, one part has such a principle in the sense of being obedient to one, the other in the sense of possessing one and exercising thought. And, as "life of the rational element" also has two meanings, we must state that life in the sense of activity is what we mean; for this seems to be the more proper sense of the term. Now if the function of man is an activity of soul which follows or implies a rational principle, and if we say "a so-and-so" and "a good so-and-so" have a function which is the same in kind, e.g. a lyre-player and a good lyre-player, and so without qualification in all cases, eminence in respect of goodness being added to the name of the function (for the function of a lyre-player is to play the lyre, and that of a good lyre-player is to do so well): if this is the case, [and we state the function of man to be a certain kind of life, and this to be an activity or actions of the soul implying a rational principle, and the function of a good man to be the good and noble performance of these, and if any action is well performed when it is performed in accordance with the appropriate excellence: if this is the case,] human good turns out to be activity of soul in accordance with virtue, and if there are more than one virtue, in accordance with the best and most complete.

But we must add "in a complete life." For one swallow does not make a summer, nor does one day; and so too one day, or a short time, does not make a man blessed and happy....

Virtue too is distinguished into kinds in accordance with this difference; for we say that some of the virtues are intellectual and others moral, philosophic wisdom and understanding and practical wisdom being intellectual, liberality and temperance moral. For in speaking about a man's character we do not say that he is wise or has understanding but that he is good-tempered or temperate; yet we praise the wise man also with respect to his state of mind; and of states of mind we call those which merit praise virtues.

Virtue, then, being of two kinds, intellectual and moral, intellectual virtue in the main owes both its birth and its growth to teaching (for which reason it requires experience and time), while moral virtue comes about as a result of habit, whence also its name (ἠθική) is one that is formed by a slight variation from the word ἔθος (habit). From this it is also plain that none of the moral virtues arises in us by nature; for nothing that exists by nature can form a habit contrary to its nature. For instance the stone which by nature moves downwards cannot be habituated to move upwards, not even if one tries to train it by throwing it up ten thousand times; nor can fire be habituated to move downwards, nor can anything else that by nature behaves in one way be trained to behave in another. Neither by nature, then, nor contrary to nature do the virtues arise in us; rather we are adapted by nature to receive them, and are made perfect by habit.

Again, of all the things that come to us by nature we first acquire the potentiality and later exhibit the activity (this is plain in the case of the senses; for it was not by often seeing or often hearing that we got these senses, but on the contrary we had them before we used them, and did not come to have them by using them); but the virtues we get by first exercising them, as also happens in the case of the arts as well. For the things we have to learn before we can do them, we learn by doing them, e.g. men become builders by building and lyre-players by playing the lyre; so too we become just by doing just acts, temperate by doing temperate acts, brave by doing brave acts.

This is confirmed by what happens in states; for legislators make the citizens good by forming habits in them, and this is the wish of every legislator, and those who do not effect it miss their mark, and it is in this that a good constitution differs from a bad one.

Again, it is from the same causes and by the same means that every virtue is both produced and destroyed, and similarly every art; for it is from playing the lyre that both good and bad lyre-players are produced. And the corresponding statement is true of builders and of all the rest; men will be good or bad builders as a result of building well or badly. For if this were not so, there would have been no need of a teacher, but all men would have been born good or bad at their craft. This, then, is the case with the virtues also; by doing the acts that we do in our transactions with other men we become just or unjust, and by doing the acts that we do in the presence of danger, and being habituated to feel fear or confidence, we become brave or cowardly. The same is true of appetites and feelings of anger; some men become temperate and good-tempered, others self-indulgent and irascible, by behaving in one way or the other in the appropriate circumstances. Thus, in one word, states of character arise out of like activities. This is why the activities we exhibit must be of a certain kind; it is because the states of character correspond to the differences between these. It makes no small difference, then, whether we form habits of one kind or of another from our very youth; it makes a very great difference, or rather *all* the difference....

If happiness is activity in accordance with virtue, it is reasonable that it should be in accordance with the highest virtue; and this will be that of the best thing in us. Whether it be reason or something else that is this element which is thought to be our natural ruler and guide and to take thought of things noble and divine, whether it be itself also divine or only the most divine element in us, the activity of this in accordance with its proper virtue will be perfect happiness. That this activity is contemplative we have already said.

Now this would seem to be in agreement both with what we said before and with the truth. For, firstly, this activity is the best (since not only is reason the best thing in us, but the objects of reason are the best of knowable objects); and, secondly, it is the most continuous, since we can contemplate truth more continuously than we can *do* anything. And we think happiness has pleasure mingled with it, but the activity of philosophic wisdom is admittedly the pleasantest of virtuous activities; at all events the pursuit of it is thought to offer pleasures marvellous for their purity and their enduringness, and it is to be expected that those who know will pass their time more pleasantly than those who inquire. And the self-sufficiency that is spoken of must belong most to the contemplative activity....

...What we said before will apply now; that which is proper to each thing is by nature best and most pleasant for each thing; for man, therefore, the life according to reason is best and pleasantest, since reason more than anything else *is* man. This life therefore is also the happiest.

But in a secondary degree the life in accordance with the other kind of virtue is happy; for the activities in accordance with this befit our human estate. Just and brave acts, and other virtuous acts, we do in relation to each other, observing our respective duties with regard to contracts and services and all manner of actions and with regard to passions; and all of these seem to be typically human. Some of them seem even to arise from the body, and virtue of character to be in many ways bound up with the passions. Practical wisdom, too, is linked to virtue of character, and this to practical wisdom, since the principles of practical wisdom are in accordance with the moral virtues and rightness in morals is in accordance with practical wisdom. Being connected with the passions also, the moral virtues must belong to our composite nature; and the virtues of our composite nature are human; so, therefore, are the life and the happiness which correspond to these. The excellence of the reason is a thing apart; we must be content to say this much about it, for to describe it precisely is a task greater than our purpose requires. It would seem, however, also to need external equipment but little, or less than moral virtue does. Grant that both need the necessaries, and do so equally, even if the statesman's work is the more concerned with the body and things of that sort; for there will be little difference there; but in what they need for the exercise of their activities there will be much difference. The liberal man will need money for the doing of his liberal deeds, and the just man too will need it for the returning of services (for wishes are hard to discern, and even people who are not just pretend to wish to act justly); and the brave man will need power if he is to accomplish any of the acts that correspond to his virtue, and the temperate man will need opportunity;

for how else is either he or any of the others to be recognized? It is debated, too, whether the will or the deed is more essential to virtue, which is assumed to involve both; it is surely clear that its perfection involves both; but for deeds many things are needed, and more, the greater and nobler the deeds are. But the man who is contemplating the truth needs no such thing, at least with a view to the exercise of his activity; indeed they are, one may say, even hindrances, at all events to his contemplation; but in so far as he is a man and lives with a number of people, he chooses to do virtuous acts; he will therefore need such aids to living a human life.

ABRAHAM H. MASLOW

*A Single Ultimate Value**

Abraham H. Maslow (1908–1972), psychologist and educator, taught at a number of schools including Brooklyn College (1937–1951) and Brandeis University (1951–1961). He was the author of articles in professional journals dealing with mental and social problems. His books include *Motivation and Personality, Toward a Psychology of Being,* and *Religious Value and Peak Experience.*

In the selection that follows, Maslow asks such questions as, What is the good life? and How can people be taught to desire and prefer the good life? He says that some values are common to all healthy persons and some other values apply to specific individuals. He describes a "single ultimate value" for all mankind, and makes suggestions for those seeking to attain this objective.

Humanists for thousands of years have attempted to construct a naturalistic, psychological value system that could be derived from man's own nature, without the necessity of recourse to authority outside the human being himself. Many such theories have been offered throughout history. They have all failed for mass purposes exactly as all other value theories have failed. We have about as many scoundrels in the world today as we have ever had, and *many more* neurotic, probably, than we have ever had.

*From "Psychological Data and Value Theory" by Abraham H. Maslow in *New Knowledge in Human Values* edited by Abraham H. Maslow, pp. 119–133.

These inadequate theories, most of them, rested on psychological assumptions of one sort or another. Today practically all of these can be shown, in the light of recently acquired knowledge, to be false, inadequate, incomplete, or in some other way lacking. But it is my belief that developments in the science and art of psychology, in the last few decades, make it possible for us for the first time to feel confident that this age-old hope may be fulfilled if only we work hard enough. We know how to criticize the old theories, we know, even though dimly, the shape of the theories to come, and, most of all, we know where to look and what to do in order to fill in the gaps in knowledge, that will permit us to answer the age-old questions, "What is the good life? What is the good man? How can people be taught to desire and prefer the good life? How ought children to be brought up to be sound adults?, etc." That is, we think that a scientific ethic may be possible, and we think we know how to go about constructing it....

BASIC NEEDS AND THEIR HIERARCHICAL ARRANGEMENT

It has by now been sufficiently demonstrated that the human being has, as part of his intrinsic construction, not only physiological needs, but also truly psychological ones. They may be considered as deficiencies which must be optimally fulfilled by the environment to avoid sickness and to avoid subjective ill-being. They can be called basic, or biological, and likened to the need for salt, or calcium or vitamin D because:

1. The person yearns for their gratification persistently.
2. Their deprivation makes the person sicken and wither, or stunts his growth.
3. Gratifying them is therapeutic, curing the deficiency-illness.
4. Steady supplies forestall these illnesses.
5. Healthy people do not demonstrate these deficiencies.

But these needs or values are related to each other in a hierarchical and developmental way, in an order of strength and of priority. Safety is a more prepotent, or stronger, more pressing, earlier appearing, more vital need than love, for instance, and the need for food is usually stronger than either. Furthermore *all* these basic needs may be considered to be simply steps along the time path to general self-actualization, under which all basic needs can be subsumed.

By taking these data into account, we can solve many value problems that philosophers have struggled with ineffectually for centuries. For one thing, it looks as if *there were* a single ultimate value for mankind, a far goal toward which all men strive. This is called variously by different authors self-actualization, self-realization, integration, psychological health, individuation, autonomy, creativity, productivity, but they all agree that this amounts to realizing the potentialities of the person, that is to say, becoming fully human, everything that the person *can* become.

But it is also true that the person himself does not know this. We, the psychologists observing and studying, have constructed this concept in order to integrate and explain lots of diverse data. So far as the person himself is concerned, all *he* knows is that he is desperate for love, and thinks he will be forever happy and content if he gets it. He does not know in advance that he will strive on *after* this gratification has come, and that gratification of one basic need opens consciousness to domination by another, "higher" need. So far as he is concerned, *the* absolute, ultimate value, synonymous with life itself, is whichever need in the hierarchy he is dominated by during a particular period. These basic needs or basic values therefore may be treated *both* as ends and as steps toward a single end-goal. It is true that there is a single, ultimate value or end of life, and *also* it is just as true that we have a hierarchical and developmental system of values, complexly interrelated.

This also helps to solve the apparent paradox of contrast between Being and Becoming. It is true that human beings strive perpetually toward ultimate humanness, which itself is anyway a different kind of Becoming and growing. It's as if we were doomed forever to try to arrive at a state to which we could never attain. Fortunately we now know this not to be true, or at least it is not the only truth. There is another truth which integrates with it. We are again and again rewarded for good Becoming by transient states of absolute Being, which I have summarized as peak-experiences. Achieving basic-need gratifications gives us many peak-experiences, each of which are absolute delights, perfect in themselves, and needing no more than themselves to validate life. This is like rejecting the notion that a Heaven lies someplace beyond the end of the path of life. Heaven, so to speak, lies waiting for us throughout life, ready to step into for a time and to enjoy before we have to come back to our ordinary life of striving. And once we have been in it, we can remember it forever, and feed ourselves on this memory and be sustained in time of stress.

Not only this, but the process of moment to moment growth is itself intrinsically rewarding and delightful in an absolute sense. If they are not mountain peak-experiences, at least they are foothill-experiences, little glimpses of absolute, self-validative delights, little moments of Being. Being and Becoming are *not* contradictory or mutually exclusive. Approaching and arriving are both in themselves rewarding.

I should make it clear here that I want to differentiate the Heaven ahead (of growth and transcendence) from the "Heaven" behind (of regression). The "high Nirvana" is very different in important ways from the "low Nirvana" even though most clinicians confuse them because they are also similar in some ways.

SELF-ACTUALIZATION: GROWTH

I have published in another place a survey of all the evidence that forces us in the direction of a concept of healthy growth or of self-actualizing tendencies. This is partly deductive evidence in the sense of pointing out that, unless we postulate such a concept, much of human behavior makes no sense. This is on the same scientific principle that led to the discovery of a hitherto unseen planet that *had* to be there in order to make sense of a lot of other observed data.

There is also some direct evidence, or rather the beginnings of direct evidence which needs much more research, to get to the point of certainty. The only direct study of self-actualizing people I know is the one I made, and it is a very shaky business to rest on just one study made by just one person when we take into account the known pitfalls of sampling error, of wish-fulfillment, of projection, etc. However, the conclusions of this study have been so strongly paralleled in the clinical and philosophical conclusions of Rogers, of Fromm, of Goldstein, of Angyal, of Murray, of C. Bühler, of Horney, Jung, Nuttin, and many others that I shall proceed under the assumption that more careful research will not contradict my findings radically. We can certainly now assert that at least a reasonable, theoretical, and empirical case has been made for the presence within the human being of a tendency toward, or need for, growing in a direction that can be summarized in general as self-actualization, or psychological health or maturation, and specifically as growth toward each and all of the subaspects of self-actualization. That is to say, the human being has within him a pressure (among other pressures) toward unity of personality, toward spontaneous expressiveness, toward full individuality and identity, toward seeing the truth rather than being blind, toward being creative, toward being good, and a lot else. That is, the human being is so constructed that he presses toward fuller and fuller being and this means pressing toward what most people would call good values, toward serenity, kindness, courage, knowledge, honesty, love, unselfishness, and goodness.

Few in number though they be, we can learn a great deal from the direct study of these highly evolved, most mature, psychologically healthiest individuals, and from the study of the peak moments of average individuals, moments in which they became transiently self-actualized. This is because they are in very real empirical and theoretical ways, *most fully human.* For instance, they are people who have retained and developed all their human capacities, especially those capacities which define the human being and differentiate him from let us say the monkey. (This accords with Hartman's axiological approach to the same problem of defining the good human being as the one who has more of the characteristics which define the concept "human being.") From a developmental point of view, they are more fully evolved because not fixated at immature or incomplete levels of growth. This is no more mysterious, or *a priori,* or question-begging than the selection of a type specimen of butterfly by a taxonomist or the most physically healthy young man by the physician. They both look for the "perfect or mature or magnificent specimen" for the exemplar, and so have I. One procedure is as repeatable in principle as the other.

Full humanness can be defined not only in terms of the degree to which the definition of the concept "human" is fulfilled, *i.e.,* the species norm. It also has a descriptive, cataloguing, measurable, psychological definition. We now have from a few research beginnings and from countless clinical experiences some notion of the characteristics both of the fully evolved human being and of the well-growing human being. These characteristics are not only neutrally describable; they are also subjectively rewarding, and pleasurable and reinforcing.

Among the objectively describable and measurable characteristics of the healthy human specimen are:

1. Clearer, more efficient perception of reality.
2. More openness to experience.
3. Increased integration, wholeness, and unity of the person.
4. Increased spontaneity, expressiveness; full functioning; aliveness.
5. A real self; a firm identity; autonomy; uniqueness.
6. Increased objectivity, detachment, transcendence of self.
7. Recovery of creativeness.
8. Ability to fuse concreteness and abstractness, primary and secondary process cognition, etc.
9. Democratic character structure.
10. Ability to love, etc.

These all need research confirmation and exploration but it is clear that such researches are feasible.

In addition, there are subjective confirmations or reinforcements of self-actualization or of good growth toward it. These are the feelings of zest in living, of happiness or euphoria, of serenity, of joy, of calmness, of responsibility, of confidence in one's ability to handle stresses, anxieties, and problems. The subjective signs of self-betrayal, of fixation, of regression, and of living by fear rather than by growth are such feelings as anxiety, despair, boredom, inability to enjoy, intrinsic guilt, intrinsic shame, aimlessness, feelings of emptiness, of lack of identity, etc.

These subjective reactions are also susceptible of research exploration. We have clinical techniques available for studying them.

It is the free choices of such self-actualizing people (in those situations where real choice is possible from among a variety of possibilities) that I claim can be descriptively studied as a naturalistic value system with which the hopes of the observer absolutely have nothing to do, *i.e.,* it is "scientific." I do not say "He *ought* to choose this or that" but only "Healthy people, permitted to choose, are *observed* to choose this or that." This is like asking "What *are* the values of the best human beings" rather than "What *should* be their values?" or "What *ought* they do?" (Compare this with Aristotle's belief that "it is the things which are valuable and pleasant to a good man that are really valuable and pleasant.")

Furthermore I think these findings can be generalized to most of the human species because it looks to me (and to others) as if *all* or most people tend toward self-actualization (this is seen most clearly in the experiences in psychotherapy, especially of the uncovering sort), and as if, in principle at least, all people are capable of self-actualization.

If the various extant religions may be taken as expressions of human aspiration, *i.e.,* what people would *like* to become if only they could, then we can see here too a validation of the affirmation that all people yearn toward self-actualization or tend toward it. This is so because our description of the actual characteristics of self-actualizing people parallels at many points the ideals urged by the religions, *e.g.,* the transcendence of self, the fusion of the true, the good and the beautiful, contribution to others, wisdom, honesty and naturalness, the transcendence of selfish and personal motivations, the giving up of "lower" desires in favor of "higher" ones, the easy differentiation between ends (tranquility, serenity, peace) and means (money, power, status), the decrease of hostility, cruelty and destructiveness and the increase of friendliness, gentleness and kindness, etc.

1. One conclusion from all these free choice experiments, from developments in dynamic motivation theory and from examination of psychotherapy is a very revolutionary one that no other large culture has ever arrived at, namely, that our deepest needs are *not,* in themselves, dangerous or evil or bad. This opens up the prospect of resolving the dichotomy between Apollonian and Dionysian, classical and romantic, scientific and poetic, between reason and impulse, work and play, verbal and preverbal, maturity and childlikeness, masculine and feminine, growth and regression.

2. The main social parallel to this change in our philosophy of human nature is the rapidly growing tendency to perceive the culture as an instrument of need-gratification as well as of frustration and control. We can now reject, as a localism, the almost universal mistake that the interests of the individual and of society are *of necessity* mutually exclusive and antagonistic, or that civilization is primarily a mechanism for controlling and policing human instinctoid impulses. All these age-old axioms are swept away by the new possibility of defining the main function of a healthy culture and each of its institutions as the fostering of universal self-actualization.

3. In healthy people only is there a good correlation between subjective delight in the experience, impulse to the experience, or wish for it, and

"basic need" for the experience (it's good for him in the long run). Only such people uniformly yearn for what is good for them and for others, and then are able wholeheartedly to enjoy it, and approve of it. For such people virtue is its own reward in the sense of being enjoyed in itself. They spontaneously tend to do right because that is what they *want* to do, what they *need* to do, what they enjoy, what they approve of doing, and what they will continue to enjoy.

It is this unity, this network of positive intercorrelation that falls apart into separateness and conflict as the person gets psychologically sick. Then what he wants to do may be bad for him; even if he does it he may not enjoy it; even if he enjoys it he may simultaneously disapprove of it so that the enjoyment is itself poisoned or may disappear quickly. What he enjoys at first he may not enjoy later. His impulses, desires, and enjoyments then become a poor guide to living. He must accordingly mistrust and fear the impulses and the enjoyments which lead him astray, and so he is caught in conflict, dissociation, indecision; in a word, he is caught in civil war.

So far as philosophical theory is concerned, many historical dilemmas and contradictions are resolved by this finding. Hedonistic theory *does* work for healthy people; it does *not* work for sick people. The true, the good and the beautiful *do* correlate some, but only in healthy people do they correlate strongly.

4. Self-actualization is a relatively achieved "state of affairs" in a few people. In most people, however, it is rather a hope, a yearning, a drive, a "something" wished for but not yet achieved, showing itself clinically as drive toward health, integration, growth, etc. The projective tests are also able to detect these trends as potentialities rather than as overt behavior, just as an X-ray can detect incipient pathology before it has appeared on the surface.

This means for us that that which the person *is* and that which the person *could be* exist simultaneously for the psychologist, thereby resolving the dichotomy between Being and Becoming. Potentialities not only *will* be or could be; they also *are*. Self-actualization values as goals exist and are real even though not yet actualized. The human being is simultaneously that which he is and that which he yearns to be....

THE PROBLEM OF CONTROLS AND LIMITS

Another problem confronting the morals-from-within theorists is to account for the easy self-discipline which is customarily found in self-actualizing, authentic, genuine people and which is *not* found in average people.

In these healthy people we find duty and pleasure to be the same thing, as are also work and play, self-interest and altruism, individualism and selflessness. We know they *are* that way, but not how they *get* that way. I have the clear impression that such authentic, fully human persons are the actualization of what *any* human being could be. And yet we are confronted with the sad fact that so few people achieve this goal, perhaps only one in a hundred, or two hundred. We can be hopeful for mankind because in principle anyone *could* become a good and healthy man. But we must also feel sad because so few actually *do* become good men. If we wish to find out why some do and some don't, then the research problem presents itself of studying the life history of self-actualizing men to find out how they get that way.

We know already that the main prerequisite of healthy growth is gratification of the basic needs, especially in early life. (Neurosis is very often a deficiency disease, like avitaminosis.) But we have *also* learned that unbridled indulgence and gratification has its own dangerous consequences, *e.g.*, psychopathic personality, irresponsibility, inability to bear stress, spoiling, immaturity, certain character disorders. Research findings are rare, but there is now available a large store of clinical and educational experience which allows us to make a reasonable guess that the young child needs not only gratification; he needs also to learn the limitations that the physical world puts upon his gratifications, and he has to learn that other human beings seek for gratifications, too, even his mother and father, *i.e.*, they are not only means to his ends. This means control, delay, limits, renunciation, frustration-tolerance, and discipline. Only to the self-disciplined and responsible person can we say, "Do as you will, and it will probably be all right."

WILLIAM K. FRANKENA

*Moral Values**

William K. Frankena (b. 1908) has taught philosophy at the University of Michigan since 1937. He has written a considerable number of articles and has contributed essays to a number of books edited by others. His books include *Ethics, Philosophy of Education, Three Historical Philosophies of Education,* and *Some Beliefs About Justice.*

*William K. Frankena, *Ethics* © 1963. Reprinted by permission of Prentice-Hall, Inc., Englewood Cliffs, New Jersey. Pages 47–52 with omissions.

In order to help clarify our thinking on the subject of what is morally good or bad, Frankena begins the following essay by carefully distinguishing moral values from moral principles and nonmoral values. In light of this distinction, he goes on to question what moral traits of character men should seek to cultivate in themselves. Compare the standard he uses to determine the greatest values in life with those used by Aristotle and Maslow in the preceding selections.

MORAL AND NONMORAL SENSES OF "GOOD"

Moral value (moral goodness and badness) must be distinguished, not only from moral obligatoriness, rightness, and wrongness, but also from nonmoral value. Moral values or things that are morally good must be distinguished from nonmoral values or things that are good in a nonmoral sense. . . . Partly, it is a matter of the difference in the *objects* that are called good or bad. The sorts of things that may be morally good or bad are persons, groups of persons, traits of character, dispositions, emotions, motives, and intentions —in short, persons, groups of persons, and elements of personality. All sorts of things, on the other hand, may be nonmorally good or bad, for example: physical objects like cars and paintings; experiences like pleasure, pain, knowledge, and freedom; and forms of government like democracy. It does not make sense to call most of these things morally good or bad, unless we mean that it is morally right or wrong to pursue them.

Of course, the same thing may be both morally good and nonmorally good. Love of fellow man, for example, is a morally good disposition or emotion; it is normally also a source of happiness and so is good in a nonmoral sense. But the *ground* or *reason* for its being good is different in the two judgments. Consider also the expressions "a good life" and "the good life." We sometimes say of a man that he "*had* a good life;" we also sometimes say that he "*led* a good life." In both cases we are saying that his life was good; but in the second case we are saying that it was morally good, or useful, or virtuous, while in the first we are saying, in effect, that it was happy or satisfying, that is, that it was good but in a nonmoral sense (which, again, is not to say that it was immoral). It will, therefore, be convenient for our purposes to speak of "the morally good life" on the one hand, and of "the nonmorally good life" on the other. Since the latter expression seems rather odd, I shall hereafter use the phrase "the good life" to mean the nonmorally good life.

In view of this and other distinctions already made, it seems to me deplorable that terms like "values" and "moral values" (or "moral and spiritual values") are so ambiguously and vaguely used as they are today.

They are used as if they indiscriminately cover all the sorts of things that are morally right or obligatory, morally good, and nonmorally good. Hence I propose that we distinguish:

1. *principles* or kinds of action that are right or obligatory, e.g., the principles of justice and beneficence;
2. *moral values* or things that are morally good, e.g., the virtues and certain motives;
3. *values* or things that are nonmorally good, whether "spiritual" like knowledge or communion with God, or "material" like cars and houses, whether intrinsically or extrinsically good, etc.

Making and sticking to this set of distinctions or some similar one would do a great deal to clarify our thinking and to enlighten our action. Some things may come under more than one of these headings; justice is both a principle and a virtuous disposition, and liberty is both a principle and a value. But even in these cases, we must try to understand clearly the aspect in which they are being considered in a given context.

MORALITY AND CULTIVATION OF TRAITS

Our present interest, then, is not in moral principles nor in nonmoral values, but in moral values, in what is morally good or bad. Throughout its history morality has been concerned about the cultivation of certain dispositions, or traits, among which are "character" and such "virtues" (an old-fashioned but still useful term) as honesty, kindness, and conscientiousness. None of these dispositions or traits are innate; they must all be acquired by teaching and practice. They are also traits of "character," rather than traits of "personality" like charm or shyness. They are all dispositions to do certain kinds of action in certain kinds of situations, not just to think or feel in certain ways.

In fact, it has been suggested that morality is or should be conceived as primarily concerned, not with rules or principles, but with the cultivation of such dispositions or traits of character. Plato and Aristotle seem to conceive of morality in this way, for they talk mainly in terms of virtues and the virtuous, rather than in terms of what is right or obligatory. David Hume uses similar terms, although he mixes in some nonmoral traits like cheerfulness and wit along with moral ones like benevolence and justice. More recently, Leslie Stephen stated the view in these words,

> . . . morality is internal. The moral law . . . has to be expressed in the form, "be this," not in the form, "do this."... the true moral law says "hate not,"

> instead of "kill not." . . . the only mode of stating the moral law must be as a rule of character.

This view has a certain truth, as we shall see shortly; however, whether the view is true or not, we may still ask what moral traits are to be cultivated. In a way, the answer is easy; with only a little thought, most of us could make up a long list which would include the traits already mentioned and many more. But we cannot be satisfied with a list of virtues in answer to our question, any more than Socrates was when he asked Meno, "What is virtue?" We want to know the standard by which we are to determine what traits we are to cultivate in ourselves and our children. In Stephen's terms, what rules of character are we to follow, what are we to *be*?...

... [T]he most adequate theory of moral value is a mixed one which advocates cultivating those traits that tend most fully to express themselves in benevolent and/or just action.

Among these, of course, will be benevolence and justice themselves, considered now as dispositions or traits of character rather than as principles of prima facie duty. In fact, in our view, benevolence and justice are the two "cardinal" moral virtues. By a set of cardinal virtues, we mean a set of virtues which are such that (1) they cannot be derived from one another and (2) all other moral virtues can be derived from or shown to be forms of them. Plato and other Greeks thought there were four cardinal virtues in this sense: wisdom, courage, temperance, and justice. Christianity is traditionally regarded as having seven cardinal virtues: three "theological" virtues—faith, hope, and love; and four "human" virtues—prudence, fortitude, temperance, and justice. This was essentially St. Thomas Aquinas' view; since St. Augustine regarded the last four as forms of love, only the first three were really cardinal for him. However, many moralists, among them Schopenhauer, have taken benevolence and justice to be the cardinal moral virtues, as does our view. It seems to me that all of the usual virtues (such as love, courage, temperance, honesty, gratitude, and considerateness), at least insofar as they are *moral* virtues, can be derived from these two and therefore should be cultivated. Insofar as they cannot be derived from benevolence and justice, I should try to argue either that they are not moral virtues (e.g., I take faith, hope, and wisdom to be religious or intellectual, not moral, virtues) or that they should not be cultivated.

We must, however, notice that besides first-order virtues like honesty, gratitude, and most of the others mentioned, there are certain other virtues which also ought to be cultivated, which are in a way more abstract and general and may be called second-order virtues. Conscientiousness is one such virtue; it is not limited to a certain sector of the moral life, as gratitude and honesty are, but it is a virtue covering the whole of the moral life.

Moral courage, or courage when moral issues are at stake, is another such second-order virtue; it belongs to all sectors of the moral life. Others which overlap with these are integrity and good-will, understanding good-will in Kant's sense of respect for the moral law. In view of what was said in a previous chapter, I must underline two others: a disposition to find out and respect the relevant facts and a disposition to think clearly. These two virtues are not limited to the moral life, but insofar as they are, they are morally desirable or rather imperative. Still other second-order qualities which are abilities rather than virtues but which must be cultivated for moral living, and so may, perhaps, best be mentioned here, are moral autonomy, the ability to make moral decisions and to revise one's principles if necessary, and the ability to realize vividly, in imagination and feeling, the "inner lives" of others. Of these second-order qualities, the first two have been referred to on occasion and will be again, but something should be said about the last.

If our morality is to be more than a conformity to internalized rules and principles, if it is to include and rest on an understanding of the point of these rules and principles, and certainly if it is to involve *being* a certain kind of person and not merely *doing* certain kinds of things, then we must somehow attain and develop an ability to be aware of others as persons, as important to themselves as we are to ourselves, and to have a lively and sympathetic representation in imagination of their interests and of the effects of our actions on their lives. The need for this is particularly stressed by Josiah Royce and William James. Both men point out how we usually go our own busy and self-concerned ways, with only an external awareness of the presence of others, much as if they were things, and without any realization of their inner and peculiar worlds of personal experience; and both emphasize the need and the possibility of a "higher vision of an inner significance" which pierces this "certain blindness in human beings" and enables us to realize the existence of others in a wholly different way, as we do our own.

> What then is thy neighbor? He too is a mass of states, of experiences, thoughts and desires, just as real as thou art ... thy neighbor is as actual, as concrete, as thou art.... Dost thou believe this? Art thou sure what it means? This is for thee the turning-point of thy whole conduct towards him.

These are Royce's quaint old-fashioned words. Here are James' more modern ones.

> This higher vision of an inner significance in what, until then, we had realized only in the dead external way, often comes over a person suddenly; and, when it does so, it makes an epoch in his history.

Royce calls this more perfect recognition of our neighbors "the moral insight" and James says that its practical consequence is "the well-known democratic respect for the sacredness of individuality." It is hard to see how either a benevolent (loving) or a just (equalitarian) disposition could come to fruition without it. To quote James again,

> We ought, all of us, to realize each other in this intense, pathetic, and important way.

Ethical Theories

IMMANUEL KANT

*The Right and Our Duty**

Immanuel Kant (1724–1804), one of the most influential thinkers in Western philosophy, lived all his life in Königsberg, Germany, where he taught in the University. Physically Kant was a small man; intellectually he was a giant whose thoughts and writings brought the most far-reaching changes in modern philosophy. Living in an age of skepticism, he read the writings of Voltaire and Hume, and claimed that the latter stirred him out of his dogmatic slumbers. His problem became, What can we know? What are the nature and the limits of knowledge? He spent much of his life studying the ways in which the mind structures the raw materials of experience. While he wrote on a variety of subjects, including peace and war, his major works are his three critiques: *Critique of Pure Reason,* dealing with the knowing process, on which he worked for fifteen years; *Critique of Practical Reason,* dealing with moral philosophy; and *Critique of Judgment,* which supplements his earlier works.

The following selection goes to the heart of Kant's moral philosophy. While there are many things that we may call good, nothing can be called good without qualifications except a Good Will. Kant elaborates on the nature of this Good Will, as well on reason, means and ends, duty and inclination, happiness, and the like. His discussion leads to his famous three formulations of the categorical imperative or the Moral Law.

Nothing can possibly be conceived in the world, or even out of it, which can be called good, without qualification, except a Good Will. Intelligence, wit, judgment, and the other *talents* of the mind, however they may be named, or courage, resolution, perseverance, as qualities of temperament,

*Immanuel Kant, from *Critique of Practical Reason and Other Works on the Theory of Ethics,* trans. Thomas Kingsmill Abbott (London: Longmans, Green, 1909), pp. 9–53 with omissions.

are undoubtedly good and desirable in many respects; but these gifts of nature may also become extremely bad and mischievous if the will which is to make use of them, and which, therefore, constitutes what is called *character,* is not good. It is the same with the *gifts of fortune.* Power, riches, honour, even health, and the general well-being and contentment with one's condition which is called *happiness,* inspire pride, and often presumption, if there is not a good will to correct the influence of these on the mind, and with this also to rectify the whole principle of acting, and adapt it to its end. The sight of a being who is not adorned with a single feature of a pure and good will, enjoying unbroken prosperity, can never give pleasure to an impartial rational spectator. Thus a good will appears to constitute the indispensable condition even of being worthy of happiness.

There are even some qualities which are of service to this good will itself, and may facilitate its action, yet which have no intrinsic unconditional value, but always presuppose a good will, and this qualifies the esteem that we justly have for them, and does not permit us to regard them as absolutely good. Moderation in the affections and passions, self-control, and calm deliberation are not only good in many respects, but even seem to constitute part of the intrinsic worth of the person; but they are far from deserving to be called good without qualification, although they have been so unconditionally praised by the ancients. For without the principles of a good will, they may become extremely bad; and the coolness of a villain not only makes him far more dangerous, but also directly makes him more abominable in our eyes than he would have been without it.

A good will is good not because of what it performs or effects, not by its aptness for the attainment of some proposed end, but simply by virtue of the volition, that is, it is good in itself, and considered by itself is to be esteemed much higher than all that can be brought about by it in favour of any inclination, nay, even of the sum-total of all inclinations. Even if it should happen that, owing to special disfavour of fortune, or the niggardly provision of a step-motherly nature, this will should wholly lack power to accomplish its purpose, if with its greatest efforts it should yet achieve nothing, and there should remain only the good will (not, to be sure, a mere wish, but the summoning of all means in our power), then, like a jewel, it would still shine by its own light, as a thing which has its whole value in itself. Its usefulness or fruitlessness can neither add to nor take away anything from this value. It would be, as it were, only the setting to enable us to handle it the more conveniently in common commerce, or to attract to it the attention of those who are not yet connoisseurs, but not to recommend it to true connoisseurs, or to determine its value....

...[R]eason is imparted to us as a practical faculty, *i.e.* as one which is to have influence on the *will,* therefore, admitting that nature generally in the distribution of her capacities has adapted the means to the end, its true destination must be to produce a *will,* not merely good as a *means* to something else, but *good in itself,* for which reason was absolutely necessary. This will then, though not indeed the sole and complete good, must be the supreme good and the condition of every other, even of the desire of happiness. Under these circumstances, there is nothing inconsistent with the wisdom of nature in the fact that the cultivation of the reason, which is requisite for the first and unconditional purpose, does in many ways interfere, at least in this life, with the attainment of the second, which is always conditional, namely, happiness. Nay, it may even reduce it to nothing, without nature thereby failing of her purpose. For reason recognizes the establishment of a good will as its highest practical destination, and in attaining this purpose is capable only of a satisfaction of its own proper kind, namely, that from the attainment of an end, which end again is determined by reason only, notwithstanding that this may involve many a disappointment to the ends of inclination.

We have then to develop the notion of a will which deserves to be highly esteemed for itself, and is good without a view to anything further, a notion which exists already in the sound natural understanding, requiring rather to be cleared up than to be taught, and which in estimating the value of our actions always takes the first place, and constitutes the condition of all the rest. In order to do this, we will take the notion of duty....

[The first proposition is: That to have moral worth an action must be done from duty.]

The second proposition is: That an action done from duty derives its moral worth, *not from the purpose* which is to be attained by it, but from the maxim by which it is determined, and therefore does not depend on the realization of the object of the action, but merely on the *principle of volition* by which the action has taken place, without regard to any object of desire. It is clear from what precedes that the purposes which we may have in view in our actions, or their effects regarded as ends and springs of the will, cannot give to actions any unconditional or moral worth. In what, then, can their worth lie, if it is not to consist in the will and in reference to its expected effect? It cannot lie anywhere but in the *principle of the will* without regard to the ends which can be attained by the action....

The third proposition, which is a consequence of the two preceding, I would express thus: *Duty is the necessity of acting from respect for the law.* I may have *inclination* for an object as the effect of my proposed action, but I cannot have *respect* for it, just for this reason, that it is an effect and not an energy of will. Similarly, I cannot have respect for inclination, whether my own or another's; I can at most, if my own, approve it; if another's, sometimes even love it; *i.e.* look on it as favourable to my own interest. It is only what is connected with my will as a principle, by no means as an effect—what does not subserve my inclination, but overpowers it, or at least in case of choice excludes it from its calculation—in other words, simply the law of itself, which can be an object of respect, and hence a command. Now an action done from duty must wholly exclude the influence of inclination, and with it every object of the will, so that nothing remains which can determine the will except objectively the *law,* and subjectively *pure respect* for this practical law, and consequently the maxim that I should follow this law even to the thwarting of all my inclinations....

But what sort of law can that be, the conception of which must determine the will, even without paying any regard to the effect expected from it, in order that this will may be called good absolutely and without qualification? As I have deprived the will of every impulse which could arise to it from obedience to any law, there remains nothing but the universal conformity of its actions to law in general, which alone is to serve the will as a principle, *i.e.* I am never to act otherwise than so *that I could also will that my maxim should become a universal law*. Here, now, it is the simple conformity to law in general, without assuming any particular law applicable to certain actions, that serves the will as its principle, and must so serve it, if duty is not to be a vain delusion and a chimerical notion. The common reason of men in its practical judgments perfectly coincides with this, and always has in view the principle here suggested. Let the question be, for example: May I when in distress make a promise with the intention not to keep it? I readily distinguish here between the two significations which the question may have: Whether it is prudent, or whether it is right, to make a false promise? The former may undoubtedly often be the case. I see clearly indeed that it is not enough to extricate myself from a present difficulty by means of this subterfuge, but it must be well considered whether there may not hereafter spring from this lie much greater inconvenience than that from which I now free myself, and as, with all my supposed *cunning,* the consequences cannot be so easily foreseen, but that credit once lost may be much more injurious to me than any mischief which I seek to avoid at present, it should be considered whether it would not be more *prudent* to act herein according to a universal maxim, and to make it a habit to promise nothing except with the intention of keeping it. But it is soon clear to me that such a maxim will still only be based on the fear of consequences. Now it is a wholly different thing to be truthful from duty, and to be so from apprehension of injurious consequences. In the first case, the very notion of the action already implies a law for me; in the second case, I must first look about elsewhere to see what results may be combined with it which would affect myself. For to deviate from the principle of duty is beyond all doubt wicked; but to be unfaithful to my maxim of prudence may often be very advantageous to me, although to abide by it is certainly safer. The shortest way, however, and an unerring one, to discover the answer to this question whether a lying promise is consistent with duty, is to ask myself, Should I be content that my maxim (to extricate myself from difficulty by a false promise) should hold good as a universal law, for myself as well as for others? and should I be able to say to myself, "Every one may make a deceitful promise when he finds himself in a difficulty from which he cannot otherwise extricate himself"? Then I presently become aware that while I can will the lie, I can by no means will that lying should be a universal law. For with such a law there would be no promises at all, since it would be in vain to allege my intention in regard to my future actions to those who would not believe this allegation, or if they over-hastily did so, would pay me back in my own coin. Hence my maxim, as soon as it should be made a universal law, would necessarily destroy itself.

I do not, therefore, need any far-reaching penetration to discern what I have to do in order that my will may be morally good. Inexperienced in the course of the world, incapable of being prepared for all its contingencies, I only ask myself: Canst thou also will that thy maxim should be a universal law? If not, then it must be rejected, and that not because of a disadvantage accruing from it to myself or even to others, but because it cannot enter as a principle into a possible universal legislation, and reason extorts from me immediate respect for such legislation. I do not indeed as yet *discern* on what this respect is based (this the philosopher may inquire), but at least I understand this, that it is an estimation of the worth which far outweighs all worth of what is recommended by inclination, and that the necessity of acting from *pure* respect for the practical law is what constitutes duty, to which every other motive must give place, because it is the condition of a will being good *in itself,* and the worth of such a will is above everything. . . .

Since every practical law represents a possible action as good, and on this account, for a subject who is practically determinable by reason, necessary, all imperatives are formulae determining an action which is necessary according to the principle of a will good in some respects. If now the action is good only as a means *to something else,* then the imperative is *hypothetical;* if it is conceived as good *in itself* and consequently as being necessarily the principle of a will which of itself conforms to reason, then it is *categorical. . . .*

There is therefore but one categorical imperative, namely, this: *Act only on that maxim whereby thou canst at the same time will that it should become a universal law. . . .*

Now if all imperatives of duty can be deduced from this one imperative as from their principle, then, although it should remain undecided whether what is called duty is not merely a vain notion, yet at least we shall be able to show what we understand by it and what this notion means.

Since the universality of the law according to which effects are produced constitutes what is properly called *nature* in the most general sense (as to form)—that is, the existence of things so far as it is determined by general laws—the imperative of duty may be expressed thus: *Act as if the maxim of thy action were to become by thy will a universal law of nature.*

We will now enumerate a few duties, adopting the usual division of them into duties to ourselves and to others, and into perfect and imperfect duties.

1. A man reduced to despair by a series of misfortunes feels wearied of life, but is still so far in possession of his reason that he can ask himself whether it would not be contrary to his duty to himself to take his own life. Now he inquires whether the maxim of his action could become a universal law of nature. His maxim is: From self-love I adopt it as a principle to shorten my life when its longer duration is likely to bring more evil than satisfaction. It is asked then simply whether this principle founded on self-love can become a universal law of nature. Now we see at once that a system of nature of which it should be a law to destroy life by means of the very feeling whose special nature it is to impel to the improvement of life would contradict itself, and therefore could not exist as a system of nature; hence that maxim cannot possibly exist as a universal law of nature, and consequently would be wholly inconsistent with the supreme principle of all duty.

2. Another finds himself forced by necessity to borrow money. He knows that he will not be able to repay it, but sees also that nothing will be lent to him unless he promises stoutly to repay it in a definite time. He desires to make this promise, but he has still so much conscience as to ask himself: Is it not unlawful and inconsistent with duty to get out of a difficulty in this way? Suppose, however, that he resolves to do so, then the maxim of his action would be expressed thus: When I think myself in want of money, I will borrow money and promise to repay it, although I know that I never can do so. Now this principle of self-love or of one's own advantage may perhaps be consistent with my whole future welfare; but the question now is, Is it right? I change then the suggestion of self-love into a universal law, and state the question thus: How would it be if my maxim were a universal law? Then I see at once that it could never hold as a universal law of nature, but would necessarily contradict itself. For supposing it to be a universal law that everyone when he thinks himself in a difficulty should be able to promise whatever he pleases, with the purpose of not keeping his promise, the promise itself would become impossible, as well as the end that one might have in view in it, since no one would consider that anything was promised to him, but would ridicule all such statements as vain pretenses.

3. A third finds in himself a talent which with the help of some culture might make him a useful man in many respects. But he finds himself in comfortable circumstances and prefers to indulge in pleasure rather

than to take pains in enlarging and improving his happy natural capacities. He asks, however, whether his maxim of neglect of his natural gifts, besides agreeing with his inclination to indulgence, agrees also with what is called duty. He sees then that a system of nature could indeed subsist with such a universal law, although men (like the South Sea islanders) should let their talents rest and resolve to devote their lives merely to idleness, amusement, and propagation of their species—in a word, to enjoyment; but he cannot possibly *will* that this should be a universal law of nature, or be implanted in us as such by a natural instinct. For, as a rational being, he necessarily wills that his faculties be developed, since they serve him, and have been given him, for all sorts of possible purposes.

4. A fourth, who is in prosperity, while he sees that others have to contend with great wretchedness and that he could help them, thinks: What concern is it of mine? Let everyone be as happy as Heaven pleases, or as he can make himself; I will take nothing from him nor even envy him, only I do not wish to contribute anything to his welfare or to his assistance in distress! Now no doubt, if such a mode of thinking were a universal law, the human race might very well subsist, and doubtless even better than in a state in which everyone talks of sympathy and good-will, or even takes care occasionally to put it into practice, but, on the other side, also cheats when he can, betrays the rights of men, or otherwise violates them. But although it is possible that a universal law of nature might exist in accordance with that maxim, it is impossible to *will* that such a principle should have the universal validity of a law of nature. For a will which resolved this would contradict itself, inasmuch as many cases might occur in which one would have need of the love and sympathy of others, and in which, by such a law of nature, sprung from his own will, he would deprive himself of all hope of the aid he desires....

If then there is a supreme practical principle or, in respect of the human will, a categorical imperative, it must be one which being drawn from the conception of that which is necessarily an end for everyone because it is *an end in itself,* constitutes an *objective* principle of will, and can therefore serve as a universal practical law. The foundation of this principle is: *rational nature exists as an end in itself.* Man necessarily conceives his own existence as being so: so far then this is a *subjective* principle of human actions. But every other rational being regards its existence similarly, just on the same rational principle that holds for me: so that it is at the same time an objective principle, from which as a supreme practical law all laws of the will must be capable of being deduced. Accordingly the practical imperative will be as follows: *So act as to treat humanity, whether in thine own person or in that of any other, in every case as an end withal, never as means only....*

This principle, that humanity and generally every rational nature is *an end in itself* (which is the supreme limiting condition of every man's freedom of action), is not borrowed from experience....

On this principle all maxims are rejected which are inconsistent with the will being itself universal legislator. Thus the will is not subject simply to the law, but so subject that it must be regarded *as itself giving the law,* and on this ground only, subject to the law (of which it can regard itself as the author)....

The conception of every rational being as one which must consider itself as giving in all the maxims of its will universal laws, so as to judge itself and its actions from this point of view—this conception leads to another which depends on it and is very fruitful, namely, that of a *kingdom of ends.*

By a *kingdom* I understand the union of different rational beings in a system by common laws. Now since it is by laws that ends are determined as regards their universal validity, hence, if we abstract from the personal differences of rational beings, and likewise from all the content of their private ends, we shall be able to conceive all ends combined in a systematic whole (including both rational beings as ends in themselves, and also the special ends which each may propose to himself), that is to say, we can conceive a kingdom of ends, which on the preceding principles is possible.

For all rational beings come under the *law* that each of them must treat itself and all others *never merely as means,* but in every case *at the same time as ends in themselves.* Hence results a systematic union of rational beings by common objective laws, *i.e.,* a kindgom which may be called a kingdom of ends, since what these laws have in view is just the relation of these beings to one another as ends and means. It is certainly only an ideal.

A rational being belongs as a *member* to the kingdom of ends when, although giving universal laws in it, he is also himself subject to these laws. He belongs to it *as sovereign* when, while giving laws, he is not subject to the will of any other.

A rational being must always regard himself as giving law either as member or as sovereign in a kingdom of ends which is rendered possible by the freedom of will. He cannot, however, maintain the latter position merely by the maxims of his will but only in case he is a completely independent being without wants and with unrestricted power adequate to his will.

Morality consists then in the reference of all action to the legislation which alone can render a kingdom of ends possible. This legislation must be capable of existing in every rational being, and of emanating from his will, so that the principle of this will is, never to act on any maxim which could not without contradiction be also a universal law, and accordingly always so to act *that the will could at the same time regard itself as giving in its maxims universal laws....*

The practical necessity of acting on this principle, *i.e.* duty, does not rest at all on feelings, impulses, or inclinations, but solely on the relation of rational beings to one another, a relation in which the will of a rational being must always be regarded as *legislative,* since otherwise it could not be conceived as *an end in itself*. Reason then refers every maxim of the will, regarding it as legislating universally, to every other will and also to every action towards oneself; and this not on account of any other practical motive or any future advantage, but from the idea of the *dignity* of a rational being, obeying no law but that which he himself also gives.

JOHN STUART MILL

*The Greatest Happiness Principle**

John Stuart Mill (1806–1873) was an eminent English philosopher, political thinker, and administrator. He never attended school, but received a remarkable and intensive private education under his distinguished father, James Mill. By age fourteen he had read most of the major Greek and Latin classics as well as much history, logic, and mathematics. He became a spokesman and defender of the basic principles of nineteenth-century liberalism and utilitarianism. His writings in these fields, as well as on logic, brought him great distinction in the English-speaking world.

Mill was a disciple of Jeremy Bentham (1748–1832) who claimed that every person, as a matter of nature, seeks his own pleasure (psychological hedonism) and that pleasure can be measured quantitatively. Bentham maintained that "the greatest happiness for the greatest number" was the ideal goal of society. In defending the happiness principle, Mill modifies this position and stresses the view that while human beings do not always seek happiness, they ought to do so (ethical hedonism). Mill furthermore stresses the quality, not the quantity, of happiness and insists that some kinds of pleasure are more desirable and more valuable than others. He maintains that men ought to seek the highest pleasures but moreover the general happiness (universalistic ethical hedonism).

A passing remark is all that needs be given to the ignorant blunder of supposing that those who stand up for utility as the test of right and wrong use the term in that restricted and merely colloquial sense in which utility

*John Stuart Mill, from *Utilitarianism* (1863), Chapters II and IV with omissions.

is opposed to pleasure. An apology is due to the philosophical opponents of utilitarianism for even the momentary appearance of confounding them with anyone capable of so absurd a misconception; which is the more extraordinary, inasmuch as the contrary accusation, of referring everything to pleasure, and that, too, in its grossest form, is another of the common charges against utilitarianism: and, as has been pointedly remarked by an able writer, the same sort of persons, and often the very same persons, denounce the theory "as impracticably dry when the word 'utility' precedes the word 'pleasure,' and as too practicably voluptuous when the word 'pleasure' precedes the word 'utility.'" Those who know anything about the matter are aware that every writer, from Epicurus to Bentham, who maintained the theory of utility meant by it, not something to be contradistinguished from pleasure, but pleasure itself, together with exemption from pain; and instead of opposing the useful to the agreeable or the ornamental, have always declared that the useful means these, among other things....

The creed which accepts as the foundation of morals "utility" or the "greatest happiness principle" holds that actions are right in proportion as they tend to promote happiness; wrong as they tend to produce the reverse of happiness. By happiness is intended pleasure and the absence of pain; by unhappiness, pain and the privation of pleasure. To give a clear view of the moral standard set up by the theory, much more requires to be said; in particular, what things it includes in the ideas of pain and pleasure, and to what extent this is left an open question. But these supplementary explanations do not affect the theory of life on which this theory of morality is grounded—namely, that pleasure and freedom from pain are the only things desirable as ends; and that all desirable things (which are as numerous in the utilitarian as in any other scheme) are desirable either for pleasure inherent in themselves or as means to the promotion of pleasure and the prevention of pain.

Now such a theory of life excites in many minds, and among them in some of the most estimable in feeling and purpose, inveterate dislike. To suppose that life has (as they express it) no higher end than pleasure—no better and nobler object of desire and pursuit—they designate as utterly mean and groveling, as a doctrine worthy only of swine, to whom the followers of Epicurus were, at a very early period, contemptuously likened; and modern holders of the doctrine are occasionally made the subject of equally polite comparisons by its German, French, and English assailants.

When thus attacked, the Epicureans have always answered that it is not they, but their accusers, who represent human nature in a degrading light, since the accusation supposes human beings to be capable of no pleasures except those of which swine are capable. If this supposition were true, the charge could not be gainsaid, but would then be no longer an imputation; for if the sources of pleasure were precisely the same to human beings and to swine, the rule of life which is good enough for the one would be good enough for the other. The comparison of the Epicurean life to that of beasts is felt as degrading, precisely because a beast's pleasures do not satisfy a human being's conceptions of happiness. Human beings have faculties more elevated than the animal appetites and, when once made conscious of them, do not regard anything as happiness which does not include their gratification. I do not, indeed, consider the Epicureans to have been by any means faultless in drawing out their scheme of consequences from the utilitarian principle. To do this in any sufficient manner, many Stoic, as well as Christian, elements require to be included. But there is no known Epicurean theory of life which does not assign to the pleasures of the intellect, of the feelings and imagination, and of the moral sentiments a much higher value as pleasures than to those of mere sensation. It must be admitted, however, that utilitarian writers in general have placed the superiority of mental over bodily pleasures chiefly in the greater permanency, safety, uncostliness, etc., of the former—that is, in their circumstantial advantages rather than in their intrinsic nature. And on all these points utilitarians have fully proved their case; but they might have taken the other and, as it may be called, higher ground with entire consistency. It is quite compatible with the principle of utility to recognize the fact that some kinds of pleasure are more desirable and more valuable than others. It would be absurd that, while in estimating all other things quality is considered as well as quantity, the estimation of pleasure should be supposed to depend on quantity alone.

If I am asked what I mean by difference of quality in pleasures, or what makes one pleasure more valuable than another, merely as a pleasure, except its being greater in amount, there is but one possible answer. Of two pleasures, if there be one to which all or almost all who have experience of both give a decided preference, irrespective of any feeling of moral obligation to prefer it, that is the more desirable pleasure. If one of the two is, by those who are competently acquainted with both, placed so far above the other that they prefer it, even though knowing it to be attended with a greater amount of discontent, and would not resign it for any quantity of the other pleasure which their nature is capable of, we are justified in ascribing to the preferred enjoyment a superiority in quality so far outweighing quantity as to render it, in comparison, of small account.

Now it is an unquestionable fact that those who are equally acquainted with and equally capable of appreciating and enjoying both do give a most marked preference to the manner of existence which employs their higher faculties. Few human creatures would consent to be changed into any of the lower animals for a promise of the fullest allowance of a beast's pleasures; no intelligent human being would consent to be a fool, no instructed person would be an ignoramus, no person of feeling and conscience would be selfish and base, even though they should be persuaded that the fool, the dunce, or the rascal is better satisfied with his lot than they are with theirs. . . . It is better to be a human being dissatisfied than a pig satisfied; better to be Socrates dissatisfied than a fool satisfied. And if the fool, or the pig, are of a different opinion, it is because they only know their own side of the question. The other party to the comparison knows both sides.

It may be objected that many who are capable of the higher pleasures occasionally, under the influence of temptation, postpone them to the lower. But this is quite compatible with a full appreciation of the intrinsic superiority of the higher. Men often, from infirmity of character, make their election for the nearer good, though they know it to be the less valuable; and this no less when the choice is between two bodily pleasures than when it is between bodily and mental. They pursue sensual indulgences to the injury of health, though perfectly aware that health is the greater good. It may be further objected that many who begin with youthful enthusiasm for everything noble, as they advance in years, sink into indolence and selfishness. But I do not believe that those who undergo this very common change voluntarily choose the lower description of pleasures in preference to the higher. I believe that, before they devote themselves exclusively to the one, they have already become incapable of the other. Capacity for the nobler feelings is in most natures a very tender plant, easily killed, not only by hostile influences, but by mere want of sustenance; and in the majority of young persons it speedily dies away if the occupations to which their position in life has devoted them, and the society into which it has thrown them, are not favorable to keeping that higher capacity in exercise. Men lose their high aspirations as they lose their intellectual tastes, because they have not time or opportunity for indulging them; and they addict themselves to inferior pleasures, not because they deliberately prefer them, but because they are either the only ones to which they have access or the only ones which they are any longer capable of enjoying. It may be questioned whether anyone who has remained equally susceptible to both classes of pleasures ever knowingly and calmly preferred the lower, though many, in all ages, have broken down in an ineffectual attempt to combine both.

From this verdict of the only competent judges, I apprehend there can be no appeal. On a question which is the best worth having of two pleasures, or which of two modes of existence is the most grateful to the feelings, apart from its moral attributes and from its consequences, the judgment of those who are qualified by knowledge of both, or, if they differ, that of the majority among them, must be admitted as final. And there needs be the less hesitation to accept this judgment respecting the quality of pleasures, since there is no other tribunal to be referred to even on the question of quantity. What means are there of determining which is the acutest of two pains, or the intensest of two pleasurable sensations, except the general suffrage of those who are familiar with both? Neither pains nor pleasures are homogeneous, and pain is always heterogeneous with pleasure. What is there to decide whether a particular pleasure is worth purchasing at the cost of a particular pain, except the feelings and judgment of the experienced? When, therefore, those feelings and judgment declare the pleasures derived from the higher faculties to be preferable *in kind,* apart from the question of intensity, to those of which the animal nature, disjoined from the higher faculties, is susceptible, they are entitled on this subject to the same regard....

It has already been remarked that questions of ultimate ends do not admit of proof, in the ordinary acceptation of the term. To be incapable of proof by reasoning is common to all first principles, to the first premises of our knowledge, as well as to those of our conduct. But the former, being matters of fact, may be the subject of a direct appeal to the faculties which judge of fact—namely, our senses and our internal consciousness. Can an appeal be made to the same faculties on questions of practical ends? Or by what other faculty is cognizance taken of them?

Questions about ends are, in other words, questions [about] what things are desirable. The utilitarian doctrine is that happiness is desirable, and the only thing desirable, as an end; all other things being only desirable as means to that end. What ought to be required of this doctrine, what conditions is it requisite that the doctrine should fulfill—to make good its claim to be believed?

The only proof capable of being given that an object is visible is that people actually see it. The only proof that a sound is audible is that people hear it; and so of the other sources of our experience. In like manner, I apprehend, the sole evidence it is possible to produce that anything is desirable is that people do actually desire it. If the end which the utilitarian doctrine proposes to itself were not, in theory and in practice, acknowledged to be an end, nothing could ever convince any person that it was so. No reason can be given why the general happiness is desirable, except that each person, so far as he believes it to be attainable, desires his own happiness. This, however, being a fact, we have not only all the proof which the case admits of, but all which it is possible to require, that happiness is a good, that each person's happiness is a good to that person, and the general happiness, therefore, a good to the aggregate of all persons. Happiness has made out its title as *one* of the ends of conduct and, consequently, one of the criteria of morality.

But it has not, by this alone, proved itself to be the sole criterion. To do that, it would seem, by the same rule, necessary to show, not only that people desire happiness, but that they never desire anything else. Now it is palpable that they do desire things which, in common language, are decidedly distinguished from happiness. They desire, for example, virtue and the absence of vice no less really than pleasure and the absence of pain. The desire of virtue is not as universal, but it is as authentic a fact as the desire of happiness. And hence the opponents of the utilitarian standard deem that they have a right to infer that there are other ends of human action besides happiness, and that happiness is not the standard of approbation and disapprobation.

But does the utilitarian doctrine deny that people desire virtue, or maintain that virtue is not a thing to be desired? The very reverse. It maintains not only that virtue is to be desired, but that it is to be desired disinterestedly, for itself. Whatever may be the opinion of utilitarian moralists as to the original conditions by which virtue is made virtue, however they may believe (as they do) that actions and dispositions are only virtuous because they promote another end than virtue, yet this being granted, and it having been decided, from considerations of this description, what *is* virtuous, they not only place virtue at the very head of the things which are good as means to the ultimate end, but they also recognize as a psychological fact the possibility of its being, to the individual, a good in itself, without looking to any end beyond it; and hold that the mind is not in a right state, not in a state conformable to utility, not in the state most conducive to the general happiness, unless it does love virtue in this manner—as a thing desirable in itself, even although, in the individual instance, it should not produce those other desirable consequences which it tends to produce, and on account of which it is held to be virtue. This opinion is not, in the smallest degree, a departure from the happiness principle. The ingredients of happiness are very various, and each of them is desirable in itself, and not merely when considered as swelling an aggregate. The principle of utility does not mean that any given pleasure, as music, for instance, or any given exemption from pain, as for example health, is to be looked upon as means to a collective something termed happiness, and to be desired on that account. They are desired and desirable in and for themselves; besides being means, they are a part of the end. Virtue, according to the utilitarian doctrine, is not naturally and originally part of the end, but it is capable of becoming so; and in those who love it disinterestedly it has become so, and is desired and cherished, not as a means to happiness, but as a part of their happiness....

We have now, then, an answer to the question, of what sort of proof the principle of utility is susceptible. If the opinion which I have now stated is psychologically true—if human nature is so constituted as to desire nothing which is not either a part of happiness or a means of happiness—we can have no other proof, and we require no other, that these are the only things desirable. If so, happiness is the sole end of human action, and the promotion of it the test by which to judge of all human conduct; from whence it necessarily follows that it must be the criterion of morality, since a part is included in the whole.

JOSEPH F. FLETCHER

*Situation Ethics: The New Morality**

Joseph F. Fletcher (b. 1905) was a professor at Episcopal Theological School in Cambridge, Massachusetts, from 1944 to 1970. He has been active in many movements of social reform. His writings, mainly in the field of Christian social ethics, include *The Church and Industry, Christianity and Poverty, Morals and Medicine, Situation Ethics,* and *The Crisis in American Medicine.*

In the selection below, Fletcher outlines three approaches to making moral decisions and discusses the parts they have played in the past and continue to play today. He has described himself as a "Christian situation ethicist" who is committed to attacking legalism in any form. He suggests that when ethical judgments are made, one should sensitively seek "an understanding of the situation." The plea of the new morality is to put love first rather than law.

There are at bottom only three alternative routes or approaches to follow in making moral decisions. They are: (1) the legalistic; (2) the antinomian, the opposite extreme—i.e., a lawless or unprincipled approach; and (3) the situational. All three have played their part in the history of Western morals, legalism being by far the most common and persistent. Just as legalism triumphed among the Jews after the exile, so, in spite of Jesus' and Paul's revolt against it, it has managed to dominate Christianity constantly from very early days....

1. LEGALISM

With this approach one enters into every decision-making situation encumbered with a whole apparatus of prefabricated rules and regulations.

*From *Situation Ethics,* by Joseph Fletcher. Copyright © MCMLXVI, W. L. Jenkins. Used by permission of The Westminster Press. Pages 17–31 with omissions.

Not just the spirit but the letter of the law reigns. Its principles, codified in rules, are not merely guidelines or maxims to illuminate the situation; they are *directives* to be followed. Solutions are preset, and you can "look them up" in a book—a Bible or a confessor's manual.

Judaism, Catholicism, Protestantism—all major Western religious traditions have been legalistic. In morals as in doctrine they have kept to a spelled-out, "systematic" orthodoxy. The ancient Jews, especially under the post-exilic Maccabean and Pharisaic leadership, lived by the law or Torah, and its oral tradition (halakah). It was a code of 613 (or 621) precepts, amplified by an increasingly complicated mass of Mishnaic interpretations and applications.

Statutory and code law inevitably piles up, ruling upon ruling, because the complications of life and the claims of mercy and compassion combine—even with code legalists—to accumulate an elaborate system of exceptions and compromise, in the form of rules for breaking the rules! It leads to that tricky and tortuous now-you-see-it, now-you-don't business of interpretation that the rabbis called pilpul—a hairsplitting and logic-chopping study of the letter of the law, pyramiding from codes (e.g., the Covenant and Holiness) to Pentateuch to Midrash and Mishna to Talmud. It was a tragic death to the prophets' "pathos" (sharing God's loving concern) and "ethos" (living by love as *norm,* not program). With the prophets it had been a question of sensitively seeking "an understanding of *the situation.*"

Any web thus woven sooner or later chokes its weavers. Reformed and even Conservative Jews have been driven to disentangle themselves from it. Only Orthodoxy is still in its coils. Something of the same pilpul and formalistic complication may be seen in Christian history. With Catholics it has taken the form of a fairly ingenious moral theology that, as its twists and involutions have increased, resorts more and more to a casuistry that appears (as, to its credit, it does) to evade the very "laws" of right and wrong laid down in its textbooks and manuals. Love, even with the most stiff-necked of system builders, continues to plead mercy's cause and to win at least partial release from law's cold abstractions. Casuistry is the homage paid by legalism to the love of persons, and to realism about life's relativities.

Protestantism has rarely constructed such intricate codes and systems of law, but what it has gained by its simplicity it has lost through its rigidity, its puritanical insistence on moral rules. In fact, the very lack of a casuistry and its complexity, once people are committed to *even the bare principle* of legalistic morality or law ethics, is itself evidence of their blindness to the factors of doubt and perplexity. They have lost touch with the headaches and heartbreaks of life.

What can be worse, no casuistry at all may reveal a punishing and sadistic use of law to hurt people instead of helping them. How else explain burning at the stake in the Middle Ages for homosexuals (death, in the Old Testament)? Even today imprisonment up to sixty years is the penalty in one state for those who were actually consenting adults, without seduction or public disorder! This is really unavoidable whenever law instead of love is put first. The "puritan" type is a well-known example of it. But even if the legalist is truly *sorry* that the law requires unloving or disastrous decisions, he still cries, *"Fiat justitia, ruat caelum!"* (Do the "right" even if the sky falls down). He is the man Mark Twain called "a good man in the worst sense of the word."

The Christian situation ethicist agrees with Bertrand Russell and his implied judgment, "To this day Christians think an adulterer more wicked than a politician who takes bribes, although the latter probably does a thousand times as much harm." And he thoroughly rejects Cardinal Newman's view: "The Church holds that it were better for sun and moon to drop from heaven, for the earth to fail, and for all the many millions who are upon it to die of starvation in extremest agony...than that one soul, I will not say should be lost, but should commit one single venial sin."....

Legalism in the Christian tradition has taken two forms. In the Catholic line it has been a matter of legalistic *reason,* based on nature or natural law. These moralists have tended to adumbrate their ethical rules by applying human reason to the facts of nature, both human and subhuman, and to the lessons of historical experience. By this procedure they claim to have adduced universally agreed and therefore valid "natural" moral laws. Protestant moralists have followed the same adductive and deductive tactics. They have taken Scripture and done with it what the Catholics do with nature. Their Scriptural moral law is, they argue, based on the words and sayings of the Law and the Prophets, the evangelists and apostles of the Bible. It is a matter of legalistic *revelation.* One is rationalistic, the other Biblicistic; one natural, the other Scriptural. But both are legalistic.

Even though Catholic moralists deal also with "revealed law" (e.g., "the divine positive law of the Ten Commandments") and Protestants have tried to use reason in interpreting the sayings of the Bible (hermeneutics), still both by and large have been committed to the doctrines of law ethics.

2. ANTINOMIANISM

Over against legalism, as a sort of polar opposite, we can put antinomianism. This is the approach with which one enters into the decision-making situation armed with no principles or maxims whatsoever, to say nothing of *rules.* In every "existential moment" or "unique" situation, it declares, one must rely upon the situation of itself, *there and then,* to provide its ethical solution.

The term "antinomianism" (literally, "against law") was used first by Luther to describe Johannes Agricola's views. The ethical concept has cropped up here and there, as among some Anabaptists, some sects of English Puritanism, and some of Wesley's followers. The concept is certainly at issue in I Corinthians (e.g., ch. 6:12–20). Paul had to struggle with two primitive forms of it among the Hellenistic Jew-Christians whom he visited. They took his attacks on law morality too naïvely and too literally.

One form was libertinism—the belief that by grace, by the new life in Christ and salvation by faith, law or rules no longer applied to Christians. Their ultimate happy fate was now assured, and it mattered no more *what* they did. (Whoring, incest, drunkenness, and the like are what they did, therefore! This explains the warning in I Peter 2:16, "Live as free men, yet without using your freedom as a pretext for evil; but live as servants of God." This license led by inevitable reaction to an increase of legalism, especially in sex ethics, under which Christians still suffer today.) The other form, less pretentious and more enduring, was a Gnostic claim to special knowledge, so that neither principles nor rules were needed any longer even as guidelines and direction pointers. They would just *know* what was right when they needed to know. They had, they claimed, a superconscience. It is this second "gnostic" form of the approach which is under examination here.

While legalists are preoccupied with law and its stipulations, the Gnostics are so flatly opposed to law—even in principle—that their moral decisions are random, unpredictable, erratic, quite anomalous. Making moral decisions is a matter of spontaneity; it is literally unprincipled, purely *ad hoc* and casual. They follow no forecastable course from one situation to another. They are, exactly, anarchic—i.e., without a rule. They are not only "unbound by the chains of law" but actually sheer extemporizers, impromptu and intellectually irresponsible. They not only cast the old Torah aside; they even cease to think seriously and *care-fully* about the demands of love as it has been shown in Christ, the love norm itself. The baby goes out with the bath water!

This was the issue Paul fought over with the antinomians at Corinth and Ephesus. They were repudiating all law, as such, and all principles, relying in all moral action choices solely upon guidance in the situation....

Another version of antinomianism, on the whole much subtler philosophically and perhaps more admirable, is the ethics of existentialism. Sartre speaks of "nausea," which is our anxious experience of the *incoherence* of reality. For him any belief in coherence (such as the Christian doctrine of the unity of God's creation and his Lordship over history) is "bad faith." In every moment of moral choice or decision "we have no excuses behind us and no justification before us." Sartre refuses to admit to any *generally* valid principles at all, nothing even ordinarily valid, to say nothing of universal *laws*....

3. SITUATIONISM

A third approach, in between legalism and antinomian unprincipledness, is situation ethics. (To jump from one polarity to the other would be only to go from the frying pan to the fire.) The situationist enters into every decision-making situation fully armed with the ethical maxims of his community and its heritage, and he treats them with respect as illuminators of his problems. Just the same he is prepared in any situation to compromise them or set them aside *in the situation* if love seems better served by doing so.

Situation ethics goes part of the way with natural law, by accepting reason as the instrument of moral judgment, while rejecting the notion that the good is "given" in the nature of things, objectively. It goes part of the way with Scriptural law by accepting revelation as the source of the norm while rejecting all "revealed" norms or laws but the one command—to love God in the neighbor. The situationist follows a moral law or violates it according to love's need. For example, "Almsgiving is a good thing *if*..." The situationist never says, "Almsgiving is a good thing. Period!" His decisions are hypothetical, not categorical. Only the commandment to love is categorically good. "Owe no one anything, except to love one another." (Rom. 13:8.) If help to an indigent only pauperizes and degrades him, the situationist refuses a handout and finds some other way. He makes no law out of Jesus' "Give to every one who begs from you." It is only one step from that kind of Biblicist literalism to the kind that causes women in certain sects to refuse blood transfusions even if death results—even if they are carrying a quickened fetus that will be lost too. The legalist says that even if he tells a man escaped from an asylum where his intended victim is, if he finds and murders him, at least only one sin has been committed (murder), not two (lying as well)! ...

William Temple put it this way: "Universal obligation attaches not to particular judgments of conscience but to conscientiousness. What acts are right may depend on circumstances ... but there is an absolute obligation to will whatever may on each occasion be right." Our obligation is relative *to* the situation, but obligation *in* the situation is absolute. We are only "obliged" to tell the truth, for example, if the situation calls for it; if a murderer asks us his victim's whereabouts, our duty might be to lie.... Situation ethics aims at a contextual appropriateness—not the "good" or the "right" but the *fitting*....

One competent situationist, speaking to students, explained the position this way. Rules are "like 'Punt on fourth down,' or 'Take a pitch when the count is three balls.' These rules are part of the wise player's know-how, and distinguish him from the novice. But they are not unbreakable. The best players are those who know when to ignore them. In the game of bridge, for example, there is a useful rule which says 'Second hand low.' But have you ever played with anyone who followed the rule slavishly? You say to him (in exasperation), 'Partner, why didn't you play your ace? We could have set the hand.' And he replies, unperturbed, 'Second hand low!' What is wrong? The same thing that was wrong when Kant gave information to the murderer. He forgot the purpose of the game.... He no longer thought of winning the hand, but of being able to justify himself by invoking the rule." ...

There are various names for this approach: situationism, contextualism, occasionalism, circumstantialism, even actualism. These labels indicate, of course, that the core of the ethic they describe is a healthy and primary awareness that "circumstances alter cases"—i.e., that in actual problems of conscience the situational variables are to be weighed as heavily as the normative or "general" constants.

The situational factors are so primary that we may even say "circumstances alter rules and principles." It is said that when Gertrude Stein lay dying she declared, "It is better to ask questions than to give answers, even good answers." This is the temper of situation ethics. It is empirical, fact-minded, data conscious, inquiring. It is antimoralistic as well as antilegalistic, for it is sensitive to variety and complexity....

It is necessary to insist that situation ethics is willing to make full and respectful use of principles, to be treated as maxims but not as laws or precepts. We might call it "principled relativism." To repeat the term used above, principles or maxims or general rules are *illuminators*. But they are not *directors*. The classic rule of moral theology has been to follow laws but do it *as much as possible* according to love and according to reason (*secundum caritatem et secundum rationem*). Situation ethics, on the other hand, calls upon us to keep law in a subservient place, so that *only* love and reason really count when the chips are down![1]

1. This selection by Joseph Fletcher is one of many statements on "the new morality." It has been widely criticized as well as defended. For a collection of critical reactions see Harvey Cox, ed., *The Situation Ethics Debate* (Philadelphia: Westminster Press, 1968). [Ed.]

Liberty, Law, and Civil Disobedience

JOHN STUART MILL

*On Liberty**

See the biographical note on p. 119.

The selection below is likely to be quoted wherever questions of human freedom, repression, and tyranny are under discussion. In this essay, Mill discusses the rights of the individual in relation to the demands of organized life in society. He is regarded as the main spokesman of the position that the only purpose for which power can rightfully be exercised over the individual against his will is to prevent his doing harm to others.

I. INTRODUCTORY

The subject of this Essay is not the so-called Liberty of the Will, so unfortunately opposed to the misnamed doctrine of Philosophical Necessity; but Civil, or Social Liberty: the nature and limits of the power which can be legitimately exercised by society over the individual. A question seldom stated, and hardly ever discussed, in general terms, but which profoundly influences the practical controversies of the age by its latent presence, and is likely soon to make itself recognized as the vital question of the future. It is so far from being new, that, in a certain sense, it has divided mankind, almost from the remotest ages; but in the stage of progress into which the more civilized portions of the species have now entered, it presents itself under new conditions and requires a different and more fundamental treatment....

*John Stuart Mill, from *On Liberty* (1859), Parts I–IV with omissions.

The object of this Essay is to assert one very simple principle, as entitled to govern absolutely the dealings of society with the individual in the way of compulsion and control, whether the means used be physical force in the form of legal penalties, or the moral coercion of public opinion. That principle is, that the sole end for which mankind are warranted, individually or collectively, in interfering with the liberty of action of any of their number, is self-protection. That the only purpose for which power can be rightfully exercised over any member of a civilized community, against his will, is to prevent harm to others. His own good, either physical or moral, is not a sufficient warrant. He cannot rightfully be compelled to do or forbear because it will be better for him to do so, because it will make him happier, because, in the opinions of others, to do so would be wise, or even right. These are good reasons for remonstrating with him, or reasoning with him, or persuading him, or entreating him, but not for compelling him, or visiting him with any evil in case he do otherwise. To justify that, the conduct from which it is desired to deter him, must be calculated to produce evil to some one else. The only part of the conduct of any one, for which he is amenable to society, is that which concerns others. In the part which merely concerns himself, his independence is, of right, absolute. Over himself, over his own body and mind, the individual is sovereign....

...When I say only himself, I mean directly, and in the first instance: for whatever affects himself, may affect others *through* himself; and the objection which may be grounded on this contingency, will receive consideration in the sequel. This, then, is the appropriate region of human liberty. It comprises, first, the inward domain of consciousness; demanding liberty of conscience, in the most comprehensive sense; liberty of thought and feeling; absolute freedom of opinion and sentiment on all subjects, practical or speculative, scientific, moral, or theological. The liberty of expressing and publishing opinions may seem to fall under a different principle, since it belongs to that part of the conduct of an individual which concerns other people; but, being almost of as much importance as the liberty of thought itself, and resting in great part on the same reasons, is practically inseparable from it. Secondly, the principle requires liberty of tastes and pursuits; of framing the plan of our life to suit our own character; of doing as we like, subject to such consequences as may follow: without impediment from our fellow-creatures, so long as what we do does not harm them, even though they should think our conduct foolish, perverse, or wrong. Thirdly, from this liberty of each individual, follows the liberty, within the same limits, of combination among individuals; freedom to unite, for any purpose not involving harm to others: the persons combining being supposed to be of full age, and not forced or deceived.

No society in which these liberties are not, on the whole, respected, is free, whatever may be its form of government; and none is completely free in which they do not exist absolute and unqualified. The only freedom which deserves the name, is that of pursuing our own good in our own way, so long as we do not attempt to deprive others of theirs, or impede their efforts to obtain it. Each is the proper guardian of his own health, whether bodily, or mental and spirtual. Mankind are greater gainers by suffering each other to live as seems good to themselves, than by compelling each to live as seems good to the rest.

Though this doctrine is anything but new, and, to some persons, may have the air of a truism, there is no doctrine which stands more directly opposed to the general tendency of existing opinion and practice. Society has expended fully as much effort in the attempt (according to its lights) to compel people to conform to its notions of personal, as of social excellence....

...The disposition of mankind, whether as rulers or as fellow-citizens, to impose their own opinions and inclinations as a rule of conduct on others, is so energetically supported by some of the best and by some of the worst feelings incident to human nature, that it is hardly ever kept under restraint by anything but want of power; and as the power is not declining, but growing, unless a strong barrier of moral conviction can be raised against the mischief, we must expect, in the present circumstances of the world, to see it increase.

It will be convenient for the argument, if, instead of at once entering upon the general thesis, we confine ourselves in the first instance to a single branch of it, on which the principle here stated is, if not fully, yet to a certain point, recognised by the current opinions. This one branch is the Liberty of Thought: from which it is impossible to separate the cognate liberty of speaking and of writing....

II. OF THE LIBERTY OF THOUGHT AND DISCUSSION

The time, it is to be hoped, is gone by, when any defence would be necessary of the "liberty of the press" as one of the securities against corrupt or tyrannical government. No argument, we may suppose, can now be needed, against permitting a legislature or an executive, not identified in interest with the people, to prescribe opinions to them, and determine what doctrines or what arguments they shall be allowed to hear....Let us suppose, therefore, that the government is entirely at one with the people, and never thinks of exerting any power of coercion unless in agreement with what it conceives to be their voice. But I deny the right of the people to exercise such coercion, either by themselves or by their government. The power itself is illegitimate. The best government has no more title to it than the worst. It is as noxious, or more noxious, when exerted in accordance with public opinion, than when in opposition to it. If all mankind minus one, were of one opinion, and only one person were of the contrary opinion, mankind would be no more justified in silencing that one person, than he, if he had the power, would be justified in silencing mankind. Were an opinion a personal possession of no value except to the owner; if to be obstructed in the enjoyment of it were simply a private injury, it would make some difference whether the injury was inflicted only on a few persons or on many. But the peculiar evil of silencing the expression of an opinion is, that it is robbing the human race; posterity as well as the existing generation; those who dissent from the opinion, still more than those who hold it. If the opinion is right, they are deprived of the opportunity of exchanging error for truth: if wrong, they lose, what is almost as great a benefit, the clearer perception and livelier impression of truth, produced by its collision with error.

It is necessary to consider separately these two hypotheses, each of which has a distinct branch of the argument corresponding to it. We can never be sure that the opinion we are endeavouring to stifle is a false opinion; and if we were sure, stifling it would be an evil still....

...It is a piece of idle sentimentality that truth, merely as truth, has any inherent power denied to error, of prevailing against the dungeon and the stake. Men are not more zealous for truth than they often are for error, and a sufficient application of legal or even of social penalties will generally succeed in stopping the propagation of either. The real advantage which truth has, consists in this: that when an opinion is true, it may be extinguished once, twice or many times, but in the course of ages there will generally be found persons to rediscover it, until some one of its reappearances falls on a time when from favourable circumstances it escapes persecution until it has made such head as to withstand all subsequent attempts to suppress it....

We...recognis[e] the necessity to the mental well-being of mankind (on which all their other well-being depends) of freedom of opinion, and freedom of the expression of opinion, on four distinct grounds....

First, if any opinion is compelled to silence, that opinion may, for aught we can certainly know, be true. To deny this is to assume our own infallibility.

Secondly, though the silenced opinion be an error, it may, and very commonly does, contain a portion of truth; and since the general or prevailing opinion on any subject is rarely or never the whole truth, it is only by the collision of adverse opinions that the remainder of the truth has any chance of being supplied.

Thirdly, even if the received opinion be not only true, but the whole truth; unless it is suffered to be, and actually is, vigorously and earnestly contested, it will, by most of those who receive it, be held in the manner of a prejudice, with little comprehension or feeling of its rational grounds. And not only this, but, fourthly, the meaning of the doctrine itself will be in danger of being lost or enfeebled, and deprived of its vital effect on the character and conduct: the dogma becoming a mere formal profession, inefficacious for good, but cumbering the ground, and preventing the growth of any real and heartfelt conviction, from reason or personal experience....

III. OF INDIVIDUALITY, AS ONE OF THE ELEMENTS OF WELL-BEING

Such being the reasons which make it imperative that human beings should be free to form opinions, and to express their opinions without reserve; and such the baneful consequences to the intellectual, and through that to the moral nature of man, unless this liberty is either conceded, or asserted in spite of prohibition; let us next examine whether the same reasons do not require that men should be free to act upon their opinions—to carry these out in their lives, without hindrance, either physical or moral, from their fellow-men, so long as it is at their own risk and peril. This last proviso is of course indispensable. No one pretends that actions should be as free as opinions. On the contrary, even opinions lose their immunity, when the circumstances in which they are expressed are such as to constitute their expression a positive instigation to some mischievous act. An opinion that corn-dealers are starvers of the poor, or that private property is robbery, ought to be unmolested when simply circulated through the press, but may justly incur punishment when delivered orally to an excited mob assembled before the house of a corn-dealer, or when handed about among the same mob in the form of a placard. Acts, of whatever kind, which, without justifiable cause, do harm to others, may be, and in the more important cases absolutely require to be, controlled by the unfavorable sentiments, and, when needful, by the active interference of mankind. The liberty of the individual must be thus far limited; he must not make himself a nuisance to other people. But if he refrains from molesting others in what concerns them, and merely acts according to his own inclination and judgment in things which concern himself, the same reasons which show that opinion should be free, prove also that he should be allowed, without molestation, to carry his opinions into practice at his own cost. That mankind are not infallible; that their truths, for the most part, are only half-truths; that unity of opinion, unless resulting from the fullest and freest comparison of opposite opinions, is not desirable, and diversity not an evil, but a good, until mankind are much more capable than at present of recognizing all sides of the truth, are principles applicable to men's modes of action, not less than to their opinions. As it is useful that while mankind are imperfect there should be different opinions, so it is that there should be different experiments of living; that free scope should be given to varieties of character, short of injury to others; and that the worth of different modes of life should be proved practically, when any one thinks fit to try them. It is desirable, in short, that in things which do not primarily concern others, individuality should assert itself. Where, not the person's own character, but the traditions or customs of other people are the rule of conduct, there is wanting one of the principal ingredients of human happiness, and quite the chief ingredient of individual and social progress....

IV. OF THE LIMITS TO THE AUTHORITY OF SOCIETY OVER THE INDIVIDUAL

What, then, is the rightful limit to the sovereignty of the individual over himself? Where does the authority of society begin? How much of human life should be assigned to individuality, and how much to society?

Each will receive its proper share, if each has that which more particularly concerns it. To individuality should belong the part of life in which it is chiefly the individual that is interested; to society, the part which chiefly interests society.

Though society is not founded on a contract, and though no good purpose is answered by inventing a contract in order to deduce social obligations from it, every one who receives the protection of society owes a return for the benefit, and the fact of living in society renders it indispensable that each should be found to observe a certain line of conduct towards the rest. This conduct consists, first, in not injuring the interests of one another; or rather certain interests, which, either by express legal provision or by tacit understanding, ought to be considered as rights; and secondly, in each person's bearing his share (to be fixed on some equitable principle) of the labours and sacrifices incurred for defending the society or its members from injury and molestation. These conditions society is justified in enforcing, at all costs to those who endeavour to withold fulfilment. Nor is this all that society may do. The acts of an individual may be hurtful to others, or wanting in due consideration for their welfare, without going the length of violating any of their constituted rights. The offender may then be justly punished by opinion, though not by law. As soon as any part of a person's conduct affects prejudicially the interests of others, society has jurisdiction over it, and the question whether the general welfare will or will not be promoted by interfering with it, becomes open to discussion. But there is no room for entertaining any such question when a person's conduct affects the interests of no persons besides himself, or needs not affect them unless they like (all the persons concerned being of full age, and the ordinary amount of understanding). In all such cases there should be perfect freedom, legal and social, to do the action and stand the consequences.

It would be a great misunderstanding of this doctrine to suppose that it is one of selfish indifference, which pretends that human beings have no business with each other's conduct in life, and that they should not concern themselves about the well-doing or well-being of one another, unless their own interest is involved. Instead of any diminution, there is need of a great increase of disinterested exertion to promote the good of others. But disinterested benevolence can find other instruments to persuade people to their good, than whips and scourges, either of the literal or the metaphorical sort. I am the last person to undervalue the self-regarding virtues; they are only second in importance, if even second, to the social. It is equally the business of education to cultivate both. But even education works by conviction and persuasion as well as by compulsion, and it is by the former only that, when the period of education is past, the self-regarding virtues should be inculcated. Human beings owe to each other help to distinguish the better from the worse, and encouragement to choose the former and avoid the latter. They should be for ever stimulating each other to increased exercise of their higher faculties, and increased direction of their feelings and aims towards wise instead of foolish, elevating instead of degrading, objects and contemplations....

ALEXANDER B. SMITH and HARRIET POLLACK

*Should We Attempt to Police our Morals?**

Alexander B. Smith (b. 1909) is professor of sociology at John Jay College of Criminal Justice of the City University of New York. A native of New York, he was a practicing attorney and a consultant for the President's Commission on Juvenile Deliquency, the Commission on Marijuana and Drug Abuse, and the Commission on Obscenity and Pornography. In addition to many articles on various aspects of the field of criminal justice, his writings include *New Direc-*

*Alexander B. Smith and Harriet Pollack, from "Crimes Without Victims," in *Saturday Review,* 54 (December 5, 1971), pp. 27–29. Used by permission of the authors and the publisher.

tions in Police Community Relations and *Treating the Criminal Offender*. He is also co-author of *Crime and Justice in a Mass Society*.

Harriet Pollack (b. 1925), a native of New York, holds a Ph.D. in Political Science from Columbia University. She is Professor of Government at John Jay College of Criminal Justice and chairman of the Department of Government and Public Administration. In addition to articles on constitutional law and criminal justice, she has written *Some Sins Are Not Crimes* and is co-author of *Crime and Justice in a Mass Society*.

In the selection below, the authors ask whether police action against offenses such as gambling, drug-addiction, and prostitution is effective in producing a decent and stable society. Should such moral offenses, in which there are no victims, be considered crimes to be regulated by the police? What is the relationship between such attempted enforcement and a denial of civil liberties, the increase in corruption, and the overburdening of our courts?

Few people would dispute that crime probably heads today's list of troubles besetting our urban population. City-dwellers are afraid of being mugged, robbed, raped, or murdered. In addition, they are disgusted: by the blatant soliciting from prostitutes; by gay bars; by seedy pornography shops; by openly sold heroin and marijuana; and by crooked cops. The response on the part of our law enforcement agencies has been to attempt better surveillance of high crime areas in order to protect people against assault and robbery, and to mount campaigns to clean up the downtown neighborhoods where pimps, female and male prostitutes, bookies, pornographers, et al., assemble.

Whatever the merits and feasibility of increased police patrols to handle street crime, there is at least no doubt that citizens need to be protected against thieves and murderers. There is a real question, however, whether campaigns against gamblers, prostitutes, and dope pushers are not actually counter-productive in terms of producing a decent, stable society.

Despite the attractiveness of the notion of a "clean" Times Square or Loop as morally pure as the more genteel sections of New York City or Chicago, are there hidden social costs to such clean-ups that society may not care to pay? Is there some relationship between the use of the criminal justice system to police our morals and its failure to protect our persons? Is how to handle prostitutes and pornographers the problem, or is it the larger question of whether morals offenses should be considered as crimes? Will a fresh look at the penal code be more fruitful in the long run than arguing over whether displaced prostitutes or pornographers will be likely to go to the suburbs if hounded out of the inner cities?

Conceptually, our penal code prohibits two kinds of acts: those that are *malum in se* (evil in themselves) and those that are *malum prohibitum* (evil because prohibited). *Malum in se* acts (murder, rape, arson, assault) are true crimes in the sense that no society can tolerate such conduct and survive. But a large part of our penal code is concerned with acts that are not universally considered evil, but that we, at this moment in time, for a variety of reasons, have labeled as sufficiently undesirable to be punished by the criminal justice system. In New York State, for example, gambling is prohibited by law, and the police, courts, and jails are expected to deal with numbers runners, bookies, and the like. At the same time, the state itself not only permits gambling at the race tracks and runs a lottery based on the outcome of the horse races, but has set up OTB, a corporation for handling off-track bets, from which the state expects to derive revenue. Nevada, among other states, licenses and taxes casinos and similar gambling establishments. Clearly, nothing in gambling per se is inconsistent with a viable society; yet the resources of our criminal justice system are diverted to the enforcement of anti-gambling laws.

Our attitudes toward drug use are equally inconsistent: We forbid the use of marijuana and heroin; yet we tolerate the limited use of amphetamines and barbiturates, and we encourage, through ubiquitous advertising, the indiscriminate sale of pills for every conceivable purpose, physiological and psychological. Hundreds of sections of the criminal law are concerned with acts that are criminal mainly because society at large says they are: homosexual activity between consenting adults, prostitution, gambling, possession of obscene and pornographic materials, to name a few. The enforcement of these laws takes the lion's share of our criminal justice resources. For every murderer arrested and prosecuted, literally dozens of gamblers, prostitutes, dope pushers, and derelicts crowd our courts' dockets. If we took the numbers runners, the kids smoking pot, and the winos out of the criminal justice system, we would substantially reduce the burden on the courts and the police. If we permitted the sale of heroin on a controlled prescription basis (as the British do, and as we do with other dangerous drugs), we would probably eliminate well over half of the cases going through our criminal courts. Myths to the contrary, there is no scientific evidence that the use of heroin, in and of itself, causes criminal conduct. By cutting off all legal access to heroin, however, we have driven the price so high that experienced observers estimate that more than half the crimes in New York City are committed by addicts seeking drugs or the money for drugs. The greater part of the social evil incident to the use of heroin, thus, comes not from its use, but from the laws that make it impossible to obtain the drug legally. This is not to say, of course, that the use of heroin is not harmful to the addict. It is only that our penal code has extended that harm from the user himself to those who are victimized by his crime. In short, the net effect of our drug laws is highly counter-productive in that they create more anti-social conduct than they prevent.

Morals laws that do not reflect contemporary mores or that cannot be enforced should be removed from the penal code through legislative action, because, at best, they undermine respect for the law, and, at worst, as in the case of our drug laws, they exacerbate a tragic situation. Admittedly, such a deliberate legislative policy would fly in the face of all historical American experience. As Morris Ernst once remarked, Americans do not repeal morals legislation; they simply allow such laws to fall into desuetude. Sunday blue laws are a classic example of this process. The New York State Sunday Closing Law currently on the books has in the past been read to forbid movie, stage, and radio performances on Sunday. Of course, this interpretation is archaic at present; the courts have simply stopped interpreting this law in so restrictive a manner. The police also have become so unconcerned with enforcing it that they ignore violations. In 1970, the New York City police commissioner, recognizing that no one any longer cared about the Sunday Closing Law, announced that his men would not even attempt to enforce it. Such forthrightness on the part of an administrative official is unusual; most laws go unenforced by default rather than by deliberate policy.

More important, despite the commissioner's candor and despite the inutility of this law, the legislature has not bothered to repeal it. The reasons are obvious: Any such attempt would lead to an outcry by small but militant minority groups who would convert a simple act of legislative housekeeping into a debate over morality. No legislator wants to be cast in the role of the defender of immorality, even in the case of a custom widely accepted and practiced by a good part of his constituency. It is much easier, and politically more sensible, simply to sweep the issue under the rug by ignoring it.

Unfortunately, we can no longer afford the luxury of waiting for administrative action (or inaction) to catch up with public morality. Possibly because we live in an era that has seen great changes in public mores in a relatively short time, we have too many laws that the police are attempting to enforce and the courts to handle that large segments of the public simply will not obey. Gambling laws are an obvious example, as are those forbidding prostitution, homosexual acts between adults, and possession of pornographic materials. The most troublesome morals laws, however, are those forbidding the possession and sale of marijuana, heroin, LSD, and other similar drugs.

There is something very frightening to most people in advocating repeal of morals laws. It is as though, by advocating repeal, the conduct that heretofore has been forbidden is being endorsed. Nothing could be further from the truth. In repealing morals laws, the legislature is not proposing that people become immoral; it is simply declaring that the criminal sanction will no longer be used to enforce a particular mode of conduct. Most human conduct, after all, is regulated by non-legal institutions: the home, the school, the church, the family, the peer group. Most husbands work hard and support their wives and children because they respond to cultural demands, not because they could be put in jail for nonsupport if they failed to do so. The unpalatable truth is that passing a law does not mean that it will be obeyed or that it can be enforced. Conversely, the repeal of a law does not necessarily mean an increase in undesirable conduct.

Prohibition is probably the most clear cut example of the effect of enacting and then repealing a morals law. The Eighteenth Amendment had virtually no effect in reducing per capita alcohol consumption in this country, and its repeal did not increase either the amount of drinking or the problems of alcoholism. The only effect the Eighteenth Amendment had was to create a flourishing bootlegging industry, and it was this spin-off—the rise in serious crime due to an unenforceable law—that constituted one of the principal reasons for repeal.

We are in a similar position today. Our gambling and drug laws particularly have created a situation in which an enormous organized crime industry thrives on satisfying a consumer demand that cannot be met legitimately. Worse yet, the effort to cope with the crime wave resulting from our unenforceable drug and gambling laws is destroying our criminal justice system and rendering it incapable of dealing with criminals who violate laws that might, under better circumstances, be reasonably enforceable.

While the chances for legislative modification of morals laws are still poor, there are signs that public opinion is beginning to recognize the need for change, especially in the areas of gambling and consensual adult sex practices. Proposed repeal of drug laws (even those relating to marijuana) has aroused far more anxiety, and there are still virtually no prominent public figures willing to openly advocate the legalization of heroin. There is probably some risk in repealing the ban on heroin. Many policemen, among others, believe that if the ban were lifted, a substantial number of people (especially youngsters), eager to try forbidden fruit, would be hooked into an addiction that would last the rest of their lives. Removing heroin from the penal code does not, however, mean permitting its sale in every candy store. As with many other pharmaceuticals, distribution could be regulated by prescription. But more than that, almost everyone familiar with the drug scene (especially the police) agrees that the present law has not deterred anyone who doesn't want to be deterred. It is easy to get heroin in New York City today, despite the law and the entire criminal justice system arrayed in support of the law. Apparently, those who are not using heroin are abstaining voluntarily, in which case repeal carries minimal risks.

Not only are morals laws frequently counter-productive in terms of their causing more crime than they prevent, but their enforcement is particularly dangerous to civil liberties since crimes resulting from their violation have no victims. The prostitute's client has not been forcibly seduced; the housewife who bets a quarter on the numbers has not been robbed; the dope user has harmed only himself. Because there are no victims available to testify for the state, the burden of producing enough evidence for the prosecution rests entirely on the police. It is this need for evidence to make morals offense violations "stick" that traditionally has produced the greatest number of civil liberties violations by the police. Prostitutes, for example, are frequently victims of entrapment by plainclothesmen. If their customers will not testify, who besides the plainclothesmen can? And what better way of establishing a case than by offering an obviously willing girl a little "encouragement"? Official police records indicate that an incredible number of gamblers and drug pushers "drop" gambling slips and narcotics at the mere approach of a policeman. This so-called dropsie evidence is frequently a euphemism for an illegal search. The amount of dropsie evidence has increased markedly since 1961 when the Supreme Court in *Mapp* v. *Ohio* banned the use of overtly, illegally seized evidence in state courts.

Such violations of civil liberties occur not because the police prefer to act illegally, but because it is difficult to build a legitimate case where there is no real victim. At the Supreme Court level, it is noteworthy that most of the decisions censuring police conduct deal with state and local enforcement procedures rather than federal ones. This is not because FBI agents are inherently more civil libertarian or cognizant of legalities than local policemen. It is because they deal with different kinds of wrongdoings. In such crimes as kidnaping, bank robbery, or counterfeiting, there are real victims, and federal agents can build their cases in an ethical, professional manner: obtaining statements from victims, interviewing eyewitnesses, obtaining fingerprints, weapons, contraband, etc. Local police, in dealing with pimps, numbers runners, and dope pushers, are not afforded this luxury. They must make a case the best way they can, and frequently this involves illegal snooping, searching, and arrests.

The enforcement of morals laws not only involves the police in violations of civil liberties but is the source of most of the corruption within police departments. All police departments are plagued with a small number of rogues who join forces with the criminals they are supposed to apprehend and participate in burglaries, extortion, etc. This kind of corruption is relatively rare and usually not difficult to eliminate. Seldom does it extend to the top administrative levels. The most common type of police corruption is the pay-offs policemen receive (and pass along to their superior officers) from criminals involved with drugs, gambling, or prostitution. This sort of graft is almost impossible to eradicate, partly because the illegal activities involved are so profitable and the payoffs so lucrative, and partly because the activities themselves do not seem terribly immoral to the police, possibly because the crimes have no real victims. Such corruption spreads, moreover, throughout entire departments, from the patrolman on the beat through top administrators and sometimes even to the commissioner, mayor, or other elected officials. Periodic exposés reveal a pattern that has varied little from the pattern laid bare at the turn of the century by Lincoln Steffens in *The Shame of the Cities;* however, the waves of reform following such exposés lead to little more than temporary remissions. No way has yet been found to eliminate this kind of corruption as long as the public wants to gamble, take illegal drugs, frequent prostitutes, etc., and as long as immense profits can be earned by criminals meeting these desires.

Perhaps the most important benefit that would result from the elimination of morals offenses from the penal code would be the relief of the criminal justice system. Prison riots, inordinately delayed trials, crimes committed by defendants out on bail, a clamor for preventive detention—all testify to the dangerously strained conditions of our criminal justice institutions. No one knows how much time is spent by the police, prosecutors, and courts in processing morals defendants, but it has been estimated that as little as 10 per cent of the courtroom hours available in our criminal courts are now devoted to the processing of serious crimes. If we were free to devote the remaining 90 per cent of our courtroom hours to the handling of dangerous offenders or serious crimes of property, we would be able to overcome most of the shortcomings of our present criminal justice system. With fewer offenders to concern them, police work could be more thorough and legitimate. The decongestion of court calendars would reduce the pressure for plea bargaining, as would, incidentally, more carefully prepared cases based on legally gathered evidence. The burden on probation and parole officers would also be lessened, and if the likelihood of arrest were greater due to better police work, then prison sentences might be more likely to act as a deterrent.

At the moment, proposals to repeal morals legislation are neither popular nor acceptable. Such proposals are attacked from both ends of the morality spectrum. On the one hand, guardians of public order are outraged at the prospect of "legalizing" gambling, drug sales, and sexual soliciting. "How would you feel if it were your sixteen-year-old daughter who became hooked on heroin?" "Terrible. But thousands are hooked now, and if she does become hooked, at least she will not have to steal, prostitute herself, victimize other people, or die of an overdose." The response in the imaginary colloquy is correct, but probably unconvincing to those who look at the printed word of the law as an amulet to ward off evil. The police, on the whole, do not favor the repeal of morals laws, in part because they see repeal as an admission of their limited role in society, i.e., that they can enforce only those laws the general public is willing to obey. Such an admission is not only ego-bruising but a distinct handicap in the annual race for their share of the public budget.

On the other hand, many people are making a very good living out of dope peddling, gambling, etc., and they are not likely to give up their livelihood without a struggle. What the ties of the underworld to elected and appointed officials are, no one really knows, but they exist, and organized crime is certainly capable of exerting pressure behind the scenes to discourage unfavorable legislation.

One can only hope that the uncommitted majority will come to realize the price we pay in corruption, the denial of civil liberties, and the overburdening of our criminal justice system for the luxury of using our penal code to enforce our currently fashionable behavior preferences. We need courage enough to admit that certain kinds of behavior cannot be controlled through the punitive sanction, and faith enough to believe that cultural pressure (or innate decency) will suffice to keep us from mass dissipation and self-destruction. And we need political leaders with guts enough to get up and say so.

HENRY DAVID THOREAU

*Civil Disobedience**

Henry David Thoreau (1817–1862) was born at Concord, Massachusetts. He graduated from Harvard University, taught school for a short time, then devoted himself to the study of literature and nature. He has been called many things: a natural philosopher, a transcendentalist, a mystic, an anarchist, and a revolutionary who created a literature of revolt. For a time he lived in a hut on the shore of Walden Pond. His *Walden* or *Life in the Woods* and his essays "Civil Disobedience," "Walking," and "Life Without Principle" are among his well-known works. His essay on civil disobedience is said to have helped Gandhi work out his doctrine of passive resistance in India.

In this essay Thoreau asserts that "action from principle" or a man's own perception of what is right may lead him to passive resistance or at times even to active rebellion against the state. Indirect democratic means and on occasion direct action may be taken against abuses and evils such as slavery, war, and excessive taxation.

I heartily accept the motto,—"That government is best which governs least"; and I should like to see it acted up to more rapidly and systematically.

*Henry David Thoreau, from "Civil Disobedience" in *Aesthetic Papers,* No. 1, ed. Elizabeth Peabody (Boston, 1849).

Carried out, it finally amounts to this, which also I believe,—"That government is best which governs not at all"; and when men are prepared for it, that will be the kind of government which they will have. Government is at best but an expedient; but most governments are usually, and all governments are sometimes, inexpedient. The objections which have been brought against a standing army, and they are many and weighty, and deserve to prevail, may also at last be brought against a standing government. The standing army is only an arm of the standing government. The government itself, which is only the mode which the people have chosen to execute their will, is equally liable to be abused and perverted before the people can act through it. Witness the present Mexican war, the work of comparatively a few individuals using the standing government as their tool; for, in the outset, the people would not have consented to this measure.

This American government,—what is it but a tradition, though a recent one, endeavoring to transmit itself unimpaired to posterity, but each instant losing some of its integrity? It has not the vitality and force of a single living man; for a single man can bend it to his will. It is a sort of wooden gun to the people themselves. But it is not the less necessary for this; for the people must have some complicated machinery or other, and hear its din, to satisfy that idea of government which they have. Governments show thus how successfully men can be imposed on, even impose on themselves, for their own advantage. It is excellent, we must all allow. Yet this government never of itself furthered any enterprise, but by the alacrity with which it got out of its way. *It* does not keep the country free. *It* does not settle the West. *It* does not educate. The character inherent in the American people has done all that has been accomplished; and it would have done somewhat more, if the government had not sometimes got in its way. For government is an expedient by which men would fain succeed in letting one another alone; and, as has been said, when it is most expedient, the governed are most let alone by it....

But, to speak practically and as a citizen, unlike those who call themselves no-government men, I ask for, not at once no government, but *at once* a better government. Let every man make known what kind of government would command his respect, and that will be one step toward obtaining it.

After all, the practical reason why, when the power is once in the hands of the people, a majority are permitted, and for a long period continue, to rule is not because they are most likely to be in the right, nor because this seems fairest to the minority, but because they are physically the strongest. But a government in which the majority rule in all cases cannot be based on justice, even as far as men understand it. Can there not be a government in which majorities do not virtually decide right and wrong, but conscience? —in which majorities decide only those questions to which the rule of expediency is applicable? Must the citizen ever for a moment, or in the least degree, resign his conscience to the legislator? Why has every man a conscience, then? I think that we should be men first, and subjects afterward. It is not desirable to cultivate a respect for the law, so much as for the right. The only obligation which I have a right to assume is to do at any time what I think right. It is truly enough said, that a corporation has no conscience; but a corporation of conscientious men is a corporation *with* a conscience. Law never made men a whit more just; and, by means of their respect for it, even the well-disposed are daily made the agents of injustice. A common and natural result of an undue respect for law is, that you may see a file of soldiers, colonel, captain, corporal, privates, powder-monkeys, and all, marching in admirable order over hill and dale to the wars, against their wills, ay, against their common sense and consciences, which makes it very steep marching indeed, and produces a palpitation of the heart. They have no doubt that it is a damnable business in which they are concerned; they are all peaceably inclined. Now, what are they? Men at all? or small movable forts and magazines, at the service of some unscrupulous man in power? ...

He who gives himself entirely to his fellow-men appears to them useless and selfish; but he who gives himself partially to them is pronounced a benefactor and philanthropist.

How does it become a man to behave toward this American government to-day? I answer, that he cannot without disgrace be associated with it. I cannot for an instant recognize that political organization as *my* government which is the *slave's* government also.

All men recognize the right of revolution; that is, the right to refuse allegiance to, and to resist, the government, when its tyranny or its inefficiency are great and unendurable. But almost all say that such is not the case now. But such was the case, they think, in the Revolution of '75. If one were to tell me that this was a bad government because it taxed certain foreign commodities brought to its ports, it is most probable that I should not make an ado about it, for I can do without them. All machines have their friction; and possibly this does enough good to counterbalance the evil. At any rate, it is a great evil to make a stir about it. But when the friction comes to have its machine, and oppression and robbery are organized, I say, let us not have such a machine any longer. In other words, when a sixth of the population of a nation which has undertaken to be the refuge of liberty are slaves, and a whole country is unjustly overrun and conquered by a foreign army, and subjected to military law, I think that it is not too soon for honest men to rebel and revolutionize. What makes this duty the more urgent is the fact that the country so overrun is not our own, but ours is the invading army....

...Practically speaking, the opponents to a reform in Massachusetts are not a hundred thousand politicians at the South, but a hundred thousand merchants and farmers here, who are more interested in commerce and agriculture than they are in humanity, and are not prepared to do justice to the slave and to Mexico, *cost what it may*. I quarrel not with far-off foes, but with those who, near at home, coöperate with, and do the bidding of, those far away, and without whom the latter would be harmless. We are accustomed to say, that the mass of men are unprepared; but improvement is slow, because the few are not materially wiser or better than the many. It is not so important that many should be as good as you, as that there be some absolute goodness somewhere; for that will leaven the whole lump. There are thousands who are *in opinion* opposed to slavery and to the war, who yet in effect do nothing to put an end to them; who, esteeming themselves children of Washington and Franklin, sit down with their hands in their pockets, and say that they know not what to do, and do nothing; who even postpone the question of freedom to the question of free-trade, and quietly read the prices-current along with the latest advices from Mexico, after dinner, and, it may be, fall asleep over them both. What is the price-current of an honest man and patriot to-day? They hesitate, and they regret, and sometimes they petition; but they do nothing in earnest and with effect. They will wait, well disposed, for others to remedy the evil, that they may no longer have it to regret. At most, they give only a cheap vote, and a feeble countenance and God-speed, to the right, as it goes by them. There are nine hundred and ninety-nine patrons of virtue to one virtuous man. But it is easier to deal with the real possessor of a thing than with the temporary guardian of it.

All voting is a sort of gaming, like checkers or backgammon, with a slight moral tinge to it, a playing with right and wrong, with moral questions; and betting naturally accompanies it. The character of the voters is not staked. I cast my vote, perchance, as I think right; but I am not vitally concerned that that right should prevail. I am willing to leave it to the majority. Its obligation, therefore, never exceeds that of expediency. Even voting *for the right* is *doing* nothing for it. It is only expressing to men feebly your desire that it should prevail. A wise man will not leave the right to the mercy of chance, nor wish it to prevail through the power of the majority. There is but little virtue in the action of masses of men. When the majority shall at length vote for the abolition of slavery, it will be because they are indifferent to slavery, or because there is but little slavery left to be abolished by their vote. *They* will then be the only slaves. Only *his* vote can hasten the abolition of slavery who asserts his own freedom by his vote....

As for adopting the ways which the state has provided for remedying the evil, I know not of such ways. They take too much time, and a man's life will be gone. I have other affairs to attend to. I came into this world, not chiefly to make this a good place to live in, but to live in it, be it good or bad. A man has not everything to do, but something; and because he cannot do *everything,* it is not necessary that he should do *something* wrong. It is not my business to be petitioning the Governor or the Legislature any more than it is theirs to petition me; and if they should not hear my petition, what should I do then? But in this case the state has provided no way: its very Constitution is the evil. This may seem to be harsh and stubborn and unconciliatory; but it is to treat with the utmost kindness and consideration the only spirit that can appreciate or deserves it. So is all change for the better, like birth and death, which convulse the body.

I do not hesitate to say, that those who call themselves Abolitionists should at once effectually withdraw their support, both in person and property, from the government of Massachusetts and not wait till they constitute a majority of one, before they suffer the right to prevail through them. I think that it is enough if they have God on their side, without waiting for that other one. Moreover, any man more right than his neighbors constitutes a majority of one already....

Under a government which imprisons any unjustly, the true place for a just man is also a prison. The proper place to-day, the only place which Massachusetts has provided for her freer and less desponding spirits, is in her prisons, to be put out and locked out of the State by her own act, as they have already put themselves out by their principles. It is there that the fugitive slave, and the Mexican prisoner on parole, and the Indian come to plead the wrongs of his race should find them; on that separate, but more free and honorable ground, where the State places those who are not *with* her, but *against* her,— the only house in a slave State in which a free man can abide with honor. If any think that their influence would be lost there, and their voices no longer afflict the ear of the State, that they would not be as an enemy within its walls, they do not know by how much truth is stronger than error, nor how much more eloquently and effectively he can combat injustice who has experienced a little in his own person. Cast your whole vote, not a strip of paper merely, but your whole influence. A minority is powerless while it conforms to the majority; it is not even a minority then; but it is irresistible when it clogs by its whole weight. If the alternative is to keep all just men in prison, or give up war and slavery, the State will not hesitate which to choose. If a thousand men were not to pay their tax-bills this year, that would not be a violent and bloody measure, as it would be to pay them, and enable the State to commit violence and shed innocent blood. This is, in fact, the definition of a peaceable revolution, if any such is possible. If the tax-gatherer, or any other public officer, asks me, as one has done, "But what shall I do?" my answer is, "If you really wish to do anything, resign your office." When the subject has refused allegiance, and the officer has resigned his office, then the revolution is accomplished. But even suppose blood should flow. Is there not a sort of blood shed when the conscience is wounded? Through this wound a man's real manhood and immortality flow out, and he bleeds to an everlasting death....

I have paid no poll-tax for six years. I was put into a jail once on this account, for one night; and, as I stood considering the walls of solid stone, two or three feet thick, the door of wood and iron, a foot thick, and the iron grating which strained the light, I could not help being struck with the foolishness of that institution which treated me as if I were mere flesh and blood and bones, to be locked up. I wondered that it should have concluded at length that this was the best use it could put me to, and had never thought to avail itself of my services in some way. I saw that, if there was a wall of stone between me and my townsmen, there was a still more difficult one to climb or break through before they could get to be as free as I was. I did not for a moment feel confined, and the walls seemed a great waste of stone and mortar. I felt as if I alone of all my townsmen had paid my tax. They plainly did not know how to treat me, but behaved like persons who are underbred. In every threat and in every compliment there was a blunder; for they thought that my chief desire was to stand the other side of that stone wall. I could not but smile to see how industriously they locked the door on my meditations, which followed them out again without let or hindrance, and *they* were really all that was dangerous. As they could not reach me, they had resolved to punish my body; just as boys, if they cannot come at some person against whom they have a spite, will abuse his dog. I saw that the State was half-witted, that it was timid as a lone woman with her silver spoons, and that it did not know its friends from its foes, and I lost all my remaining respect for it, and pitied it....

The authority of government, even such as I am willing to submit to,—for I will cheerfully obey those who know and can do better than I, and in many things even those who neither know nor can do so well,—is still an impure one: to be strictly just, it must have the sanction and consent of the governed. It can have no pure right over my person and property but what I concede to it. The progress from an absolute to a limited monarchy, from a limited monarchy to a democracy, is a progress toward a true respect for the individual. Even the Chinese philosopher was wise enough to regard the individual as the basis of the empire. Is a democracy, such as we know it, the last improvement possible in government? Is it not possible to take a step further towards recognizing and organizing the rights of man? There will never be a really free and enlightened State until the State comes to recognize the individual as a higher and independent power, from which all its own power and authority are derived, and treats him accordingly. I please myself with imagining a State at last which can afford to be just to all men, and to treat the individual with respect as a neighbor; which even would not think it inconsistent with its own repose if a few were to live aloof from it, not meddling with it, nor embraced by it, who fulfilled all the duties of neighbors and fellow-men. A State which bore this kind of fruit, and suffered it to drop off as fast as it ripened, would prepare the way for a still more perfect and glorious State, which also I have imagined, but not yet anywhere seen.

CHARLES FRANKEL

*Is It Ever Right to Break the Law?**

Charles Frankel (b. 1917), professor of philosophy at Columbia University, served as Assistant Secretary of State for Educational and Cultural Affairs from 1965 to 1967. He has engaged in various educational and social organizations or movements and is the author of many papers and books, including *The Faith of Reason, The Case for Modern Man, The Democratic Prospect, The Neglected Aspect of Foreign Affairs,* and *High on Foggy Bottom.*

After giving some examples of instances in the past when the law was broken in the name of moral principles, the author of the following article asks if the individual ever has the right, or perhaps the duty at times, to disobey the law. He goes on to discuss some of the principal issues raised by civil disobedience and to expose some of the more common mistakes that are made when thinking about questions of this kind. Under certain circumstances, Frankel argues, civil disobedience may sometimes be justified.

Our period in history is frequently described as "materialistic" and "conformist," an age in which governments have enormous powers to crush the bodies and anesthetize the minds of their subjects, and in which the great masses of men and women—presumably in contrast with men and women of other times—prefer to play it safe rather than raise questions of basic moral principle. It is to the point to note, however, that massive resistance to law, justified in the name of higher moral principles like "freedom," "equality" and "national independence," has been a conspicuous feature of our period, and one of its most effective techniques of social action. Millions of ordinary people with no pretensions to being either heroes or saints

*Charles Frankel, from "Is It Ever Right to Break the Law?", in *New York Times Magazine,* January 12, 1964, pp. 17, 36, 39, 41. Copyright © 1964 by The New York Times Company. Reprinted by permission of the author and the publisher.

have employed it in India, in South Africa, in the resistance movements against the Nazis and in the struggle for equality for Negroes in the United States.

Moreover, such massive resistance to law is by no means confined only to supremely glorious or dangerous causes; nor is it used only by revolutionaries, underdogs or outsiders. During Prohibition, a large number of respectable, conservative Americans dutifully broke the law in defense of what they regarded as an inalienable human right. In this case, doing one's duty happened also to be agreeable and even fashionable, but this does not change the fact that many right-thinking citizens, who today condemn pacifists or integrationists for using illegal methods to advance their cause, have themselves used such methods happily and unashamedly.

When is it justified, then, for the citizen to act as his own legislator, and to decide that he will or will not obey a given law?

An answer that covers all the issues this question raises cannot be given here, nor can a set of principles be proposed that will allow anyone to make automatic and infallible judgments concerning the legitimacy or illegitimacy of specific acts of civil disobedience. Such judgments require detailed knowledge of the facts of specific cases, and such knowledge is often unavailable to the outsider. Nevertheless, it is possible to indicate some of the principal issues that are raised by civil disobedience, some of the more common mistakes that are made in thinking about these issues, and, at least in outline, the approach that one man would take toward such issues.

We can begin, it seems to me, by rejecting one extreme position. This is the view that disobedience to the law can never be justified in any circumstances. To take this position is to say one or two things: either every law that exists is a just law, or a greater wrong is always done by breaking the law. The first statement is plainly false. The second is highly doubtful. If it is true, then the signers of the Declaration of Independence, and those Germans who refused to carry out Hitler's orders, committed acts of injustice.

It is possible, however, to take a much more moderate and plausible version of this position, and many quite reasonable people do. Such people concede that disobedience to the law can sometimes be legitimate and necessary under a despotic regime. They argue, however, that civil disobedience can never be justified in a democratic society, because such a society provides its members with legal instruments for the redress of their grievances.

This is one of the standard arguments that is made, often quite sincerely, against the activities of people like supporters of the Congress of Racial Equality, who set about changing laws they find objectionable by dramatically breaking them. Such groups are often condemned for risking disorder and for spreading disrespect for the law when, so it is maintained, they could accomplish their goals a great deal more fairly and patriotically by staying within the law, and confining themselves to the courts and to methods of peaceful persuasion.

Now it is perfectly true, I believe, that there is a stronger case for obedience to the law, including bad law, in a democracy than in a dictatorship. The people who must abide by the law have presumably been consulted, and they have legal channels through which to express their protests and to work for reform. One way to define democracy is to say that it is a system whose aim is to provide alternatives to civil disobedience. Nevertheless, when applied to the kind of situation faced, say, by CORE, these generalizations, it seems to me, become cruelly abstract.

The basic fallacy in the proposition that, in a democracy, civil disobedience can never be justified, is that it confuses the *ideals* or *aims* of democracy with the inevitably less than perfect accomplishments of democracy at any given moment. In accordance with democratic ideals, the laws of a democracy may give rights and powers to individuals which, in theory, enable them to work legally for the elimination of injustices.

In actual fact, however, these rights and powers may be empty. The police may be hostile, the courts biased, the elections rigged—and the legal remedies available to the individual may be unavailing against these evils.

Worse still, the majority may have demonstrated, in a series of free and honest elections, that it is unwavering in its support of what the minority regards as an unspeakable evil. This is obviously the case today in many parts of the South, where the white majority is either opposed to desegregation or not so impatient to get on with it as is the Negro minority. Are we prepared to say that majorities never err? If not, there is no absolutely conclusive reason why we must invariably give the results of an election greater weight than considerations of elementary justice.

It is true, of course, that one swallow does not make a summer, and that the test of legal democratic processes is not this or that particular success or failure, but rather the general direction in which these processes move over the long run. Still, the position that violation of the law is never justifiable so long as there are legal alternatives overstates this important truth. It fails to face at least three important exceptions to it.

In the first place, dramatic disobedience to the law by a minority may be the only effective way of catching the attention or winning the support of the majority. Most classic cases of civil disobedience, from the early Christians to Gandhi and his supporters, exemplify this truth. Civil disobedience, like almost no other technique, can shame a majority and make it ask itself just how far it is willing to go, just how seriously it really is committed to defending the status quo.

Second, there is the simple but painful factor of time. If a man is holding you down on a bed of nails, it is all very well for a bystander to say that you live in a great country in which there are legal remedies for your condition, and that you ought, therefore, to be patient and wait for these remedies to take effect. But your willingness to listen to this counsel will depend, quite properly, on the nature of the injury you are suffering.

Third, it is baseless prejudice to assume that observance of the law is *always* conducive to strengthening a democratic system while disobedience to the law can never have a salutary effect. A majority's complacent acquiescence in bad laws can undermine the faith of a minority in the power of democratic methods to rectify manifest evils; yet a vigorous democracy depends on the existence of minorities holding just such a faith.

Disobedience to bad laws can sometimes jolt democratic processes into motion. Which strengthens one's hope for democracy more—the behavior of the Negroes in Birmingham who broke municipal ordinances when they staged their protest marches, or the behavior of the police, using dogs and fire hoses to assert their legal authority? . . .

Civil disobedience is not simply like other acts in which men stand up courageously for their principles. It involves violation of the law. And the law can make no provision for its violation except to hold the offender liable to punishment. This is why President Kennedy was in such a delicate position . . . at the time of the Negro demonstrations in Birmingham. He gave many signs that, as an individual, he was in sympathy with the goals of the demonstrators. As a political leader, he probably realized that these goals could not be attained without dramatic actions that crossed the line into illegality. But as Chief Executive he could not give permission or approval to such actions.

We may admire a man like Martin Luther King, who [was] prepared to defy the authorities in the name of a principle, and we may think that he is entirely in the right; just the same, his right to break the law cannot be officially recognized. No society, whether free or tyrannical, can give its citizens the right to break its laws: To ask it to do so is to ask it to proclaim, as a matter of law, that its laws are not laws.

In short, if anybody ever has a right to break the law, this cannot be a legal right under the law. It has to be a moral right against the law. And this moral right is not an unlimited right to disobey any law which one regards as unjust. It is a right that is hedged about, it seems to me, with important restrictions.

First of all, the exercise of this right is subject to standards of just and fair behavior. I may be correct, for example, in thinking that an ordinance against jaywalking is an unnecessary infringement on my rights. This does not make it reasonable, however, for me to organize a giant sit-down strike in the streets which holds up traffic for a week. Conformity to the concept of justice requires that there be some proportion between the importance of the end one desires to attain and the power of the means one employs to attain it.

When applied to civil disobedience, this principle constitutes a very large restriction. Civil disobedience is an effort to change the law by making it impossible to enforce the law, or by making the price of such enforcement extremely high. It is a case, as it were, of holding the legal system to ransom. It can arouse extreme passions on one side or the other, excite and provoke the unbalanced, and make disrespect for the law a commonplace and popular attitude.

Although violence may be no part of the intention of those who practice civil disobedience, the risks of violence are present, and are part of what must be taken into account when a program of civil disobedience is being contemplated.

In short, civil disobedience is a grave enterprise. It may sometimes be justified, but the provocation for it has to be equally grave. Basic principles have to be at issue. The evils being combated have to be serious evils that are likely to endure unless they are fought. There should be reasonable grounds to believe that legal methods of fighting them are likely to be insufficient by themselves.

Nor is this the only limitation on the individual's moral right to disobey the law. The most important limitation is that his cause must be a just one. It was right for General de Gaulle to disobey Marshal Pétain; it was wrong for the commanders of the French Army in Algeria, twenty years later, to disobey General de Gaulle.

Similarly, if it is absolutely necessary, and if the consequences have been properly weighed, then it is right to break the law in order to eliminate inequalities based on race. But it can never be necessary, and no weighing of consequences can ever make it right, to break the law in the name of Nazi principles.

In sum, the goals of those who disobey the law have to lie at the very heart of what we regard as morality before we can say that they have a moral right to do what they are doing.

But who is to make these difficult decisions? Who is to say that one man's moral principles are right and another man's wrong? We come here to the special function that civil disobedience serves in a society. The man who breaks the law on the ground that the law is immoral asks the rest of us, in effect, to trust him, or to trust those he trusts, in preference to the established conventions and authorities of our society.

He has taken a large and visible chance, and implicitly asked us to join him in taking that chance, on the probity of his personal moral judgment. In doing so, he has put it to us whether we are willing to take a similar chance on the probity of our own judgment.

Thomas Hobbes, who knew the trouble that rebels and dissenters convinced of their rectitude can cause, once remarked that a man may be convinced that God has commanded him to act as he has, but that God, after all, does not command other men to believe that this is so. The man who chooses to disobey the law on grounds of principle may be a saint, but he may also be a madman. He may be a courageous and lonely individualist, but he may also merely be taking orders and following his own crowd. Whatever he may be, however, his existence tends to make us painfully aware that we too are implicitly making choices, and must bear responsibility for the ones we make.

This, indeed, may be the most important function of those who practice civil disobedience. They remind us that the man who obeys the law has as much of an obligation to look into the morality of his acts and the rationality of his society as does the man who breaks the law. The occurrence of civil disobedience can never be a happy phenomenon; when it is justified, something is seriously wrong with the society in which it takes place.

But the man who puts his conscience above the law, though he may be right or he may be wrong, does take personal moral responsibility for the social arrangements under which he lives. And so he dramatizes the fascinating and fearful possibility that those who obey the law might do the same. They might obey the law and support what exists, not out of habit or fear, but because they have freely chosen to do so, and are prepared to live with their consciences after having made that choice.

Aesthetics and Art

C. J. DUCASSE

*Aesthetics and the Aesthetic Activities**

See the biographical note on page 71.

In the following article, Ducasse clarifies the meaning of terms used in discussions of art and aesthetic experience. He goes on to distinguish the three basic aesthetic activities of creation, contemplation, and appreciation, and considers the place of such activities in the life of man. He analyzes the role of philosophy in dealing with art and the aesthetic activities and sees his own article as an example of this role.

From ancient times in the history of thought, man has speculated as to the nature of man. His conceptions of its distinctive essence have been many, but the one most often met with today is that man is *Homo Sapiens* —the animal endowed with reason. This conception, it is true, is rather hard to accept when one observes the countless follies of which human beings are guilty. But then, one should bear in mind that no animal, but only a man, can be a fool; for folly is failure to obey the voice of reason, and is therefore possible only to a being possessed of reason.

Besides reason, however, man obviously also has other capacities—among them, in particular, the capacity for artistic creation and for aesthetic enjoyment. Whether or not it depends on the exercise of the reasoning powers is an interesting question, which I shall not attempt to answer. But it would be raised, if in no other way, by Oscar Wilde's remark that there are two ways of disliking art—one, to dislike it; and the other, to like

*C. J. Ducasse, from "Aesthetics and the Aesthetic Activities," *The Journal of Aesthetics & Art Criticism,* 5 (March, 1947), pp. 165–170, 171–172, 174–176. (Presidential address, read at the third annual meeting of The American Society for Aesthetics, September 6, 1946, at the Chicago Art Institute.) Used by permission of the author and The Society.

it rationally. For there are certain persons—historians, philosophers, critics, and other such addicts of rationality—whose relation to art consists, like mine at this moment, in talking and talking about it rather than in practising it or enjoying its products; and one may therefore well wonder whether they really like art. Certainly, it often looks as if their interest in it were of the same ghoulish sort as that with which an inveterate anatomist might be looking at his friends!

In any case, the fact remains that the idea most of us have of the nature of reason is pretty vague—so vague that, by means of it, we should find it difficult to tell a man from an ape if both looked exactly alike and the ape had the parrot's ability to utter words. It is by what we assume reason does, rather than by an abstract notion of what it is, that we recognize its presence in man. For life, in so far as it is specifically human, is marked by certain kinds of activity of which animals seem incapable or capable only in rudimentary degree; and it is chiefly because we have previously been led to believe man the only rational animal, that we now call rational all the activities peculiar to him. Science evidently is one of them. Philosophy, education, religion, are others. So are manufacture and trade. And, as already noted, art and aesthetic experience constitute still another, as distinctively human as any of the rest.

But to carry further profitably our scrutiny of the relation between the aesthetic activities and the nature of man, we must pause here for a moment to say something as to the meaning of the word "art" and of the adjective "aesthetic," which we have already employed several times and will need to use again in the sequel. For both of these words are commonly employed rather loosely as well as in a variety of senses, and if we do not specify with some precision the meaning we attach to them, misunderstandings and confusion inevitably arise.

"Art," in its most inclusive sense, simply means skill; and skill is ability to control a purposive activity well enough to make it attain its intended purpose. We speak, therefore, not only of the fine and the decorative arts, but also of the practical or useful arts, and of the arts of play. But, when art is mentioned without explicit qualification, what most often is meant is *aesthetic art,* which includes not only painting, sculpture, music, poetry, the theater, and the other fine arts, but also the decorative arts. "Art" in this sense is then the name of a certain sort of *creative activity,* namely, activity that creates objects intended for aesthetic contemplation, no matter whether or not they happen to be also objects of practical use.

The word art, however, is often used also to denote the *products* of such creative activity. But it is better to call these products more explicitly *works* of art, for this distinguishes them at once both from the activity itself, which creates them, and from another category of aesthetic objects, namely those that are products or works not of art but of nature.

As regards now the adjective "aesthetic," we find that it cannot be defined quite as simply. It is true that the French aesthetician, Lalo, has proposed to make it synonymous with "beautiful"; but this is too glaring a violation of the linguistic proprieties to be acceptable, since the word "aesthetic" comes from the Greek *aisthetikos,* which means perceptive or perceptible, capable of being apprehended by the senses. In contemporary usage, the adjective "aesthetic" has come to have a meaning both broader and narrower than this—broader in that it is not restricted to sensory perception; and narrower in that not all sensory perception is called aesthetic. Elucidation of that meaning, however, is possible only in the light of a clear understanding of the nature of a certain psychological attitude commonly called the aesthetic attitude, or aesthetic contemplation.

Various descriptions of it have been given by the many writers that have scrutinized it. Most of these descriptions stress in one way or another that it demands surrender for the time being both of scientific curiosity and of preoccupation with moral or practical considerations. Abstraction from the latter in particular is implied by the metaphor "psychic distance," by which Bullough describes the aesthetic attitude; for, in physical matters, it is distance in time or space that typically bars a person from practical participation in events and forces him into the spectator's position.

But we need to understand not only thus what aesthetic contemplation is not, but also what, positively, it is. It consists in the combination of attention with a certain interest: To contemplate aesthetically an object one attends to is to be at the moment interested in, and as it were to listen for, the particular sensations, feelings, moods, emotions, sentiments, or other *directly intuitable* qualities, which the object exhibits or expresses.

The concept of aesthetic contemplation is of fundamental importance in aesthetics, and it will therefore probably be well to repeat in slightly different and fuller terms the account of it just given in summary form. Attention to an object, then, is aesthetic contemplation in so far as this attention is governed by interest in certain aspects of the object and coupled with receptiveness to them. These aspects are on the one hand the sensible qualities and patterns of qualities, which the object exhibits or perhaps wholly consists of; and on the other, the moods, emotions, sentiments, and other feelings the object expresses. Aesthetic contemplation means, moreover, that the interest one is taking in these aspects of the object is not at the moment scientific or practical interest, but is interest in them for their own sakes—that it is direct and terminal as ordinarily is one's interest in the taste of a piece of candy or in the odor of a rose. Indeed, attentive interest simply in the quality of an odor, or a taste, tone, or color, is itself genuinely aesthetic contemplation, notwithstanding that the object contemplated is then only a very simple one. Aesthetic contemplation,—or for short hereafter, contemplation—is thus not a rare or delicate sort of activity possible only to persons specially gifted. On the contrary, it is one in which all of us engage spontaneously at times—whenever, for instance, we attend to something we are finding beautiful or ugly; or again, whenever we are at the point of reaching a decision of taste.

This brief analysis of aesthetic contemplation was necessary at this place to enable us to clarify the meaning of certain terms, too vague in current usage, which we shall need to employ. One of them is *aesthetic object,* which now we can define as anything taken as object of aesthetic contemplation. Another is *aesthetic feeling,* which means any feeling an object communicates in aesthetic contemplation. Again, the *aesthetic value* of an object is the pleasingness, or the opposite, which it is found to have in aesthetic contemplation. Further, *aesthetic appreciation,* whether analytical or ingenuous, is valuation of an object in terms of the pleasure or displeasure it gives us in the mere contemplation. And *aesthetic art,* we may say, is art—that is, skilled creation—in so far as its products are intended for contemplation rather than for use as implements or as stimuli to curiosity.

Finally, we may now agree that whenever—as for instance in the title of the present address—we speak of *the aesthetic activities,* what we shall be referring to will be three things: one of them, the creating of works of aesthetic art; another, aesthetic contemplation; and the third, aesthetic appreciation—each of these as just characterized.

With these various relatively precise terms at our disposal, let us now return to the question of the place of the aesthetic activities in the life of man. We asserted earlier that they are intrinsic to it, but it might be contended that although only man is capable of them, nevertheless they are accidental rather than essential parts of his life. For after all, the vast majority of human beings never visit museums of art, never participate in or attend symphony concerts or ballets, never read or write poetry, never paint pictures; and yet their lives remain human lives. Hence it might be urged that the aesthetic activities are only a luxury—something it is well enough to have for moments of leisure, but really of little human importance.

To this, however, I must reply that if we call these activities luxuries, then we shall have to redefine man as the animal for whom certain luxuries are necessities. For, in the objection I have just quoted, the basis on which the aesthetic activities were argued to be of little importance in the life of man was far too narrow to support this conclusion.

For one thing, the range of objects aesthetically contemplated and aesthetically enjoyed by human beings comprises not only those to be found in museums, galleries, concert halls, and the like, but a vastly greater number of others—including not only other works of art, but also innumerable things in nature. And, in parenthesis, it may be mentioned that, to the taste of some of us, many works of nature are aesthetically more rewarding to contemplate than are certain works of art.

But further, the works of aesthetic art include much beyond the products of what are commonly called the fine arts; for whenever, in the creating of an object, the maker introduces some feature simply at the behest of his taste, then he is at the moment truly an artist, not just an artisan; and the thing he creates is to that extent truly a work of art, not just an artifact.

Unless this is kept in mind, one cannot get a fair view of the extent to which human beings actually engage in the creating of works of aesthetic art. For a fair view of it, moreover, it is also essential to remember that something may be genuinely a work of aesthetic art and yet be not an ambitious but only a very humble one. And further, one needs to recall again and again that the term "work of art" is not synonymous with "*good* work of art"; for, as pointed out earlier, "work of art" simply means "product of skill," and skill is something that has degrees. Hence it is perfectly possible for something to be truly a work of art, and of aesthetic art, and yet—whether ambitious or humble—to be a poor one rather than a good one.

If now we bear these remarks in mind and look about us, we then perceive innumerable works of aesthetic art, which otherwise would have escaped our notice. Consider, for example, the man who, coming home at the end of his day's work, gets out the lawn mower and painstakingly clips his lawn. Why does he do it? Evidently, because, in the context of houses and streets, he finds the smooth green surface of the close-cut lawn more pleasing to contemplate than would be rough wild grass. Thus, he is devoting time and effort to the end of creating the sort of appearance his taste demands. Hence, even if only at a humble level, he is in so far a creative artist as genuinely as the professional landscape architect, or the mural painter.

But to go even farther, consider that every man who combs his hair or shaves his chin, every woman who paints her face or stains her nails, and every person whose purchase of a garment is determined or influenced by his taste as to colors and shapes, is likewise exercising his taste creatively in the constructing of some particular sort of personal appearance; and in so far making that appearance truly a work of aesthetic art. This remains true irrespective of what may be the factors, social or other, that influence a person's taste, and irrespective also of the social functions, such, perhaps, as sex attraction, which an aesthetically pleasing personal appearance performs.

It is only when one thus takes into account such modest and often rather poor but immensely numerous works of aesthetic art—and not alone the lofty and excellent ones—that he truly realizes how various are the possible media of aesthetic art, how nearly universal is the practice of it, and what enormous amounts of time, effort, and treasure mankind actually devotes to the aesthetic activities. Then, however, the contention that these activities are only an accidental and dispensable feature of human life is seen to be completely untenable. Rather, the inescapable fact is that a life wholly devoid of them would be not human, but only animal.

But my topic is not only the aesthetic activities, but also aesthetics; and to make clear the relation between the two, I must now call attention to another characteristic, in respect to which also man is unique among the animals. Man, namely, is the animal that looks at himself in mirrors! He alone is capable of and interested in observing himself—his physical appearance, his behavior, and his various experiences and activities, mental as well as physical. The human individual is both performer, and spectator of his own performance. He not only thinks, perceives, acts, experiences, wills, feels, desires, and so on, but also watches himself doing so. He is curious about all these manifestations of his life and is capable of studying them, of appraising them, and then to some extent of regulating them.

Among the activities he thus observes in himself are of course those we have called the aesthetic activities, namely, once more, the creation of works of aesthetic art, aesthetic contemplation of them and of other objects, and aesthetic appreciation of the objects contemplated. But what must now be specially emphasized is that to engage concretely in these activities is one thing, and to observe and study them and their products is another and very different thing. The *study* of them is *aesthetics*. It is an intellectual, not an aesthetic activity. It is a manifestation of *curiosity about* the aesthetic activities, but is not itself one of them. This is true even if it is also true that, to be in position to answer some of the questions this curiosity prompts about the aesthetic activities, one must have some time oneself concretely engaged in them....

The task of the philosophical aesthetician, as I conceive it, is... to analyze and state with some precision the objective meaning of the key terms employed in discussions of the aesthetic activities.

But here it might be asked whether it is not up to the psychologist rather than the philosopher to say what, for instance, "aesthetic contemplation" really means. Let us see what the psychologist, proceeding experimentally, would do. He would, we may take it, confront a number of persons with some work of art—say, a painting—and note the responses it actually elicits in them. I happen to have the record of a large number of spontaneous responses so obtained, and, as might be expected, they are of very diverse sorts. One observer liked the painting, which was a farm yard, because it reminded him of a place where he had been happy; another, because he found it a very realistic representation; another, because he liked animals; another, because he thought he had seen that particular farm; another, because the colors were harmonious and bright; another, because the principal objects were in the middle; another, because of the mood it engendered in him; and so on.

But, now that we know how these people actually did respond to a given painting, do we know *eo ipso* what aesthetic contemplation is? Obviously, the question still remains as to *which* of these responses are to be described as *aesthetic* responses, and which as responses of kinds *other than aesthetic.* And, for an answer to *this* question, what we have to observe is evidently something else, namely, language. That is, we have to start from the fact, as a matter of ordinary usage, *some* of the responses would be called aesthetic responses, and others not. And we have then to discover what latent characteristics of them are determining us unawares to call the ones "aesthetic" and to deny this name to the others.

Any answer we offer to this question is a theory of the nature of aesthetic response, i.e., of aesthetic contemplation. It is a conjecture as to what we *mean* when we spontaneously judge a given response to be "aesthetic" response, and a given other non-aesthetic. Moreover, let it be well noted, *anyone* who talks at all about aesthetic contemplation does so on the basis of some assumptions as to its nature. His only choice is as to whether they will remain unconscious, and therefore both vague and dogmatic; or whether on the contrary they will be brought to consciousness, critically scrutinized, and purged of errors and confusions. But since knowledge rather than just opinion is what all branches of aesthetics aim at, the second choice is the one forced upon us; and to do what it demands is the philosopher's task. All other questions of philosophical aesthetics are ultimately of this same general type.

In the light of this description of the nature of philosophical inquiry in matters of aesthetics, it is now evident that we have actually been engaged in it at many points in what has preceded. For example, when we attempted to analyze the meaning of "aesthetic" in the expressions "aesthetic object," "aesthetic feeling," "aesthetic value," and so on. Also, when we analyzed briefly the meaning of the word "art," and that of "aesthetic" art as distinguished from practical and from sportive art. And also, indeed, when we turned from the aesthetic activities themselves to aesthetics; defined the latter as the study of the former; distinguished the principal branches of aesthetics; and defined the nature of each in terms of the types of questions it investigates.

This means that my remarks not only have been *about* aesthetics and the aesthetic activities, but also have themselves constituted an illustration of the nature of the philosopher's own type of activity in the field of aesthetics. But they may thereby perhaps also, in some small measure, have helped to dispel some of the hostilities, confusions, and misunderstandings so common in matters relating to aesthetics. If so, then my remarks will have provided a modest concrete demonstration of the very practical kind of service philosophy is called upon to render in this field. For, it has been rightly said, truth emerges more easily even out of error than it does out of confusion.

GEORGE SANTAYANA

*The Nature of Beauty**

George Santayana (1863–1952), philosopher, poet, literary critic, and novelist, was born in Spain and came to the United States at the age of nine when his family settled in Boston. He obtained his Ph.D. degree from Harvard University in 1886 and returned two years later to teach there until his retirement in 1912. He traveled extensively and settled in Italy where he spent the later years of his life writing. His publications include *The Life of Reason, Skepticism and Animal Faith,* and *Realms of Being (Realm of Essence, Realm of Matter, Realm of Truth,* and *Realm of Spirit).*

The following selection is taken from Santayana's early work that grew out of his lectures on beauty at Harvard. According to Santayana, beauty and the aesthetic experience spring from the emotional or the irrational side of man's nature, rather than from his intellectual and rational faculties. The basis of aesthetic experience and enjoyment is inherent in human nature and grows out of vital interest.

INTRODUCTION

The sense of beauty has a more important place in life than aesthetic theory has ever taken in philosophy. The plastic arts, with poetry and music, are the most conspicuous monuments of this human interest, because they appeal only to contemplation, and yet have attracted to their service, in all civilized ages, an amount of effort, genius, and honour, little inferior to that given to industry, war, or religion. The fine arts, however, where aesthetic feeling appears almost pure, are by no means the only sphere in which men show their susceptibility to beauty. In all products of human industry we notice the keenness with which the eye is attracted to the mere appearance of things: great sacrifices of time and labour are made to it in the most vulgar manufactures; nor does man select his dwelling, his clothes, or his companions without reference to their effect on his aesthetic senses. Of late we have even learned that the forms of many animals are due to the survival by sexual selection of the colours and forms most attractive to the eye. There must therefore be in our nature a very

*George Santayana, from *The Sense of Beauty* (New York: Charles Scribner's Sons, 1896), Introduction and Chapter 1 with omissions.

radical and wide-spread tendency to observe beauty, and to value it. No account of the principles of the mind can be at all adequate that passes over so conspicuous a faculty....

THE PHILOSOPHY OF BEAUTY IS A THEORY OF VALUES

It would be easy to find a definition of beauty that should give in a few words a telling paraphrase of the word. We know on excellent authority that beauty is truth, that it is the expression of the ideal, the symbol of divine perfection, and the sensible manifestation of the good. A litany of these titles of honor might easily be compiled, and repeated in praise of our divinity. Such phrases stimulate thought and give us momentary pleasure, but they hardly bring any permanent enlightenment. A definition that should really define must be nothing less than the exposition of the origin, place, and elements of beauty as an object of human experience. We must learn from it, as far as possible, why, when, and how beauty appears, what conditions an object must fulfill to be beautiful, what elements of our nature make us sensible of beauty, and what the relation is between the constitution of the object and the excitement of our susceptibility. Nothing less will really define beauty or make us understand what aesthetic appreciation is....

The historical titles of our subject may give us a hint towards the beginning of such a definition. Many writers of the last century called the philosophy of beauty *Criticism,* and the word is still retained as the title for the reasoned appreciation of works of art. We could hardly speak, however, of delight in nature as criticism. A sunset is not criticized; it is felt and enjoyed. The word "criticism," used on such an occasion, would emphasize too much the element of deliberate judgment and of comparison with standards. Beauty, although often so described, is seldom so perceived, and all the greatest excellences of nature and art are so far from being approved of by a rule that they themselves furnish the standard and ideal by which critics measure inferior effects.

This age of science and of nomenclature has accordingly adopted a more learned word, *Aesthetics,* that is, the theory of perception or of susceptibility. If criticism is too narrow a word, pointing exclusively to our more artificial judgments, aesthetics seems to be too broad and to include within its sphere all pleasures and pains, if not all perceptions whatsoever. Kant used it, as we know, for his theory of time and space as forms of all perception; and it has at times been narrowed into an equivalent for the philosophy of art.

If we combine, however, the etymological meaning of criticism with that of aesthetics, we shall unite two essential qualities of the theory of beauty. Criticism implies judgment, and aesthetics perception. To get the common ground, that of perceptions which are critical, or judgments which are perceptions, we must widen our notion of deliberate criticism so as to include those judgments of value which are instinctive and immediate, that is, to include pleasures and pains; and at the same time we must narrow our notion of aesthetics so as to exclude all perceptions which are not appreciations, which do not find a value in their objects. We thus reach the sphere of critical or appreciative perception, which is, roughly speaking, what we mean to deal with. And retaining the word "aesthetics," which is now current, we may therefore say that aesthetics is concerned with the perception of values. The meaning and conditions of value is, then, what we must first consider.

Since the days of Descartes it has been a conception familiar to philosophers that every visible event in nature might be explained by previous visible events, and that all the motions, for instance, of the tongue in speech, or of the hand in painting, might have merely physical causes. If consciousness is thus accessory to life and not essential to it, the race of man might have existed upon the earth and acquired all the arts necessary for its subsistence without possessing a single sensation, idea, or emotion. Natural selection might have secured the survival of those automata which made useful reactions upon their environment. An instinct of self-preservation would have been developed, dangers would have been shunned without being feared, and injuries revenged without being felt.

In such a world there might have come to be the most perfect organization. There would have been what we should call the expression of the deepest interests and the apparent pursuit of conceived goods. For there would have been spontaneous and ingrained tendencies to avoid certain contingencies and to produce others; all the dumb show and evidence of thinking would have been patent to the observer. Yet there would surely have been no thinking, no expectation, and no conscious achievement in the whole process.

The onlooker might have feigned ends and objects of forethought, as we do in the case of the water that seeks its own level, or in that of the vacuum which nature abhors. But the particles of matter would have remained unconscious of their collocation, and all nature would have been insensible of their changing arrangement. We only, the possible spectators of that process, by virtue of our own interests and habits, could see any progress or culmination in it. We should see culmination where the result attained satisfied our practical or aesthetic demands, and progress wherever such a satisfaction was approached. But apart from ourselves, and our human bias, we can see in such a mechanical world no element of value whatever. In removing consciousness, we have removed the possibility of worth.

But it is not only in the absence of all consciousness that value would be removed from the world; by a less violent abstraction from the totality of human experience, we might conceive beings of a purely intellectual cast, minds in which the transformations of nature were mirrored without any emotion. Every event would then be noted, its relations would be observed, its recurrence might even be expected; but all this would happen without a shadow of desire, of pleasure, or of regret. No event would be repulsive, no situation terrible. We might, in a word, have a world of idea without a world of will. In this case, as completely as if consciousness were absent altogether, all value and excellence would be gone. So that for the existence of good in any form it is not merely consciousness but emotional consciousness that is needed. Observation will not do, appreciation is required.

PREFERENCE IS ULTIMATELY IRRATIONAL

We may therefore at once assert this axiom, important for all moral philosophy and fatal to certain stubborn incoherences of thought, that there is no value apart from some appreciation of it, and no good apart from some preference of it before its absence or its opposite. In appreciation, in preference, lies the root and essence of all excellence. Or, as Spinoza clearly expresses it, we desire nothing because it is good, but it is good only because we desire it....

Values spring from the immediate and inexplicable reaction of vital impulse, and from the irrational part of our nature. The rational part is by its essence relative; it leads us from data to conclusions, or from parts to wholes; it never furnishes the data with which it works....

It is evident that beauty is a species of value, and what we have said of value in general applies to this particular kind. A first approach to a definition of beauty has therefore been made by the exclusion of all intellectual judgments, all judgments of matter of fact or of relation. To substitute judgments of fact for judgments of value, is a sign of a pedantic and borrowed criticism. If we approach a work of art or nature scientifically, for the sake of its historical connexions or proper classification, we do not approach it aesthetically....

In an opposite direction the same substitution of facts for values makes its appearance, whenever the reproduction of fact is made the sole standard of artistic excellence. Many half-trained observers condemn the work of some naive or fanciful masters with a sneer, because, as they truly say, it is out of drawing. The implication is that to be correctly copied from a model is the prerequisite of all beauty. Correctness is, indeed, an element of effect and one which, in respect to familiar objects, is almost indispensable, because its absence would cause a disappointment and dissatisfaction incompatible with enjoyment. We learn to value truth more and more as our love and knowledge of nature increase. But fidelity is a merit only because it is in this way a factor in our pleasure. It stands on a level with all other ingredients of effect. When a man raises it to a solitary pre-eminence and becomes incapable of appreciating anything else, he betrays the decay of aesthetic capacity. The scientific habit in him inhibits the artistic.

That facts have a value of their own, at once complicates and explains this question. We are naturally pleased by every perception, and recognition and surprise are particularly acute sensations. When we see a striking truth in any imitation, we are therefore delighted, and this kind of pleasure is very legitimate, and enters into the best efforts of all the representative arts. Truth and realism are therefore aesthetically good, but they are not all-sufficient, since the representation of everything is not equally pleasing and effective. The fact that resemblance is a source of satisfaction, justifies the critic in demanding it, while the aesthetic insufficiency of such veracity shows the different value of truth in science and in art. Science is the response to the demand for information, and in it we ask for the whole truth and nothing but the truth. Art is the response to the demand for entertainment, for the stimulation of our senses and imagination, and truth enters into it only as it subserves these ends.

Even the scientific value of truth is not, however, ultimate or absolute. It rests partly on practical, partly on aesthetic interests. As our ideas are gradually brought into conformity with the facts by the painful process of selection,—for intuition runs equally into truth and into error, and can settle nothing if not controlled by experience,—we gain vastly in our command over our environment. This is the fundamental value of natural science, and the fruit it is yielding in our day. We have no better vision of nature and life than some of our predecessors, but we have greater material resources. To know the truth about the composition and history of things is good for this reason. It is also good because of the enlarged horizon it gives us, because the spectacle of nature is a marvellous and fascinating one, full of a serious sadness and large peace, which gives us back our birthright as children of the planet and naturalizes us upon the earth. This is the poetic value of the scientific *Weltanschauung*. From these two benefits, the practical and the imaginative, all the value of truth is derived.

Aesthetic and moral judgments are accordingly to be classed together in contrast to judgments intellectual; they are both judgments of value, while intellectual judgments are judgments of fact. If the latter have any value, it is only derivative, and our whole intellectual life has its only justification in its connexion with our pleasures and pains.

CONTRAST BETWEEN MORAL AND AESTHETIC VALUES

The relation between aesthetic and moral judgments, between the spheres of the beautiful and the good, is close, but the distinction between them is important. One factor of this distinction is that while aesthetic judgments are mainly positive, that is perceptions of good, moral judgments are mainly and fundamentally negative, or perceptions of evil. Another factor of the distinction is that whereas, in the perception of beauty, our judgment is necessarily intrinsic and based on the character of the immediate experience, and never consciously on the idea of an eventual utility in the object, judgments about moral worth, on the contrary, are always based, when they are positive, upon the consciousness of benefits probably involved. Both these distinctions need some elucidation.

Hedonistic ethics have always had to struggle against the moral sense of mankind. Earnest minds, that feel the weight and dignity of life, rebel against the assertion that the aim of right conduct is enjoyment. Pleasure usually appears to them as a temptation, and they sometimes go so far as to make avoidance of it a virtue. The truth is that morality is not mainly concerned with the attainment of pleasure; it is rather concerned, in all its deeper and more authoritative maxims, with the prevention of suffering. There is something artificial in the deliberate pursuit of pleasure; there is something absurd in the obligation to enjoy oneself. We feel no duty in that direction; we take to enjoyment naturally enough after the work of life is done, and the freedom and spontaneity of our pleasures is what is most essential to them.

The sad business of life is rather to escape certain dreadful evils to which our nature exposes us,—death, hunger, disease, weariness, isolation, and contempt. By the awful authority of these things, which stand like spectres behind every moral injunction, conscience in reality speaks, and a mind which they have duly impressed cannot but feel, by contrast, the hopeless triviality of the search for pleasure. It cannot but feel that a life abandoned to amusement and to changing impulse must run unawares into fatal dangers. The moment, however, that society emerges from the early pressure of the environment and is tolerably secure against primary evils, morality grows lax. The forms that life will further assume are not to be imposed by moral authority, but are determined by the genius of the race, the opportunities of the movement, and the tastes and resources of individual minds. The reign of duty gives place to the reign of freedom, and the law and the covenant to the dispensation of grace.

The appreciation of beauty and its embodiment in the arts are activities which belong to our holiday life, when we are redeemed for the moment from the shadow of evil and the slavery to fear, and are following the bent of our nature where it chooses to lead us. The values, then, with which we here deal are positive; they were negative in the sphere of morality. The ugly is hardly an exception, because it is not the cause of any real pain. In itself it is rather a source of amusement. If its suggestions are vitally repulsive, its presence becomes a real evil towards which we assume a practical and moral attitude. And, correspondingly, the pleasant is never, as we have seen, the object of a truly moral injunction....

ALL VALUES ARE IN ONE SENSE AESTHETIC

In this second and subjective sense, then, work is the disparaging term and play the eulogistic one. All who feel the dignity and importance of the things of the imagination, need not hesitate to adopt the classification which designates them as play. We point out thereby, not that they have no value, but that their value is intrinsic, that in them is one of the sources of all worth. Evidently all values must be ultimately intrinsic. The useful is good because of the excellence of its consequences; but these must somewhere cease to be merely useful in their turn, or only excellent as means; somewhere we must reach the good that is good in itself and for its own sake, else the whole process is futile, and the utility of our first object illusory. We here reach the second factor in our distinction between aesthetic and moral values, which regards their immediacy.

If we attempt to remove from life all its evils, as the popular imagination has done at times, we shall find little but aesthetic pleasures remaining to contitute unalloyed happiness. The satisfaction of the passions and the appetites, in which we chiefly place earthly happiness, themselves take on an aesthetic tinge when we remove ideally the possibility of loss or variation. What could the Olympians honor in one another or the seraphim worship in God except the embodiment of eternal attributes, of essences which, like beauty, make us happy only in contemplation? The glory of heaven could not be otherwise symbolized than by light and music. Even the knowledge of truth which the most sober theologians made the essence of the beatific vision, is an aesthetic delight; for when the truth has no further practical utility, it becomes a landscape. The delight of it is imaginative and the value of it aesthetic.

This reduction of all values to immediate appreciations, to sensuous or vital activities, is so inevitable that it has struck even the minds most courageously rationalistic. Only for them, instead of leading to the liberation of aesthetic goods from practical entanglements and their establishment as the only pure and positive values in life, this analysis has led rather to the denial of all pure and positive goods altogether. Such thinkers naturally assume that moral values are intrinsic and supreme; and since these moral values would not arise but for the existence or imminence of physical evils, they embrace the paradox that without good no evil whatever is conceivable.

The harsh requirements of apologetics have no doubt helped them to this position, from which one breath of spring or the sight of one well-begotten creature should be enough to dislodge them. Their ethical temper and the fetters of their imagination forbid them to reconsider their original assumption and to conceive that morality is a means and not an end; that it is the price of human non-adaptation, and the consequence of the original sin of unfitness. It is the compression of human conduct within the narrow limits of the safe and possible. Remove danger, remove pain, remove the occasion of pity, and the need of morality is gone. To say "thou shalt not" would then be an impertinence.

But this elimination of precept would not be a cessation of life. The senses would still be open, the instincts would still operate, and lead all creatures to the haunts and occupations that befitted them. The variety of nature and the infinity of art, with the companionship of our fellows, would fill the leisure of that ideal existence. These are the elements of our positive happiness, the things which, amid a thousand vexations and vanities, make the clear profit of living....

THE DEFINITION OF BEAUTY

We have now reached our definition of beauty, which, in the terms of our successive analysis and narrowing of the conception, is value positive, intrinsic, and objectified. Or, in less technical language, Beauty is pleasure regarded as the quality of a thing.

This defintion is intended to sum up a variety of distinctions and identifications which should perhaps be here more explicitly set down. Beauty is a value, that is, it is not a perception of a matter of fact or of a relation: it is an emotion, an affection of our volitional and appreciative nature. An object cannot be beautiful if it can give pleasure to nobody: a beauty to which all men were forever indifferent is a contradiction in terms.

In the second place, this value is positive, it is the sense of the presence of something good, or (in the case of ugliness) of its absence. It is never the perception of a positive evil, it is never a negative value. That we are endowed with the sense of beauty is a pure gain which brings no evil with it. When the ugly ceases to be amusing or merely uninteresting and becomes disgusting, it becomes indeed a positive evil: but a moral and practical, not an aesthetic one. In aesthetics that saying is true—often so disingenuous in ethics—that evil is nothing but the absence of good: for even the tedium and vulgarity of an existence without beauty is not itself ugly so much as lamentable and degrading. The absence of aesthetic goods is a moral evil: the aesthetic evil is merely relative, and means less of aesthetic good than was expected at the place and time. No form in itself gives pain, although some forms give pain by causing a shock of surprise even when they are really beautiful: as if a mother found a finc bull pup in her child's cradle, when her pain would not be aesthetic in its nature.

Further, this pleasure must not be in the consequence of the utility of the object or event, but in its immediate perception; in other words, beauty is an ultimate good, something that gives satisfaction to a natural function, to some fundamental need or capacity of our minds. Beauty is therefore a positive value that is intrinsic; it is a pleasure. These two circumstances sufficiently separate the sphere of aesthetics from that of ethics. Moral values are generally negative, and always remote. Morality has to do with the avoidance of evil and the pursuit of good: aesthetics only with enjoyment.

Finally, the pleasures of sense are distinguished from the perception of beauty, as sensation in general is distinguished from perception; by the objectification of the elements and their appearance as qualities rather of things than of consciousness. The passage from sensation to perception is gradual, and the path may be sometimes retraced: so it is with beauty and the pleasures of sensation. There is no sharp line between them, but it depends upon the degree of objectivity my feeling has attained at the moment whether I say "It pleases me," or "It is beautiful." If I am self-conscious and critical, I shall probably use one phrase; if I am impulsive and susceptible, the other. The more remote, interwoven, and inextricable the pleasure is, the more objective it will appear; and the union of two pleasures often makes one beauty. In Shakespeare's LIVth sonnet are these words:

> Oh how much more doth beauty beauteous seem
> By that sweet ornament which truth doth give!
> The rose looks fair, but fairer we it deem
> For that sweet odor which doth in it live.
> The canker-blooms have full as deep a dye
> As the perfumèd tincture of the roses,
> Hang on such thorns, and play as wantonly
> When summer's breath their maskèd buds discloses.
> But, for their beauty only is their show,
> They live unwooed and unrespected fade;
> Die to themselves. Sweet roses do not so:
> Of their sweet deaths are sweetest odors made.

One added ornament, we see, turns the deep dye, which was but show and mere sensation before, into an element of beauty and reality; and as truth is here the cooperation of perceptions, so beauty is the cooperation of pleasures. If color, form, and motion are hardly beautiful without the sweetness of the odor, how much more necessary would they be for the sweetness itself to become a beauty! If we had the perfume in a flask, no one would think of calling it beautiful: it would give us too detached and controllable a sensation. There would be no object in which it could be easily incorporated. But let it float from the garden, and it will add another sensuous charm to objects simultaneously recognized, and help to make them beautiful. Thus beauty is constituted by the objectification of pleasure. It is pleasure objectified.

What is History?

CARL L. BECKER

*What Are Historical Facts?**

Carl L. Becker (1873–1945) taught at Pennsylvania State College, Dartmouth, and the University of Kansas before going to Cornell University in 1917 where he taught history for many years. He was the author of essays and books, including *The Heavenly City of the Eighteenth-Century Philosophers, Modern Democracy, New Liberties for Old,* and *How New Will the Better World Be?*

In the following essay, Becker attempts to show that the term "historical facts" is not as simple as first appears. Each fact seems to be tied by innumerable lines of connection to other facts, and may become a symbol whose meaning leads to controversy. History is not just a presentation of the external world; it is in part imaginatively recreated. Five implications of this point of view are presented in this essay.

History is a venerable branch of knowledge, and the writing of history is an art of long standing. Everyone knows what history is, that is, everyone is familiar with the word, and has a confident notion of what it means. In general, history has to do with the thought and action of men and women who lived in past times. Everyone knows what the past is too. We all have a comforting sense that it lies behind us, like a stretch of uneven country we have crossed; and it is often difficult to avoid the notion that one could easily, by turning round, walk back into this country of the past. That, at all events, is what we commonly think of the historian as doing: he works in the past, he explores the past in order to find out what men did and thought in the past. His business is to discover and set forth the "facts" of history.

*Carl L. Becker, from "What Are Historical Facts?" *The Western Political Quarterly,* 8 (September, 1955): 327–329, 330–334, 335–336, 337–340. Used by permission of the publisher.

When anyone says "facts" we are all there. The word gives us a sense of stability. We know where we are when, as we say, we "get down to the facts"—as, for example, we know where we are when we get down to the facts of the structure of the atom, or the incredible movement of the electron as it jumps from one orbit to another. It is the same with history. Historians feel safe when dealing with the facts. We talk much about the "hard facts" and the "cold facts," about "not being able to get around the facts," and about the necessity of basing our narrative on a "solid foundation of fact." By virtue of talking in this way, the facts of history come in the end to seem something solid, something substantial like physical matter (I mean matter in the common sense, not matter defined as "a series of events in the ether"), something possessing definite shape, and clear persistent outline—like bricks or scantlings; so that we can easily picture the historian as he stumbles about in the past, stubbing his toe on the hard facts if he doesn't watch out. That is his affair of course, a danger he runs; for his business is to dig out the facts and pile them up for someone to use. Perhaps he may use them himself; but at all events he must arrange them conveniently so that someone—perhaps the sociologist or the economist—may easily carry them away for use in some structural enterprise.

Such (with no doubt a little, but not much, exaggeration to give point to the matter) are the common connotations of the words historical facts, as used by historians and other people. Now, when I meet a word with which I am entirely unfamiliar, I find it a good plan to look it up in the dictionary and find out what someone thinks it means. But when I have frequently to use words with which everyone is perfectly familiar—words like "cause" and "liberty" and "progress" and "government"—when I have to use words of this sort which everyone knows perfectly well, the wise thing to do is to take a week off and think about them. The result is often astonishing; for as often as not I find that I have been talking about words instead of real things. Well, "historical fact" is such a word; and I suspect it would be worthwhile for us historians at least to think about this word more than we have done. For the moment therefore, leaving the historian moving about in the past piling up the cold facts, I wish to inquire whether the historical fact is really as hard and stable as it is often supposed to be.

And this inquiry I will throw into the form of three simple questions. I will ask the questions, I can't promise to answer them. The questions are: (1) What is the historical fact? (2) Where is the historical fact? (3) When is the historical fact? Mind I say *is* not *was*. I take it for granted that if we are interested in, let us say, the fact of the Magna Carta, we are interested in it for our own sake and not for its sake; and since we are living now and not in 1215 we must be interested in the Magna Carta, if at all, for what it is and not for what it was.

First then, What is the historical fact? Let us take a simple fact, as simple as the historian often deals with, viz.: "In the year 49 B.C. Caesar crossed the Rubicon." A familiar fact this is, known to all, and obviously of some importance since it is mentioned in every history of the great Caesar. But is this fact as simple as it sounds? Has it the clear, persistent outline which we commonly attribute to simple historical facts? When we say that Caesar crossed the Rubicon we do not of course mean that Caesar crossed it alone, but with his army. The Rubicon is a small river, and I don't know how long it took Caesar's army to cross it; but the crossing must surely have been accompanied by many acts and many words and many thoughts of many men. That is to say, a thousand and one lesser "facts" went to make up the one simple fact that Caesar crossed the Rubicon; and if we had someone, say James Joyce, to know and relate all these facts, it would no doubt require a book of 794 pages to present this one fact that Caesar crossed the Rubicon. Thus the simple fact turns out to be not a simple fact at all. It is the statement that is simple—a simple generalization of a thousand and one facts.

Well, anyhow Caesar crossed the Rubicon. But what of it? Many other people at other times crossed the Rubicon. Why charge it up to Caesar? Why for two thousand years has the world treasured this simple fact that in the year 49 B.C. Caesar crossed the Rubicon? What of it indeed? If I, as historian, have nothing to give you but this fact taken by itself with its clear outline, with no fringes or strings tied to it, I should have to say, if I were an honest man, why nothing of it, nothing at all. It may be a fact but it is nothing to us. The truth is, of course, that this simple fact *has* strings tied to it, and that is why it has been treasured for two thousand years. It is tied by these strings to innumerable other facts, so that it can't mean anything except by losing its clear outline. It can't mean anything except as it is absorbed into the complex web of circumstances which brought it into being. This complex web of circumstances was the series of events growing out of the relation of Caesar to Pompey, and the Roman Senate, and the Roman Republic, and all the people who had something to do with these. Caesar had been ordered by the Roman Senate to resign his command of the army in Gaul. He decided to disobey the Roman Senate. Instead of resigning his command, he marched on Rome, gained the mastery of the Republic, and at last, as we are told, bestrode the narrow world like a colossus. Well, the Rubicon happened to be the boundary between Gaul and Italy, so that by the act of crossing the Rubicon with his army Caesar's treason became an accomplished fact and the subsequent great events followed in due course. Apart from these great events and complicated relations, the crossing of the Rubicon means nothing, is not an historical fact properly speaking at all. In itself it is nothing for us; it becomes something for us, not in itself, but as a symbol of something else, a symbol standing for a long series of events which have to do with the most intangible and immaterial realities, viz.: the relation between Caesar and the millions of people of the Roman world.

Thus the simple historical fact turns out to be not a hard, cold something with clear outline, and measurable pressure, like a brick. It is so far as we can know it, only a *symbol,* a simple statement which is a generalization of a thousand and one simpler facts which we do not for the moment care to use, and this generalization itself we cannot use apart from the wider facts and generalizations which it symbolizes. And generally speaking, the more simple an historical fact is, the more clear and definite and provable it is, the less use it is to us in and for itself....

What then is the historical fact? Far be it from me to define so illusive and intangible a thing! But provisionally I will say this: the historian may be interested in anything that has to do with the life of man in the past—any act or event, any emotion which men have expressed, any idea, true or false, which they have entertained. Very well, the historian is interested in some event of this sort. Yet he cannot deal directly with this event itself, since the event itself has disappeared. What he can deal with directly is a *statement about the event.* He deals in short not with the event, but with a statement which affirms *the fact that the event occurred.* When we really get down to the hard facts, what the historian is always dealing with is an *affirmation*—an affirmation of the fact that something is true. There is thus a distinction of capital importance to be made: the distinction between the ephemeral event which disappears, and the affirmation about the event which persists. For all practical purposes it is this affirmation about the event that constitutes for us the historical fact. If so the historical fact is not the past event, but a symbol which enables us to recreate it imaginatively. Of a symbol it is hardly worthwhile to say that it is cold or hard. It is dangerous to say even that it is true or false. The safest thing to say about a symbol is that it is more or less appropriate.

This brings me to the second question—Where is the historical fact? I will say at once, however brash it sounds, that the historical fact is in someone's mind or it is nowhere. To illustrate this statement I will take an event familiar to all. "Abraham Lincoln was assassinated in Ford's Theater in Washington on the 14th of April, 1865." That *was* an actual event, occurrence, fact at the moment of happening. But speaking now... we say it *is* an historical fact. We don't say that it *was* an historical fact, for that would imply that it no longer is one. We say that it *was* an actual event, but *is now* an historical fact. The actual occurrence and the historical fact, however closely connected, are two different things. Very well, if the assassination of Lincoln is an historical fact, where is this fact now? Lincoln is not being assassinated now in Ford's Theater, or anywhere else (except perhaps in propagandist literature!). The actual occurrence, the event, has passed, is gone forever, never to be repeated, never to be again experienced or witnessed by any living person. Yet this is precisely the sort of thing the historian is concerned with—events, acts, thoughts, emotions that have forever vanished as actual occurrences. How can the historian deal with vanished realities? He can deal with them because these vanished realities give place to pale reflections, impalpable images or ideas of themselves, and these pale reflections, and impalpable images which cannot be touched or handled are all that is left of the actual occurrence. These are therefore what the historian deals with. These are his "material." He has to be satisfied with these, for the very good reason that he has nothing else. Well then, where are they—these pale reflections and impalpable images of the actual? Where are these facts? They are, as I said before, in his mind, or in somebody's mind, or they are nowhere.

Ah, but they are in the records, in the sources, I hear someone say. Yes, in a sense, they are in the sources. The historical fact of Lincoln's assassination is in the records—in contemporary newspapers, letters, diaries, etc. In a sense the fact is there, but in what sense? The records are after all only paper, over the surface of which ink has been distributed in certain patterns. And even these patterns were not made by the actual occurrence, the assassination of Lincoln. The patterns are themselves only "histories" of the event, made by someone who had in *his* mind an image or idea of Lincoln's assassination. Of course we, you and I, can, by looking at these inky patterns, form in *our* minds images or ideas more or less like those in the mind of the person who made the patterns. But if there were now no one in the world who could make any meaning out of the patterned records or sources, the fact of Lincoln's assassination would cease to be an historical fact. You might perhaps call it a dead fact; but a fact which is not only dead, but not known ever to have been alive, or even known to be now dead, is surely not much of a fact. At all events, the historical facts lying dead in the records can do nothing good or evil in the world. They become historical facts, capable of doing work, of making a difference, only when someone, you or I, brings them alive in our minds by means of pictures, images, or ideas of the actual occurrence. For this reason I say that the historical fact is in someone's mind, or it is nowhere, because when it is in no one's mind it lies in the records inert, incapable of making a difference in the world.

But perhaps you will say that the assassination of Lincoln has made a difference in the world, and that this difference is now effectively working, even if, for a moment, or an hour or a week, no one in the world has the image of the actual occurrence in mind. Quite obviously so, but why? Quite obviously because after the actual event people remembered it, and because ever since they have continued to remember it, by repeatedly forming images of it in their minds. If the people of the United States had been incapable of enduring memory, for example, like dogs (as I assume;

not being a dog I can't be sure) would the assassination of Lincoln be now doing work in the world, making a difference? If everyone had forgotten the occurrence after forty-eight hours, what difference would the occurrence have made, then or since? It is precisely because people have long memories, and have constantly formed images in their minds of the assassination of Lincoln, that the universe contains the historical fact which persists as well as the actual event which does not persist. It is the persisting historical fact, rather than the ephemeral actual event, which makes a difference to us now; and the historical fact makes a difference only because it is, and so far as it is, in human minds.

Now for the third question—When is the historical fact? If you agree with what has been said (which is extremely doubtful) the answer seems simple enough. If the historical fact is present, imaginatively, in someone's mind, then it is now, a part of the present. But the word present is a slippery word, and the thing itself is worse than the word. The present is an indefinable point in time, gone before you can think it; the image or idea which I have now present in mind slips instantly into the past. But images or ideas of past events are often, perhaps always, inseparable from images or ideas of the future. Take an illustration. I awake this morning, and among the things my memory drags in to enlighten or distress me is a vague notion that there was something I needed particularly to remember but cannot—a common experience surely. What is it that I needed to remember I cannot recall; but I can recall that I made a note of it in order to jog my memory. So I consult my little pocket memorandum book—a little Private Record Office which I carry about, filled with historical sources. I take out my memorandum book in order to do a little historical research; and there I find (Vol. I, p. 20) the dead historical fact—"Pay Smith's coal bill today: $1,016." The image of the memorandum book now drops out of mind, and is replaced by another image—an image of what? Why an image, an idea, a picture (call it what you will) made up of three things more or less inseparable. First the image of myself ordering coal from Smith last summer; second, the image of myself holding the idea in mind that I must pay the bill; third, the image of myself going down to Smith's office at four o'clock to pay it. The image is partly of things done in the past, and partly of things to be done in the future; but it is more or less all one image now present in mind.

Someone may ask, "Are you talking of history or of the ordinary ills of every day that men are heir to?" Well, perhaps Smith's coal bill is only my personal affair, of no concern to anyone else, except Smith to be sure. Take then another example. I am thinking of the Congress of Berlin, and that is without doubt history—the real thing. The historical facts of the Congress of Berlin I bring alive in memory, imaginatively. But I am making an image of the Congress of Berlin for a purpose; and indeed without a purpose no one would take the trouble to bring historical facts to mind. My purpose happens to be to convey this image of the Congress of Berlin to my class in History 42, in Room C, tomorrow afternoon at 3 o'clock. Now I find that inseparable from this image of the Congress of Berlin, which occurred in the past, are flitting images of myself conveying this image of the Congress of Berlin to my class tomorrow in Room C. I picture myself standing there monotonously talking, I hear the labored sentences painfully issuing forth, I picture the students' faces alert or bored as the case may be; so that images of this future event enter into the imagined picture of the Congress of Berlin, a past event; enter into it, coloring and shaping it too, to the end that the performance may do credit to me, or be intelligible to immature minds, or be compressed within the limits of fifty minutes, or to accomplish some other desired end. Well, this living historical fact, this mixed image of the coal bill or the Congress of Berlin—is it past, present, or future? I cannot say. Perhaps it moves with the velocity of light, and is timeless. At all events it is real history to me, which I hope to make convincing and real to Smith, or to the class in Room C.

I have now asked my three questions, and have made some remarks about them all. I don't know whether these remarks will strike you as quite beside the mark, or as merely obvious, or as novel. If there is any novelty in them, it arises, I think, from our inveterate habit of thinking of the world of history as part of the external world, and of historical facts as actual events. In truth the actual past is gone; and the world of history is an intangible world, recreated imaginatively, and present in our minds. If, as I think, this is true, then there are certain important implications growing out of it; and if you are not already exhausted I should like to touch upon a few of these implications. I will present them "firstly," "secondly," and so on, like the points of a sermon, without any attempt at coordination.

One implication is that by no possibility can the historian present in its entirety any actual event, even the simplest. You may think this a commonplace, and I do too; but still it needs to be often repeated because one of the fondest illusions of nineteenth century historians was that the historian, the "scientific" historian, would do just that: he would "present all the facts and let them speak for themselves." The historian would contribute nothing himself, except the sensitive plate of his mind, upon which the objective facts would register their own unimpeachable meaning....

Well, for twenty years I have taken it for granted that no one could [any] longer believe so preposterous an idea. But the notion continues to bob up regularly; and only the other day, riding on the train to the meeting of the Historical Association, Mr. A. J. Beveridge, eminent and honored historian, assured me dogmatically (it would be dogmatically) that the historian has nothing to do but "present all the facts and let them speak for themselves." And so I repeat, what I have been teaching for twenty years, that this notion is preposterous; first, because it is impossible to present all the facts; and second, because even if you could present all the facts the miserable things wouldn't say anything, would say just nothing at all....

...It is the historian who speaks, who imposes a meaning.

A second implication follows from this. It is that the historian cannot eliminate the personal equation. Of course, no one can; not even, I think, the natural scientist. The universe speaks to us only in response to our purpose; and even the most objective constructions, those, let us say, of the theoretical physicist, are not the sole possible constructions, but only such as are found most convenient for some human need or purpose. Nevertheless, the physicist can eliminate the personal equation to a greater extent, or at least in a different way, than the historian, because he deals, as the historian does not, with an external world directly. The physicist presides at the living event, the historian presides only at the inquest of its remains. If I were alone in the universe and gashed my finger on a sharp rock, I could never be certain that there was anything there but my conciousness of the rock and gashed finger. But if ten other men in precisely the same way gash their fingers on the same sharp rock, we can, by comparing impressions, infer that there is something there besides consciousness. There is an external world there. The physicist can gash his finger on the rock as many times as he likes, and get others to do it, until they are all certain of the facts. He can, as Eddington says, make pointer-readings of the behavior of the physical world as many times as he likes for a given phenomenon, until he and his colleagues are satisfied. When their minds all rest satisfied they have an explanation, what is called the truth. But suppose the physicist had to reach his conclusions from miscellaneous records, made by all sorts of people, of experiments that had been made in the past, each experiment made only once, and none of them capable of being repeated. The external world he would then have to deal with would be the records. That is the case of the historian. The only external world he has to deal with is the records. He can indeed look at the records as often as he likes, and he can get dozens of others to look at them: and some things, some "facts," can in this way be established and agreed upon, as, for example, the fact that the document known as the Declaration of Independence was voted on July 4, 1776. But the meaning and significance of this fact cannot be thus agreed upon, because the series of events in which it has a place cannot be enacted again and again, under varying conditions, in order to see what effect the variations would have. The historian has to judge the significance of the series of events from the one single performance, never to be repeated, and never, since the records are incomplete and imperfect, capable of being fully known or fully affirmed. Thus into the imagined facts and their meaning there enters the personal equation. The history of any event is never precisely the same thing to two different persons; and it is well known that every generation writes the same history in a new way, and puts upon it a new construction....

A third implication is that no one can profit by historical research, or not much, unless he does some for himself. Historical knowledge, however richly stored in books or in the minds of professors of history, is no good to me unless I have some of it. In this respect, historical research differs profoundly from research in the natural sciences, at least in some of them. For example, I know no physics, but I profit from physical researches every night by the simple act of pressing an electric light button. And everyone can profit in this way from researches in physics without knowing any physics, without knowing even that there is such a thing as physics. But with history it is different. Henry Ford, for example, can't profit from all the historical researches of two thousand years, because he knows so little history himself. By no pressing of any button can he flood the spare rooms of his mind with the light of human experience.

A fourth implication is more important than the others. It is that every normal person does know some history, a good deal in fact. Of course we often hear someone say: "I don't know any history; I wish I knew some history; I must improve my mind by learning some history." We know what is meant. This person means that he has never read any history books, or studied history in college; and so he thinks he knows no history. But it is precisely this conventional notion of history as something external to us, as a body of dull knowledge locked up in books, that obscures its real meaning. For, I repeat (it will bear repeating) every normal person—every man, woman, and child—does know some history, enough for his immediate purposes; otherwise he would be a lost soul indeed. I suppose myself, for example, to have awakened this morning with loss of memory. I am all right otherwise; but I can't remember anything that happened in the past. What is the result? The result is that I don't know who I am, where I am, where to go, or what to do. I can't attend to my duties at the university, I can't read this paper before the Research Club. In short, my present would be unintelligible and my future meaningless. Why? Why, because I had suddenly ceased to know any history. What happens when I wake up in the morning is that my memory reaches out into the past and gathers together those images of past events, of objects seen, of words spoken and of thoughts thought in the past, which are necessary to give me an ordered world to live in, necessary to orient me in my personal world. Well, this collection of images and ideas of things past in history, my command of living history, a series of images of the past which shifts and reforms at every moment of the day in response to the exigencies of my daily living. Every man has a knowledge of history in this sense, which is the only vital sense in which he can have a knowledge of history. Every man has some knowledge of past events, more or less accurate; knowledge enough, and accurate enough, for his purposes, or what he regards as such. How much and how accurate, will depend on the man and his purposes. Now, the point is that history in the formal sense, history as we commonly think of it, is only an extension of memory. Knowledge or history, insofar as it is living history and not dead knowledge locked up in notebooks, is only an enrichment of our minds with the multiplied images of events, places, peoples, ideas, emotions outside our personal experience, an enrichment of our experience by bringing into our minds memories of the experience of the community, the nation, the race. Its chief value, for the individual, is doubtless that it enables a man to orient himself in a larger world than the merely personal, has the effect for him of placing the petty and intolerable present in a longer perspective, thus enabling him to judge the acts and thoughts of men, his own included, on the basis of an experience less immediate and restricted.

A fifth implication is that the kind of history that has most influence upon the life of the community and the course of events is the history that common men carry around in their heads. It won't do to say that history has no influence upon the course of events because people refuse to read history books. Whether the general run of people read history books or not, they inevitably picture the past in some fashion or other, and this picture, however little it corresponds to the real past, helps to determine their ideas about politics and society. This is especially true in times of excitement, in critical times, in time of war above all. It is precisely in such times that they form (with the efficient help of official propaganda!) an idealized picture of the past, born of their emotions and desires working on fragmentary scraps of knowledge gathered, or rather flowing in upon them, from every conceivable source, reliable or not matters nothing. Doubtless the proper function of erudite historical research is to be forever correcting the common image of the past by bringing it to the test of reliable information. But the professional historian will never get his own chastened and corrected image of the past into common minds if no one reads his books. His books may be as solid as you like, but their social influence will be nil if people do not read them and not merely read them, but read them willingly and with understanding.

ARNOLD J. TOYNBEE

*Does History Repeat Itself?**

Arnold J. Toynbee (1889-1975) was a famous English historian whose *Study of History* appeared in twelve volumes between 1934 and 1960. This work deals with the origin, growth, and breakdown of the known civilizations (sixteen to twenty-one of them, depending on the definition). Educated at Oxford, he became a fellow and tutor in ancient history. From 1925 until his retirement in 1955 he was research professor and director of studies at the Royal Institute of International Affairs in London. Besides *A Study of History,* his writings include *Greek Civilization and Character, An Historian's Approach to Religion* and *The World and the West.*

The selection below, from Toynbee's book of essays, raises questions about the prospects for the future of our civilization. Other civilizations have declined; is there anything to prevent Western civilization from following historical precedent and committing social suicide? What must we do to avoid that fate? Can our technical "know-how" save us?

Does history repeat itself? In our Western world in the eighteenth and nineteenth centuries, this question used to be debated as an academic exercise. The spell of well-being which our civilization was enjoying at the time had dazzled our grandfathers into the quaint pharisaical notion that they were "not as other men are"; they had come to believe that our Western society was exempt from the possibility of falling into those mistakes and mishaps that have been the ruin of certain other civilizations whose history, from beginning to end, is an open book. To us, in our generation, the old question has rather suddenly taken on a new and very practical significance. We have awakened to the truth (how, one wonders, could we ever have been blind to it?) that Western man and his works are no more invulnerable than the now extinct civilizations of the Aztecs and the Incas, the Sumerians and the Hittites. So to-day, with some anxiety, we are searching the scriptures of the past to find out whether they contain a lesson that we can decipher. Does history give us any information about our own prospects? And, if it does, what is the burden of it? Does it spell out for us an inexorable doom, which we can merely await with folded hands—resigning

*Arnold J. Toynbee, from *Civilization on Trial* (New York: Oxford University Press, 1948), Chapters 2 and 3 with omissions. Used by permission of the publisher.

ourselves, as best we may, to a fate that we cannot avert or even modify by our own efforts? Or does it inform us, not of certainties, but of probabilities, or bare possibilities, in our own future? The practical difference is vast, for, on this second alternative, so far from being stunned into passivity, we should be roused to action. On this second alternative, the lesson of history would not be like an astrologer's horoscope; it would be like a navigator's chart, which affords the seafarer who has the intelligence to use it a much greater hope of avoiding shipwreck than when he was sailing blind, because it gives him the means, if he has the skill and courage to use them, of steering a course between charted rocks and reefs.

It will be seen that our question needs defining before we plunge into an attempt to answer it. When we ask ourselves "Does history repeat itself?" do we mean no more than "Does history turn out to have repeated itself, on occasions, in the past?" Or are we asking whether history is governed by inviolable laws which have not only taken effect in every past case to which they have applied but are also bound to take effect in every similar situation that may arise in the future? On this second interpretation, the word "does" would mean "must"; on the other interpretation it would mean "may." On this issue, the writer of the present article may as well put his cards on the table at once. He is not a determinist in his reading of the riddle of human life. He believes that where there is life there is hope, and that, with God's help, man is master of his own destiny, at least to some extent in some respects.

But as soon as we have taken our stand on this issue between freedom and necessity that is raised by the ambiguous word "does," we find ourselves called upon to define what we mean by the word "history." If we have to limit the field of history to events that are wholly within the control of human wills, then, to be sure, for a non-determinist no difficulty would arise. But do such events ever actually occur in real life? In our personal experience, when we are making a decision, do we not always find ourselves only partly free and partly bound by past events and present facts in our own life and in our social and physical environment? Is not history itself, in the last analysis, a vision of the whole universe on the move in the four-dimensional framework of space-time? And, in this all-embracing panorama, are there not many events that the most staunch believer in the freedom of the human will would admit, as readily as the most thoroughgoing determinist, to be inexorably recurrent and precisely predictable?

Some events of this undisputedly recurrent predictable order may have little apparent bearing upon human affairs—as, for example, the repetitions of history in nebulae outside the system of the Milky Way. There are, however, some very obvious cyclic movements in physical nature that do affect human affairs in the most intimate fashion—as, for example, the recurrent predictable alternations of day and night and of the seasons of the year. The day-and-night cycle governs all human work; it dictates the schedules of the transporation systems of our cities, sets the times of their rush hours, and weighs on the minds of the commuters whom it shuttles to and fro, twice in every twenty-four hours, between "dormitory" and "workshop." The cycle of the seasons governs human life itself by governing our food supply.

It is true that man, by taking thought, can win a measure of freedom from these physical cycles that is beyond the reach of birds and beasts. Though the individual cannot break the tyranny of the day-and-night cycle by leading a waking life for twenty-four hours in the day, like the legendary Egyptian Pharaoh Mycerinus, human society can achieve Mycerinus' mythical feat collectively by a planned co-operation and a division of labour. Industrial plants can be operated for twenty-four hours in the day by successive shifts of workers, and the labours of workers who work by day can be prepared for and be followed up by the labours of other workers who rest by day and work by night. The tyranny of the seasons, again, has been broken by a Western society that has expanded from the northern temperate zone into the tropics and the southern temperate zone and has devised a technique of refrigeration. Nevertheless, these triumphs of man's mind and will over the tyranny of the two physical cycles of the day and the year are comparatively small gains for human freedom, remarkable though these triumphs are. On the whole, these recurrent predictable events in physical nature remain masters of human life—even at the present level of Western man's technology—and they show their mastery by subduing human affairs, as far as their empire over them extends, to their own recurrent predictable pattern....

In the formation, in the modern Western world, of a number of federal unions, and in the industrialization of these and other countries, we see history repeating itself in the sense of producing a number of more or less contemporary examples of the same human achievement. The contemporaneity of the different instances is, however, no more than approximate. The industrial revolution occurred as an apparently unique event in Great Britain at least two generations before its occurrence in America, and Germany proved it to be a repetitive phenomenon. The insecurely welded pre-Civil-War United States had existed for "four score and seven years," and the ramshackle post-Napoleonic German Confederation for half a century, before the crucial events of the eighteen-sixties proved that federal union was a repetitive pattern which was to recur not only in Canada but in Australia, South Africa, and Brazil. Contemporaneity is not an essential condition for the repetition of history on the political and cultural plane of human affairs. The historical events that repeat themselves may be strictly contemporary or they may overlap in time or they may be entirely non-contemporaneous with one another.

The picture remains the same when we turn to the consideration of the greatest human institutions and experiences that are known to us: the civilizations in their births and growths, their breakdowns, declines, and falls; the higher religions in their foundation and evolution. Measured by our subjective personal measuring rod of the average span of the memory of a single human being who lives to a normal old age, the time interval that divides our present generation from the date of the emergence of the Sumerian civilization in the fourth millennium B.C. or from the date of the beginning of the Christian era itself seems, no doubt, a very long one. Yet it is infinitesimally small on the objective time scale that has recently been given to us by the discoveries of our geologists and astronomers. Our modern Western physical science tells us that the human race has been in existence on this planet for at least 600,000 and perhaps a million years, life for at least 500 million and perhaps 800 million years, and the planet itself for possibly 2000 million years. On this time scale the last five or six thousand years that have seen the births of civilizations, and the last three or four thousand years that have seen the births of higher religions are periods of such infinitesimal brevity that it would be impossible to show them, drawn to scale, on any chart of the whole history of this planet up to date. On this true time scale, these events of "ancient history" are virtually contemporary with our own lifetime, however remote they may appear to be when viewed through the magnifying lens of the individual human midget's subjective mental vision.

The conclusion seems to be that human history does turn out, on occasions, to have repeated itself up to date in a significant sense even in spheres of human activity in which the human will is at its nearest to being master of the situation and is least under domination of cycles in physical nature. Must we go on to conclude that, after all, the determinists are right and that what looks like free will is an illusion? In the present writer's opinion, the correct conclusion is just the opposite. As he sees it, this tendency towards repetition, which thus asserts itself in human affairs, is an instance of one of the well-known devices of the creative faculty. The works of creation are apt to occur in bunches: a bunch of representatives of a species, a bunch of species of a genus. And the value of such repetitions is, after all, not difficult to discern. Creation could hardly make any headway at all if each new form of creature were not represented by numerous eggs distributed among numerous baskets. How else could a creator, human or divine, provide himself with sufficient materials for bold and fruitful experiment and with effective means of retrieving inevitable failures? If human history repeats itself, it does so in accordance with the general rhythm of the universe; but the significance of this pattern of repetition lies in the scope that it gives for the work of creation to go forward. In this light, the repetitive element in history reveals itself as an instrument for freedom of creative action, and not as an indication that God and man are the slaves of fate.

What is the bearing of these conclusions about history in general on the particular question of the prospects of our Western civilization? As we observed at the beginning of this paper, the Western world has become rather suddenly very anxious about its own future, and our anxiety is a natural reaction to the formidableness of the situation in which we now find ourselves. Our present situation is formidable indeed. A survey of the historical landscape in the light of our existing knowledge shows that, up to date, history has repeated itself about twenty times in producing human societies of the species to which our Western society belongs, and it also shows that, with the possible exception of our own, all these representatives of the species of society called civilizations are already dead or moribund. Moreover, when we study the histories of these dead and moribund civilizations in detail, and compare them with one another, we find indications of what looks like a recurring pattern in the process of their breakdowns, declines, and falls. We are naturally asking ourselves to-day whether this particular chapter of history is bound to repeat itself in our case. Is that pattern of decline and fall in store for us in our turn, as a doom from which no civilization can hope to escape? In the writer's opinion, the answer to this question is emphatically in the negative. The effort to create a new manifestation of life—be it a new species of mollusc or a new species of human society—seldom or never succeeds at the first attempt. Creation is not so easy an enterprise as that. It wins its ultimate successes through a process of trial and error; and accordingly the failure of previous experiments, so far from dooming subsequent experiments to fail in their turn in the same way, actually offers them their opportunity of achieving success through the wisdom that can be gained from suffering. Of course a series of previous failures does not guarantee success to the next comer, any more than it condemns him to be a failure in his turn. There is nothing to prevent our Western civilization from following historical precedent, if it chooses, by committing social suicide. But we are not doomed to make history repeat itself; it is open to us, through our own efforts, to give history, in our case, some new and unprecedented turn. As human beings, we are endowed with this freedom of choice, and we cannot shuffle off our responsibility upon the shoulders of God or nature. We must shoulder it ourselves. It is up to us.

What shall we do to be saved? In politics, establish a constitutional co-operative system of world government. In economics, find working compromises (varying according to the practical requirements of different places and times) between free enterprise and socialism. In the life of the spirit, put the secular super-structure back onto religious foundations. Efforts are being made in our Western world to-day to find our way towards each of these goals. If we had arrived at all three of them, we might fairly feel that we had won our present battle for our civilization's survival. But these are, all of them, ambitious undertakings, and it will call for the hardest work and the highest courage to make any progress at all towards carrying any one of them through to achievement.

Of the three tasks, the religious one is, of course, in the long run by far the most important, but the other two are the more urgent, because, if we were to fail in these in the short run, we might lose for ever our opportunity of achieving a spiritual rebirth which cannot just be whistled for at our convenience, but will only come, if it comes at all, at the unhurrying pace at which the deepest tides of spiritual creation flow.

The political task is the most urgent of all. The immediate problem here is a negative one. Faced, as we are, with the prospect that—given our present interdependence and present weapons—the world is now on the eve of being unified politically by one means or another, we have to stave off the disastrous dénouement of unification by force of arms: the familiar method of the forcible imposition of a *Pax Romana* which is probably the line of least resistance for the resolution of the formidable political forces in whose grip our own world finds itself to-day. Can the United States and the other Western countries manage to co-operate with the Soviet Union through the United Nations? If the United Nations organization could grow into an effective system of world government, that would be much the best solution of our political crux. But we have to reckon with the possibility of this enterprise's failing, and to be ready, should it fail, with an alternative to fall back upon. Could the United Nations split, *de facto,* into two groups without a breach of the peace? And, supposing that the whole face of the planet could be partitioned peacefully into an American and a Russian sphere, could two worlds on one planet live side by side on a footing of "non-violent non-co-operation" for long enough to give a chance for a gradual mitigation of the present differences in their social and ideological climates? The answer to this question would depend on whether, on these terms, we could buy the time needed to carry out our economic task of finding a middle way between free enterprise and socialism.

These riddles may be hard to read, but they do tell us plainly what we most need to know. They tell us that our future largely depends upon ourselves. We are not just at the mercy of an inexorable fate.

The Aims of Education

JOHN DEWEY

*Traditional vs. Progressive Education**

John Dewey (1859–1952) graduated from the University of Vermont and later received his Ph.D. degree from Johns Hopkins University. After teaching at the universities of Michigan, Minnesota, and Chicago, he taught from 1904 until his retirement in 1930 at Columbia University. His influence spread throughout the world, and he lectured in many countries, including China, Turkey, Mexico, and Russia. A bibliography of his writings runs to more than 150 pages. In addition to the various fields of philosophy, his interests included democracy and politics, education, science, and art.

The contrast between traditional and progressive education has been a topic of controversy for some decades. In the following selection, Dewey, the leader of the Progressive Education Movement, states the issue from his point of view.

Mankind likes to think in terms of extreme opposites. It is given to formulating its beliefs in terms of *Either-Ors,* between which it recognizes no intermediate possibilities. When forced to recognize that the extremes cannot be acted upon, it is still inclined to hold that they are all right in theory but that when it comes to practical matters circumstances compel us to compromise. Educational philosophy is no exception. The history of educational theory is marked by opposition between the idea that education is development from within and that it is formation from without; that it is based upon natural endowments and that education is a process of overcoming natural inclination and substituting in its place habits acquired under external pressure.

At present, the opposition, so far as practical affairs of the school are concerned, tends to take the form of contrast between traditional and

*John Dewey, from *Experience and Education* (New York: Macmillan Company, 1938), pages 1–17 with omissions. Reprinted by permission of the publisher.

progressive education. If the underlying ideas of the former are formulated broadly, without the qualifications required for accurate statement, they are found to be about as follows: The subject-matter of education consists of bodies of information and of skills that have been worked out in the past; therefore, the chief business of the school is to transmit them to the new generation. In the past, there have also been developed standards and rules of conduct; moral training consists in forming habits of action in conformity with these rules and standards. Finally, the general pattern of school organization (by which I mean the relations of pupils to one another and to the teachers) constitutes the school a kind of institution sharply marked off from other social institutions. Call up in imagination the ordinary schoolroom, its time-schedules, schemes of classification, of examination and promotion, of rules of order, and I think you will grasp what is meant by "pattern of organization." If then you contrast this scene with what goes on in the family, for example, you will appreciate what is meant by the school being a kind of institution sharply marked off from any other form of social organization.

The three characteristics just mentioned fix the aims and methods of instruction and discipline. The main purpose or objective is to prepare the young for future responsibilities and for success in life, by means of acquisition of the organized bodies of information and prepared forms of skill which comprehend the material of instruction. Since the subject-matter as well as standards of proper conduct are handed down from the past, the attitude of pupils must, upon the whole, be one of docility, receptivity, and obedience. Books, especially textbooks, are the chief representatives of the lore and wisdom of the past, while teachers are the organs through which pupils are brought into effective connection with the material. Teachers are the agents through which knowledge and skills are communicated and rules of conduct enforced.

I have not made this brief summary for the purpose of criticizing the underlying philosophy. The rise of what is called new education and progressive schools is of itself a product of discontent with traditional education. In effect it is a criticism of the latter. When the implied criticism is made explicit it reads somewhat as follows: The traditional scheme is, in essence, one of imposition from above and from outside. It imposes adult standards, subject-matter, and methods upon those who are only growing slowly toward maturity. The gap is so great that the required subject-matter, the methods of learning and of behaving are foreign to the existing capacities of the young. They are beyond the reach of the experience the young learners already possess. Consequently, they must be imposed; even though good teachers will use devices of art to cover up the imposition so as to relieve it of obviously brutal features.

But the gulf between the mature or adult products and the experience and abilities of the young is so wide that the very situation forbids much active participation by pupils in the development of what is taught. Theirs is to do—and learn, as it was the part of the six hundred to do and die. Learning here means acquisition of what already is incorporated in books and in the heads of the elders. Moreover, that which is taught is thought of as essentially static. It is taught as a finished product, with little regard either to the ways in which it was originally built up or to changes that will surely occur in the future. It is to a large extent the cultural product of societies that assumed the future would be much like the past, and yet it is used as educational food in a society where change is the rule, not the exception.

If one attempts to formulate the philosophy of education implicit in the practices of the new education, we may, I think, discover certain common principles amid the variety of progressive schools now existing. To imposition from above is opposed expression and cultivation of individuality; to external discipline is opposed free activity; to learning from texts and teachers, learning through experience; to acquisition of isolated skills and techniques by drill, is opposed acquisition of them as means of attaining ends which make direct vital appeal; to preparation for a more or less remote future is opposed making the most of the opportunities of present life; to static aims and materials is opposed acquaintance with a changing world....

It is not too much to say that an educational philosophy which professes to be based on the idea of freedom may become as dogmatic as ever was the traditional education which is reacted against. For any theory and set of practices is dogmatic which is not based upon critical examination of its own underlying principles. Let us say that the new education emphasizes the freedom of the learner. Very well. A problem is now set. What does freedom mean and what are the conditions under which it is capable of realization? Let us say that the kind of external imposition which was so common in the traditional school limited rather than promoted the intellectual and moral development of the young. Again, very well. Recognition of this serious defect sets a problem. Just what is the role of the teacher and of books in promoting the educational development of the immature? Admit that traditional education employed as the subject-matter for study facts and ideas so bound up with the past as to give little help in dealing with the issues of the present and future. Very well. Now we have the problem of discovering the connection which actually exists *within* experience between the achievements of the past and the issues of the present. We have the problem of ascertaining how acquaintance with the past may be translated into a potent instrumentality for dealing effectively with the future. We may reject knowledge of the past as the *end* of education and thereby only emphasize its importance as a *means*. When we do that we have a problem that is new in the story of education: How shall the young become acquainted with the past in such a way that the acquaintance is a potent agent in appreciation of the living present? . . .

The belief that all genuine education comes about through experience does not mean that all experiences are genuinely or equally educative. Experience and education cannot be directly equated to each other. For some experiences are mis-educative. Any experience is mis-educative that has the effect of arresting or distorting the growth of further experience. An experience may be such as to engender callousness; it may produce lack of sensitivity and of responsiveness. Then the possibilities of having richer experience in the future are restricted. Again, a given experience may increase a person's automatic skill in a particular direction and yet tend to land him in a groove or rut; the effect again is to narrow the field of further experience. An experience may be immediately enjoyable and yet promote the formation of a slack and careless attitude; this attitude then operates to modify the quality of subsequent experiences so as to prevent a person from getting out of them what they have to give. Again, experiences may be so disconnected from one another that, while each is agreeable or even exciting in itself, they are not linked cumulatively to one another. Energy is then dissipated and a person becomes scatter-brained. Each experience may be lively, vivid, and "interesting," and yet their disconnectedness may artificially generate dispersive, disintegrated, centrifugal habits. The consequence of formation of such habits is inability to control future experiences. They are then taken, either by way of enjoyment or of discontent and revolt, just as they come. Under such circumstances, it is idle to talk of self-control.

Traditional education offers a plethora of examples of experiences of the kinds just mentioned. It is a great mistake to suppose, even tacitly, that the traditional schoolroom was not a place in which pupils had experiences. Yet this is tacitly assumed when progressive education as a plan of learning by experiences is placed in sharp opposition to the old. The proper line of attack is that the experiences which were had, by pupils and teachers alike, were largely of a wrong kind. How many students, for example, were rendered callous to ideas, and how may lost the impetus to learn because of the way in which learning was experienced by them? How many acquired special skills by means of automatic drill so that their power of judgment and capacity to act intelligently in new situations was limited? How many came to associate the learning process with ennui and boredom? How many found what they did learn so foreign to the situations of life outside the school as to give them no power of control over the latter? How many came to associate books with dull drudgery, so that they were "conditioned" to all but flashy reading matter?

If I ask these questions, it is not for the sake of wholesale condemnation of the old education. It is for quite another purpose. It is to emphasize the fact, first, that young people in traditional schools do have experiences; and, secondly, that the trouble is not the absence of experiences, but their defective and wrong character—wrong and defective from the standpoint of connection with further experience. The positive side of this point is even more important in connection with progressive education. It is not enough to insist upon the necessity of experience, nor even of activity in experience. Everything depends upon the *quality* of the experience which is had. The quality of any experience has two aspects. There is an immediate aspect of agreeableness or disagreeableness, and there is its influence upon later experiences. The first is obvious and easy to judge. The *effect* of an experience is not borne on its face. It sets a problem to the educator. It is his business to arrange for the kind of experiences which, while they do not repel the student, but rather engage his activities are, nevertheless, more than immediately enjoyable since they promote having desirable future experiences. Just as no man lives or dies to himself, so no experience lives and dies to itself. Wholly independent of desire or intent, every experience lives on in further experiences. Hence the central problem of an education based upon experience is to select the kind of present experiences that live fruitfully and creatively in subsequent experiences.

JAMES A. MICHENER

*When Does Education Stop?**

James A. Michener (b. 1907) has engaged in a wide range of activities including research, teaching, and governmental posts. He has received the Pulitzer Prize for fiction and is most widely known for his many essays and novels. His books include *Tales of the South Pacific, Hawaii,* and *The Source.*

In the following essay, an outstanding writer is interviewed by a student seeking help on a three-thousand-word term paper on the writer's books. The conversation soon turns to the kind of education young persons must seek in order to face great challenges and make real contributions in life.

During the summer vacation a fine-looking young man, who was majoring in literature at a top university, asked for an interview, and before we had talked for five minutes, he launched into his complaint.

*James A. Michener, "When Does Education Stop?" Copyright © 1962 by Reader's Digest Association, Inc. Copyright 1973 by Random House, Inc. and the Reader's Digest Association, Inc. Reprinted from *A Michener Miscellany: 1950–1970,* by James A. Michener, by permission of Random House, Inc.

"Can you imagine?" he lamented. "During vacation I have to write a three-thousand-word term paper about your books." He felt very sorry for himself.

His whimpering irritated me, and on the spur of the moment I shoved at him a card which had become famous in World War II. It was once used on me while I was "bitching" to a chaplain on Guadalcanal. It read:

Young man, your sad story
is truly heartbreaking.
Excuse me while I fetch a
crying towel.

My complaining visitor reacted as I had done twenty years earlier. He burst into laughter and asked, "Did I sound that bad?"

"Worse!" I snapped. Then I pointed to a novel of mine which he was using as the basis for his term paper. "You're bellyaching about a three-thousand-word paper which at most will occupy you for a month. When I started work on *Hawaii,* I faced the prospect of a three-million-word term paper. And five years of work. Frankly, you sound silly."

This strong language encouraged an excellent discussion of the preparation it takes to write a major novel. Five years of research, months of character development, extensive work on plot and setting, endless speculation on psychology and concentrated work on historical backgrounds.

"When I was finally ready to write," I replied under questioning, "I holed up in a bare-wall, no-telephone Waikiki room and stuck at my typewriter every morning for eighteen months. Seven days a week I wrestled with the words that would not come, with ideas that refused to jell. When I broke a tooth, I told the dentist I'd have to see him at night. When DeWitt Wallace, the editor of the *Reader's Digest* and a man to whom I am much indebted, came to Hawaii on vacation, I wanted to hike with him but had to say, 'In the late afternoon. In the morning I work.' "

I explained to my caller that I write all my books slowly, with two fingers on an old typewriter, and the actual task of getting the words on paper is difficult. Nothing I write is good enough to be used in first draft, not even important personal letters, so I am required to rewrite everything at least twice. Important work, like a novel, must be written over and over again, up to six or seven times. For example, *Hawaii* went very slowly and needed constant revision. Since the final version contained about 500,000 words, and since I wrote it all many times, I had to type in my painstaking fashion about 3,000,000 words.

At this news, my visitor whistled and asked, "How many research books did you have to consult?"

"Several thousand. When I started the actual writing, there were about five hundred that I kept in my office."

"How many personal interviews?"

"About two hundred. Each two or three hours long."

"Did you write much that you weren't able to use?"

"I had to throw away about half a million words."

The young scholar looked again at the chaplain's card and returned it reverently to my desk. "Would you have the energy to undertake such a task again?" he asked.

"I would always like to be engaged in such tasks," I replied, and he turned to other questions.

Young people, especially those in college who should know better, frequently fail to realize that men and women who wish to accomplish anything must apply themselves to tasks of tremendous magnitude. A new vaccine may take years to perfect. A Broadway play is never written, cast and produced in a week. A foreign policy is never evolved in a brief time by diplomats relaxing in Washington, London or Geneva.

The good work of the world is accomplished principally by people who dedicate themselves unstintingly to the big job at hand. Weeks, months, years pass, but the good workman knows that he is gambling on an ultimate achievement which cannot be measured in time spent. Responsible men and women leap to the challenge of jobs that require enormous dedication and years to fulfill, and are happiest when they are so involved.

This means that men and women who hope to make a real contribution to American life must prepare themselves to tackle big jobs, and the interesting fact is that no college or university in the world can give anyone the specific education he will ultimately need. Adults who are unwilling to reeducate themselves periodically are doomed to mediocrity.

For in American life, the average man—let's leave out doctors and highly specialized scientists—can expect to work in three radically different fields before he retires. The trained lawyer is dragged into a business reorganization and winds up a college president. The engineer uses his slide rule for a short time, finds himself a sales expert and ends his career in labor relations. The schoolteacher becomes a principal and later on heads the town's Buick agency.

Obviously no college education could prepare a young man for all that he will have to do in his years of employment. The best a college can do is to inspire him with the urge to reeducate himself constantly.

I first discovered this fact on Guadalcanal in 1945, when the war had passed us by and we could see certain victory ahead. Relieved of pressure, our top admirals and generals could have been excused if they loafed, but the ones I knew well in those days took free time and gave themselves orderly courses in new fields. One carrier admiral studied everything he could get on tank warfare. The head of our outfit, William Lowndes Calhoun, spent six hours a day learning French.

I asked him about this. "Admiral, what's this big deal with French?"

"How do I know where I'll be sent when the war's over?" he countered.

But what impressed me most was the next tier of officers, the young Army colonels and the Navy commanders. They divided sharply into two groups: those who spent their spare time learning something and those who didn't. In the years that followed, I noticed in the newspapers that whenever President Truman or President Eisenhower chose men for military positions of great power, they always picked from the officers who had re-educated themselves.

More significant to me personally was my stay with the brilliant doctors of an Army hospital in the jungles of Espiritu Santo. The entire staff of a general hospital in Denver, Colorado, had been picked up and flown out to care for our wounded, and they experienced days of overwork followed by weeks of tedium. In the latter periods the doctors organized voluntary study groups by which to further their professional competence.

By good luck, I was allowed to participate in a group that was analyzing alcoholism, and one night the leader asked me, as we were breaking up, "What are you studying, Michener?" The question stunned me, for I had been studying exactly nothing.

I drove back through the jungle and that very night started working on something that I had been toying with for some months. In a lantern-lit, mosquito-filled tin shack, I started writing *Tales of the South Pacific*.

I have been the typical American in that I have had widely scattered jobs: teacher, businessman, soldier, traveler, writer. And my college education gave me no specific preparation for any of these jobs.

But it gave me something much better. I attended Swarthmore College, outside Philadelphia, and by fantastic luck, I got there just as the college was launching an experiment which was to transform the institution and those of us who participated. At the end of my sophomore year the faculty assembled a group of us and said, "Life does not consist of taking courses in small segments. A productive life consists of finding huge tasks and mastering them with whatever tools of intelligence and energy we have. We are going to turn you loose on some huge tasks. Let's see what you can do with them."

Accordingly, we were excused from all future class attendance and were told, "Pick out three fields that interest you." I chose logic, English history and the novel. The faculty said, "For the next two years go to the library and learn what you can about your fields. At the end of two years we'll bring in some outside experts from Harvard and Yale, whom you've never seen, and they will determine whether or not you have educated yourselves."

What followed was an experience in intellectual grandeur. The Swarthmore professors, realizing that when I was tested they would be tested too, helped me to gain as thorough an education as a young man could absorb. For it was in their interest to see that I understood the fine points of the fields I had chosen.

When the two years ended, the visiting experts arrived and for a week they probed and tested and heckled. At the end of this exciting time one of the examiners told me, "You have the beginning of a real education."

He was right. Nothing that I studied in college has been of use to me in my various jobs. But what I did learn was how to learn, how to organize, how to write term papers. If my education had ended the week I stood before those strange examiners, I would have proved a fairly useless citizen.

While I was reflecting on these matters, my young scholar asked, "If you were a young man today and wanted to be a writer, what kind of education would you seek?"

I replied, "I'd choose some very difficult field and try to master it. I'd seek out professors who really poured it on. Long term papers and many of them, tough laboratory work."

"Why?" he pressed.

"Because we learn only those things at which we have to work very hard. It's ridiculous to give a bright fellow like you a three-thousand-word term paper. It ought to be fifteen thousand words—or thirty. Tackle a real job. Then, when you're through, you're on the way to facing big jobs in adult life."

My visitor made a few marks in his notebook, then asked, "When you were in college, the scientific revolution hadn't occurred yet. Today, would you stick with liberal arts—things like logic and history—or would you switch to science, where the good jobs are?"

I didn't hesitate a minute on this one. "Unless I had extraordinary aptitude in the sciences, I'd stick with liberal arts every time. The pay isn't as good. The jobs aren't waiting when you graduate. And when you want to get married, it's tough to tell your girl's father, 'I'm studying philosophy.' But forty years from now the scientists in your class will be scientists. And the liberal arts men will be governing the world."

The idea was so startling that my young visitor wished to discuss it further. "You mean there's a chance for fellows like me?"

"Every year your prospects grow brighter," I insisted. "The more complex the world becomes, the more desperately it needs men trained in liberal arts. For the government of the world must always rely upon the man with broad human knowledge. And the government of a business or a university or a newspaper requires the same kind of man."

"Why?" he asked, forgetting his notebook.

"Because governing anything requires knowledge of men, a balanced judgment, a gift for conciliation and, above all, a constant weighing of good versus bad. Only men with broad educations can perform such tasks."

"Can't scientists do this?" he asked.

"They surely can. If, after they graduate, they give themselves courses in the humanities."

I finished our interview by telling a story. "In 1942 the United States Navy was hungry for talent, and four of us were taken into a small room where we sat around shivering in our shorts. A grim-faced selection committee asked the first would-be officer, 'What can you do?' and the man replied, 'I'm a buyer for Macy's, and I can judge very quickly between markets and prices and trends.' The selection board replied, 'But you can't do anything practical?' The man said no, and he was shunted off to one side.

"The next man was a lawyer, and when the board asked him if he could do anything practical, he had to confess, 'I can weigh evidence and organize information,' and he was rejected.

"I was the third in line, and when I answered, 'I know language and a good deal of history,' the board groaned and I was sent shivering away.

"But when the fourth man said boldly, 'I'm from Georgia Tech and I can overhaul diesel engines,' the committee jumped up, practically embraced him and made him an officer on the spot."

"That's what I mean," my young scholar pointed out.

"At the end of the war," I continued, "the buyer from Macy's was assistant to the Secretary of the Navy, in charge of many complex responsibilities requiring instant good judgment. He gave himself courses in naval management and government procedures until he became one of the nation's real experts.

"The lawyer wound up as assistant to Admiral Halsey, and in a crucial battle, deduced where the Japanese fleet had to be. He came out covered with medals.

"I was given the job of naval secretary to several Congressional committees who were determining the future of America in the South Pacific. And what was the engineer doing at the end of the war? He was still overhauling diesel engines."

"You're sure there's hope for the liberal-arts man?" the young scholar repeated.

"If he learns to tackle the big jobs—the big ones historically or morally or culturally or politically."

We parted on that note, but when he had gone, I realized that I had not made my statement nearly strong enough. I should have said, "The world is positively hungry for young men who have dedicated themselves to big jobs. If your present professors aren't training you for such work, quit them and find others who will drive you. If your present college isn't making you work to the limit of your ability, drop out and go to another that will. Because if you don't discipline your brain now, you'll never be prepared for the years when it's a question of work or perish."

Parents or professors who do not encourage their young to tackle big jobs commit a moral crime against those young people. For we know that when the young are properly challenged, they will rise to the occasion and they will prepare themselves for the great work that remains to be done.

BRAND BLANSHARD

*Values: The Polestar of Education**

Brand Blanshard (b. 1892) has taught philosophy at a number of schools including Swarthmore College (1925–1945) and Yale University (1945–1961). He has received many honors and given many series of lectures, including the Gifford Lectures at St. Andrews University in Scotland, and the Carus Lectures for the American Philosophical Association. He has written many articles and books, including *The Nature of Thought* (2 volumes), *Reason and Goodness,* and *Reason and Analysis.*

After setting forth his basic thesis, Blanshard in the selection below defines and explains what he means by values and the things that different values have in common. In asking about the place of values in education, he gives some interesting examples and states his own conviction that the purpose of education is to make us creators and centers of value.

In the midst of the universal clamor for more and better technology, too little is heard about the place of values in higher education....

What do we mean by a value? To define the term is surprisingly hard; many thinkers have thought it impossible. But it is easy enough to give examples. As examples of minor values, we could cite such experiences as toasting one's toes before a pleasant fire, having tea in the midst of a seminar, watching a world series game on television, and taking a cool plunge on a hot day. As examples of major values, we could cite the love of Damon for Pythias or of Darby for Joan, the hearing with full understanding of Beethoven's Fifth Symphony, the experience of Keats on first looking into Chapman's Homer, the experience of Schweitzer in ministering to his African Negroes. Is there anything that all these values have in common? Yes, three things, I think.

*Excerpted by permission of the author and publishers from "Values: The Polestar of Education" by Brand Blanshard, a chapter in *The Goals of Higher Education,* Willis D. Weatherford, ed., Cambridge, Mass.: Harvard University Press, © 1960 by the President and Fellows of Harvard College.

In the first place they are all experiences. You may say that there are many things that are valuable besides experiences, and it is true that we commonly talk that way. For economists anything has value that can be exchanged for something else one wants—for example, money or a diamond ring or a grandfather clock. But why should anyone else want these things, and why should you want things they will exchange for? The answer in both cases is the same. It is because these things are means to experiences that are wanted for their own sakes. If somebody wants your grandfather clock, it is because he can set it in his front hall and look at it and gloat over it. Things are always wanted for the sake of experiences, never experiences for the sake of things....

Secondly, these values are not only experiences; they are pleasant experiences. I am inclined to think that every experience valued for its own sake is suffused with a flush of agreeable feeling. This does not mean, of course, that hard work, mental and physical, or even the acute suffering of a bad illness or a bad conscience is not good in a sense; only it is good in a different sense. If we call these things good, it is not because we seek them out for their own sakes, but because they are the means to later states of mind that *are* thus sought; in short, they are instrumental, not intrinsic goods. We admire people who can face suffering with Spartan firmness in the interests of a cause. But if we found a man who cultivated illness or pain for its own sweet sake, we should choose our gambit warily in approaching him; we should assume that he was a crank, and not improbably a psychopath. Indeed, I doubt whether even psychopaths attain this pitch of oddity....

Our conclusion so far is that all goods involve pleasant experiences. Is there anything more that is essential to them? I think there is. And perhaps the best way to see it is to take an example which perplexed John Stuart Mill, one familiar to all students of ethics. He began by saying that pleasure, and pleasure alone, was what made anything good. But he was brought up short by reflecting on the comparative value that this doctrine would assign to the lives of Socrates and a pig. Take first a month in the life of a pig, and make it no ordinary pig but a porcine gourmet whose every gustatory whim is satisfied with the most exquisite dainties of the trough. Then take a month in the life of Socrates, and make it a month in which the good man is tormented by doubt, taxes, and Xanthippe. Which life would Mill rather live? Being a singularly honest man, he voted for Socrates, thereby making untold trouble for himself. For he was by no means certain that Socrates' life was a pleasanter life, while he had no doubt at all that it was more worth living. There must, then, be something other than pleasure that makes it more worth living. What was this? I will not remind you of Mill's answer because, by pretty general agreement, it was wrong. The right answer, I suggest is this: Socrates' life was better because, whether more pleasant or not, it involved a completer fulfillment of powers. Grant the pig as generous a gastronomic capacity as one wishes, still one must admit that its intellectual, moral, and aesthetic horizons are limited, while those of Socrates are all but unlimited. What gave Socrates' life its value was the free play of a magnificent mind, the fulfillment in thought, feeling, and practice of a great intellect and a great heart.

This gives us the clue, I think, to the third component of all values. Besides experience, and pleasant experience, there must be fulfillment of natural faculties or powers.... Values are not adventitious to human nature. A value is a value because it speaks to our condition, answers our need, meets and completes some demand of our nature. And the more central and fundamental the demand, the greater is the value attaching to its fulfillment.

In the light of all this, we may describe a value as an experience that is at once pleasant and fulfilling. And our question is, What is the place of values, so conceived, in education?

The answer is that they should form the polestar of education. For the aim of education is to secure a more worth-while life, in the first instance for those who receive it, in the second for others affected by these; and a more worth-while life is one that is richer in values. But while education should aim at the production of values, it has two branches that serve this purpose in very different ways. The aim of *liberal* education is to qualify us directly to realize such values; the aim of *technological* education is to qualify us for them indirectly....

Now there is a difference between a technologist and a scientist. What is this difference? Presumably, that the technologist studies nature for the sake of controlling it, while the scientist studies it for the sake of understanding it. Thus the horizon of the scientist is wider than that of the technologist; for if a certain kind of knowledge gives no promise of application, the technologist's interest fades while that of the scientist may remain as lively as ever....

This brings us to the second of the two values to be found in the liberal pursuit of science, taken in the broad sense. The first was illumination. The second is discipline. Our education ought to supply us with a habit and a method of attacking problems, a habit of orderliness, clearness, persistence, and precision. How often we must endure performances by persons, too often with degrees after their names, which require an agonizing re-appraisal of their being educated at all: political speeches without form and void, radio sermons full of sound and fury, signifying nothing; after-dinner oratory in which the point, if there is one, is fathoms deep in half-relevant anecdotage! And what a satisfaction it is, when we are hunting for light on some complicated issue, to find an article that puts the issue simply, offers its evidence economically, faces difficulties fairly, and draws a firm conclusion! The ability to do that is one of the most infallible marks of the educated mind....

We have been considering the disciplines that aim at knowledge. But what about the study of literature, music, and art? These are now a recognized part of a liberal education, and their primary aim is plainly not knowledge. Their aim is to satisfy and educate feeling. We sometimes forget that feeling is as educable as intelligence and that, so far as happiness is concerned, its cultivation is even more important. What does the education of feeling mean? Someone has given the answer in the remark that culture is the adjustment of feeling to its objects and that education is learning to like and dislike the right things. Such education is one of our most conspicuous needs. Americans are a people of strong feelings, freely expressed; they have been called the Latin branch of the Anglo-Saxon family. Many of us seem to like excitement for its own sake, and if there is insufficient outward occasion for it, we are adroit at generating it *ad hoc*. When Shriners or Legionnaires get together, or a birthday or the New Year is to be celebrated, Americans have an inexhaustible repertory of first aids to excitement: brass bands, paper hats, ticker tape, horns and whistles, snake dances, fancy costumes, and drum majorettes; and at big games there are trained cheerleaders to work up our emotions and give them organized vent. Of course exuberance and high spirits are excellent things. But this hardly implies that the value of an experience depends on how exciting it is. May I quote two or three wise sentences from the philosopher A. E. Taylor? "The mere identification of *any* fundamental activity of the human spirit with emotion, cut loose from a *specific* object, is the degradation and, in the end, the paralysis of the emotion itself. Emotions of all kinds so manifestly derive their value for human life from the character of the object on which they are directed. Emotion inappropriate or disproportionate to the objective situation by which it is evoked is the bane of life."...

We have considered values of the intellect and values of appreciation, but have said nothing about the values of conduct or practice. Is not life largely action, and should not college prepare us to act as well as to think and feel? Now if action means mere behavior, the play of arm and leg, there are no values of action, for values are in the mind. Still, we all know that the man of action—the Napoleon of the army or industry or public life—is a distinct type from the thinker or the artist, and a vastly important type who is often lost in the shuffle when education is under review. Can a college turn out such men, or even do much to help them? This is my last question.

Of course there are schools of business administration and welfare work and diplomacy, but no college can reproduce the conditions in which the man of affairs is going to work. So when liberal arts colleges are criticized because their graduates on entering business have to learn it from the ground up, the charge is both true and negligible. No curriculum ever devised will guarantee a Churchill or a Henry Ford. But that a college can do something even here is suggested by the fact that little Merton College, Oxford, with less than a hundred and fifty students, produced, if I remember rightly, seven archbishops of Canterbury in one century, and that Balliol under Jowett poured out administrators to every part of the empire.

The chief points about the office of the college in training men of action seem to me to be these. First, a training of intelligence *is* a training of will. As William James pointed out, a firm will is largely a matter of controlled attention, of fixing our thought firmly on what must be done, and hence a discipline of thought is itself a preparation for action. Secondly, college life on the practical side is not wholly divorced from the rest of life. It exacts hard tasks, it sets deadlines, it requires the ordering of one's time and the budgeting of one's energies. Teachers are sometimes slack and indulgent about these things, as doting parents are, but the student ought not to be so toward himself. He is enjoying a great privilege which he ought to take most seriously, and if he keeps himself to the mark, that alone will equip him to meet the deadlines of the world. Thirdly, American colleges, rightly I think, value athletics; and the participation in competitive games, if wisely conducted, gives an admirable discipline in taking success modestly, in taking defeat and hard knocks uncomplainingly, and in developing respect for justice, since sportsmanship is justice in play. If Yorktown was lost, as has been alleged, on the playing fields of Eton, at least Waterloo was something. Fourthly, as in the realms of intelligence and appreciation, so too in the realm of action college can marshal models across the stage for whom we feel a self-revealing repulsion or affinity. Here history is the chief resource, not so much social or constitutional history as the old-fashioned kind that makes it largely the biography of great men. We all find it intelligible that General Eisenhower, traversing Napoleon's field of action, should have remarked, "I should have liked to tangle with that fellow," or that he and Montgomery should have gone over Gettysburg together and come up with a reappraisal of Lee. What is more significant is that such people as Goethe, Hegel, and Emerson should also be fascinated by Napoleon; that Mommsen, Froude, and Thornton Wilder should have been fascinated by Caesar; and that Carlyle should have worshiped at the shrines of Cromwell and Frederick. These men of action had deep moral flaws, but they were, after all, among the "quarto and folio editions of mankind," and to read in them is to expand one's ideas of what a mere human being can do. Finally, education not only can inspire action, it can give it perspective and goals. How different the world would be if Napoleon and Hitler had been cultivated minds instead of being the one an outsized Corsican brigand and the other a guttersnipe of genius!

We have reached the end of our argument, and it proves to be as simple as it has been long. Values, we have argued, are experiences that are at once satisfying and fulfilling. The purpose of education is to make us creators and centers of value. Technological education does that indirectly by supplying us tools for the exploiting of nature. Liberal education on its intellectual side provides the values of understanding, which makes us at home in our world. Liberal education on its appreciative side makes us responsive to the best that has been said and painted and built and sung. Liberal education on its practical side puts the wind of emulation in our sails and gives direction to our voyage. Values are the stars by which education may and should steer its course.

The Ways of Knowing

ELMER SPRAGUE

*Matters of Fact and Matters of Logic**

Elmer Sprague (b. 1924) holds a Doctorate of Philosophy from Oxford University, where he was a Rhodes Scholar. He has taught philosophy at Brooklyn College since 1953.

The following selection examines two types of statement and the differences between them. This distinction, stemming from earlier philosophers such as Leibniz and Hume, has played an important role in many current philosophical discussions, especially those of the analytic school. You will find this distinction recurring in other readings, including the selection from A. J. Ayer.

In this chapter I shall discuss man's powers to know and the kinds of knowledge which these powers guarantee. The discussion will center on two kinds of knowledge: matters of fact, which depend on man's senses, or his powers of perceiving; and matters of logic, which depend on man's reason, or his powers of conceiving. This chapter is a necessary preface to all the rest. If what is said here seems formal, empty, and uninteresting, I must beg the reader to remember that until we settle questions about the *ways* in which we can know, we cannot settle questions about *what* we can know. This is one of the central problems in philosophy, and one to which philosophers turn again and again as the key to all of their other problems.

In what follows I shall consider knowledge as declarative sentences or statements, which someone knows how to prove or to use. There is more than one way of proving and using declarative sentences, but the example of the Pythagorean Theorem will illustrate my point in a general way. The theorem: "In any right-angled triangle, the square which is described on

*Elmer Sprague, from "Philosophy and Man: Intellectual Powers." From *What is Philosophy? A Short Introduction* by Elmer Sprague. Copyright © 1961 by Oxford University Press, Inc. Reprinted by permission. Pages 13–29 with omissions.

the side opposite the right angle is equal to the squares described on the sides which contain the right angle." Now I may be said to know the theorem when I can prove it by appeal to the necessary definitions, postulates, axioms, and preceding theorems in Euclidean geometry, when I can use it to prove further theorems, and when I can use it to find the length of unknown sides, and so on.

Knowledge may also be spoken of as knowing some object. For example, philosophers like to talk about our knowledge of material objects; and they like to talk in general about objects of knowledge. But talk about objects of knowledge can always be translated into talk about knowing whether a statement about the object is true or false. The reader will find it a salutary move to translate an awesome question like "Can I really know material objects?" into the more manageable question, "How do I know that the statement, 'There is a tea cup on my desk,' is true?" What is more, talk about knowledge as statements puts us in a favorable position to deal with the social aspect of knowledge. Whatever my object of knowledge, if I want to call someone's attention to it or to discuss it with him, I must make statements about it. Statements are the medium for exchanging knowledge; and this consideration makes them additionally interesting as a clue to man's powers to know.

MATTER-OF-FACT STATEMENTS

We may begin with matter-of-fact statements, and see what can be made of them in their own right. Later, when we have also examined matter-of-logic statements, we may consider the differences between the two kinds of statement. Here are some sample matter-of-fact statements:

The cows are in the corn field.
Alice always talks too much.
The sun will rise tomorrow.
Aristotle gave philosophy lectures.
Alexander swam the Hellespont.
The Eiffel Tower is in New York City.

These statements differ in many ways. All are about different subjects. Some are in the present tense, while others are about the past and the future. Some are statements about a particular subject at a particular time. Some are generalizations about a particular subject, and thus are meant to describe that subject at all times (e.g. Alice always talks too much). But despite their many differences, the characteristic which these statements have in common is that they may be proved true or false by experience.

It is easy to say that matter-of-fact statements are confirmed or disproved by experience; but it is not easy to give any general account of what is meant by experience. What is usually meant is that someone who wants to confirm a matter-of-fact statement must use his senses in some way to find out whether the statement does describe the world. When we find that a matter-of-fact statement does describe the world, we say that it is confirmed. When we find that a matter-of-fact statement fails to describe the world, we say that it is disproved. Here, we may consider the following examples which are meant to illustrate in a general way the confirmation of a matter-of-fact statement by experience.

(1) When someone tells me, "The cows are in the corn field," I look in the corn field to see whether I can find the cows there. If they are in the corn field, my finding them there has confirmed the statement. My failing to find them in the corn field would disprove it. But I must not minimize the difficulties in proving this statement false, or, to put the matter another way, the difficulties in proving that the statement "The cows are not in the corn field" is true. To be sure, I must have searched, and searched carefully. Of course, looking for cows in a corn field requires less care than hunting for a needle in a haystack; but nonetheless I must be certain that I have looked in all those places big enough to conceal a herd of cows before I can assert confidently that there are no cows in the corn field in question. The proof of the affirmative statement "The cows are in the corn field" is, however, fairly easy. All I have to do is find the cows. But the proof of the negative statement is more difficult. No matter how exhaustive a search I conduct before I conclude that the cows are not in the corn field, it is still possible that they might be hidden in a spot that I have missed.

(2) While riding with me in my car, someone tells me, "The radiator is boiling." I can neither see nor hear anything unusual from the direction of the radiator; so I look at the temperature gauge. If the indicator is in the red section of its arc, I agree with my passenger. His statement is true. But here confirmation by experience is more complicated than in the case above, where I looked into the corn field and saw the cows. Why does my seeing the temperature indicator in the red section prove true the statement "The radiator is boiling"? It proves it for me because I believe another statement, which links the behavior of the indicator and the behavior of the radiator: "If the indicator is in the red, the radiator is boiling." And why do I believe this last statement? I believe it because in the past each time the indicator has gone into the red section of its arc, I have found the car's radiator to be boiling. So now when I find the indicator in the red I believe that the radiator must be boiling.

But one may very well ask why my memory of the indicator's riding in the red when the radiator was boiling in the past in any way guarantees that my radiator is now boiling because the indicator is riding in the red section. Strictly speaking, there is no guarantee that there is now a connection between the position of the indicator and my radiator's boiling. Matter-of-fact statements are meant to describe the world, and it is possible that the world may have changed since I last experienced a link between the position of the indicator and the radiator's boiling. My temperature gauge may now be broken, to name the most probable way in which the world may have changed. But even though there is no guarantee that there is a connection between the position of the indicator and my radiator's boiling, it usually happens in cases of this kind that our belief that the present resembles the past outweighs our knowledge that the world may have changed. Our belief about a particular kind of connection grows stronger each time we experience it. On the other hand, those occasions when experience disproves our matter-of-fact statements (The gauge was broken. The radiator was not even hot.) are salutary reminders that matter-of-fact statements are meant to describe the world rather than to prescribe it.

(3) "The sun will rise tomorrow" is yet another and different example of a statement that we say is true because of experience. But here there is no present experience comparable to looking at an indicator in the red portion of its arc, that leads from the seen to belief in the unseen. It is the regularity of our past experience of sunrises that leads us to expect that the sun will rise tomorrow, and thus leads us to say that the statement is true. Of course, neither my past experience of sunrises nor the expectation it engenders makes the statement true. Only the sun's rising on the morrow can do that.

These three examples show that confirmation of a matter-of-fact statement by experience may have at least three meanings: (1) I am directly observing what the statement describes, and what I observe justifies my saying that the statement is true. (2) I am directly observing one thing, which I have regularly found to be conjoined with the state of affairs described by the statement, and this observation leads me to believe that the state of affairs which the statement describes, but which I have not observed, does exist; and I say that the statement is true. In principle we argue for the truth of statements about the past or the future in the same way when we say that what we can see implies the existence of past events which we have not seen or when we argue that what we can see implies the probability of events yet to come. (3) I remember something that I have regularly observed in the past; and I am led to believe that a similar state of affairs which the statement describes, but which I have not yet observed, will exist; and I say that the statement is true.

To these remarks about confirming by experience must be added the rule that no one can confirm a matter-of-fact statement who does not know what observations will confirm it. If I do not know the difference between cows and the rest of the world, and corn fields and the rest of the world, the statement "The corn field is in the cows" will make as much sense to me as the statement "The cows are in the corn field." Philosophers say that someone who does not know how to confirm a matter-of-fact statement does not understand it. To him, it is meaningless. To him, it makes no sense.

After this consideration of proving and disproving matter-of-fact statements, we are in a position to notice one of their characteristics that is their defining characteristic. For every matter-of-fact statement, its denial is as meaningful as the statement itself. For instance, "The cows are not in the corn field" is as meaningful as "The cows are in the corn field." It is because each is as meaningful as the other that we must appeal to experience to determine which is true. Later we shall find this characteristic to be of the greatest importance in distinguishing matter-of-fact statements from matter-of-logic statements.

THE SENSES AND KNOWLEDGE

Matter-of-fact statements are the kind of knowledge we may gain by the use of our senses; but not all philosophers have thought that our senses are fit instruments for gaining knowledge of the world. Their views deserve some notice. At the outset, however, I wish to announce that I am not claiming that the only knowledge we have is knowledge confirmed by our senses. Therefore, neither does the position I am describing hold its place by belittling other sources of knowledge, nor does it deserve belittlement for the purpose of enhancing other sources of knowledge.

The criticism of the senses as powers for knowing falls under two main heads: the claim that the fallibility of the senses makes all sensory knowledge untrustworthy; and the claim that the senses can never be used to gain knowledge of the real world.

The claim that the senses are fallible rests on evidence that the senses deceive. The classic examples fall into two varieties: the failure to perceive things as they are, and the mistake of perceiving things that are not. Examples of the failure to perceive things as they are, are the straight stick that looks bent in water; the penny at one's feet that turns out to be a bottle cap; the mountain that seems quite near but turns out to be a hundred miles away; the man in the night who turns out to be a wind-blown bush; and the burglar's footsteps that turn into a dripping faucet. The problems in these examples arise largely from assuming more than the sensory evidence warrants. The fault lies not with the senses but with the hasty assumption; and its avoidance lies not in abandoning the senses because they are untrustworthy, but in seeking more sensory knowledge to confirm or disprove one's first assumption. What is more, as soon as one learns the tricks one's senses can play, one learns to be careful in judging water effects, distance, and shadows.

But if we pursue the fallibility of the senses a little further, we discover that a good part of the trouble comes from personifying the senses: from my thinking of my use of my senses as a communication between *me* and my senses. I say, "My eyes deceived me," when I ought to say, "*I* should have taken another look." I say, "My ears tricked me," when I ought to say, "*I* should have listened more carefully." I say, "My nose knows," when I ought to say, "*I* smell it." The problem of the fallibility of the senses turns into the problem of the careless observer when we make ourselves the subject of verbs of sense. Then we know that we have only ourselves to blame for our perceptual mistakes. Ordinary people know this; but philosophers have to be reminded from time to time.

The mistake of perceiving things that are not is exemplified by mirages, unrecognized mirror images, and the one-legged man who still feels rheumatic pains in his amputated member. The solution of the problems raised by these examples requires again a greater use of the senses. Three tests are possible: the test of two or more observers; the test of observations at different times; and the test of two or more senses. Do I see an oasis or do I see a mirage? If I can see it at different times, and if my fellow travelers can see it at the same times I do, my answer is a tentative "Oasis." Tentative, because the test of an optical experience is, can I touch what I see? It may be objected, of course, that sensory tests are circular. Touch confirms sight, and sight confirms touch. One illusion leads to another, and all is illusion. This objection leads us to the second main head under which criticism of the senses is made: The senses can never be used to gain knowledge of the real world.

"Real" is a loaded word. If it is used to describe a world that transcends the powers of our senses, then by definition we can never learn anything of that world by our senses. But here I understand the denial of sensory knowledge of a real world to be a claim that the world is a creation of one's senses, and that one cannot tell what to credit to the world and what to attribute to one's senses. The claim is that the knower and his knowledge run together indistinguishably.

The distinction between the knower and the known is not always an easy one to make; and it often depends on where the philosopher wants to draw the line. Consider, for example, the Wizard of Oz and his Emerald City. To achieve the absolute greenness of Oz, the Wizard equipped all of his subjects and visitors with green spectacles, which they were compelled to wear at all times. Now here is a nice philosophical question: Was the city of Oz really green or was its greenness merely in the eyes of its beholders? (Said eyes being properly assisted by green spectacles, of course.) Whether or not a philosopher says that Oz was really green depends on where he draws the line between the beholders and the world. If the philosopher says that Oz was really not green, he is ready to argue that if the inhabitants had taken off their colored spectacles, they would have found the city to be not wholly green. Such a philosopher is answering the question from a viewpoint above the relation of the beholder to the city; and thus he finds green not in the world but in the eye of the beholder. On the other hand, a philosopher might argue that the question about Oz's greenness must always be answered from within the relationship of the beholder and the world. For such a philosopher, when someone says, "Oz isn't really green," he is only saying, "I am not looking at Oz through green spectacles." So, from the point of view of those subject to the Wizard's spectacles, Oz is really green.

The philosophical moral is that only when we can distinguish between two different ways of knowing the world (without green spectacles and with green spectacles) are we in any position to distinguish between what is the world and what is a condition for knowing the world. Without the correction of other perceptions—in the way that clear-eyed observers can penetrate the Wizard of Oz's color-scheming—the world of sense is as real as we perceive it. There is some truth in saying that we are the prisoners of our senses; but we may take consolation in the fact that our prison is not a cave-like dungeon, but a house of correction.

MATTER-OF-LOGIC STATEMENTS

I want now to turn to matter-of-logic statements. As always, it will be best to proceed by way of examples:

The whole is equal to the sum of its parts.
In any right-angled triangle the square which is described on the side opposite the right angle is equal to the squares described on the sides which contain the right angle. (Pythagorean Theorem)
Three times five is equal to one-half of thirty.
That which is red is colored.

Why do we accept or reject these statements? In a general way, the answer is that matter-of-logic statements are confirmed by an appeal to the way in which we use the words in the statement. How does this sort of confirmation work? I shall illustrate it by considering "The whole is equal to the sum of its parts."

In the case of "The whole is equal to the sum of its parts," the appeal is to the way in which we are to use the words "whole," "part," and "equal to" in this statement. That into which a whole can be divided is its parts. That into which parts can be assembled is a whole. Further, there is a question of the kind of whole that we will allow this statement to describe. The rough rule is that the wholes and their parts must be subject to some system of measurement as of area or weight or volume. What "equal to" means in

"The whole is equal to the sum of its parts" is that whatever quantitative measurement can be applied to the whole can also be applied to the sum of the parts. Now the confirmation of "The whole is equal to the sum of its parts" depends solely on my understanding the way in which these words are to be used and by agreeing to use them in this way. This is why I call such a statement a matter-of-logic statement, for our "logic" comes from the Greek *logos* meaning "word." In addition, I must digress for a moment to give a little perspective to what I have spoken of as "understanding the way in which words are to be used." For a very long time, philosophers thought about matter-of-logic statements as being about ideas or concepts rather than about words. This was their way of distinguishing between matter-of-fact statements, which were about perceptions, and matter-of-logic statements, which were about conceptions. In addition, just as perceptions were perceived by the senses, so a faculty called reason was thought of as conceiving conceptions, or ideas. Thus many philosophers speak of confirming matter-of-logic statements as an appeal to reason; but I want to follow those philosophers who speak of confirming matter-of-logic statements as reminding ourselves of the ways in which we may use these statements.

We can carry our understanding of matter-of-logic statements a little further if we consider the way in which we use "The whole is equal to the sum of its parts." This matter-of-logic statement is really a rule which allows me the convenience of mentioning the whole rather than listing all of the parts. For example, when you ask me how much money I have, I can tell you that I have two dollars and thirty-six cents rather than having to say that I have three nickels, two dimes, a penny, two quarters, and three half-dollars. But notice that the confirmation of "The whole is equal to the sum of its parts" never depends on any example of its usefulness. I do not say that the statement is true because my pocketful of coins is the same as two dollars and thirty-six cents. I say that the statement is true because I understand the way in which the words are used. On the other hand, I never allow that any example can disprove the statement either. My tactics are to show that any example which someone believes disproves "The whole is equal to the sum of its parts" is really not a case to which the rule can be applied; and anyone who supposes that it is such a case misunderstands the way in which the rule is to be used. An example will illustrate my point.

Suppose that someone argues in the following way: I can show you that the whole is not equal to the sum of its parts. Look at this medicine dropper full of liquid. Now, I squeeze it ten times, and let ten drops fall into this saucer; and they run together to make one drop. That shows you that the whole is not equal to the sum of its parts, for the sum of the parts is ten drops, but the whole in the saucer is only one drop.

My reply to this argument must be that I am being taken in a numbers game. When I said that the whole is equal to the sum of its parts, I never meant to claim that one is equal to ten. Indeed, enumerative equality is not the sort of equality which can be sought between a whole and its parts, since the whole will always be one, and the number of its parts will always be greater than one. What has happened is that the drops case has been presented in such a way that it does not fit the rule. So it can in no way disprove my claim that the whole is equal to the sum of its parts. I can, however, turn the example to my own account by showing how it can be made to fit the rule. I can talk about the volume of the drop in the saucer and the volume of the ten drops that were squeezed from the medicine dropper. When their volume is considered, the whole is equal to the sum of the parts. What is required here is discretion in summing. Notice, however, that by showing how the drops case can be made to fit the rule, I am not appealing to the case to confirm the matter-of-logic statement, "The whole is equal to the sum of its parts." What I am doing is showing a case in which the rule can be used.

I now want to distinguish two sorts of matter-of-logic statements. The sorts which I have in mind are exemplified by "That which is red is colored," and the Pythagorean Theorem. To bring out their characteristics, I shall discuss each of these statements in turn. Notice that the statement, "That which is red is colored," is always true, for its denial, "That which is red is *not* colored," is a self-contradiction, granting that as we ordinarily use the color word "red," to say that something is red is to say that it is colored. For the same reason, of course, the self-contradictory statement, "Red objects are *not* colored," is a self-contradiction, granting that as we ordinarily use the color word "red," to say that something is red is to say that it is colored. For the same reason, of course, the self-contradictory statement, "Red objects are *not* colored," will always be false.

Now consider the Pythagorean Theorem, which I wish to discuss because it exemplifies those matter-of-logic statements which are part of a logical system of statements, as that theorem is a part of Euclidean geometry. It is the case that this sort of matter-of-logic statement is also always true; indeed it is this characteristic which leads us to classify these statements, too, as matter-of-logic statements. However, these statements are not said to be always true because their denials are self-contradictory, as is the case with "That which is red is colored." A longer explanation is required. We say that the Pythagorean Theorem is true because we can prove it within the context of Euclidean geometry. We appeal to the relevant definitions, postulates, and axioms laid down in the beginning, and to any relevant theorems that were proved earlier, and our claim is that all of these taken together imply the truth of the Pythagorean Theorem. The principle of our proof is that we can show the Pythagorean Theorem to be consistent with the rest of Euclidean geometry. If we then counted it as false, we should be contradicting ourselves, in the light of our adherence to the rest of Euclidean geometry. Valuing self-consistency, we therefore count the Pythagorean Theorem as true and its denial as false. Could its denial ever be true? Yes, if we invented an alternative geometry into which it could fit; and that such a geometry is conceivable is what makes us refrain from calling the denial of the Pythagorean Theorem a self-contradiction. We only say that within Euclidean geometry it cannot be true.

There is another way to bring out the reason for classifying both "Red objects are colored" and the Pythagorean Theorem as matter-of-logic statements. It is that we disallow the denial of each for a logical reason: in the first case because it is a self-contradiction and in the second because of inconsistency with our original principles. We may then formulate rules for detecting each of the different sorts of matter-of-logic statement. The first is that if a statement's denial is a self-contradiction, then it is a matter-of-logic statement. The second is that if the assertion of a statement's denial is disallowed because of its inconsistency with the logical system of statements into which the statement itself fits, then it is a matter-of-logic statement. Notice that if the application of one rule is inconclusive, the other must be applied before one can be satisfied about whether a given statement belongs in the matter-of-logic category.

We may now notice another characteristic of matter-of-logic statements. They do not describe the world. Consider, for example, "That which is red is colored." The statement makes no claim that there is anything red in the world. It is only an assertion that if there are red things in the world, then they are colored. But even though matter-of-logic statements do not describe the world, they may have a great deal to do with the way in which we look at the world. Consider, for example, the usefulness of "The whole is equal to the sum of its parts," a matter-of-logic statement I have already discussed. We do not want to say that this statement describes the world in the sense that it can be confirmed or disproved by experience. But in our use of the statement it is clearly not unrelated to experience, for we do order appropriate parts of our experiences in accordance with it. This is not to say, however, that all matter-of-logic statements are, or need to be, useful in the ordering of experience. For instance, many geometries have been invented simply because of the charm which their elegant self-consistency has exercised on the minds of their inventors; and no thought is given to the question of whether they describe any discoverable space.

MATTERS OF FACT AND LOGIC

From what I have written thus far, my readers may suppose that all statements come neatly labeled "matter-of-fact" or "matter-of-logic," and there can be no trouble in deciding into which basket a given statement should be sorted. Unfortunately this orderly picture is inaccurate, and the kind of puzzle about which a philosopher is most likely to work his head to the bone is one generated by the ins and outs of classifying some statement. There are, however, ways of testing statements that help to decide whether they are to be classified as matter-of-fact or matter-of-logic. I have already described the rules for testing for matter-of-logic statements. I want now to show how points made earlier provide a test for identifying matter-of-fact statements.

Consider the statement, "My collar button is on the bureau." Now even though my collar button is on the bureau, and thus the statement is true, I know what it would be like for its denial, "My collar button is *not* on the bureau," to be true. As I have described things, the denial is, of course, false; but notice that if I did not know how to find out the truth of both statements, I could not find out the truth of either. To find that my collar button is on the bureau, I must also know what it would be like for it not to be on the bureau, or else how could I start looking for it? Should the reader doubt what I have said, he may set himself the task of finding out the truth of the statement, "There is a xonygl in the next room." His first question must be, "What is a xonygl?" If he does not know how to tell the difference between xonygls and everything else in the next room, he is in no position to check on the presence of xonygls. Philosophers like to speak of this as knowing the difference between xonygls and non-xonygls. When someone knows this difference, he will be able to find out the truth of either "There is a xonygl in the next room" or "There is *not* a xonygl in the next room."

The denials of matter-of-fact statements, then, may be either true or false, and a look at the world is required in order to decide whether a given matter-of-fact statement or its denial is true. Here, then, is our test for matter-of-fact statements: Their denials are as conceivable as the original statements, and we can decide which is true only by an appeal to experience. Here too is a basis for our distinction between matter-of-fact and matter-of-logic statements. The denial of the first sort of matter-of-logic statement we noticed is inconceivable because it is a self-contradiction; and the denial of the second sort is not to be allowed because it is inconsistent with the logical system of statements into which the original statement fits.

EDITORS' NOTE: We agree with the author and his publisher that, in ending our selection here, we do not adequately represent his full view and that, as he writes in the concluding section, part of which has been omitted by us, "the tangle of fact and logic is such that there are some statements which we sometimes allow to be matter-of-fact and at other times count as matter-of-logic. It would seem that our distinctions depend not only on the outcome of our tests, but also upon which test we want to make." The reader is urged to consult pages 26–29 of Dr. Spragues' *What is Philosophy? A Short Introduction,* Oxford University Press, 1961, to get the full force of his views.

BERTRAND RUSSELL

*Knowledge of Facts and Knowledge of Laws**

Bertrand Russell (1872–1970) was a British mathematician, logician, and philosopher who throughout a long and active life devoted his attention to a wide spectrum of philosophical and social issues. He stimulated his fellow philosophers through his more technical writings and attracted (and at times upset) a wide public through his more popular works and by his championing of controversial causes.

In the following selection, Russell considers the alternatives to a complete skepticism in regard to all the inferences we draw at the common-sense level and in the sciences. He believes that the only escape from such skepticism is the possession of a stock of knowledge that is not inferred from anything else. He argues that such knowledge consists in part of "data" (and Russell uses this term in a rather special sense) and in part of a general law or rule which permits us to make inferences from matters of fact.

When we examine our beliefs as to matters of fact, we find that they are sometimes based directly on perception or memory, while in other cases they are inferred. To common sense this distinction presents little difficulty: the beliefs that arise immediately from perception appear to it indubitable, and the inferences, though they may sometimes be wrong, are thought, in such cases, to be fairly easily rectified except where peculiarly dubious matters are concerned. I know of the existence of Napoleon because I have heard and read about him, and I have every reason to believe in the veracity of my teachers. I am somewhat less certain about Hengist and Horsa, and much less certain about Zoroaster, but these uncertainties are still on a common-sense level, and do not seem, at first sight, to raise any philosophical issue.

This primitive confidence, however, was lost at a very early stage in philosophical speculation, and was lost for sound reasons. It was found that what I know by perception is less than had been thought, and that the inferences by which I pass from perceived to unperceived facts are open to question. Both these sources of skepticism must be investigated.

*Bertrand Russell, from *Human Knowledge, Its Scope and Limits* (New York: Simon & Schuster, 1948), Chapter I, Part 3, pp. 165–175. Copyright, 1948, by Bertrand Russell. Reprinted by permission of Simon & Schuster, Inc. and George Allen & Unwin Ltd., London.

There is, to begin with, a difficulty as to what is inferred and what is not. I spoke a moment ago of my belief in Napoleon as an inference from what I have heard and read, but there is an important sense in which this is not quite true. When a child is being taught history, he does not argue: "My teacher is a person of the highest moral character, paid to teach me facts; my teacher says there was such a person as Napoleon; therefore probably there was such a person." If he did, he would retain considerable doubt, since his evidence of the teacher's moral character is likely to be inadequate, and in many countries at many times teachers have been paid to teach the opposite of facts. The child in fact, unless he hates the teacher, spontaneously believes what he is told. When we are told anything emphatically or authoritatively, it is an effort not to believe it, as anyone can experience on April Fool's Day. Nevertheless there is still a distinction, even on a common-sense level, between what we are told and what we know for ourselves. If you say to the child, "How do you know about Napoleon?", the child may say, "Because my teacher told me." If you say, "How do you know your teacher told you?", the child may say, "Why, of course, because I heard her." If you say, "How do you know you heard her?", he may say, "Because I remember it distinctly." If you say, "How do you know you remember it?", he will either lose his temper or say, "Well, I do remember it." Until you reach this point, he will defend his belief as to a matter of fact by belief in another matter of fact, but in the end he reaches a belief for which he can give no further reason.

There is thus a distinction between beliefs that arise spontaneously and beliefs for which no further reason can be given. It is the latter class of beliefs that are of most importance for theory of knowledge, since they are the indispensable minimum of premises for our knowledge of matters of fact. Such beliefs I shall call "data." In ordinary thinking they are *causes* of other beliefs rather than *premises* from which other beliefs are inferred; but in a critical scrutiny of our beliefs as to matters of fact we must whenever possible translate the causal transitions of primitive thinking into logical transitions, and only accept the derived beliefs to the extent that the character of the transitions seems to justify. For this there is a common-sense reason, namely, that every such transition is found to involve some risk of error, and therefore data are more nearly certain than beliefs derived from them. I am not contending that data are ever completely certain, nor is this contention necessary for their importance in theory of knowledge.

There is a long history of discussions as to what was mistakenly called "skepticism of the senses." Many appearances are deceptive. Things seen in a mirror may be thought to be "real." In certain circumstances, people see double. The rainbow seems to touch the ground at some point, but if you go there you do not find it. Most noteworthy in this connection are dreams: however vivid they may have been, we believe, when we wake up, that the objects which we thought we saw were illusory. But in all these cases the core of data is not illusory, but only the derived beliefs. My visual sensations, when I look in a mirror or see double, are exactly what I think they are. Things at the foot of the rainbow do really look colored. In dreams I have all the experiences that I seem to have; it is only things outside my mind that are not as I believe them to be while I am dreaming. There are in fact no illusions of the senses, but only mistakes in interpreting sensational data as signs of things other than themselves. Or, to speak more exactly, there is no evidence that there are illusions of the senses.

Every sensation which is of a familiar kind brings with it various associated beliefs and expectations. When, say, we see and hear an airplane, we do not merely have the visual sensation and the auditory sensation of a whirring noise; spontaneously and without conscious thought we interpret what we see and hear and fill it out with customary adjuncts. To what an extent we do this becomes obvious when we make a mistake—for example, when what we thought was an airplane turns out to be a bird. I knew a road, along which I used often to go in a car, which had a bend at a certain place, and a whitewashed wall straight ahead. At night it was very difficult not to see the wall as a road going straight on up a hill. The right interpretation as a house and the wrong interpretation as an uphill road were both, in a sense, inferences from the sensational datum, but they were not inferences in the logical sense, since they occurred without any conscious mental process.

I gave the name "animal inference" to the process of spontaneous interpretation of sensations. When a dog hears himself called in tones to which he is accustomed, he looks around and runs in the direction of the sound. He may be deceived, like the dog looking into the gramophone in the advertisement of "His Master's Voice." But since inferences of this sort are generated by the repeated experiences that give rise to habit, his inference must be one which has usually been right in his past life, since otherwise the habit would not have been generated. We thus find ourselves, when we begin to reflect, expecting all sorts of things that in fact happen, although it would be logically possible for them not to happen in spite of the occurrence of the sensations which give rise to the expectations. Thus reflection upon animal inference gives us an initial store of scientific laws, such as "Dogs bark." These initial laws are usually somewhat unreliable, but they help us to take the first steps toward science.

Everyday generalizations, such as "Dogs bark," come to be explicitly believed after habits have been generated which might be described as a pre-verbal form of the same belief. What sort of habit is it that comes to be expressed in the words "Dogs bark"? We do not expect them to bark at all times, but we do expect that *if* they make a noise it will be a bark or a growl. Psychologically, induction does not proceed as it does in the textbooks, where we are supposed to have observed a number of occasions on which dogs barked, and then proceeded consciously to generalize. The fact is that the generalization, in the form of a habit of expectation, occurs at a lower level than that of conscious thought, so that, when we begin to think consciously, we find ourselves believing the generalization, not, explicitly, on the basis of the evidence, but as expressing what is implicit in our habit of expectation. This is a history of the belief, not a justification of it.

Let us make this state of affairs somewhat more explicit. First comes the repeated experience of dogs barking, then comes the habit of expecting a bark, then, by giving verbal expression to the habit, comes belief in the general proposition "Dogs bark." Last comes the logician, who asks not "Why do I believe this?" but "What reason is there for supposing this true?" Clearly the reason, if any, must consist of two parts: first, the facts of perception consisting of the various occasions on which we have heard dogs bark; second, some principle justifying the generalization from observed instances to a law. But this logical process comes historically after, not before, our belief in a host of common-sense generalizations.

The translation of animal inferences into verbal generalizations is carried out very inadequately in ordinary thinking, and even in the thinking of many philosophers. In what counts as perception of external objects there is much that consists of habits generated by past experience. Take, for example, our belief in the permanence of objects. When we see a dog or a cat, a chair or a table, we do not suppose that we are seeing something which has a merely momentary existence; we are convinced that what we are seeing has a past and a future of considerable duration. We do not think this about everything that we see; a flash of lightning, a rocket, or a rainbow is expected to disappear quickly. But experience has generated in us the expectation that ordinary solid objects, which can be touched as well as seen, usually persist, and can be seen and touched again on suitable occasions. Science reinforces this belief by explaining away apparent disappearances as transformations into gaseous forms. But the belief in quasi-permanence, except in exceptional cases, antedates the scientific doctrine of the indestructibility of matter, and is itself antedated by the animal expectation that common objects can be seen again if we look in the right place.

The filling out of the sensational core by means of animal inferences, until it becomes what is called "perception," is analogous to the filling out of telegraphic press messages in newspaper offices. The reporter telegraphs the one word "King," and the newspaper prints "His Gracious Majesty King George VI." There is some risk of error in this proceeding, since the reporter may have been relating the doings of Mr. Mackenzie King. It is true that the context would usually reveal such an error, but one can imagine circumstances in which it would not. In dreams, we fill out the bare sensational message wrongly, and only the context of waking life shows us our mistake.

The analogy to abbreviated press telegrams is very close. Suppose, for instance, you see a friend at the window of an incoming train, and a little later you see him coming toward you on the platform. The physical causes of your perceptions (and of your interpretation of them) are certain light signals passing between him and your eyes. All that physics, by itself, entitles you to infer from the receipt of these signals is that, somewhere along the line of sight, light of the appropriate colors has been emitted or reflected or refracted or scattered. It is obvious that the kind of ingenuity which has produced the cinema could cause you to have just these sensations in the absence of your friend, and that in that case you would be deceived. But such sources of deception cannot be frequent, or at least cannot have been frequent hitherto, since, if they were, you would not have formed the habits of expectation and belief in context that you have in fact formed. In the case supposed, you are confident that it is your friend, that he has existed throughout the interval between seeing him at the window and seeing him on the platform, and that he has pursued a continuous path through space from the one to the other. You have no doubt that what you saw was something solid, not an intangible object like a rainbow or a cloud. And so, although the message received by the senses contains (so to speak) only a few key words, your mental and physical habits cause you, spontaneously and without thought, to expand it into a coherent and amply informative dispatch.

This expansion of the sensational core to produce what goes by the somewhat question-begging name of "perception" is obviously only trustworthy in so far as our habits of association run parallel to processes in the external world. Clouds looked down upon from a mountain may look so like the sea or a field of snow that only positive knowledge to the contrary prevents you from so interpreting your visual sensations. If you are not accustomed to the gramophone, you will confidently believe that the voice you hear on the other side of the door proceeds from a person in the room that you are about to enter. There is no obvious limit to the invention of ingenious apparatus capable of deceiving the unwary. We know that the people we see on the screen in the cinema are not really there, although they move and talk and behave in a manner having some resemblance to that of human beings; but if we did not know it, we might at first find it hard to believe. Thus what we seem to know through the senses may be deceptive whenever the environment is different from what our past experience has led us to expect.

From the above considerations it follows that we cannot admit as data all that an uncritical acceptance of common sense would take as given in perception. Only sensations and memories are truly data for our knowledge of the external world. We must exclude from our list of data not only the things that we consciously infer, but all that is obtained by animal inference, such as the imagined hardness of an object seen but not touched. It is true that our "perceptions," in all their fullness, are data for psychology: we do in fact have the experience of believing in such-and-such an object. It is only for knowledge of things outside our own minds that it is necessary to regard only sensations as data. This necessity is a consequence of what we know of physics and physiology. The same external stimulus, reaching the brains of two men with different experiences, will produce different results, and it is only what these different results have in common that can be used in inferring external causes. If it is objected that the truth of physics and physiology is doubtful, the situation is even worse; for if they are false, nothing whatever as to the outer world can be inferred from my experiences. I am, however, throughout this work, assuming that science is broadly speaking true.

If we define "data" as "those matters of fact of which, independently of inference, we have a right to feel most nearly certain," it follows from what has been said that all my data are events that happen to me, and are, in fact, what would commonly be called events in my mind. This is a view which has been characteristic of British empiricism, but has been rejected by most Continental philosophers, and is not now accepted by the followers of Dewey or by most of the logical positivists. As the issue is of considerable importance, I shall set forth the reasons which have convinced me, including a brief repetition of those that have already been given.

There are, first, arguments on the common-sense level, derived from illusions, squinting, reflection, refraction, etc., but above all from dreams. I dreamed last night that I was in Germany, in a house which looked out on a ruined church; in my dream I supposed at first that the church had been bombed during the recent war, but was subsequently informed that its destruction dated from the wars of religion in the sixteenth century. All this, so long as I remained asleep, had all the convincingness of waking life. I did really have the dream, and did really have an experience intrinsically indistinguishable from that of seeing a ruined church when awake. It follows that the experience which I call "seeing a church" is not conclusive evidence that there is a church, since it may occur when there is no such external object as I suppose in my dream. It may be said that, though when dreaming I may *think* that I am awake, when I wake up I *know* that I am awake. But I do not see how we are to have any such certainty; I have frequently dreamed that I woke up; in fact once, after ether, I dreamed it about a hundred times in the course of one dream. We condemn dreams, in fact, because they do not fit into a proper context, but this argument can be made inconclusive, as in Calderon's play *La Vida es Sueño*. I do not believe that I am now dreaming, but I cannot prove that I am not. I am, however, quite certain that I am having certain experiences, whether they be those of a dream or those of waking life.

We come now to another class of arguments, derived from physics and physiology. This class of arguments came into philosophy with Locke, who used it to show that secondary qualities are subjective.[1] This class of arguments is capable of being used to throw doubt on the truth of the physics and physiology, but I will first deal with them on the hypothesis that science, in the main, is true.

We experience a visual sensation when light waves reach the eye, and an auditory sensation when sound waves reach the ear. There is no reason to suppose that light waves are at all like the experience which we call seeing something, or sound waves at all like the experience which we call hearing a sound. There is no reason whatever to suppose that the physical sources of light and sound waves have any more resemblance to our experiences than the waves have. If the waves are produced in unusual ways, our experience may lead us to infer subsequent experiences which it turns out that we do not have; this shows that even in normal perception interpretation plays a larger part than common sense supposes, and that interpretation sometimes leads us to entertain false expectations.

Another difficulty is connected with time. We see and hear now, but what (according to common sense) we are seeing and hearing occurred some time ago. When we both see and hear an explosion, we see it first and hear it afterward. Even if we could suppose that the furniture of our room is exactly what it seems, we cannot suppose this of a nebula millions of light-years away, which looks like a speck but is not much smaller than the Milky Way, and of which the light that reaches us now started before human beings began to exist. And the difference between the nebula and the furniture is only one of degree.

Then there are physiological arguments. People who have lost a leg may continue to feel pain in it. Dr. Johnson, disproving Berkeley, thought the pain in his toe when he kicked a stone was evidence for the existence of the stone, but it appears that it was not even evidence for the existence of his toe, since he might have felt it even if his toe had been amputated. Speaking generally, if a nerve is stimulated in a given manner, a certain sensation results, whatever may be the source of the stimulation. Given sufficient skill, it ought to be possible to make a man see the starry heavens by tickling his optic nerve, but the instrument used would bear little resemblance to the august bodies studied by astronomers.

The above arguments, as I remarked before, may be interpreted skeptically, as showing that there is no reason to believe that our sensations have external causes. As this interpretation concedes what I am at present engaged in maintaining—namely, that sensations are the sole data for physics—I shall

1. Secondary qualities are sense qualities such as color, sound, taste, and odor. Primary qualities, on the other hand, such as extension, solidity, motion, and number, are said to exist independently of the knower (and hence are "objective"). [Ed.]

not, for the moment, consider whether it can be refuted, but shall pass on to a closely similar line of argument which is related to the method of Cartesian doubt. This method consists in searching for data by provisionally rejecting everything that it is found possible to call in question.

Descartes argues that the existence of sensible objects might be uncertain, because it would be possible for a deceitful demon to mislead us. *We* should substitute for a deceitful demon a cinema in technicolor. It is, of course, also possible that we may be dreaming. But he regards the existence of our thoughts as wholly unquestionable. When he says, "I think, therefore I am," the primitive certainties at which he may be supposed to have arrived are particular "thoughts," in the large sense in which he uses the term. His own existence is an inference from his thoughts, an inference whose validity does not at the moment concern us. In the context, what appears certain to him is that there is doubting, but the experience of doubting has no special prerogative over other experiences. When I see a flash of lightning I may, it is maintained, be uncertain as to the physical character of lightning and even as to whether anything external to myself has happened, but I cannot make myself doubt that there has been the occurrence which is called "seeing a flash of lightning," though there may have been no flash outside my seeing.

It is not suggested that I am certain about all my own experiences; this would certainly be false. Many memories are dubious, and so are many faint sensations. What I am saying—and in this I am expounding part of Descartes's argument—is that there are some occurrences that I cannot make myself doubt, and that these are all of the kind that, if we admit a not-self, are part of the life of myself. Not all of them are sensations; some are abstract thoughts, some are memories, some are wishes, some are pleasures or pains. But all are what we should commonly describe as mental events in me.

My own view is that this point of view is in the right in so far as it is concerned with data that are matters of fact. Matters of fact that lie outside my experience can be made to seem doubtful, unless there is an argument showing that their existence follows from matters of fact within my experience together with laws of whose certainty I feel reasonably convinced. But this is a long question, concerning which, at the moment, I wish to say only a few preliminary words.

Hume's skepticism with regard to the world of science resulted from (a) the doctrine that all my data are private to me, together with (b) the discovery that matters of fact, however numerous and well selected, never logically imply any other matter of fact. I do not see any way of escaping from either of these theses. The first I have been arguing; I may say that I attach especial weight in this respect to the argument from the physical causation of sensations. As to the second, it is obvious as a matter of syntax to anyone who has grasped the nature of deductive arguments. A matter of fact which is not contained in the premises must require for its assertion a proper name which does not occur in the premises. But there is only one way in which a new proper name can occur in a deductive argument, and that is when we proceed from the general to the particular, as in "All men are mortal, therefore Socrates is mortal." Now, no collection of assertions of matters of fact is logically equivalent to a general assertion, so that, if our premises concern only matters of fact, this way of introducing a new proper name is not open to us. Hence the thesis follows.

If we are not to deduce Hume's skepticism from the above two premises, there seems to be only one possible way of escape, and that is to maintain that among the premises of our knowledge, there are some general propositions, or there is at least one general proposition, which is not analytically necessary, i.e., the hypothesis of its falsehood is not self-contradictory. A principle justifying the scientific use of induction would have this character. What is needed is some way of giving probability (not certainty) to the inferences from known matters of fact to occurrences which have not yet been, and perhaps never will be, part of the experience of the person making the inference. If an individual is to know anything beyond his own experiences up to the present moment, his stock of uninferred knowledge must consist not only of matters of fact but also of general laws, or at least a law, allowing him to make inferences from matters of fact; and such law or laws must, unlike the principles of deductive logic, be synthetic, i.e., not proved true by their falsehood being self-contradictory. The only alternative to this hypothesis is complete skepticism as to all the inferences of science and common sense, including those which I have called animal inferences.

A. C. EWING

*The Criteria of Truth**

A. C. Ewing (1899–1973), a former Fellow of the British Academy, taught philosophy for many years at the University of Cambridge and was a visiting professor in numerous American universities. He published many articles in

*Reprinted with permission of Macmillan Publishing Co., Inc., from *The Fundamental Questions of Philosophy* by A. C. Ewing. First published in 1951 by Routledge & Kegan Paul, Ltd. From "Criteria of Truth," pp. 59–67.

professional journals and a dozen books, including *Idealism, A Critical Survey; The Individual, the State, and World Government; The Definition of the Good;* and *Non-Linguistic Philosophy*.

In the following selection, Ewing argues the need for distinguishing what truth is (its definition) from the tests of truth (its criteria). He then proceeds to examine and evaluate the tests that have been proposed and argues that we cannot do with just one. He concludes by explaining why he does not believe that the pragmatic test of truth can be regarded as an ultimate one.

We shall now turn to the question of the criterion or criteria of truth. This question has not always been carefully separated from the question of the definition of truth, but I think it ought to be. The question, what truth is, is in itself different from the question how we are to find out whether a proposition is true. If we know that truth is to be defined as *A*, it may be thought that this at once gives us also the criterion of truth, because we could then always look for the characteristic *A* in order to decide whether a proposition was true. But it might well be the case that *A* was something which we could not thus directly discover but must determine by indirect means. For instance, only at the best in a minority of cases could we claim to see by direct inspection whether a proposition corresponded to the real, since to do so we should have to have an immediate awareness of the latter, whereas most of the propositions which we believe are established by inference and not thus immediately seen to be true. Yet this admission would not necessarily contradict the view that correspondence constituted the definition of truth. So we had better handle separately the question of the criterion and the question of the definition of truth. The only way of determining the criterion or criteria is to investigate the different kinds of well-authenticated knowledge and belief we have and see what the criteria are that convince us of their truth. There is no means of proving *a priori* what the criteria should be apart from such an investigation of what we find we must actually believe in ordinary cases.

We might well speak of "correspondence" as the criterion of truth in cases of straightforward sense-experience or introspection. We can then observe the fact in question immediately and see whether our judgment corresponds. But, as we shall discover later, it is difficult to hold that we ever directly sense external physical objects; and in any case most of our judgments about them certainly go beyond anything we experience immediately.

What is to be the criterion of these? It may be contended that the best single word to describe it is "coherence." Certainly something that we may describe as a coherence test is needed to decide between rival scientific theories or even to distinguish illusion from genuine perception. Many of our sense-perceptions are unhesitatingly rejected just because they do not fit into a coherent system. That is the case with dreams. Why do we not believe our dreams when awake? Because they do not cohere with the perceptions of waking life. *A* dreamt that he was hanged last night, but that does not agree (cohere) with the fact that he is still alive. I sometimes dream that I am in a place hundreds or thousands of miles away from where I am when I wake, though no known means of locomotion can have transported me from there. The lack of coherence with waking life would be still more obvious if somebody else were in the room at the time I dreamt and could observe my presence. Again, if we always believed in the sense-perceptions even of waking life, we should have to suppose that the same physical thing had all manner of different shapes, since the shape varies with the position of the observer, and rather than do this we reject very many of our perceptions as illusory. In water an oar appears bent, but to assume that it is really bent would not agree (cohere) well with the fact that we can use it to row effectively. All this can be cited to show the very important part which coherence plays in our actual thinking as a test of truth. It may be said to be the sole criterion by which we distinguish illusions and correct perceptions.

A great deal of stress has rightly been laid on the supreme importance for science of observation, but it may be doubted whether there is a single accepted proposition of science which could be established by observation alone, and I do not think this is altered when we add to observation deductive logic and mathematics. An obstinate person could aways adopt the course of the opponents of Galileo when the latter claimed to have discovered the satellites of Jupiter. When they denied the existence of these bodies, Galileo challenged them to look through the newly invented telescope and see them for themselves. They replied that they knew already there were no such satellites and would not look through the telescope because, if they did, the devil might make them see them although they were not there. This is ridiculous enough, but it must be admitted both that the view is logically possible and that a similar course is adopted by all of us in regard to the objects of dreams and other appearances condemned as illusory (except that we do not attribute the deception to the devil but to our sense-organs). These objects do not conform to our intellectual standards of coherence, and so we just say they were not really there, though we have seen them perfectly well. (Of course we do not mean they are not real at all. We give them reality as sort of mental images, but not as physical things.) Even without resorting to such heroic expedients as Galileo's opponents, most physical theories that have been held at any time could avoid outright refutation if a sufficient number of arbitrary *ad hoc* assumptions were made. Take the Ptolemaic theory, for instance. If we relied on observation primarily, the right reply to Copernicus's suggestion would be that put by Bernard Shaw in the mouth of a medieval soldier: "The utter fool! Why could not he use his eyes?" It may be retorted that the Ptolemaic theory, although in accordance with experiences such as that of seeing the sun rise, was logically incompatible with observations of a more recondite order, so that these latter refuted it. But this is not the case: it would be possible to maintain the Ptolemaic system compatibly with the evidence of the senses provided we made sufficient arbitrary *ad hoc* assumptions unconnected by any principle. This was what was done in face of the first criticisms of Copernicans, but eventually as the number of such assumptions became greater the Ptolemaic theory became less and less plausible until it was quite dead, although never strictly refuted, and this is what happens with most discarded theories of science.

Advocates of the coherence theory are well aware that complete coherence must be regarded as an unattainable ideal, but views may still be judged according to their greater or less distance from it. The nearest approach to it is to be found in mathematics. Here the different propositions are so connected that each follows necessarily from others and that you could not deny any one without contradicting a vast number of others. If we assumed that 2 + 2 was equal to 5 we could, I think, without making any further mistake draw conclusions which contradicted every arithmetical truth there is about any number. Other sciences cannot attain to this degree of coherence, but in any science we assume that of two theories, equally compatible with observed facts, the one which brings us nearer to this ideal is the more likely to be the true. To be successful a theory must not be inconsistent with empirical facts, but coherence must not be interpreted in terms of mere consistency. Two truths might be quite compatible and yet quite independent and logically unconnected, e.g. that Washington is the capital of the United States and that I have a pain in my big toe. A successful theory must not just enumerate logically compatible facts without connecting them or causally explaining them. It must, if possible, bring them under laws, and the only evidence for the laws may be said to be their coherence with experience. We bring together into a coherent system what previously appeared unconnected by deducing different facts from the same set of laws, e.g. the fall of apples in an orchard and the movements of the stars. We may have no insight into the causal laws governing nature, but nevertheless in deciding what these laws are we can be swayed only by two considerations. Either we must see the laws accepted to be those which can easiest be reconciled with our experience, i.e. cohere best with it. Or we must see that they increase the coherence of our experience by bringing different elements of it together under the same law, instead of two separate unconnected laws. It is difficult to see what other criteria there could be for a scientific law, and these certainly can be brought under the heading of the principle of coherence. In our psychological interpretation of people's actions and testimony we similarly apply the coherence test, accepting the explanation which we say "makes the best sense" of their actions. We presuppose it even in a detective story, for the correct theory as to origin of the crime will be the one which accounts for the facts and fits them into a coherent system. The fundamental principles of logic themselves can be justified by this criterion on the ground that there could be no coherent system at all without these principles. But the argument does not in any way support the view that coherence by itself is the sole criterion, but rather *coherence with experience.* This would probably be admitted by most advocates of the coherence theory, but it may then be urged that "coherence with experience" really means "coherence with propositions based on experience," so that we have now admitted a second set of propositions not themselves based on coherence but on the mere fact that we can see them to correspond to our experience. The coherence criterion cannot without being thus supplemented by the correspondence criterion ever do justice to the empirical element in our knowledge. Only we must not think of the empirical data as known completely quite apart from the use of the coherence test and thus serving as an altogether independent starting-point already there in its entirety. In order really to know the empirical data, we must have already fitted them into some rough kind of system. We cannot know them, still less communicate our knowledge, without classifying them and bringing them under universal concepts, and this already presupposes a conceptual system in the light of which we make all our judgments and which is tested by its ability to give a coherent interpretation of our empirical data. We must remember that with the exception of proper names almost every word we use stands for a universal concept of one sort or other, and this means that it is part of a conceptual system which men have gradually built up in order to describe their experiences to each other and interpret them to themselves.

There are other gaps in a purely coherence theory of truth besides its inability to deal with empirical data. It is true that the coherence theory cannot get on without admitting immediate empirical cognitions not just based on coherence. But it is true also that it cannot get on without immediate cognitions of a different sort. The advocates of the coherence theory reject the view that any propositions are self-evident in their own right. They would say that the fundamental logical propositions, like the law of contradiction, which seem self-evident, are validated not by their self-evidence, but by the fact that they are presupposed if there is to be any knowledge or any coherent system at all. Of subordinate principles they would say that they must be accepted as true because, although these are not themselves necessary presuppositions of knowledge, they follow from general principles which are. But I find it hard to believe that we only know the law of contradiction because we see that without it we could have no knowledge or that we only know that numbers can be summed because we see that otherwise we could have no arithmetic or no consistent arithmetic. But, however that may be, there is in any case a definite proof that the coherence theory cannot dispense altogether with the notion of self-evidence or intuition. Suppose a belief is accepted or a proposition known because it coheres with the system. But how do we see that it coheres with the system? We might see it as the result of a process of mediate inference, but that could not go on *ad infinitum*. Sooner or later we should have to come to a proposition of which we could only say that it is evident that it coheres with the others or that we just see immediately that it coheres....

Again, I do not see how, if we were never immediately aware of the presence of goodness or badness, rightness or wrongness in any particular instance, we could ever establish any ethical proposition by the coherence test. Ethical propositions cannot be proved by argument from non-ethical, so some ethical propositions must be known immediately if we are to know any at all. Finally, I do not see how the coherence theory can give a satisfactory account of memory judgments. These are clearly not inferences, they are not established, though they may be confirmed, by coherence; they are as much given as the data of sense-perception. They represent still another kind, and a very important and all-pervasive kind of immediate cognitions.

It seems to me therefore that "coherence with experience" is not a formula adequate to cover the whole of knowledge and justified belief. There are other immediate cognitions besides those of objects of our present introspection and sense-experience. But a parallel formula might be found to cover all cases. We might say that the criterion is "coherence with direct cognitions in general." By an "immediate cognition" or "direct awareness" I mean a "cognition otherwise than by inference," thus covering alike sense-perception, introspection, memory, intuition of the logically self-evident and of immediately apprehended ethical propositions. To say that correspondence was the sole criterion would be to try to bring all criteria under the heading of this direct awareness, but the correspondence theory has to admit that we are able to make inferences beyond our immediate experience or memory. Similarly, the coherence theory has to admit that coherence by itself is not the sole criterion, but at least coherence with experience, and, I should say, "coherence with immediate cognitions in general." When this has been admitted, either theory has left a place for the other, and the difference between them has become one of relative emphasis.

It is clear in any case that we cannot do with just one criterion of truth. Neither sense-experience nor coherence can fulfil this role for all truths, if only because there are both *a priori* and empirical propositions. Intuition we have to introduce as a third criterion, if only because all inference presupposes intuitions by which we see that a stage in the inference follows from the preceding one. Since intuitions are usually concerned with facts of a kind that could not be confirmed or refuted by sense-experience or memory, coherence provides a specially valuable test for them; but coherence is also absolutely essential for building up our ordinary conception of the physical world and of human minds. Nor can we dispense with memory as a fourth means of attaining knowledge and justified belief. Memory is not sense-perception or present introspection, nor is it inference, and it can rightly claim to be its own adequate guarantee in a vast multitude of cases. Memory, introspection and perception of the immediate object of sense may perhaps be all appropriately brought under the correspondence formula as cases where we just see immediately that the propositions believed or known correspond to the facts, but it seems less appropriate to apply this formula to knowledge by inference.

The discussion has brought out the fact that there are two elements in knowledge and true belief to both of which it is essential to give an adequate place in our philosophy, (1) active construction and systematizing by the mind, (2) an objectively given basis independent of the first element and the foundation of its work. Extreme empiricism neglects the former element, most forms of the coherence and pragmatist theories the latter.

Are we to add to the other criteria the pragmatic test of which so much is said nowadays? Now no doubt a belief in a true proposition will usually (though not always) work well and a belief in a false proposition badly, and therefore practical success may commonly serve as a criterion which will at least make it likely that the proposition in question is true. But I cannot regard this criterion as an ultimate one. How are we to know that a belief works badly? Because the consequences which should follow if the belief were true do not in fact occur? But this is a direct theoretical refutation which every theory recognizes. The point which shows the belief false is not its practical bearing, i.e. that it injures somebody, but the fact that it conflicts with experience. A false belief might be refuted by a conflict with experience of a kind which was highly agreeable to the believer, as when he has a pleasant surprise. And it may be urged that we know by perception and inference a great many propositions without seeing how they work at all. To this it may be retorted that, since we do not assume all our perceptions to be correct and do not see the canons of at least inductive arguments to be logically self-evident, we must in judging what we perceive and making inductive inferences at any rate presuppose certain general principles which can only be justified by their working. The question is not whether a particular propsition works, but whether it is a consistent deduction from the application of principles of inference which have worked in dealing with experience and are justified by their working. But we may reply that this is a vicious circle. What the pragmatist is trying to justify is the belief in induction, i.e. the argument from what we have observed to the unobserved, and the argument offered to justify it is that the belief has worked in the past. But this is no argument that it will work in the future unless he already assumes the principles of induction which he is trying to justify. And, since he has not shown that they will work, these principles must be assumed independently of any test by their working. We may of course interpret "working" as "systematizing empirical facts," but then we shall be falling back on the coherence test. The question is: Can the mere fact that some belief produces good consequences, apart from any further argument which shows that the belief in question would not be likely to produce good consequences if it were not true, itself supply a criterion of truth? I am not clear why it should. If we were perfectly adjusted to the real, true beliefs would perhaps always work better than false, but then nobody can claim that we are perfectly adjusted.

The Structure of Science

NORMAN CAMPBELL

*What Is Science?**

Norman Campbell (1880–1949), an English physicist and philosopher of science, was educated at Eton and Cambridge and worked as a research assistant for a time at the Cavendish Laboratory. He spent some time on research in physics at Leeds University, and from 1919 to 1944 was a member of the research staff of the General Electric Company. His writings include *The Principles of Electricity; Physics: The Elements; Measurements and Calculations;* and the small popular work, *What is Science?* from which our selection is taken.

After distinguishing in the following essay between two forms of science, the author criticizes a common definition of science and proposes one which he holds avoids the difficulties. He then examines the nature of scientific laws and the development of these laws.

There are two forms or aspects of science. First, science is a body of useful and practical knowledge and a method of obtaining it. It is science of this form which played so large a part in the destruction of war and, it is claimed, should play an equally large part in the beneficent restoration of peace. It can work for good or for evil. If practical science made possible gas warfare, it was also the means of countering its horrors. If it was largely responsible for the evils of the industrial revolution, it has already cured many of them by decreasing the expenditure of labour and time that are necessary for the satisfaction of our material needs. In its second form or aspect, science has nothing to do with practical life and cannot affect

*Norman Campbell, from *What is Science?* (New York: Dover Publications, Inc., 1952), pp. 1–46 with omissions. Used by permission of the publisher.

it, except in the most indirect manner, either for good or for ill. Science of this form is a pure intellectual study. It is akin to painting, sculpture, or literature rather than to the technical arts. Its aim is to satisfy the needs of the mind and not those of the body; it appeals to nothing but the disinterested curiosity of mankind....

...[T]hough pure and practical science are inseparable and merely different aspects of the same study, it is necessary to remember the difference between them. And I want to point out here, once and for all, that what we are going to study directly is pure science; that the motive of our study is supposed to be intellectual curiosity without any ulterior end; and that our criterion will be always the satisfaction of our intellectual needs and not the interests of practical life. This procedure would be necessary even if our ultimate concern were rather with practical science. For it is only if we understand the nature of pure science that we can interpret with confidence the knowledge that it offers and apply it rightly to practical problems. Science, like everything else, has its limitations; there are problems, even practical problems, on which science can offer no advice whatever. One of the greatest hindrances to the proper application of science to the needs of the community lies in a failure to realize those limitations; if science is sometimes ignored, it is often because it has been discredited by an attempt to extend it to regions far beyond its legitimate province....

A DEFINITION OF SCIENCE

This discussion was started by the suggestion that we could answer our question, What is Science? by saying that science consists in the study of the external world of nature....I propose to reject that definition of science. In its place I propose to put another....This definition is: Science is the study of those judgments concerning which universal agreement can be obtained.

The connexion between this definition and the ideas that we have been considering is obvious. It is the fact that there are things concerning which universal agreement can be obtained which gives rise to our belief in an external world, and it is the judgments which are universally agreed upon which are held to give us information about that world. According to the definition proposed, the things which science studies are very closely allied to those which make up the external world of nature. Indeed, it may seem at first sight, that we are practically reverting to the definition of science as the study of nature and that there is little difference except in words between the definition which is proposed and that which has been rejected....

...It is true that the popular belief in the external world is founded primarily upon the fact of agreement about sensations; but, in deciding what part of our experience is to be referred to that external world, common sense does not adhere at all strictly to the criterion on which that belief is ultimately based. We do not ordinarily refuse to regard as part of the external world everything about which there is not universal agreement. A very simple example will illustrate this point. A moment ago a book fell from my table to the floor: I heard a sound and, looking round, saw the book on the floor. Now I had no hesitation in referring that experience to something happening in the external world; but there was not, and there cannot be, universal agreement about it or indeed any agreement at all. For I am alone in the room and nobody but myself has ever had, or can ever have, any share in that experience. Accordingly our definition of science excludes that experience of mine from the judgments which science studies, although to common sense it was certainly an event in the external world....

...All the early struggles of science for separate recognition, Bacon's revolt against mediæval learning and the nineteenth-century struggle of the "rationalists" against the domination of orthodox theology, can be interpreted ...as a demand for the acceptance of the strictly applied criterion of universal agreement as the basis for one of the branches of pure learning.

IS THERE UNIVERSAL AGREEMENT?

But objections are probably crowding in upon the reader's mind. The more he thinks about the matter, the more impossible it will appear to him that truly and perfectly universal agreement can be obtained about anything. The scientific criterion, he will think, may be an ideal, but surely even the purest and most abstract science cannot really live up to it in a world of human fallibility. Let us consider for the moment some of the objections that will probably occur to him.

In the first place, he may say that it is notorious that men of science differ among themselves, that they accuse each other of being wrong, and that their discussions are quite as acrimonious as those of their philosophical or linguistic colleagues. This is quite true, but the answer is simple. I do not say that all the propositions of science are universally accepted—nothing is further from my meaning; what I say is that the judgments which science studies and on which its final propositions are based are universally accepted. Difference of opinion enters, not with the subject-matter, but with the conclusions that are based on them.

In the second place, he may say that, if absolutely universal agreement is necessary for the subject-matter of science, a single cantankerous person who chose, out of mere perversity, to deny what every one else accepted could overthrow with one stroke the whole fabric of science; agreement would cease to be universal! Now this objection raises an important issue. How do we judge what other people think, and how do we know whether they do agree? ...We judge men's thoughts by their actions. In common life we generally use for this purpose one particular form of action, namely, speech: if a man says "I see a table" I conclude that the thoughts in his mind are the same as those in my mind when I say "I see a table." And men are generally so truthful that we do not often need to examine further. But sometimes we may suspect that a man is wilfully lying and that the relation between his words and thoughts is not normal (although it is again a relation of which we have some experience in our minds), and we can often detect the lie by examining other actions of his. Thus, if he says that he cannot see a table, we may not be able to make him change his assertion; but we may be able to induce him to walk across the room, after having distracted his attention from the matter, and then note that he, like ourselves, walks round the table and does not try to walk through it. Such tricks are familiar enough in attempts to detect malingerers in medical examinations. But what I want to point out here is that the method can only be applied to detect lies about a certain class of matters. If a man says that he does not believe that 2 and 2 make 4, or holds that an object can be both round and square, I do not see that we have any way whatsoever to prove that he does not believe what he says he believes. And the distinction is clear between the matters in which lying and imposture can be detected and those in which it can not. As we detect imposture by examining a man's actions, it is only in thoughts and beliefs that affect his actions that we can find out certainly what he thinks or believes. There may be actually universal agreement on the proposition that 2 and 2 make 4, but in this case the objection that we are considering is valid. A single denier could upset that universal agreement, and we should have no way of discounting his assertion and proving that the agreement really is universal. Accordingly, in defining science as the study of judgments concerning which universal agreement can be obtained, we are limiting science to judgments which affect action and deliberately excluding matters which, though they may actually be the subject of universal agreement, do not affect action. This conclusion is important, because it enables us to separate science clearly from pure mathematics and logic; but space cannot be spared to pursue this line of thought beyond a bare reference to it....

WHY DOES SCIENCE STUDY LAWS?

There was quoted [earlier] an example of an experience which could not be the subject-matter of science, according to our definition, because there would not be universal agreement about it. A book fell on the floor when only one person was in a position to observe the fall. Now it may be urged that this example is typical, not of a small and peculiar class of events occurring in the external world of nature and perceived by the senses, but of all such events. No event whatever has been observed by more than a very small minority of mankind, even if we include only persons who are all alive at the same time; if we include—and our definition suggests that we ought to include—all men, past, present, and future, it is still more obvious that there can be no event concerning which they can all agree; for there is no event which they can all perceive. Are we then to take the view that no event whatever is the proper subject-matter for science? And, if we take that view, what is there left in the external world which can properly be such subject-matter?

The answer is that we *are* to exclude every particular event from the subject-matter of science. It is here that science is distinguished from history; history studies particular events, but science does not. What then does science study? Science studies certain relations between particular events. It may be possible for every one to observe two events each of a particular kind, and to judge that there is some relation between those events; although the particular events of that kind which they observe are different. Thus, in our example, it is impossible for everyone to observe that a particular book fell to the floor and made a noise on striking it; but it is possible for every one to observe that, *if* a book is pushed over the edge of the table, it *will* fall to the floor and *will* make a noise on striking it. Concerning that judgment there can be universal agreement; and that agreement will not be upset, even if somebody has never actually observed a book fall; so long as he agrees when at last he is placed in the necessary circumstances, that a book will fall and that, when it falls, it will make a noise, then universal agreement is secured....

Our definition then limits science to the study of these special relations between events. And this conclusion, though the form in which it has been expressed and the reasons alleged for it may be unfamiliar, is very well known and widely recognized. For the relation of which we have spoken is often called that of "cause and effect"; to say that, if a book falls off the table, it will make a noise when it strikes the floor is much the same as to say that the noise is the effect of the fall, and the fall the cause of the noise. Again, assertions of cause and effect in nature are often called "laws" or "laws of nature"; in fact, the assertion that a book, or any other object, will fall if unsupported is one of the most familiar instances that is often offered of one of the most widely known laws, namely the law of gravitation. Accordingly, all that we have said is that science studies cause and effect and that it studies the laws of nature; nothing can be more trite than such a statement of the objects of science. Indeed, I expect that some readers thought that a great deal of unnecessary fuss was made in the previous chapter and that all our difficulties about the relations between science and nature would have vanished, if it had been said simply that science studied, not nature, but the laws of nature.

However here, as so often, the popular view, though it contains a large measure of truth, is not the whole truth. The meaning popularly attached to "cause and effect" and to "laws" is too loose and vague; "cause and effect," in the conversational sense, includes some relations which are not studied by science and excludes some that are; the assertions which are popularly regarded as laws are not invariably scientific laws, and there are many scientific laws which are not popularly termed so. The value of our definition is that it will enable us to give a more precise meaning to these terms, and to show clearly why and where scientific and popular usage differ....

THE DEVELOPMENT OF LAWS

First, we may note that there is an apparent difference between the popular conception of the part played by laws in science and that laid down by our definition. It is probably usually thought that it is the aim and object of science to discover laws, that laws are its final result. But according to our view nothing can be admitted to the domain of science at all unless it is a law, for it is only the relations expressed by laws that are capable of universal agreement. Laws are the raw material, not the final product. There is nothing inconsistent in these two statements, but the mode in which they are to be reconciled is important. Laws are both the raw material and the finished product. Science begins from laws, and on them bases other laws.

To understand how this may be let us take an example of a law; that used already is not very suitable for the purpose; the following will serve better: A steel object will rust if exposed to damp air. This is a law; it states that if one event happens another will follow; although it is the result of common observation, it would usually be regarded as lying definitely within the province of science. But now let us ask what we mean by a steel object, or by "steel." We may say that steel is a hard, shining, white substance, the hardness of which can be altered by suitable tempering, and which is attracted by a magnet. But, if we express what we mean by steel in this way, we are in effect asserting another law. We are saying that there is a substance which is *both* shining, white, *and* capable of being tempered, *and* attracted by a magnet; and that, *if* it is found to be white and capable of tempering, *then* it will be magnetic. The very idea of "steel" implies that these properties are invariably associated, and it is just these invariable associations, whether of "properties" or of "events," that are expressed by laws. In the same way "rust" implies another set of associated properties and another law; rust would not be rust, unless a certain colour were associated with a powdery form and insolubility in water.

And we can proceed further and apply the same analysis to the ideas that were employed in stating that the properties of steel are invariably associated, or, in other words, that there is such a thing as steel. For instance, we spoke of a magnet. When we say that a body is a magnet, we are again asserting an invariable association of properties; the body will deflect a compass needle and it will generate an electric current in a coil of wire rotated rapidly in its neighbourhood. The statement that there are magnets is a law asserting that these properties are invariably associated. And so we could go on finding that the things between which laws assert invariable relations are themselves characterized by other invariably associated properties.

This, then, is one of the ways in which laws may be both the original subject-matter and the final result of science. We find that certain events or certain properties, A and B, are invariably associated; the fact that they are so associated enables us to define a kind of object, or a kind of event, which may be the proper subject-matter of science. If the object or the event consisted of A and B without any invariable association between them, it might be a particular object or a particular event, and might form an important part of the popular conception of the external world, but it would not be proper subject-matter for science. Thus the man Napoleon and the battle of Waterloo are an object and an event consisting of various properties and events; but these properties and events are not invariably associated. We cannot, by placing ourselves in such circumstances that we observe some of the properties (for instance short stature, black hair, and a sallow complexion), make sure that we shall observe the other properties of Napoleon. On the other hand, iron is a kind of object suitable for the contemplation of science, and not a particular object, because, if we place ourselves in a position to observe some of the properties of iron, we can always observe the other properties. Now, having found an A and B invariably associated in this way, and therefore defining a kind of object, we seek another set of associated properties, C and D, which are again connected by a law, and form another kind of object. We now discover that the kind of object which consists of A and B invariably associated is again invariably associated with the kind of object which consists of C and D invariably associated; we can then state a new law, asserting this invariable association of (AB) with (CD); and this law marks a definite step forward in science....

...[We now turn to] a process in the development of science precisely contrary to that which we considered before. We were then considering the process by which science, starting from a relatively small number of laws, found relations between the objects of which they are the laws, and so arrived at new and more complex laws. In the second process, science takes these simple laws, analyses them, shows that they are not truly laws, and divides them up into a multitude of yet simpler laws. These two processes have been going on concurrently throughout the history of science; in one science at one time one of the processes will be predominant; in another science at another time, the other. But on the whole the first process is the earlier in time. Science started, as we have seen, from the ordinary everyday knowledge of common sense. Common sense recognizes kinds of objects and kinds of events, distinguished from particular objects and particular events by the feature we have just discussed; they imply the assertion of a law. Thus all "substances," iron, rust, water, air, wood, leather, and so on, are such kinds of objects; so again are the various kinds of animals, horses, sparrows, flies, and so on. Similarly common sense recognizes kinds of events, thunder and wind, life and death, melting and freezing, and so on; all such general terms imply some invariable association and thus are, if the association is truly invariable, proper matter for the study of science. And science in its earlier stages assumed that the association was invariable, and on that assumption proceeded to build up laws by the first process. It found that *iron* in damp *air* produced *rust;* that *poison* would cause *death.*

But, as soon as this process was well under way, the second process of analysis began; it was found that the association stated by the laws implied by the recognition of such objects was not truly invariable. This discovery was a direct consequence of the first process. Thus, until we have discovered that steel in general rusts, we are not in a position to notice that there are some steels which do not rust. When we have found that there are certain substances, otherwise like steel, but differing from other steels by being rustless, we are for the first time in a position to divide steels into two classes, those which do and those which do not rust, and so to analyse the single law implied by the use of the term "steel" into two laws, one implied by the term rusting steel, and the other by the term rustless steel. And so, again, when we have found that steel is attracted by a magnet, we are first in the position to notice that different objects, hitherto all called magnets, differ somewhat in their power of attracting steel; we can break up the single law, There are magnets, into a whole series of laws asserting the properties of all the various magnets which are distinguished by their different power of attracting steel.

This is actually the history of scientific development, so far as the discovery of laws is concerned. And now we can see why it is so difficult to say what are the fundamental and irresolvable laws on which science is ultimately built. Science is always assuming, for the time being, that certain laws are irresolvable; the law of steel, for example, in the early stages of chemistry. But later it resolves these laws, and uses for the purpose of the resolution laws which have been discovered on the assumption that they are irresolvable. At no stage is it definitely and finally asserted that the limits of analysis have been reached; it is not asserted even in the most advanced sciences of to-day; it is always recognized that a law which at present appears complete may later be shown to state an association which is not truly invariable. Moreover, the intermingling of the two processes leads to the result that a law which is regarded as final in one connexion is not regarded as final in another. We use the law that there is steel to assert the law that there are magnets, and at the same time use the law that there are magnets to assert the law that there is steel!

MORRIS R. COHEN & ERNEST NAGEL

*The Nature of Scientific Method**

Morris R. Cohen (1880–1947) taught philosophy for many years at the College of the City of New York. Among his outstanding works are *Reason and Nature, A Preface to Logic,* and *The Meaning of Human History.*

Ernest Nagel (b. 1901) taught philosophy at Columbia University from 1931 to 1970. He was editor of the *Journal of Symbolic Logic,* 1939–1945; the *Journal of Philosophy,* 1940–1956, and *Philosophy of Science,* 1956–1959. Among his books are *Principles of the Theory of Probability, Sovereign Reason,* and *The Structure of Science.*

In the following joint chapter from their text on logic, the authors clarify the meaning of scientific method and the part played by facts, evidence, hypotheses, and common sense. They point out the sense in which science is self-corrective, and indicate the abstract nature of scientific theories and their role in the explanation of events and phenomena.

§ *1. What Is Scientific Method?*

. . . [We have] asserted that the method of science is free from the limitations and willfulness of the alternative methods for settling doubt which

*Abridged from *An Introduction to Logic and Scientific Method* by Morris R. Cohen and Ernest Nagel, copyright, 1934, by Harcourt Brace Jovanovich, Inc.; copyright, 1962, by Ernest Nagel and Leonora Cohen Rosenfield.

we . . . rejected. Scientific method, we declared, is the most assured technique man has yet devised for controlling the flux of things and establishing stable beliefs. What are the fundamental features of this method? . . .

FACTS AND SCIENTIFIC METHOD

The method of science does not seek to impose the desires and hopes of men upon the flux of things in a capricious manner. It may indeed be employed to satisfy the desires of men. But its successful use depends upon seeking, in a deliberate manner, and irrespective of what men's desires are, to recognize, as well as to take advantage of, the structure which the flux possesses.

1. Consequently, scientific method aims to discover what the facts truly are, and the use of the method must be guided by the discovered facts. But, as we have repeatedly pointed out, what the facts are cannot be equated to the brute immediacy of our sensations. When our skin comes into contact with objects having high temperatures or with liquid air, the immediate experiences may be similar. We cannot, however, conclude without error that the temperatures of the substances touched are the same. Sensory experience sets the problem for knowledge, and just because such experience is immediate and final it must become informed by reflective analysis before knowledge can be said to take place.

2. Every inquiry arises from some felt problem, so that no inquiry can even get under way unless some selection or sifting of the subject matter has taken place. Such selection requires . . . some hypothesis, preconception, prejudice, which guides the research as well as delimits the subject matter of inquiry. Every inquiry is specific in the sense that it has a definite problem to solve, and such solution terminates the inquiry. It is idle to collect "facts" unless there is a problem upon which they are supposed to bear.

3. The ability to formulate problems whose solution may also help solve other problems is a rare gift, requiring extraordinary genius. The problems which meet us in daily life can be solved, if they can be solved at all, by the application of scientific method. But such problems do not, as a rule, raise far-reaching issues. The most striking applications of scientific method are to be found in the various natural and social sciences.

4. The "facts" for which every inquiry reaches out are propositions for whose truth there is considerable evidence. Consequently what the "facts" are must be determined by inquiry, and cannot be determined antecedently to inquiry. Moreover, what we believe to be the facts clearly depends upon the stage of our inquiry. There is therefore no sharp line dividing facts from guesses or hypotheses. During any inquiry the status of a proposition may change from that of hypothesis to that of fact, or from that of

fact to that of hypothesis. Every so-called fact, therefore, may be challenged for the evidence upon which it is asserted to be a fact, even though no such challenge is actually made.

HYPOTHESES AND SCIENTIFIC METHOD

The method of science would be impossible if the hypotheses which are suggested as solutions could not be elaborated to reveal what they imply. The full meaning of a hypothesis is to be discovered in its implications.

1. Hypotheses are suggested to an inquirer by something in the subject matter under investigation, and by his previous knowledge of other subject matters. No rules can be offered for obtaining fruitful hypotheses, any more than rules can be given for discovering significant problems.

2. Hypotheses are required at every stage of an inquiry. It must not be forgotten that what are called general principles or laws (which may have been confirmed in a previous inquiry) can be applied to a present, still unterminated inquiry only with some risk. For they may not in fact be applicable. The general laws of any science function as hypotheses, which guide the inquiry in all its phases.

3. Hypotheses can be regarded as suggestions of possible connections between actual facts or imagined ones. The question of the truth of hypotheses need not, therefore, always be raised. The necessary feature of a hypothesis, from this point of view, is that it should be statable in a determinate form, so that its implications can be discovered by logical means.

4. The number of hypotheses which may occur to an inquirer is without limit, and is a function of the character of his imagination. There is a need, therefore, for a technique to choose between the alternative suggestions, and to make sure that the alternatives are in fact, and not only in appearance, *different* theories. Perhaps the most important and best explored part of such a technique is the technique of formal inference....

5. It is convenient to have on hand—in storage, so to speak—different hypotheses whose consequences have been carefully explored. It is the task of mathematics to provide and explore alternative hypotheses. Mathematics receives hints concerning what hypotheses to study from the natural sciences; and the natural sciences are indebted to mathematics for suggestions concerning the type of order which their subject matter embodies.

6. The deductive elaboration of hypotheses is not the sole task of scientific method. Since there is a plurality of possible hypotheses, it is the task of inquiry to determine which of the possible explanations or solutions of the problem is in best agreement with the facts. Formal considerations are therefore never sufficient to establish the material truth of any theory.

7. No hypothesis which states a general proposition can be demon-

strated as absolutely true. We have seen that all inquiry which deals with matters of fact employs probable inference. The task of such investigations is to select that hypothesis which is the most probable on the factual evidence; and it is the task of further inquiry to find other factual evidence which will increase or decrease the probability of such a theory.

EVIDENCE AND SCIENTIFIC METHOD

Scientific method pursues the road of systematic doubt. It does not doubt *all* things, for this is clearly impossible. But it does question whatever lacks adequate evidence in its support.

1. Science is not satisfied with psychological certitude, for the mere intensity with which a belief is held is no guarantee of its truth. Science demands and looks for logically adequate grounds for the propositions it advances.

2. No single proposition dealing with matters of fact is beyond every significant doubt. No proposition is so well supported by evidence that other evidence may not increase or decrease its probability. However, while no single proposition is indubitable, the body of knowledge which supports it, and of which it is itself a part, is better grounded than any alternative body of knowledge.

3. Science is thus always ready to abandon a theory when the facts so demand. But the facts must really demand it. It is not unusual for a theory to be modified so that it may be retained in substance even though "facts" contradicted an earlier formulation of it. Scientific procedure is therefore a mixture of a willingness to change, and an obstinacy in holding on to, theories apparently incompatible with facts.

4. The verification of theories is only approximate. Verification simply shows that, within the margin of experimental error, the experiment is *compatible* with the verified hypothesis.

SYSTEM IN THE IDEAL OF SCIENCE

The ideal of science is to achieve a systematic interconnection of facts. Isolated propositions do not constitute a science. Such propositions serve merely as an opportunity to find the logical connection between them and other propositions.

1. "Common sense" is content with a miscellaneous collection of information. As a consequence, the propositions it asserts are frequently vague, the range of their application is unknown, and their mutual compatibility is generally very questionable. The advantages of discovering a system

among facts are therefore obvious. A condition for achieving a system is the introduction of accuracy in the assertions made. The limit within which propositions are true is then clearly defined. Moreover, inconsistencies between propositions asserted become eliminated gradually because propositions which are part of a system must support and correct one another. The extent and accuracy of our information is thus increased. In fact scientific method differs from other methods in the accuracy and number of facts it studies.

2. When, as frequently happens, a science abandons one theory for another, it is a mistake to suppose that science has become "bankrupt" and that it is incapable of discovering the structure of the subject matter it studies. Such changes indicate rather that the science is progressively realizing its ideal. For such changes arise from correcting previous observations or reasoning, and such correction means that we are in possession of more reliable facts.

3. The ideal of system requires that the propositions asserted to be true should be connected without the introduction of further propositions for which the evidence is small or nonexistent. In a system the number of unconnected propositions and the number of propositions for which there is no evidence are at a minimum. Consequently, in a system the requirements of simplicity, as expressed in the principle of Occam's razor, are satisfied in a high degree. For that principle declares that entities should not be multiplied beyond necessity. This may be interpreted as a demand that whatever is capable of proof should be proved. But the ideal of system requires just that.

The evidence for propositions which are elements in a system accumulates more rapidly than that for isolated propositions. The evidence for a proposition may come from its own verifying instances, or from the verifying instances of *other* propositions which are connected with the first in a system. It is this systematic character of scientific theories which gives such high probabilities to the various individual propositions of a science.

THE SELF-CORRECTIVE NATURE OF SCIENTIFIC METHOD

Science does not desire to obtain conviction for its propositions in *any* manner and at *any* price. Propositions must be supported by logically acceptable evidence, which must be weighed carefully and tested by the well-known canons of necessary and probable inference. It follows that the *method* of science is more stable, and more important to men of science, than any particular result achieved by its means.

1. In virtue of its method, the enterprise of science is a self-corrective process. It appeals to no special revelation or authority whose deliverances are indubitable and final. It claims no infallibility, but relies upon the methods of developing and testing hypotheses for assured conclusions. The canons

of inquiry are themselves discovered in the process of reflection, and may themselves become modified in the course of study. The method makes possible the noting and correction of errors by continued application of itself.

2. General propositions can be established only by the method of repeated sampling. Consequently, the propositions which a science puts forward for study are either confirmed in all possible experiments or modified in accordance with the evidence. It is this self-corrective nature of the method which allows us to challenge any proposition, but which also assures us that the theories which science accepts are more probable than any alternative theories. By not claiming more certainty than the evidence warrants, scientific method succeeds in obtaining more logical certainty than any other method yet devised.

3. In the process of gathering and weighing evidence, there is a continuous appeal from facts to theories or principles, and from principles to facts. For there is nothing intrinsically indubitable, there are no absolutely first principles, in the sense of principles which are self-evident or which must be known prior to everything else.

4. The method of science is thus essentially circular. We obtain evidence for principles by appealing to empirical material, to what is alleged to be "fact"; and we select, analyze, and interpret empirical material on the basis of principles. In virtue of such give and take between facts and principles, everything that is dubitable falls under careful scrutiny at one time or another.

THE ABSTRACT NATURE OF SCIENTIFIC THEORIES

No theory asserts *everything* that can possibly be asserted about a subject matter. Every theory selects certain aspects of it and excludes others. Unless it were possible to do this—either because such other aspects are irrelevant or because their influence on those selected is very minute—science as we know it would be impossible.

1. All theories involve abstraction from concrete subject matter. No rule can be given as to which aspects of a subject matter should be abstracted and so studied independently of other aspects. But in virtue of the goal of science—the achievement of a systematic interconnection of phenomena—in general those aspects will be abstracted which make a realization of this goal possible. Certain common elements in the phenomenon studied must be found, so that the endless variety of phenomena may be viewed as a system in which their structure is exhibited.

2. Because of the abstractness of theories, science often seems in patent contradiction with "common sense." In "common sense" the unique character and the pervasive character of things are not distinguished, so that the

attempt by science to disclose the invariant features often gives the appearance of artificiality. Theories are then frequently regarded as "convenient fictions" or as "unreal." However, such criticisms overlook the fact that it is just certain *selected invariant relations* of things in which science is interested, so that many familiar properties of things are necessarily neglected by the sciences. Moreover, they forget that "common sense" itself operates in terms of abstractions, which are familiar and often confused, and which are inadequate to express the complex structure of the flux of things....

Scientific explanation consists in subsuming under some rule or law which expresses an invariant character of a group of events, the particular events it is said to explain. Laws themselves may be explained, and in the same manner, by showing that they are consequences of more comprehensive theories. The effect of such progressive explanation of events by laws, laws by wider laws or theories, is to reveal the interconnection of many apparently isolated propositions. . . .

§ 2. *The Limits and the Value of Scientific Method*

The desire for knowledge for its own sake is more widespread than is generally recognized by anti-intellectualists. It has its roots in the animal curiosity which shows itself in the cosmological questions of children and in the gossip of adults. No ulterior utilitarian motive makes people want to know about the private lives of their neighbors, the great, or the notorious. There is also a certain zest which makes people engage in various intellectual games or exercises in which one is required to find out something. But while the desire to know is wide, it is seldom strong enough to overcome the more powerful organic desires, and few indeed have both the inclination and the ability to face the arduous difficulties of scientific method in more than one special field. The desire to know is not often strong enough to sustain critical inquiry. Men generally are interested in the results, in the story or romance of science, not in the technical methods whereby these results are obtained and their truth continually is tested and qualified. Our first impulse is to accept the plausible as true and to reject the uncongenial as false. We have not the time, inclination, or energy to investigate everything. Indeed, the call to do so is often felt as irksome and joy-killing. And when we are asked to treat our cherished beliefs as mere hypotheses, we rebel as violently as when those dear to us are insulted. This provides the ground for various movements that are hostile to rational scientific procedure (though their promoters do not often admit that it is science to which they are hostile)....

Scientific method is the only effective way of strengthening the love of truth. It develops the intellectual courage to face difficulties and to overcome illusions that are pleasant temporarily but destructive ultimately. It settles differences without any external force by appealing to our common rational nature. The way of science, even if it is up a steep mountain, is open to all. Hence, while sectarian and partisan faiths are based on personal choice or temperament and divide men, scientific procedure unites men in something nobly devoid of all pettiness. Because it requires detachment, disinterestedness, it is the finest flower and test of a liberal civilization.

JOHN DEWEY

*The Influence of Darwinism on Philosophy**

See the biographical note on p. 188.

In the following selection, Dewey discusses the influence of Darwin's "Origin of Species" on the intellectual outlook of the modern world. Within a comparatively short time man's thinking moved from an emphasis on fixity and permanence to the study of change and transition in nature, life, mind, and morals. Discussions of chance and design, mind and its place in nature, values and purpose took on a new urgency.

I

That the publication of the "Origin of Species" marked an epoch in the development of the natural sciences is well known to the layman. That the combination of the very words origin and species embodied an intellectual revolt and introduced a new intellectual temper is easily overlooked by the expert. The conceptions that had reigned in the philosophy of nature and knowledge for two thousand years, the conceptions that had become the familiar furniture of the mind, rested on the assumption of the superiority of the fixed and final; they rested upon treating change and origin as signs of defect and unreality. In laying hands upon the sacred ark of absolute permanency, in treating the forms that had been regarded as types of fixity

*John Dewey, from *The Influence of Darwin on Philosophy,* Copyright 1910, 1938 Holt, Rinehart and Winston, Inc. Reprinted by permission. Pp. 1–19 with omissions.

and perfection as originating and passing away, the "Origin of Species" introduced a mode of thinking that in the end was bound to transform the logic of knowledge, and hence the treatment of morals, politics, and religion....

II

Few words in our language foreshorten intellectual history as much as does the word species. The Greeks, in initiating the intellectual life of Europe, were impressed by characteristic traits of the life of plants and animals; so impressed indeed that they made these traits the key to defining nature and to explaining mind and society. And truly, life is so wonderful that a seemingly successful reading of its mystery might well lead men to believe that the key to the secrets of heaven and earth was in their hands. The Greek rendering of this mystery, the Greek formulation of the aim and standard of knowledge, was in the course of time embodied in the word species, and it controlled philosophy for two thousand years. To understand the intellectual face-about expressed in the phrase "Origin of Species," we must, then, understand the long dominant idea against which it is a protest.

Consider how men were impressed by the facts of life. Their eyes fell upon certain things slight in bulk, and frail in structure. To every appearance, these perceived things were inert and passive. Suddenly, under certain circumstances, these things—henceforth known as seeds or eggs or germs—begin to change, to change rapidly in size, form, and qualities. Rapid and extensive changes occur, however, in many things—as when wood is touched by fire. But the changes in the living thing are orderly; they are cumulative; they tend constantly in one direction; they do not, like other changes, destroy or consume, or pass fruitless into wandering flux; they realize and fulfil. Each successive stage, no matter how unlike its predecessor, preserves its net effect and also prepares the way for a fuller activity on the part of its successor. In living beings, changes do not happen as they seem to happen elsewhere, any which way; the earlier changes are regulated in view of later results. This progressive organization does not cease till there is achieved a true final term, a *telos,* a completed, perfected end. This final form exercises in turn a plenitude of functions, not the least noteworthy of which is production of germs like those from which it took its own origin, germs capable of the same cycle of self-fulfilling activity.

But the whole miraculous tale is not yet told. The same drama is enacted to the same destiny in countless myriads of individuals so sundered in time, so severed in space, that they have no opportunity for mutual consultation and no means of interaction. As an old writer quaintly said, "things of the same kind go through the same formalities"—celebrate, as it were, the same ceremonial rites.

This formal activity which operates throughout a series of changes and holds them to a single course; which subordinates their aimless flux to its own perfect manifestation; which, leaping the boundaries of space and time, keeps individuals distant in space and remote in time to a uniform type of structure and function: this principle seemed to give insight into the very nature of reality itself. To it Aristotle gave the name, *eidos*. This term the scholastics translated as *species*.

The force of this term was deepened by its application to everything in the universe that observes order in flux and manifests constancy through change. From the casual drift of daily weather, through the uneven recurrence of seasons and unequal return of seed time and harvest, up to the majestic sweep of the heavens—the image of eternity in time—and from this to the unchanging pure and contemplative intelligence beyond nature lies one unbroken fulfillment of ends. Nature as a whole is a progressive realization of purpose strictly comparable to the realization of purpose in any single plant or animal....

The influence of Darwin upon philosophy resides in his having conquered the phenomena of life for the principle of transition, and thereby freed the new logic for application to mind and morals and life. When he said of species what Galileo had said of the earth, *e pur se muove,* he emancipated, once for all, genetic and experimental ideas as an organon of asking questions and looking for explanations.

III

The exact bearings upon philosophy of the new logical outlook are, of course, as yet, uncertain and inchoate. We live in the twilight of intellectual transition. One must add the rashness of the prophet to the stubborness of the partizan to venture a systematic exposition of the influence upon philosophy of the Darwinian method. At best, we can but inquire as to its general bearing—the effect upon mental temper and complexion, upon that body of half-conscious, half-instinctive intellectual aversions and preferences which determine, after all, our more deliberate intellectual enterprises. In this vague inquiry there happens to exist as a kind of touchstone a problem of long historic currency that has also been much discussed in Darwinian literature. I refer to the old problem of design *versus* chance, mind *versus* matter, as the causal explanation, first or final, of things.

As we have already seen, the classic notion of species carried with it the idea of purpose. In all living forms, a specific type is present directing the earlier stages of growth to the realization of its own perfection. Since this purposive regulative principle is not visible to the senses, it follows that it must be an ideal or rational force. Since, however, the perfect form is gradually approximated through the sensible changes, it also follows that in and through a sensible realm a rational ideal force is working out its own ultimate manifestation. These inferences were extended to nature: (a) She does nothing in vain; but all for an ulterior purpose. (b) Within natural sensible events there is therefore contained a spiritual causal force, which as spiritual escapes perception, but is apprehended by an enlightened reason. (c) The manifestation of this principle brings about a subordination of matter and sense to its own realization, and this ultimate fulfillment is the goal of nature and of man. The design argument thus operated in two directions. Purposefulness accounted for the intelligibility of nature and the possibility of science, while the absolute or cosmic character of this purposefulness gave sanction and worth to the moral and religious endeavors of man. Science was underpinned and morals authorized by one and the same principle, and their mutual agreement was eternally guaranteed.

This philosophy remained, in spite of sceptical and polemic outbursts, the official and the regnant philosophy of Europe for over two thousand years. The expulsion of fixed first and final causes from astronomy, physics, and chemistry had indeed given the doctrine something of a shock. But, on the other hand, increased acquaintance with the details of plant and animal life operated as a counterbalance and perhaps even strengthened the argument from design. The marvelous adaptations of organisms to their environment, of organs to the organism, of unlike parts of a complex organ—like the eye—to the organ itself; the foreshadowing by lower forms of the higher; the preparation in earlier stages of growth for organs that only later had their functioning—these things were increasingly recognized with the progress of botany, zoology, paleontology, and embryology. Together, they added such prestige to the design argument that by the late eighteenth century it was, as approved by the sciences of organic life, the central point of theistic and idealistic philosophy.

The Darwinian principle of natural selection cut straight under this philosophy. If all organic adaptions are due simply to constant variation and the elimination of those variations which are harmful to the struggle for existence that is brought about by excessive reproduction, there is no call for a prior intelligent causal force to plan and preordain them. Hostile critics charged Darwin with materialism and with making chance the cause of the universe....

IV

So much for some of the more obvious facts of the discussion of design *versus* chance, as causal principles of nature and of life as a whole. We brought up this discussion, you recall, as a crucial instance. What does our touchstone indicate as to the bearing of Darwinian ideas upon philosophy? In the first place, the new logic outlaws, flanks, dismisses—what you will—one type of problem and substitutes for it another type. Philosophy forswears inquiry after absolute origins and absolute finalities in order to explore specific values and the specific conditions that generate them.

Darwin concluded that the impossibility of assigning the world to chance as a whole and to design in its parts indicated the insolubility of the question. Two radically different reasons, however, may be given as to why a problem is insoluble. One reason is that the problem is too high for intelligence; the other is that the question in its very asking makes assumptions that render the question meaningless. The latter alternative is unerringly pointed to in the celebrated case of design *versus* chance. Once admit that the sole verifiable or fruitful object of knowledge is the particular set of changes that generate the object of study together with the consequences that then flow from it, and no intelligible question can be asked about what, by assumption, lies outside. To assert—as it often asserted—that specific values of particular truth, social bonds and forms of beauty, if they can be shown to be generated by concretely knowable conditions, are meaningless and in vain; to assert that they are justified only when they and their particular causes and effects have all at once been gathered up into some inclusive first cause and some exhaustive final goal, is intellectual atavism. Such argumentation is reversion to the logic that explained the extinction of fire by water through the formal essence of aqueousness and the quenching of thirst by water through the final cause of aqueousness. Whether used in the case of the special event or that of life as a whole, such logic only abstracts some aspect of the existing course of events in order to reduplicate it as a petrified eternal principle by which to explain the very changes of which it is the formalization.

When Henry Sidgwick casually remarked in a letter that as he grew older his interest in what or who made the world was altered into interest in what kind of a world it is anyway, his voicing of a common experience of our own day illustrates also the nature of that intellectual transformation effected by the Darwinian logic. Interest shifts from the wholesale essence back of special changes to the question of how special changes serve and defeat concrete purposes; shifts from an intelligence that shaped things once for all to the particular intelligences which things are even now shaping; shifts from an ultimate goal of good to the direct increments of justice and happiness that intelligent administration of existent conditions may beget and that present carelessness or stupidity will destroy or forego.

In the second place, the classic type of logic inevitably set philosophy upon proving that life *must* have certain qualities and values—no matter how experience presents the matter—because of some remote cause and eventual goal. The duty of wholesale justification inevitably accompanies all thinking that makes the meaning of special occurrences depend upon something that once and for all lies behind them. The habit of derogating from present meanings and uses prevents our looking the facts of experience in the face; it prevents serious acknowledgment of the evils they present and serious concern with the goods they promise but do not as yet fulfil. It turns thought to the business of finding a wholesale transcendent remedy for the one and guarantee for the other. One is reminded of the way many moralists and theologians greeted Herbert Spencer's recognition of an unknowable energy from which welled up the phenomenal physical process without and the conscious operations within. Merely because Spencer labeled his unknowable energy "God," this faded piece of metaphysical goods was greeted as an important and grateful concession to the reality of the spiritual realm. Were it not for the deep hold of the habit of seeking justification for ideal values in the remote and transcendent, surely this reference of them to an unknowable absolute would be despised in comparison with the demonstrations of experience that knowable energies are daily generating about us precious values.

The displacing of this wholesale type of philosophy will doubtless not arrive by sheer logical disproof, but rather by growing recognition of its futility. Were it a thousand times true that opium produces sleep because of its dormitive energy, yet the inducing of sleep in the tired, and the recovery to waking life of the poisoned, would not be thereby one least step forwarded. And were it a thousand times dialectically demonstrated that life as a whole is regulated by a transcendent principle to a final inclusive goal, none the less truth and error, health and disease, good and evil, hope and fear in the concrete, would remain just what and where they now are. To improve our education, to ameliorate our manners, to advance our politics, we must have recourse to specific conditions of generation.

Finally, the new logic introduces responsibility into the intellectual life. To idealize and rationalize the universe at large is after all a confession of inability to master the courses of things that specifically concern us. As long as mankind suffered from this impotency, it naturally shifted a burden of responsibility that it could not carry over to the more competent shoulders of the transcendent cause. But if insight into specific conditions of value and into specific consequences of ideas is possible, philosophy must in time become a method of locating and interpreting the more serious of the conflicts that occur in life, and a method of projecting ways for dealing with them: a method of moral and political diagnosis and prognosis.

The claim to formulate *a priori* the legislative constitution of the universe is by its nature a claim that may lead to elaborate dialectic developments. But it is also one that removes these very conclusions from subjection to experimental test, for, by definition, these results make no differences in the detailed course of events. But a philosophy that humbles its pretensions to the work of projecting hypotheses for the education and conduct of mind, individual and social, is thereby subjected to test by the way in which the ideas it propounds work out in practice. In having modesty forced upon it, philosophy also acquires responsibility.

Doubtless I seem to have violated the implied promise of my earlier remarks and to have turned both prophet and partizan. But in anticipating the direction of the transformations in philosophy to be wrought by the Darwinian genetic and experimental logic, I do not profess to speak for any save those who yield themselves consciously or unconsciously to this logic. No one can fairly deny that at present there are two effects of the Darwinian mode of thinking. On the one hand, there are making many sincere and vital efforts to revise our traditional philosophic conceptions in accordance with its demands. On the other hand, there is as definitely a recrudescence of absolutistic philosophies; an assertion of a type of philosophic knowing distinct from that of the sciences, one which opens to us another kind of reality from that to which the sciences give access; an appeal through experience to something that essentially goes beyond experience. This reaction affects popular creeds and religious movements as well as technical philosophies. The very conquest of the biological sciences by the new ideas has led many to proclaim an explicit and rigid separation of philosophy from science.

Old ideas give way slowly; for they are more than abstract logical forms and categories. They are habits, predispositions, deeply engrained attitudes of aversion and preference. Moreover, the conviction persists—though history shows it to be a hallucination—that all the questions that the human mind has asked are questions that can be answered in terms of the alternatives that the questions themselves present. But in fact intellectual progress usually occurs through sheer abandonment of questions together with both of the alternatives they assume—an abandonment that results from their decreasing vitality and a change of urgent interest. We do not solve them: we get over them. Old questions are solved by disappearing, evaporating, while new questions corresponding to the changed attitude of endeavor and preference take their place. Doubtless the greatest dissolvent in contemporary thought of old questions, the greatest precipitant of new methods, new intentions, new problems, is the one effected by the scientific revolution that found its climax in the "Origin of Species."

WILLIAM A. EARLE

*Science and Philosophy**

William A. Earle (b. 1919) is professor of philosophy at Northwestern University. He has been visiting lecturer at Yale and Harvard. His writings include *Christianity and Existentialism, Objectivity,* and *The Autobiographical Consciousness.* He has also translated Karl Jasper's *Reason and Existenz.*

In the following selection Earle asks, What is it that philosophy can do that nothing else can do? After showing the inadequacy of the position that science is knowledge and philosophy is merely *analytic,* the handmaiden of the sciences, he insists that philosophy has its own unique subject matter. He explains what this subject matter is and defends his position with conviction.

We have all heard the story once too ofen: science is knowledge about what is; the scientific method is self-correcting, its results cumulative, and is in fact the only way in which we can achieve publicly warrantable assertions about things in the world. If in the popular phrase, "Science says it is," then it *is;* and if Science says it isn't, then it isn't. Science therefore is knowledge. But philosophy also claims to be knowledge; and yet it obviously isn't any experimental or observational science at all. Philosophy will therefore be *analytic;* it will analyze the synthetic conceptual compositions of science, render clear the method of science, its language, how it forms concepts, how it verifies them, etc. In short, we are already on that particular toboggan which carries philosophy downhill until it reaches dead rest in the form of the philosophy of science, art, religion, history, namely, the philosophy of something which is already in operation, living its own life; and I should suppose in no need whatever of our own snooping over its shoulder to correct or analyze its method. Are we not dangerously near that particular phase where philosophers have become the somewhat meddlesome handmaidens of everybody else? Part and parcel of this view is the notion that there may still be some role for philosophy, namely that of throwing off brilliant but as yet untested hypotheses, or suggesting new sci-

*William Earle, from "Science and Philosophy" in *Science, Philosophy and our Educational Tasks,* ed. John P. Anton and George Kimball Plochmann, *Buffalo Studies:* 2. (July, 1966): 59–67. Published jointly by The University Council for Educational Administration and The School of Education, State University of New York at Buffalo. Used by permission of the author and the editors.

ences. In a word, it is conceived as "speculative" in the worst, not best sense of that term, something akin to armchair science, or dreaming, an activity which again might help those too close to their own work in the laboratory, but which has no serious right to be called knowledge until tested in that laboratory. Estheticians are thus "proud" to be of help to artists; and some artists have been known to accept that help in clearing up their own esthetics, but it is doubtful if any painting was better painted as a result. Unquestionably, some philosopher of science has found something gone astray in the work of his scientist cousins, and been useful to them, much as they might be useful to one another on occasions. But is it not time that we examine the question whether philosophy must inherently be the analysis and reflection upon the ongoing activities of others, or whether in fact it has not always had another aim, another method, if it has any at all, and its *own* proud independence from *science* and also all other forms of mind. Our question, then, is what can philosophy do that nothing else can do; and secondly, whether science, as well as the philosophy of science, should not always inherently be a derived, and secondary theme for philosophy? I am here arguing that philosophy is the king of the humanities, not a handmaiden of the sciences.

Heidegger says at the outset of *Sein und Zeit* that to define philosophy as the philosophy of *life* is as pleonastic as to speak of the "botany of plants." Perhaps there are other legitimate concerns of philosophy than life, but, for all that, it has as one of its *central* concerns life, and not every form and mode of life but *human* life, namely, our own; and further, not our own lives as seen from any and every possible perspective, such as the biological, sociological, psychological, but our lives seen from the point of view of the very men living them, ourselves, as we live them, in our own living present. Speaking in and about life so considered is a possible mode of expression; the truth is, that it is what lies closest to us as living human beings. It is, if you like, a possible "subject-matter," it has its own aims, its own forms of excellence, and it is essential, I believe, to recognize that it is inherently not a subject-matter for science, nor is its excellence that of scientific method, and its goal is certainly not that of publicly warrantable assertions. It is least of all the analysis of sentences uttered by scientists. But human life so considered is that which is closest to us in every way: since it is our life, we are speaking about ourselves, and speaking about not so much what we may or may not know about nature, but about what we have done and are about to do, what we choose, what consent to, what revolt against; instead of a purportedly value-free discourse in "law-like" sentences about what is inherently not ourselves, it is at least in effort, the attempt to gain whatever clarification might be gained about a certain perpetual problem: how to live. The clarification is not of something called "humanity," but remains personal; it is not a clarification of its problem through laws or generalities, but rather through a rendering explicit of the existing singular; its utility is not in predicting the future but in rendering evident the problem and alternatives of the perpetual present. It hardly aspires to neutral, value-free observations or descriptions, but is expressive and hortatory—if we can deprive the latter term of its empty politico-religious connotations. Now, if such an effort at articulation, exhortation, clarification of ultimate horizons in life, is not warrantable public assertion, then with *that* stipulation for "knowledge," philosophy is not knowledge. It might even aspire to be wisdom. But the capturing of the term "knowledge" by science does have the disastrous effect of leaving us with no term to characterize that philosophy which is not science except as empty emotion, attitude, or posturing. But if philosophy has always sought wisdom, whatever wisdom is, it has something to do with knowing, and if the knowing in question is not scientific knowing, then it is knowing of another sort. The wise man can hardly be regarded as a fool.

I have been trying to point to a domain which I should maintain (following Karl Jaspers) is absolutely not a province to be explored by any science, since its very character is inherently not subject to either observation or experiment. Further it is not some curious corner, left over from science, of merely private or personal concern; a somewhat messy corner, where anything can be said, so long as it is said in an urgent tone. This particular domain, I believe, happens to be nothing short of our lives, and far from being undisciplined, merely emotional, a matter of guesses and hunches, is in fact the sole domain of the arts and of philosophy, when that discourse understands itself. If it is not explorable by any natural science, and if it touches precisely what we are, then the natural sciences and philosophy conceived as an analysis of the work of natural scientists, both recede into the somewhat secondary curiosities which I believe they inherently are. It is all a question of principle, and not the "present state" of science; it is not possible in principle for psychology, sociology, or cybernetics to clarify this domain, and thereupon render its philosophical clarification either superfluous, or scientifically false or true. The domains are kept distinct; and the remainder of my remarks will be an effort to make plausible this distinctness of domain, of method, and of goal. Science has virtually nothing to do with life as it is lived, its methods and attitudes. Observation, experiment, impersonal materiality transferred to life would amount to a destruction of the appropriate attitudes we entertain towards one another, and its goal of prediction through law utterly irrelevant. Yet, this domain is where we are so long as we exist. Meanwhile, although in contrast to science, it is sometimes thought that the humanistic-philosophical clarification of existence lags behind the sciences, makes no dramatic "breakthroughs," is in effect something rather apologetic and retrospective, defining itself only negatively against the brillance of modern physics, I should like to give some evidence that the domain of life has in fact been explored with a nuance and precision not merely unattained but wholly unattainable in the natural sciences, and that its expression in poetry and philosophy represents the *clearest* form of knowledge we do or could possess. But it is not publicly warrantable assertion, additive or cumulative.

The natural sciences, first of all, must gather data, pertinent to whatever problem they wish to pose. These data obviously must be experienceable; imagined or dreamed-of experiences, or experiences which in principle only a single man could have, would hardly supply a very firm foundation for pubicly warrantable assertions. And so with experiments. Both observation and experiment must be experiences of something; they must, secondly, be repeatable experiences, repeatable by a "standard observer." As we all know, the aim of the repeatable experience is to settle some problem, and the problem is, typically, to answer the question of either how things work or why they work this particular way, in a word, a law which will describe or explain the experienced; and that law again is for the purpose of predicting the character of future experiences under similar circumstances. Some such thing I would suppose to be the method of the natural sciences, and no doubt it is remarkably successful for its proper domain, nature. But its success there is a correlate to its absolute failure elsewhere, namely, in the domain of our living existence. For, first of all, it needs experienceable data of some sort. But now, if we turn that same experiencing mode of consciousness *within,* the first thing we find is that there is *nothing* there to be experienced; secondly, that my *awareness* of my present existence is not an *experience* of it at all, but rather a *reflexive consciousness* of it. The essential characteristic of anything that should be called experience is that it is a mediated awareness of an *independent object;* my perception of the stone is not the stone itself, but rather a perception of it from where I am, with my organs of perception, operating through their own appropriate media and distances. It is precisely due to this mediated character of the perceived thing, that one and the same thing could in principle simultaneously be perceived by another, and therefore supply us with a something or other which in principle could be public and repeatable, hence a fit object for scientific observation. For if anything is clear it is that my *perceptions* can not be perceived by another, are not themselves perceivable objects, and therefore my awareness of my own perceptions is not itself another perception but a reflexive awareness in which I am *immediately* aware of my own perceptions. Hence it is false to say that we experience our experiences or that we perceive our perceptions; we are indeed *aware* of performing these acts, but not by either experience or perception, whichever term is preferred. Accordingly, acts of consciousness *as* they are enacted by the consciousness, are not fit objects for either observation or experiment. This hardly implies that we are unconscious of them; but rather that our consciousness of them is immediate, and reflexive. And, since they are given immediately to consciousness itself, there is no possibility of repeatability. Another act may be performed very much like the first; but since these acts do not have a thing-like character, the only witness to the similarity would have to be the consciousness immediately having them; and in any event, similarity between two singular acts is radically distinct from the simultaneous perspectives which a plurality of observers can take on a single, perceived thing or event.

The first reason, then, why our existence as we exist in it is not a fit object for science is that it is *wholly* inaccessible to observation and experiment. It will be at once objected that this is not strictly true; we can by observing the behavior of the *body* from the outside make perfectly legitimate inferences as to what the consciousness is conscious of. In common experience, if I see a man's face contorted, I surely am safe in concluding that he is in pain. And we are told by physiologists that inferences can be drawn from measurable brain waves to the consciousness belonging to that brain. I, for one, would be the last to deny these facts. But I think their bearing on our question is different from what might seem to be the case at first sight. What are in these instances publicly observable are faces and meter-readings. What is *not* publicly observable is the pain or the dream. The line of inference, then, is not from one publicly observable to another, but from a publicly observable to a private consciousness, *never* publicly observable. The inference then rests for its plausibility on private reports by that consciousness of its own acts, which are then correlated with the public data. Further, observation directed wholly to the observable and possessing no private reflexive awareness of itself as consciousness, if such a thing were possible, could never have the slightest inkling of what it was trying to conclude *to;* unaware of the immediate sense of its own consciousness, it would run along concluding from what was observable to another thing observable, from brain states to muscle twitches, and would never have the slightest motivation for associating these observables with any private consciousness. The very sense of consciousness would be lost. We are driven to the conclusion that consciousness as it is lived may make public manifestations, but in itself it is inherently private; it must report what it is like out of its reflection, and these reflexive reports or descriptions or expressions are not based upon experience but upon immediate reflection. Further, although private, they are communicable through expression; expression has a public vehicle, like sound, or the body, but its *sense* is not equally a perceptible public object. It demands consciousness for its interpretation. Human existence as it is lived can be reported, expressed, clarified; but any observational-experimental inference to it presupposes it; if philosophy could articulate and clarify human existence, it would not be by way of inferences or supposed laws connecting observable data to the inner lived sense of that existence.

Now if we turn our reflexive consciousness to our own living present, what do we find? I said before that we find nothing. We certainly do not find something called a mind, namely our own, painted over with certain *states* or *qualities* like "pain," "pleasure," colors, shapes, etc.; instead we find ourselves *in act;* we have just come from somewhere and are going somewhere; consciousness is as it were in flight, always aimed at something which is not the flight itself, but something in its own future. We are, in this sense, always about to become something; but we never can settle into being that thing. Sartre has described this aspect of consciousness in great detail. Consciousness is inherently intentional, and projective. And so no wonder if we find nothing there but a restlessness. This supplies another very good reason why there can be no natural science of consciousness; so long as we exist, we never *are* anything to be observed. We can certainly recall what we have done; and we can imagine what we are about to do; but the present is torn between the two, a flight from one *to* the other, hence not a thing with thing-like properties, Hence even our reflexive awareness of our lives is nothing like staring within at a datum, but is an awareness of an inner projection toward what we are about to become, our possible alternatives. Or, since existence in this sense is not a collective or public project, a projection toward what *I* am about to become. But what I am *about* to do, I have *not yet* done; I must choose it, decide it, affirm it, consent to it. And, since it appears to me in the light of a *possible* act, and not already *necessarily* implicated by my present, it is of such a sort that it could either be or not; I can always say yes or no to it. I remain free, I choose what inherently depends upon my choice for its existence; and my choice of this rather than that is identical with conferring "value" upon it. The predictability from the outside of my choice has no bearing on this internal lived freedom whatsoever; if I invariably keep my promises, in short, if I am a man of character, "reliable," then indeed I can be depended upon, I act "predictably"; but I am hardly less free for choosing consistently than in being erratic, undependable. Hence, if natural science seeks a law governing experienceables according to which the future can be predicted, nothing would prevent it, so far as I can see, from finding such a law for us. But it hardly means that it has thereby disproven our freedom; it would have established nothing more than that freedom can choose coherently and consistently, and it most frequently does that when it is satisfied with its values, and can see no reason for change. Further, if natural science now turned into psychology and sociology, should find the law, it had better keep this a well-hidden secret; knowing what it was, what would prevent any of us from violating it out of spite?

To bring these remarks together: There is a domain in which the methods of the natural sciences are inapplicable, the domain of our own lives so long as we are alive, and alive for us, not for an external observer. This domain is accessible to us in the form of reflection and not observation or experiment. And our most immediate reflection upon it uncovers it as inherently characterized by singularity, freedom, projectedness, choice, and value. Summed up, our existence is a perpetual *problem* of how to exist; there can be inherently no solution which extinguishes the problem as such except the extinction of life itself. Under these circumstances, our knowledge of ourselves is not in the least publicly warrantable assertion, but far more of the character of expression, clarification, confession, and finally valuation. But this is already within the realm of the arts. The man who speaks best of how human existence is, what it can be, what it has been, is the poet, and he gives us not an "explanation" or "general law," but rather a story and a metaphor. He makes no contribution to a general science of man but rather to our own imaginative awareness of possibilities of choice, what men have chosen, what they might choose; his dependence for this upon the imagination is notorious; neither he nor the philosopher conducts observations repeatable by others or experiments. As Husserl showed, for these purposes imagination is a far superior faculty than experience. And, unless he gets led astray into allegories, he always speaks of himself, or of other singular and unique men in singular circumstances, with singular destinies. Is this "knowledge"? But if it is only the clarification and articulation of the possibilities before us, and remains an awareness of the concrete and singular *possible,* precisely what *existent* thing does he know? Man? But man, as we take him here, is but a projection into the possible; he is not finished off in the present. And yet it is awareness. If Freud as theoretician of his science knew some generalizations about men, and therefore perhaps approached something like a natural science of certain types of man, are we simply to hold Shakespeare in contrast ignorant? Or did he, too, have knowledge, or if that term is infected with scientific implications, then at least the most extended, and subtle awareness of the possibilities latent in man?

In the domain we are trying to explore, the essential thing is singularity, uniqueness, the individual, *not* the law, the principle, the general. In Hegelian terminology we are in the domain of spirit, and that is the domain of the concrete universal, not the vacuous abstractions of science but the intelligible singularities of human existence.

If the arts in general *present* or *show* us how we are, were or could be, what is left for philosophy? But the answer is, I believe, to be drawn from

Hegel. To *show* man, or rather this and that man in his singular historical circumstances, is not quite the same thing as to *think* this or that life in its singularity. But philosophy thinks; it thinks then about what art wishes to show. This of course does not mean that it is now to be the philosophy of art, esthetics, but rather it tries to think that same spirit which the arts try to show. Nor, if we reintroduce the term "thought" at this point, is the thought in question to be that almost unavoidable tendency to skim off the general from the individual, and arrive back at some universal theory of man, in which all singularities are considered only as cases of a type; and our thought, abstracting from historical singularity, contents itself with the vacuous again. The singular can be made intelligible in its singularity, and not by way of cancelling that singularity, on the supposition, utterly misled in my opinion, that only the universal in and for itself is intelligible. The artist already shows us intelligible singularities. Shakespeare exhibits Hamlet, and not Man, and Hamlet is intelligible to us not by subsuming him under supposed general psychological laws, unknown to both Shakespeare as well as Hamlet, but in his singular circumstances where everything pertinent is shown; the play is a *whole,* and that means we are shown all that, and only that, which needs to be shown to render Hamlet's unique choice intelligible. This is certainly not "explanation" but rather presupposes at every step the freedom, that is, the humanity of Hamlet.

If philosophy then tries to *think* life, rather than exhibit it in the imagination or on the stage, that thinking must be conceived not as explanation through general principles, but as a phenomenological clarification of singular human existence; and not the existence of everyone, which is the same as the existence of no one in particular, but the existence of the thinker. Gertrude Stein wrote something she called *Everybody's Autobiography,* and had the serious project of talking about everybody; but interesting as the work is, she succeeds in writing, in the end, only her own life.

Why, then, is it outrageous if a philosopher attempts to think through to the bottom his own life, in its depth and in its singularity, and bring us something which might elucidate possibilities in our own existence—in short, write an ontological autobiography? If someone should ask, Why should anyone else be interested in the merely autobiographical, what contribution would it make to the universal science of man, the appropriate reply, I suppose, would be: Why should anyone be interested in *anything else* but a singular man who is or was, who is not mankind but only himself, and perhaps, if he is or was wise enough could elucidate some possibilities of our own, so that he could help by having been there before? Considered in this light, both the natural sciences and the philosophy of science must be considered interesting curiosities but existentially irrelevant; philosophy itself is rather a passionate attempt to explore the passionate possibilities which offer themselves to passionate men. It is autobiographical, inseparable from values and urgencies, provided with its own distinctive clarity, and for these reasons above all inherently *closest* to us.

The Religious Traditions of the West

SELECTIONS FROM THE OLD TESTAMENT*

The Old Testament, containing 39 books (Genesis to Malachi), is the scripture of Judaism. Christians accept the Old Testament and an additional 27 books (Matthew to Revelation), known collectively as the New Testament. We include selections from the Islam scripture, the Koran (Qur'an), since in it Muslims make use of Old Testament and New Testament material, and include many Old Testament leaders and Jesus of Nazareth among their prophets. Mohammed, they insist, is the last, "The Seal," of the prophets.

THE TEST OF ABRAHAM: GENESIS 22:1–18.

The time came when God put Abraham to the test. 'Abraham', he called, and Abraham replied, 'Here I am.' God said, 'Take your son Isaac, your only son, whom you love, and go to the land of Moriah. There you shall offer him as a sacrifice on one of the hills which I will show you.' So Abraham rose early in the morning and saddled his ass, and he took with him two of his men and his son Isaac; and he split the firewood for the sacrifice, and set out for the place of which God had spoken. On the third day Abraham looked up and saw the place in the distance. He said to his men, 'Stay here with the ass while I and the boy go over there; and when we have worshipped we will come back to you.' So Abraham took the wood for the sacrifice and laid it on his son Isaac's shoulder; he himself carried the fire and the knife, and the two of them went on together. Isaac said to Abraham, 'Father', and he answered, 'What is it, my son?' Isaac said,

*Selections from the Old Testament and the New Testament are from *The New English Bible,* © the Delegates of the Oxford University Press and the Syndics of the Cambridge University Press, 1961, 1970. Reprinted by permission.

'Here are the fire and the wood, but where is the young beast for the sacrifice? Abraham answered, 'God will provide himself with a young beast for a sacrifice, my son.' And the two of them went on together and came to the place of which God had spoken. There Abraham built an altar and arranged the wood. He bound his son Isaac and laid him on the altar on top of the wood. Then he stretched out his hand and took the knife to kill his son; but the angel of the LORD called to him from heaven, 'Abraham, Abraham.' He answered, 'Here I am.' The angel of the LORD said, 'Do not raise your hand against the boy; do not touch him. Now I know that you are a God-fearing man. You have not withheld from me your son, your only son.' Abraham looked up, and there he saw a ram caught by its horns in a thicket. So he went and took the ram and offered it as a sacrifice instead of his son. Abraham named that place Jehovah-jireh; and to this day the saying is: 'In the mountain of the LORD it was provided.' Then the angel of the LORD called from heaven a second time to Abraham, 'This is the word of the LORD: By my own self I swear: inasmuch as you have done this and have not withheld your son, your only son, I will bless you abundantly and greatly multiply your descendants until they are as numerous as the stars in the sky and the grains of sand on the sea-shore. Your descendants shall possess the cities of their enemies. All nations on earth shall pray to be blessed as your descendants are blessed, and this because you have obeyed me.'

THE TEN COMMANDMENTS: DEUTERONOMY 5:1–22

Moses summoned all Israel and said to them: Listen, O Israel, to the statutes and the laws which I proclaim in your hearing today. Learn them and be careful to observe them. The LORD our God made a covenant with us at Horeb. It was not with our forefathers that the LORD made this covenant, but with us, all of us who are alive and are here this day. The LORD spoke with you face to face on the mountain out of the fire. I stood between the LORD and you at that time to report the words of the LORD; for you were afraid of the fire and did not go up the mountain. And the LORD said:

I am the LORD your God who brought you out of Egypt, out of the land of slavery.

You shall have no other god to set against me.

You shall not make a carved image for yourself nor the likeness of anything in the heavens above, or on the earth below, or in the waters under the earth.

You shall not bow down to them or worship them; for I, the LORD your God, am a jealous god. I punish the children for the sins of the fathers to the third and fourth generations of those who hate me. But I keep faith with thousands, with those who love me and keep my commandments.

You shall not make wrong use of the name of the LORD your God; the LORD will not leave unpunished the man who misuses his name.

Keep the sabbath day holy as the LORD your God commanded you. You have six days to labour and do all your work. But the seventh day is a sabbath of the LORD your God; that day you shall not do any work, neither you, your son or your daughter, your slave or your slave-girl, your ox, your ass, or any of your cattle, nor the alien within your gates, so that your slaves and slave-girls may rest as you do. Remember that you were slaves in Egypt and the LORD your God brought you out with a strong hand and an outstretched arm, and for that reason the LORD your God commanded you to keep the sabbath day.

Honour your father and your mother, as the LORD your God commanded you, so that you may live long, and that it may be well with you in the land which the LORD your God is giving you.

You shall not commit murder.

You shall not commit adultery.

You shall not steal.

You shall not give false evidence against your neighbour.

You shall not covet your neighbour's wife; you shall not set your heart on your neighbor's house, his land, his slave, his slave-girl, his ox, his ass, or on anything that belongs to him.

The Commandments the LORD spoke in a great voice to your whole assembly on the mountain out of the fire, the cloud, and the thick mist; then he said no more. He wrote them on two tablets of stone and gave them to me.

ONE RIGHTEOUS GOD: PSALM 145

I will extol thee, O God my king,
    and bless thy name for ever and ever.
Every day will I bless thee
    and praise thy name for ever and ever.

Great is the LORD and worthy of all praise;
    his greatness is unfathomable.
One generation shall commend thy works to another
    and set forth thy mighty deeds.
My theme shall be thy marvellous works,
    the glorious splendour of thy majesty.
Men shall declare thy mighty acts with awe
    and tell of thy great deeds.

They shall recite the story of thy abounding goodness
and sing of thy righteousness with joy.

The LORD is gracious and compassionate,
forbearing, and constant in his love.
The LORD is good to all men,
and his tender care rests upon all his creatures.

All thy creatures praise thee, LORD,
and thy servants bless thee.
They talk of the glory of thy kingdom
and tell of thy might,
they proclaim to their fellows how mighty are thy deeds,
how glorious the majesty of thy kingdom.
Thy kingdom is an everlasting kingdom,
and thy dominion stands for all generations.

In all his promises the LORD keeps faith,
he is unchanging in all his works;
the LORD holds up those who stumble
and straightens backs which are bent.
The eyes of all are lifted to thee in hope,
and thou givest them their food when it is due;
with open and bountiful hand
thou givest what they desire to every living creature.
The LORD is righteous in all his ways,
unchanging in all that he does;
very near is the LORD to those who call to him,
who call to him in singleness of heart.
He fulfils their desire if only they fear him;
he hears their cry and saves them.
The LORD watches over all who love him
but sends the wicked to their doom.
My tongue shall speak out the praises of the LORD,
and all creatures shall bless his holy name
for ever and ever.

PROPHETS OF RIGHTEOUSNESS AND JUSTICE

The man who lives an upright life and speaks the truth,
who scorns to enrich himself by extortion,
who snaps his fingers at a bribe,

who stops his ears to hear nothing of bloodshed,
who closes his eyes to the sight of evil—
that is the man who shall dwell on the heights,
his refuge a fastness in the cliffs,
his bread secure and his water never failing.

Isaiah 33:15–16

These are the words of the Lord:
Maintain justice, do the right;
for my deliverance is close at hand,
and my righteousness will show itself victorious.
Happy is the man who follows these precepts,
happy the mortal who holds them fast,
who keeps the sabbath undefiled,
who refrains from all wrong-doing!

Isaiah 56:1–2

I hate, I spurn your pilgrim-feasts;
I will not delight in your sacred ceremonies.
When you present your sacrifices and offerings
I will not accept them,
nor look on the buffaloes of your shared-offerings.
Spare me the sound of your songs;
I cannot endure the music of your lutes.
Let justice roll on like a river
and righteousness like an ever-flowing stream.

Amos 5:21–24

God has told you what is good;
and what is it that the Lord asks of you?
Only to act justly, to love loyalty,
to walk wisely before your God.

Hark, the Lord, the fear of whose name brings success,
the Lord calls to the city.
Listen, O tribe of Judah and citizens in assembly,
can I overlook the infamous false measure,
the accursed short bushel?

Can I connive at false scales or a bag of light weights?
Your rich men are steeped in violence,
your townsmen are all liars,
and their tongues frame deceit.

Micah 6:8–12

SELECTIONS FROM THE NEW TESTAMENT

See the note on p. 262.

THE STORY OF JESUS: MATTHEW 2–3

Jesus was born at Bethlehem in Judaea during the reign of Herod. After his birth astrologers from the east arrived in Jerusalem, asking, 'Where is the child who is born to be king of the Jews? We observed the rising of his star, and we have come to pay him homage.' King Herod was greatly perturbed when he heard this; and so was the whole of Jerusalem. He called a meeting of the chief priests and lawyers of the Jewish people, and put before them the question: 'Where is it that the Messiah is to be born?' 'At Bethlehem in Judaea', they replied; and they referred him to the prophecy which reads: 'Bethlehem in the land of Judah, you are far from least in the eyes of the rulers of Judah; for out of you shall come a leader to be the shepherd of my people Israel.'

Herod next called the astrologers to meet him in private, and ascertained from them the time when the star had appeared. He then sent them on to Bethlehem, and said, 'Go and make a careful inquiry for the child. When you have found him, report to me, so that I may go myself and pay him homage.'

They set out at the king's bidding; and the star which they had seen at its rising went ahead of them until it stopped above the place where the child lay. At the sight of the star they were overjoyed. Entering the house, they saw the child with Mary his mother, and bowed to the ground in homage to him; then they opened their treasures and offered him gifts: gold, frankincense, and myrrh. And being warned in a dream not to go back to Herod, they returned home another way.

After they had gone, an angel of the Lord appeared to Joseph in a dream, and said to him, 'Rise up, take the child and his mother and escape with them to Egypt, and stay there until I tell you; for Herod is going to search for the child to do away with him.' So Joseph rose from sleep, and taking mother and child by night he went away with them to Egypt, and there he stayed till Herod's death. This was to fulfil what the Lord had declared through the prophet: 'I called my son out of Egypt.'

When Herod saw how the astrologers had tricked him he fell into a passion, and gave orders for the massacre of all children in Bethlehem and its neighbourhood, of the age of two years or less, corresponding with the time he had ascertained from the astrologers. So the words spoken through Jeremiah the prophet were fulfilled: 'A voice was heard in Rama, wailing and loud laments; it was Rachel weeping for her children, and refusing all consolation, because they were no more.'

The time came that Herod died; and an angel of the Lord appeared in a dream to Joseph in Egypt and said to him, 'Rise up, take the child and his mother, and go with them to the land of Israel, for the men who threatened the child's life are dead.' So he rose, took mother and child with him, and came to the land of Israel. Hearing, however, that Archelaus had succeeded his father Herod as king of Judaea, he was afraid to go there. And being warned by a dream, he withdrew to the region of Galilee; there he settled in a town called Nazareth. This was to fulfil the words spoken through the prophets: 'He shall be called a Nazarene.'

About that time John the Baptist appeared as a preacher in the Judaean wilderness; his theme was: 'Repent; for the kingdom of Heaven is upon you! It is of him that the prophet Isaiah spoke when he said, 'A voice crying aloud in the wilderness, "Prepare a way for the Lord; clear a straight path for him." '

John's clothing was a rough coat of camel's hair, with a leather belt round his waist, and his food was locusts and wild honey. They flocked to him from Jerusalem, from all Judaea, and the whole Jordan valley, and were baptized by him in the River Jordan, confessing their sins.

When he saw many of the Pharisees and Sadducees coming for baptism he said to them: 'You vipers' brood! Who warned you to escape from the coming retribution? Then prove your repentance by the fruit it bears; and do not presume to say to yourselves, "We have Abraham for our father." I tell you that God can make children for Abraham out of these stones here. Already the axe is laid to the roots of the trees; and every tree that fails to produce good fruit is cut down and thrown on the fire. I baptize you with water, for repentance; but the one who comes after me is mightier than I. I am not fit to take off his shoes. He will baptize you with the Holy Spirit and with fire. His shovel is ready in his hand and he will winnow his threshing-floor; the wheat he will gather into his granary, but he will burn the chaff on a fire that can never go out.'

Then Jesus arrived at the Jordan from Galilee, and came to John to be baptized by him. John tried to dissuade him. 'Do you come to me?' he said; 'I need rather to be baptized by you.' Jesus replied, 'Let it be so for the present; we do well to conform in this way with all that God requires.' John then allowed him to come. After baptism Jesus came up out of the water at once, and at that moment heaven opened; he saw the Spirit of

God descending like a dove to alight upon him; and a voice from heaven was heard saying, 'This is my Son, my Beloved, on whom my favour rests.'

THE SERMON ON THE MOUNT: MATTHEW 5–7

When he saw the crowds he went up the hill. There he took his seat, and when his disciples had gathered round him he began to address them. And this is the teaching he gave:

'How blest are those who know their need of God;
  the kingdom of Heaven is theirs.
How blest are the sorrowful;
  they shall find consolation.
How blest are those of a gentle spirit;
  they shall have the earth for their possession.
How blest are those who hunger and thirst to see right prevail;
  they shall be satisfied.
How blest are those who show mercy;
  mercy shall be shown to them.
How blest are those whose hearts are pure;
  they shall see God.
How blest are the peacemakers;
  God shall call them his sons.
How blest are those who have suffered persecution for the cause of right;
  the kingdom of Heaven is theirs.

'How blest you are, when you suffer insults and persecution and every kind of calumny for my sake. Accept it with gladness and exultation, for you have a rich reward in heaven; in the same way they persecuted the prophets before you.

'You are salt to the world. And if salt becomes tasteless, how is its saltness to be restored? It is now good for nothing but to be thrown away and trodden underfoot.

'You are light for all the world. A town that stands on a hill cannot be hidden. When a lamp is lit, it is not put under the meal-tub, but on the lamp-stand, where it gives light to everyone in the house. And you, like the lamp, must shed light among your fellows, so that, when they see the good you do, they may give praise to your Father in heaven.

'Do not suppose that I have come to abolish the Law and the prophets; I did not come to abolish, but to complete. I tell you this: so long as heaven and earth endure, not a letter, not a stroke, will disappear from the Law until all that must happen has happened. If any man therefore sets aside even the least of the Law's demands, and teaches others to do the same, he will have the lowest place in the kingdom of Heaven, whereas anyone who keeps the Law, and teaches others so, will stand high in the kingdom of Heaven. I tell you, unless you show yourselves far better men than the Pharisees and the doctors of the law, you can never enter the kingdom of Heaven.

'You have learned that our forefathers were told, "Do not commit murder; anyone who commits murder must be brought to judgment." But what I tell you is this: Anyone who nurses anger against his brother must be brought to judgment. If he abuses his brother he must answer for it to the court; if he sneers at him he will have to answer for it in the fires of hell.

'If, when you are bringing your gift to the altar, you suddenly remember that your brother has a grievance against you, leave your gift where it is before the altar. First go and make your peace with your brother, and only then come back and offer your gift.

'If someone sues you, come to terms with him promptly while you are both on your way to court; otherwise he may hand you over to the judge, and the judge to the constable, and you will be put in jail. I tell you, once you are there you will not be let out till you have paid the last farthing....

'You have learned that they were told, "Eye for eye, tooth for tooth." But what I tell you is this: Do not set yourself against the man who wrongs you. If someone slaps you on the right cheek, turn and offer him your left. If a man wants to sue you for your shirt, let him have your coat as well. If a man in authority makes you go one mile, go with him two. Give when you are asked to give; and do not turn your back on a man who wants to borrow.

'You have learned that they were told, "Love your neighbour, hate your enemy." But what I tell you is this: Love your enemies and pray for your persecutors; only so can you be children of your heavenly Father, who makes his sun rise on good and bad alike, and sends the rain on the honest and the dishonest. If you love only those who love you, what reward can you expect? Surely the tax-gatherers do as much as that. And if you greet only your brothers, what is there extraordinary about that? Even the heathen do as much. There must be no limit to your goodness, as your heavenly Father's goodness knows no bounds.

'Be careful not to make a show of your religion before men; if you do, no reward awaits you in your Father's house in heaven.

'Thus, when you do some act of charity, do not announce it with a flourish of trumpets, as the hypocrites do in synagogue and in the streets to win admiration from men. I tell you this: they have their reward already. No; when you do some act of charity, do not let your left hand know what your right is doing; your good deed must be secret, and your Father who sees what is done in secret will reward you.

'Again, when you pray, do not be like the hypocrites; they love to say their prayers standing up in synagogue and at the street-corners, for everyone to see them. I tell you this: they have their reward already. But when you pray, go into a room by yourself, shut the door, and pray to your Father who is there in the secret place; and your Father who sees what is secret will reward you.

'In your prayers do not go babbling on like the heathen, who imagine that the more they say the more likely they are to be heard. Do not imitate them. Your Father knows what your needs are before you ask him.

'This is how you should pray:

> "Our Father in heaven,
> thy name be hallowed;
> thy kingdom come,
> thy will be done,
> on earth as in heaven.
> Give us today our daily bread.
> Forgive us the wrong we have done,
> as we have forgiven those who have wronged us.
> And do not bring us to the test,
> but save us from the evil one."

For if you forgive others the wrongs they have done, your heavenly Father will also forgive you; but if you do not forgive others, then the wrongs you have done will not be forgiven by your Father....

'Pass no judgment, and you will not be judged. For as you judge others, so you will yourselves be judged, and whatever measure you deal out to others will be dealt back to you. Why do you look at the speck of sawdust in your brother's eye, with never a thought for the great plank in your own? Or how can you say to your brother, "Let me take the speck out of your eye", when all the time there is that plank in your own? You hypocrite! First take the plank out of your own eye, and then you will see clearly to take the speck out of your brother's....

'Not everyone who calls me "Lord, Lord" will enter the kingdom of Heaven, but only those who do the will of my heavenly Father. When that day comes, many will say to me, "Lord, Lord, did we not prophesy in your name, cast out devils in your name, and in your name perform many miracles?" Then I will tell them to their face, "I never knew you; out of my sight, you and your wicked ways!"...

When Jesus had finished this disclosure the people were astounded at his teaching; unlike their own teachers he taught with a note of authority.

FROM THE EPISTLES OF PAUL

Love in all sincerity, loathing evil and clinging to the good. Let love for our brotherhood breed warmth of mutual affection. Give pride of place to one another in esteem.

With unflagging energy, in ardour of spirit, serve the Lord.

Let hope keep you joyful; in trouble stand firm; persist in prayer.

Contribute to the needs of God's people, and practise hospitality.

Call down blessings on your persecutors—blessings, not curses.

With the joyful be joyful, and mourn with the mourners.

Care as much about each other as about yourselves. Do not be haughty, but go about with humble folk. Do not keep thinking how wise you are.

Never pay back evil for evil. Let your aims be such as all men count honourable. If possible, so far as it lies with you, live at peace with all men. My dear friends, do not seek revenge, but leave a place for divine retribution; for there is a text which reads 'Justice is mine, says the Lord, I will repay.' But there is another text: 'If your enemy is hungry, feed him; if he is thirsty, give him a drink; by doing this you will heap live coals on his head.' Do not let evil conquer you, but use good to defeat evil.

Romans 12:9–21

And now I will show you the best way of all.

I may speak in tongues of men or of angels, but if I am without love, I am a sounding gong or a clanging cymbal. I may have the gift of prophecy, and know every hidden truth; I may have faith strong enough to move mountains; but if I have no love, I am nothing. I may dole out all I possess, or even give my body to be burnt, but if I have no love, I am none the better.

Love is patient; love is kind and envies no one. Love is never boastful, nor conceited, nor rude; never selfish, not quick to take offence. Love keeps no score of wrongs; does not gloat over other men's sins, but delights in the truth. There is nothing love cannot face; there is no limit to its faith, its hope, and its endurance.

Love will never come to an end. Are there prophets? their work will be over. Are there tongues of ecstasy? they will cease. Is there knowledge? it will vanish away; for our knowledge and our prophecy alike are partial, and the partial vanishes when wholeness comes. When I was a child, my speech, my outlook, and my thoughts were all childish. When I grew up, I had finished with childish things. Now we see only puzzling reflections in a mirror, but then we shall see face to face. My knowledge now is partial; then it will be whole, like God's knowledge of me. In a word, there are three things that last for ever: faith, hope, and love; but the greatest of them all is love.

I Corinthians 13:1–13

We must not be conceited, challenging one another to rivalry, jealous of one another. If a man should do something wrong, my brothers, on a sudden impulse, you who are endowed with the Spirit must set him right again very gently. Look to yourself, each one of you: you may be tempted too. Help one another to carry these heavy loads, and in this way you will fulfil the law of Christ.

For if a man imagines himself to be somebody, when he is nothing, he is deluding himself. Each man should examine his own conduct for himself; then he can measure his achievement by comparing himself with himself and not with anyone else. For everyone has his own proper burden to bear.

When anyone is under instruction in the faith, he should give his teacher a share of all good things he has.

Make no mistake about this: God is not to be fooled; a man reaps what he sows. If he sows seed in the field of his lower nature, he will reap from it a harvest of corruption, but if he sows in the field of the Spirit, the Spirit will bring him a harvest of eternal life. So let us never tire of doing good, for if we do not slacken our efforts we shall in due time reap our harvest. Therefore, as opportunity offers, let us work for the good of all, especially members of the household of the faith.

Galatians 6:1–10

SELECTIONS FROM THE ISLAMIC SCRIPTURES*

See the note on p. 262.

THE MOST HIGH

Praise the name of thy Lord The Most High,
Who hath created and balanced all things,
And who hath fixed their destinies and guided them;
Who bringeth forth the pastures,
Then reduceth them to dusky stubble.
We will teach thee to recite the Koran, nor aught shalt thou forget,
Save what God pleaseth; he verily knoweth alike the manifest and what

*From *The Koran,* trans. J. M. Rodwell (London: Bernard Quaritch, 1876).

is hidden;
And we will make easy for thee the easiest way.

Warn therefore; verily the warning is profitable:
He that feareth God will receive the warning,—
And the greatest wretch only will turn aside from it,
Who shall be burned at the terrible fire;
Then shall he not die therein, and shall not live.
Happy he who is purified by Islam,
And remembereth the name of his Lord and prayeth.
But ye prefer this present life,
Though the life to come is better and more enduring.
This truly is in the books of old.
The books of Abraham and Moses.

THOSE WHO STINT

Woe to those who stint the measure:
Who when they take by measure from others, exact the full;
But when they mete to them or weigh to them, minish—
Have they no thought that they shall be raised again
For a great day,
A day when mankind shall stand before the Lord of the worlds?

MORAL AND RITUAL PRESCRIPTIONS

There is no piety in turning your faces towards the east or the west, but he is pious who believeth in God and the last day and the angels and the scriptures and the prophets; who for the love of God disburseth his wealth to his kindred, and to the orphans, and the needy, and the wayfarer, and those who ask, and for ransoming; who observeth prayer, and payeth the legal alms, and who is one of those who are faithful to their engagements when they have engaged in them, and patient under ills and hardships and in time of trouble: these are they who are just, and these are they who fear God.

O believers! retaliation for bloodshedding is prescribed to you: the free man for the free, and the slave for the slave, and the woman for the woman: but he to whom his brother shall make any remission is to be dealt with equitably; and a payment should be made to him with liberality.

This is a relaxation from your Lord and a mercy. For him therefore who after this shall transgress, a sore punishment!

But in this law of retaliation is your security for life, O men of understanding! Haply ye will fear God.

It is prescribed to you when any one of you is at the point of death, that if he leave goods, he bequeath equitably to his parents and kindred; this is binding on those who fear God:—

Whoso then after he hath heard what a bequest is shall change it, the guilt of this shall be on those only who alter it; verily, God heareth, knoweth:

But he who feareth from the testator any mistake or wrong, and shall make a settlement between the parties—that then shall be no guilt in him; verily, God is forgiving, merciful.

O believers! a fast is prescribed to you, as it was prescribed to those before you, that ye may fear God,

For certain days. But he among you who shall be sick, or on a journey, shall fast the same number of other days: and for those who are able to keep it and yet break it, there shall be as an expiation the maintenance of a poor man. And he who of his own accord performeth a good work, shall derive good from it: and that ye fast is good for you—if ye but knew it.

As to the month Ramadan in which the Koran was sent down to be man's guidance, and an explanation of that guidance, and an illumination, as soon as any one of you observeth the moon, let him set about the fast; but he who is sick, or upon a journey, shall fast a like number of other days. God wisheth you ease and wisheth not your discomfort, and that you fulfil the number of days, and that you glorify God for his guidance: and haply you will be thankful.

And when my servants ask thee concerning me, then verily will I be nigh unto them—will answer the cry of him that crieth, when he crieth unto me: but let them hearken unto me, and believe in me. Haply they will proceed aright.

You are allowed on the night of the fast to approach your wives: they are your garment and ye are their garment. God knoweth that ye have mutually defrauded yourselves therein; so he turneth unto you and remitteth unto you. Now, therefore, go in unto them with full desire for that which God hath ordained for you; and eat and drink until ye can discern a white thread from a black thread by the daybreak: afterwards fast strictly till night, and go not in unto them, but pass the time in the Mosques. These are the bounds set up by God: therefore come not near to transgress them. Thus God maketh his signs clear to men: haply they will fear him.

Consume not your wealth among yourselves in vain things; nor offer it to judges as a bribe that ye may consume a part of men's wealth unjustly, while ye know the sin which ye commit.

They will ask thee of the new moons. Say: They are periods fixed for man's service and for the pilgrimage. But there is no piety in entering your houses at the back, but piety consists in the fear of God. Enter your houses then by their doors; and fear God: haply ye shall be prosperous.

ST. ANSELM

*The Ontological Argument**

St. Anselm (1033–1109), one of the most important medieval philosophers, was born in Italy of noble parentage. He went to Normandy to study and became a Benedictine monk, an abbott, and Archbishop of Canterbury in England (1093). His works include ***Cur Deus Homo*** (Why God Became Man), the *Monologium,* dealing with the divine essence, and the ***Proslogium,*** which contains the famous "ontological argument" for the existence of God. This argument, both affirmed and denied by some outstanding minds, has been debated right down to the present.

Anselm holds that the idea of God in men's minds is evidence for a genuinely existent being. Concerned with the relation between faith and reason, he believes that reason and philosophy aid faith by answering objections and furnishing understanding.

CHAPTER II.

Truly there is a God, although the fool hath said in his heart, There is no God.

And so, Lord, do thou, who dost give understanding to faith, give me, so far as thou knowest it to be profitable, to understand that thou art as we believe; and that thou art that which we believe. And, indeed, we believe that thou are a being than which nothing greater can be conceived. Or is there no such nature, since the fool hath said in his heart, there is no God? (Psalms xiv. 1). But, at any rate, this very fool, when he hears of this being of which I speak—a being than which nothing greater can be con-

*St. Anselm, from "Proslogium," trans. Sidney Norton Deane (Chicago: Open Court, 1910), pp. 7–10.

ceived—understands what he hears, and what he understands is in his understanding; although he does not understand it to exist.

For, it is one thing for an object to be in the understanding, and another to understand that the object exists. When a painter first conceives of what he will afterwards perform, he has it in his understanding, but he does not yet understand it to be, because he has not yet performed it. But after he has made the painting, he both has it in his understanding, and he understands that it exists, because he has made it.

Hence, even the fool is convinced that something exists in the understanding, at least, than which nothing greater can be conceived. For, when he hears of this, he understands it. And whatever is understood, exists in the understanding. And assuredly that, than which nothing greater can be conceived, cannot exist in the understanding alone. For, suppose it exists in the understanding alone: then it can be conceived to exist in reality; which is greater.

Therefore, if that, than which nothing greater can be conceived, exists in the understanding alone, the very being, than which nothing greater can be conceived, is one, than which a greater can be conceived. But obviously this is impossible. Hence, there is no doubt that there exists a being, than which nothing greater can be conceived, and it exists both in the understanding and in reality.

CHAPTER III.

God cannot be conceived not to exist.—God is that, than which nothing greater can be conceived.—That which can be conceived not to exist is not God.

And it assuredly exists so truly, that it cannot be conceived not to exist. For, it is possible to conceive of a being which cannot be conceived not to exist; and this is greater than one which can be conceived not to exist. Hence, if that, than which nothing greater can be conceived, can be conceived not to exist, it is not that, than which nothing greater can be conceived. But this is an irreconcilable contradiction. There is, then, so truly a being than which nothing greater can be conceived to exist, that it cannot even be conceived not to exist; and this being thou art, O Lord, our God.

So truly, therefore, dost thou exist, O Lord, my God, that thou canst not be conceived not to exist; and rightly. For, if a mind could conceive of a being better than thee, the creature would rise above the Creator; and this is most absurd. And, indeed, whatever else there is, except thee alone, can be conceived not to exist. To thee alone, therefore, it belongs to exist more truly than all other beings, and hence in a higher degree than all others. For, whatever else exists does not exist so truly, and hence in a less degree it belongs to it to exist. Why, then, has the fool said in his heart, there is no God (Psalms xiv. 1), since it is so evident, to a rational mind, that thou dost exist in the highest degree of all? Why, except that he is dull and a fool?

CHAPTER IV.

How the fool has said in his heart what cannot be conceived.—A thing may be conceived in two ways: (1) when the word signifying it is conceived; (2) when the thing is understood. As far as the word goes, God can be conceived not to exist; in reality he cannot.

But how has the fool said in his heart what he could not conceive; or how is it that he could not conceive what he said in his heart? since it is the same to say in the heart, and to conceive.

But, if really, nay, since really, he both conceived, because he said in his heart; and did not say in his heart, because he could not conceive; there is more than one way in which a thing is said in the heart or conceived. For, in one sense, an object is conceived, when the word signifying it is conceived; and in another, when the very entity, which the object is, is understood.

In the former sense, then, God can be conceived not to exist; but in the latter, not at all. For no one who understands what fire and water are can conceive fire to be water, in accordance with the nature of the facts themselves, although this is possible according to the words. So, then, no one who understands what God is can conceive that God does not exist; although he says these words in his heart, either without any, or with some foreign, signification. For, God is that than which a greater cannot be conceived. And he who thoroughly understands this, assuredly understands that this being so truly exists, that not even in concept can it be non-existent. Therefore, he who understands that God so exists, cannot conceive that he does not exist.

I thank thee, gracious Lord, I thank thee; because what I formerly believed by thy bounty, I now so understand by thine illumination, that if I were unwilling to believe that thou dost exist, I should not be able not to understand this to be true.

ST. THOMAS AQUINAS

*The Existence of God**

St. Thomas Aquinas (1225–1274), Roman Catholic theologian and philosopher, was born in Italy. His early education was under Benedictine and Dominican monks; later he attended the universities of Naples, Paris, and Cologne. After a period of teaching at the University of Paris, he spent a decade lecturing at monasteries near Rome, then returned to Paris to teach and write. His writings, all in Latin, include *Summa Contra Gentiles,* written to aid in the conversion of the Moors in Spain, and *Summa Theologica,* written as an exposition of Christian doctrine. He studied carefully the major works of Aristotle, wrote books on twelve treatises of Aristotle and on certain books of the Bible, and engaged in many controversies. In 1323 he was canonized as a saint, and he is called the Angelic Doctor. Students for the priesthood are required by Canon Law to study two years of philosophy and four of theology, "following the teaching of St. Thomas."

The selection below dealing with the existence of God illustrates Aquinas' usual method of exposition in the *Summa Theologica.* He begins with a question to which his analysis is expected to provide an answer. Then he presents objections against the position he plans to defend. He proceeds to develop his position and replies to the objections raised. His procedure is to start from some observed facts of experience and move to what he believes is the ultimate cause of these facts.

WHETHER GOD EXISTS?

We proceed thus to the Third Article:—

Objection 1. It seems that God does not exist; because if one of two contraries be infinite, the other would be altogether destroyed. But the word "God" means that He is infinite goodness. If, therefore, God existed, there would be no evil discoverable; but there is evil in the world. Therefore God does not exist.

Obj. 2. Further, it is superfluous to suppose that what can be accounted for by a few principles has been produced by many. But it seems that everything we see in the world can be accounted for by other principles, supposing God did not exist. For all natural things can be reduced to one principle, which is nature; and all voluntary things can be reduced to one

*St. Thomas Aquinas, from "The Existence of God," in *Summa Theologica* (New York: Benziger, 1911), Part I, Question 2, Article 3.

principle, which is human reason, or will. Therefore there is no need to suppose God's existence.

On the contrary, It is said in the person of God: *I am Who am* (Exod. iii. 14).

I answer that, The existence of God can be proved in five ways.

The first and more manifest way is the argument from motion. It is certain, and evident to our senses, that in the world some things are in motion. Now whatever is in motion is put in motion by another, for nothing can be in motion except it is in potentiality to that towards which it is in motion; whereas a thing moves inasmuch as it is in act. For motion is nothing else than the reduction of something from potentiality to actuality. But nothing can be reduced from potentiality to actuality, except by something in a state of actuality. Thus that which is actually hot, as fire, makes wood, which is potentially hot, to be actually hot, and thereby moves and changes it. Now it is not possible that the same thing should be at once in actuality and potentiality in the same respect, but only in different respects. For what is actually hot cannot simultaneously be potentially hot; but it is simultaneously potentially cold. It is therefore impossible that in the same respect and in the same way a thing should be both mover and moved, *i.e.,* that it should move itself. Therefore, whatever is in motion must be put in motion by another. If that by which it is put in motion be itself put in motion, then this also must needs be put in motion by another, and that by another again. But this cannot go on to infinity, because then there would be no first mover, and, consequently, no other mover; seeing that subsequent movers move only inasmuch as they are put in motion by the first mover; as the staff moves only because it is put in motion by the hand. Therefore it is necessary to arrive at a first mover, put in motion by no other; and this everyone understands to be God.

The second way is from the nature of the efficient cause. In the world of sense we find there is an order of efficient causes. There is no case known (neither is it, indeed, possible) in which a thing is found to be the efficient cause of itself; for so it would be prior to itself, which is impossible. Now in efficient causes it is not possible to go on to infinity, because in all efficient causes following in order, the first is the cause of the intermediate cause, and the intermediate is the cause of the ultimate cause, whether the intermediate cause be several, or one only. Now to take away the cause is to take away the effect. Therefore, if there be no first cause among efficient causes, there will be no ultimate, nor any intermediate cause. But if in efficient causes it is possible to go on to infinity, there will be no first efficient cause, neither will there be an ultimate effect, nor any intermediate efficient causes; all of which is plainly false. Therefore it is necessary to admit a first efficient cause, to which everyone gives the name of God.

The third way is taken from possibility and necessity, and runs thus.

We find in nature things that are possible to be and not to be, since they are found to be generated, and to corrupt, and consequently, they are possible to be and not to be. But it is impossible for these always to exist, for that which is possible not to be at some time is not. Therefore, if everything is possible not to be, then at one time there could have been nothing in existence. Now if this were true, even now there would be nothing in existence, because that which does not exist only begins to exist by something already existing. Therefore, if at one time nothing was in existence, it would have been impossible for anything to have begun to exist; and thus even now nothing would be in existence—which is absurd. Therefore, not all beings are merely possible, but there must exist something the existence of which is necessary. But every necessary thing either has its necessity caused by another, or not. Now it is impossible to go on to infinity in necessary things which have their necessity caused by another, as has been already proved in regard to efficient causes. Therefore we cannot but postulate the existence of some being having of itself its own necessity, and not receiving it from another, but rather causing in others their necessity. This all men speak of as God.

The fourth way is taken from the gradation to be found in things. Among beings there are some more and some less good, true, noble, and the like. But "more" and "less" are predicated of different things, according as they resemble in their different ways something which is the maximum, as a thing is said to be hotter according as it more nearly resembles that which is hottest; so that there is something which is truest, something best, something noblest, and consequently, something which is uttermost being; for those things that are greatest in truth are greatest in being, as it is written in *Metaph.* ii. Now the maximum in any genus is the cause of all in that genus; as fire, which is the maximum of heat, is the cause of all hot things. Therefore there must also be something which is to all beings the cause of their being, goodness, and every other perfection; and this we call God.

The fifth way is taken from the governance of the world. We see that things which lack intelligence, such as natural bodies, act for an end, and this is evident from their acting always, or nearly always, in the same way, so as to obtain the best result. Hence it is plain that not fortuitously, but designedly, do they achieve their end. Now whatever lacks intelligence cannot move towards an end, unless it be directed by some being endowed with knowledge and intelligence; as the arrow is shot to its mark by the archer. Therefore some intelligent being exists by whom all natural things are directed to their end; and this being we call God.

Reply Obj. 1. As Augustine says (*Enchir.* xi.): *Since God is the highest good, He would not allow any evil to exist in His works, unless His omnipotence and goodness were such as to bring good even out of evil.*

This is part of the infinite goodness of God, that He should allow evil to exist, and out of it produce good.

Reply Obj. 2. Since nature works for a determinate end under the direction of a higher agent, whatever is done by nature must needs be traced back to God, as to its first cause. So also whatever is done voluntarily must also be traced back to some higher cause other than human reason or will, since these can change and fail; for all things that are changeable and capable of defect must be traced back to an immovable and self-necessary first principle, as was shown in the body of the *Article*.

WILLIAM PALEY

*The Argument from Design**

William Paley (1743–1805) was an English philosopher and theologian who studied mathematics at Cambridge University where he taught for nine years. He held different offices in the Established Church and was ordained a priest and later became an archbishop. He wrote three books that were widely read: *A View of the Evidences of Christianity, The Principles of Moral and Political Philosophy,* and *Natural Theology,* from which our selection is taken.

Paley states the argument from design, also called the teleological argument, for the existence of God. He claims that design, such as found in human artifacts like the watch and in the works of nature, can be explained only in terms of a designer.

In crossing a heath, suppose I pitched my foot against a *stone,* and were asked how the stone came to be there, I might possibly answer, that for anything I knew to the contrary it had lain there forever; nor would it, perhaps, be very easy to show the absurdity of this answer. But suppose I had found a *watch* upon the ground, and it should be inquired how the watch happened to be in that place, I should hardly think of the answer which I had before given, that for anything I knew the watch might have always been there. Yet why should not this answer serve for the watch

*William Paley, from *Natural Theology* (1802), Chapters 1 and 3 with omissions. Our selection is from a late nineteenth century edition published by The American Tract Society. Also available is an edition edited by Frederick Ferré (Indianapolis: Bobbs-Merrill, 1963). [Ed.]

as well as for the stone; why is it not as admissible in the second case as in the first? For this reason, and for no other, namely, that when we come to inspect the watch, we perceive—what we could not discover in the stone—that its several parts are framed and put together for a purpose, e.g. that they are so formed and adjusted as to produce motion, and that motion so regulated as to point out the hour of the day; that if the different parts had been differently shaped from what they are, or placed after any other manner or in any other order than that in which they are placed, either no motion at all would have been carried on in the machine, or none which would have answered the use that is now served by it. To reckon up a few of the plainest of these parts and of their offices, all tending to one result: We see a cylindrical box containing a coiled elastic spring, which, by its endeavor to relax itself, turns round the box. We next observe a flexible chain—artificially wrought for the sake of flexure—communicating the action of the spring from the box to the fusee. We then find a series of wheels, the teeth of which catch in and apply to each other, conducting the motion from the fusee to the balance and from the balance to the pointer, and at the same time, by the size and shape of those wheels, so regulating that motion as to terminate in causing an index, by an equal and measured progression, to pass over a given space in a given time. We take notice that the wheels are made of brass, in order to keep them from rust; the springs of steel, no other metal being so elastic; that over the face of the watch there is placed a glass, a material employed in no other part of the work, but in the room of which, if there had been any other than a transparent substance, the hour could not be seen without opening the case. This mechanism being observed—it requires indeed an examination of the instrument, and perhaps some previous knowledge of the subject, to perceive and understand it; but being once, as we have said, observed and understood, the inference we think is inevitable, that the watch must have had a maker—that there must have existed, at some time and at some place or other, an artificer or artificers who formed it for the purpose which we find it actually to answer, who comprehended its construction and designed its use.

I. Nor would it, I apprehend, weaken the conclusion, that we had never seen a watch made—that we had never known an artist capable of making one—that we were altogether incapable of executing such a piece of workmanship ourselves, or of understanding in what manner it was performed; all this being no more than what is true of some exquisite remains of ancient art, of some lost arts, and, to the generality of mankind, of the more curious productions of modern manufacture. Does one man in a million know how oval frames are turned? Ignorance of this kind exalts our opinion of the unseen and unknown artist's skill, if he be unseen and unknown, but raises no doubt in our minds of the existence and agency of such an artist, at some former time and in some place or other. Nor can I perceive that it varies at all the inference, whether the question arise concerning a human agent or concerning an agent of a different species, or an agent possessing in some respects a different nature.

II. Neither, secondly, would it invalidate our conclusion, that the watch sometimes went wrong or that it seldom went exactly right. The purpose of the machinery, the design, and the designer might be evident, and in the case supposed, would be evident, in whatever way we accounted for the irregularity of the movement, or whether we could account for it or not. It is not necessary that a machine be perfect, in order to show with what design it was made: still less necessary, where the only question is whether it were made with any design at all.

III. Nor, thirdly, would it bring any uncertainty into the argument, if there were a few parts of the watch, concerning which we could not discover or had yet discovered in what manner they conduced to the general effect; or even some parts, concerning which we could not ascertain whether they conduced to that effect in any manner whatever. For, as to the first branch of the case, if by the loss, or disorder, or decay of the parts in question, the movement of the watch were found in fact to be stopped, or disturbed, or retarded, no doubt would remain in our minds as to the utility or intention of these parts, although we should be unable to investigate the manner according to which, or the connection by which, the ultimate effect depended upon their action or assistance; and the more complex the machine, the more likely is this obscurity to arise. Then, as to the second thing supposed, namely, that there were parts which might be spared without prejudice to the movement of the watch, and that we had proved this by experiment, these superfluous parts, even if we were completely assured that they were such, would not vacate the reasoning which we had instituted concerning other parts. The indication of contrivance remained, with respect to them, nearly as it was before.

IV. Nor, fourthly, would any man in his senses think the existence of the watch with its various machinery accounted for, by being told that it was one out of possible combinations of material forms; that whatever he had found in the place where he found the watch, must have contained some internal configuration or other; and this configuration might be the structure now exhibited, namely, of the works of a watch, as well as a different structure.

V. Nor, fifthly, would it yield his inquiry more satisfaction, to be answered that there existed in things a principle of order, which had disposed the parts of the watch into their present form and situation. He never knew a watch made by the principle of order; nor can he even form to himself an idea of what is meant by a principle of order, distinct from the intelligence of the watchmaker.

VI. Sixthly, he would be surprised to hear that the mechanism of the watch was no proof of contrivance, only a motive to induce the mind to think so:

VII. And not less surprised to be informed, that the watch in his hand was nothing more than the result of the laws of *metallic* nature. It is a perversion of language to assign any law as the efficient, operative cause of any thing. A law presupposes an agent; for it is only the mode according to which an agent proceeds: it implies a power; for it is the order according to which that power acts. Without this agent, without this power, which are both distinct from itself, the *law* does nothing, is nothing. The expression, "the law of metallic nature," may sound strange and harsh to a philosophic ear; but it seems quite as justifiable as some others which are more familiar to him, such as "the law of vegetable nature," "the law of animal nature," or, indeed, as "the law of nature" in general, when assigned as the cause of phenomena, in exclusion of agency and power, or when it is substituted into the place of these.

VIII. Neither, lastly, would our observer be driven out of his conclusion or from his confidence in its truth, by being told that he knew nothing at all about the matter. He knows enough for his argument; he knows the utility of the end; he knows the subserviency and adaptation of the means to the end. These points being known, his ignorance of other points, his doubts concerning other points, affect not the certainty of his reasoning. The consciousness of knowing little need not beget a distrust of that which he does know.

. . . Every indication of contrivance, every manifestation of design which existed in the watch, exists in the works of nature, with the difference on the side of nature of being greater and more, and that in a degree which exceeds all computation. I mean, that the contrivances of nature surpass the contrivances of art, in the complexity, subtilty, and curiosity of the mechanism; and still more, if possible, do they go beyond them in number and variety; yet, in a multitude of cases, are not less evidently mechanical, not less evidently contrivances, not less evidently accommodated to their end or suited to their office, than are the most perfect productions of human ingenuity.

JOHN E. SMITH

*The Problem of God**

John E. Smith (b. 1921) received his Ph.D. from Columbia University and taught at Vassar College and Barnard College before moving to Yale University in 1952. From 1961 to 1964 he was chairman of the Department of Philosophy at Yale. He has been a lecturer at various universities in the United States and abroad. His writings include *Royce's Social Infinite, The Spirit of American Philosophy, Religion and Empiricism, Themes in American Philosophy,* and *The Analogy of Experience.*

The author of the following selection discusses what is meant by "the problem of God" and its meaning in philosophy. He outlines the major views of the divine nature in the Western tradition and the types of arguments that have been used by thinkers attempting to prove or to support the idea of the existence of God.

Just as the *doctrine* of God is central for religion, the *problem* of God is central for the philosophy of religion. By the "problem of God" we do not mean any single question or issue, but rather a cluster of problems inevitably arising in the encounter between religion and philosophy. What do we mean by God? Does God exist? Can the existence of God be demonstrated? Can we know God through experience? These and other questions are the proper objects of attention when we speak of the problem of God.

Of special importance in the development of modern philosophy is the problem of God's reality or existence. The present age has been described as one that has lost God and is seeking to find him again. While the reality of God is the first certainty of the religious man, for philosophers it is the final problem. Philosophers and theologians alike have been forced to pay attention to the doubts that have arisen and the difficulties that must be met if we are to maintain the reality of divinity. Closely related to the question of God's reality is the problem of the divine nature. The two obviously must go together. Just as we would not consider asking whether there are any unicorns without at least a rudimentary idea of what a unicorn is like,

*Reprinted with permission of Macmillan Publishing Co., Inc. from *Philosophy of Religion,* ed. John E. Smith. Copyright © 1965 by John E. Smith. From "The Problem of God," pp. 1–8.

we cannot consider whether God exists without possessing some idea of what we are looking for. Whether God is—in whatever form that question may be raised—cannot finally be decided unless we pay attention to *what* or *who* it is we are talking about. Stated in classical terminology, the question of existence (the "that") cannot be treated abstractly, but only in relation to the essence (the "what").

Three major conceptions of the divine nature have made their appearance in the Western tradition of philosophical and religious thought. First, there is the conception of a divine Self transcending the world and interpreted in personal terms; secondly, there is the idea of God as a wholly immanent Order or Power to which all finite reality is subject; thirdly, there is the monistic conception of God as the Absolute or all-embracing totality. The first of these conceptions is found primarily in the Judeo-Christian tradition and in the writings of certain of the ancient Greek philosophers; the second idea is found in such thinkers as Spinoza and some writers in the mystical tradition; the third conception is that of Hegel and of modern absolute idealism. The three conceptions are not mutually exclusive and they have in fact interpenetrated during the long history of Western theological thought. Since there is a measure of truth in all three conceptions, only a view comprehensive enough to harmonize them successfully will be able to maintain itself. Quite apart, however, from the problem of combining the different views is the question of the connection between any one of them and the manner in which we can come to know that God exists or is real. What we understand God to be provides clues to where we shall expect to find the presence of the divine.

The first conception—God as a divine Self transcending the world—has dominated the Western tradition; most critical approaches to God's existence have presupposed this conception, although there has been considerable disagreement as to whether God is more appropriately understood as Truth, Being, and the Ground of all things, or as the First Cause and the Necessary Being found in the conclusions of the cosmological arguments. In either case God appears as a transcendent reality standing beyond both the world and human consciousness. A complete account of the relations between the different conceptions of God and the avenue of approach to the divine existence is beyond our present purpose. The problem, nevertheless, is important, for it is ultimately impossible to indicate the sort of "existence" God is to have unless we have some clear idea about the sort of reality we intend.

At least three characteristic approaches to the problem of God have been developed in the Western tradition: first, the way of critical or rational argument aiming at either an *understanding* of what is believed (Augustine and Anselm) or at *demonstration* (Aquinas) constraining the mind to accept the divine existence and certain attributes; secondly, the *mystical* route eschewing argument in favor of immediate certainty regarding the nature and existence of God through intuition or insight; third, the *negative route* followed by those who either deny the reality of God entirely, or who claim that knowledge of such matters exceeds our powers, or again, by those, like A. J. Ayer, who claim that the term "god" is meaningless and consequently that we can say nothing significant whatever about theological topics. Naturally, there have been variations within each of these approaches. Not all who accept the way of argument have been satisfied with the same arguments. Exponents of the mystical approach have appealed to many forms of immediacy—feeling, intuition, direct experience. Defenders of the negative approach include those who explicitly deny God, those who are cautious agnostics, and various forms of indifferentism.

Within the tradition of rational argument, two chief types of argument have developed—the *ontological* and the *cosmological*. The first starts with the self, our ideas and reflective capacity, and seeks to show that the very idea of God properly conceived and understood leads us to the insight that God must be real beyond our minds and their ideas. Understanding God as "that than which nothing greater can be conceived," Anselm sought to show that such a being must exist, because if it did not we would become involved in a contradiction. His argument takes the form of claiming, *first,* that since to exist is better than not to exist, unless we understand God as existing, we would be conceiving him as imperfect, which runs counter to what we mean; *second,* that the nonexistence of God is inconceivable because it is self-contradictory prima facie to deny existence to "that than which nothing greater can be conceived."

It is now generally agreed that Anselm has two forms of his argument: first, he argues that existence is a perfection and that God conceived as above must possess that perfection and hence must exist; second, he argues that the nonexistence of God is inconceivable or self-contradictory and hence that God necessarily exists. The second form of the argument pays attention to "existence" as a *mode* of being and to the different senses in which different things may be said to exist.

The ontological way of approach does not start with some outer fact or external object, but rather with the mind reflecting on itself and its ideas. It has been called the way to God that achieves its goal by drawing our thoughts away from the world of passing things in order to contemplate the meaning of the divine idea.

The cosmological approach, as the name implies, starts with the existence of the world, or of some particular facts within it or with some feature that the world exhibits in a pervasive way (for example, the orderly arrangement of things). The logical form of this argument is different from that of the ontological. The cosmological approach requires the law of causality or principle of sufficient reason. The form of the argument is as follows: Something (an object, a particular serial order, an idea) is given or acknowledged to exist; every existing thing or feature of the world we encounter must have a ground, cause or reason why it is so and not otherwise; no finite reality (that is, something that comes into existence at a time and is able to perish) is its own ground or sufficient reason; therefore, since something is acknowledged to exist, there must be at least one reality that has its own ground or sufficient reason within itself. Unless there is God or a self-existing being, nothing could become existent at all.

As a rule the proponents of the cosmological argument rejected the ontological argument on the ground that it is circular and that it could be known to be valid only by God. The chief claim in behalf of the cosmological proofs has been that, in starting with existence as given, there is no need to attempt to derive it from concepts alone. On the other side, the defenders of the ontological argument have insisted that to argue from finite, perishable things can never lead to anything other than a finite God existing in the same order as the world of finite things. Moreover, if one holds, as there are good reasons to hold, that the cosmological arguments rest on the basic principle that is behind the ontological argument, the success or failure of the arguments from the world depends upon the final disposition of the argument from perfection. A reformulated ontological argument based on a concept of perfection that allows for change and novelty and upon a defensible theory of real necessity is very difficult to refute, except by invoking positivist principles that are equally difficult to support.

As one might expect, the arguments for God have been vigorously criticized and finally rejected by some as invalid. The grounds, however, for these rejections and the philosophical motives behind them are varied. Some critics have explicitly denied the reality of God in rejecting the proofs, while others in their criticism have meant only to express skepticism about man's capacity to attain knowledge in the theological sphere. Still others maintain a kind of agnosticism, claiming that the term "God" is meaningless and hence that theological statements are neither true nor false because they do not say anything. This position is the one held by Ayer in *Language, Truth and Logic*.

In addition to these negative responses, there is the view according to which rational proofs for God are set aside, not because of doubt about the reality of God, but because of the belief that God cannot be approached through the medium of rational argument....

First, [the mystic is required] to agree with the critics of the rational arguments who say that all arguments for God must fail. Secondly, the issue is removed from the sphere of argument entirely on the ground that God's reality is a matter of direct insight. There are thus two distinct spheres of meaning or universes of discourse—the literal, the logical, and the scientific on one side, and the symbolic, the intuitive, and the religious on the other. From within the perspective of one side, the other appears opaque and unintelligible. From the literal standpoint, the rational approach to God is seen to fail; from the standpoint of religion we find that we can neither know nor have anything to do with the world of scientific explanation. There are two realms and no bridge between them. The two spheres, nevertheless, *intersect* at a point and that point is the human consciousness. Though there is an intersection, there is no interpenetration. Neither side can criticize the other because each is wholly true within its own limits. It follows from what has been said that neither side can conflict with the other; man can live in both worlds without contradiction. God can be approached only through the immediate experience of the person; knowing God is more like the intimate understanding shared by friends than like the universal knowledge of mathematics. All attempts to reach God through universal reason are abortive; all attempts to explain the world by invoking God's existence are futile. There is no point of contact between the religious and the scientific standpoints.

The ways of argument and of insight are positive in the sense that they mark out a way that leads to God. The positivist position on the other hand is radical in its opposition to the religious perspective. Positivism means the dissolution of any religious statement purporting to be true. This uncompromising conclusion is supported largely by considerations drawn from the nature of logic and the use of language. The main thesis is that to be true or false an expression must consist of terms that are meaningful; meaningful terms are those that can be verified or exemplified in *sense experience* (the logical connectives—"if, then" "and" "or" etc.—are accorded different treatment). Terms not capable of such verification are without meaning and the compound expressions in which they occur are likewise without meaning. From this it is said to follow that all forms of expression in which the term "God" is found are without meaning and cognitive import.

Any attempt to resolve the problem of God as posed by the three general approaches sketched—the way of argument, the way of insight or immediate experience, and the way of skeptical dissolution—must take the following considerations into account. First, the positivist approach can never be conclusive in its denial of God, partly because it means ignoring crucial differences between the reality of God and that of, for example, a unicorn, and partly because, to be successful, the positivist has to show the *truth* of the claim that the only meaningful terms are transcripts of sense experience. The development of modern positivism shows how very difficult it is to sustain this claim. Second, the clear-cut distinction between the way of argument and the way of experience cannot be defended. This conclusion is suggested by the fact that further analysis of each way reveals points of dependence on the other. Both the ontological and cosmological arguments depend upon experience and tradition for their points and for the intellectual framework used to elaborate them. This means that in neither case are these arguments the deliverance of "pure reason" unmixed with a concrete content derived from contact with the world and other selves. The conception of God with which the ontological argument begins is thoroughly dependent upon a way of thinking about God that stems from the Judeo-Christian perspective. This is not to say that logical refinement of the idea plays no part; it is, however, to deny that the idea springs from reason alone. Or again, the cosmological arguments explicitly set out from experience and their use within the context of any one religion requires the *identification* of the God whose existence is proved—the First Cause, the Prime Mover, and the like—with the God of the religious tradition.

If, however, the way of argument veers around to dependence upon experience, the way of experience can be seen to require a similar move in the direction of argument. The appeal to intuition or to immediate experience cannot be sustained without some form of rational support, no matter how indirect. For the question of the *trustworthiness* of intuition inevitably arises, and once this has happened we must either allay our doubts by showing that intuition is trustworthy or we must succumb to the doubts and have done with the way of insight. This means that although intuition or immediate experience may turn out to be essential for any approach to God, it is never sufficient and self-sustaining. The history of mysticism is a history of indirect arguments aimed at showing that insight is trustworthy and that in the sphere of religion we cannot do without it. In view of the mutual involvement of the two ways of approach, it is reasonable to conclude that the problem of God can be solved only through the cooperation of both.

A final consideration concerns the nature of proof itself and the function of reason in religion. We are more aware than we once were of the impossibility of giving certain proofs for propositions purporting to refer to the actual world. (God, it should be obvious, must belong to the actual.) Proof, moreover, even if it were attainable in religion, would still be insufficient because personal engagement and commitment are essential to religious faith, and both involve the total person and not only the intellect. Proof constrains and forces the mind; the question is, can proof enlist the center of the person by the same coercion? The answer is negative; two reasons support this answer. First, proof or rational coercion all by itself cannot lead to love; without love there can be no commitment to God. Second, proof or rational demonstration does not exhaust the role of reason in religion; everything depends upon the sort of meaning through which the rational argument moves. In mathematics, where the key terms are quite clear and the meanings remain quite steady, demonstration is approached, although even in mathematics there are more uncertainties than are dreamed of by laymen. In the religious sphere, the situation is quite otherwise. The meanings of the key terms, "God," "world," "idea," and so forth are difficult to make precise and they cannot be rigorously controlled throughout a process of reasoning. Demonstration cannot be attained, but understanding can. It is possible through critical reflection to lead to conviction; first, by neutralizing the objections and then by clarifying the ideas proposed for our belief by showing their analogues in concrete experience. The role of reason in religion is to lead to understanding, not to proof.

The Religious Traditions of the East

SELECTIONS FROM HINDU WRITINGS*

The first three selections are from *The Upanishads,* "Breath of the Eternal," which represent philosophical Hinduism and the worship of Brahman. They appeared 800–600 B.C. Karma, the law of sowing and reaping, comes from the *Paranas,* a collection of eighteen books representing popular Hinduism and dating about 1–250 A.D. Selections from the *Bhagavad Gita,* "Song of the Lord," appeared near the beginning of the Christian era and had great influence on the popular religion and thought. The *Gita* is a long poem in which Krishna, a god appearing as a man, carries on a dialogue with the warrior leader Arjuna, who is awaiting the start of a great battle and is perplexed about his duty since he has friends in the ranks of the enemy.

The last selection comes from the writings of Sri Ramakrishna (1836–1886), a Hindu saint and mystic who, along with Vivekananda and others, led a reform movement within Hinduism. He has attracted many disciples from all sections of Hindu society and has established missions in many parts of the world. Reality appears in many forms, and the different religions, it is claimed, represent many paths to the same truth and the one God.

*Selections from the Upanishads are from *The Upanishads, Breath of the Eternal,* by Swami Prabhavananda and Frederick Manchester (New York: New American Library, 1957, Mentor Book MP386). Used by permission of the Vedanta Society of Southern California, copyright holder. "Karma" is from *The Garuda Purana,* Manmatha Nath Dutt, ed. (Calcutta: Society for the Resuscitation of Indian Literature, 1908). Selections from the Bhagavad Gita are from *The Bhagavad Gita,* trans. Eliot Deutsch (New York: Holt, Rinehart & Winston, 1968), pp. 36–53 with omissions. Used by permission of the publisher. "Many Paths to the One God" is from *The Sayings of Sri Ramakrishna,* comp. Swami Abhedananda (New York: The Vedanta Society, 1903).

From the Upanishads

THE INDWELLING BRAHMAN

Disciples inquire within themselves: what is the cause of this universe—is it Brahman? Whence do we come? Why do we live? Where shall we at last find rest? Under whose command are we bound by the law of happiness and its opposite?

Time, space, law, chance, matter, primal energy, intelligence—none of these, nor a combination of these, can be the final cause of the universe, for they are effects, and exist to serve the soul. Nor can the individual self be the cause, for, being subject to the law of happiness and misery, it is not free.

The seers, absorbed in contemplation, saw within themselves the ultimate reality, the self-luminous being, the one God, who dwells as the self-conscious power in all creatures. He is One without a second. Deep within all beings he dwells, hidden from sight by the coverings of the gunas—*sattwa, rajas,* and *tamas.* He presides over time, space, and all apparent causes.

This vast universe is a wheel. Upon it are all creatures that are subject to birth, death, and rebirth. Round and round it turns, and never stops. It is the wheel of Brahman. As long as the individual self thinks it is separate from Brahman, it revolves upon the wheel in bondage to the laws of birth, death, and rebirth. But when through the grace of Brahman it realizes its identity with him, it revolves upon the wheel no longer. It achieves immortality.

THE REQUIREMENTS OF DUTY

The requirements of duty are three. The first is sacrifice, study, almsgiving; the second is austerity; the third is life as a student in the home of a teacher and the practice of continence. Together, these three lead one to the realm of the blest. But he who is firmly established in the knowledge of Brahman achieves immortality.

The light that shines above the heavens and above this world, the light that shines in the highest world, beyond which there are no others—that is the light that shines in the hearts of men.

Truly has this universe come forth from Brahman. In Brahman it lives and has its being. Assuredly, all is Brahman. Let a man, freed from the taint of passion, worship Brahman alone.

A man is, above all, his will. As is his will in this life, so does he become when he departs from it. Therefore should his will be fixed on attaining Brahman.

The Self, who is to be realized by the purified mind and the illumined consciousness, whose form is light, whose thoughts are true; who, like the ether, remains pure and unattached; from whom proceed all works, all desires, all odors, all tastes; who pervades all, who is beyond the senses, and in whom there is fullness of joy forever—he is my very Self, dwelling within the lotus of my heart.

Smaller than a grain of rice is the Self; smaller than a grain of barley, smaller than a mustard seed, smaller than a canary seed, yea, smaller even than the kernel of a canary seed. Yet again is that Self, within the lotus of my heart, greater than the earth, greater than the heavens, yea, greater than all the worlds.

He from whom proceed all works, all desires, all odors, all tastes; who pervades all, who is beyond the senses, and in whom there is fullness of joy forever—he, the heart-enshrined Self, is verily Brahman. I, who worship the Self within the lotus of my heart, will attain him at death. He who worships him, and puts his trust in him, shall surely attain him.

From the Garuda Purana

KARMA

A man is the creator of his own fate, and even in his foetal life he is affected by the dynamics of the works of his prior existence. Whether confined in a mountain fastness or lulling on the bosom of a sea, whether secure in his mother's lap or held high above her head, a man cannot fly from the effects of his own prior deeds.

This human body entombs a self which is nothing if not emphatically a worker. It is the works of this self in a prior existence which determine the nature of its organism in the next, as well as the character of the diseases, whether physical or mental, which it is to fall a prey to.

A man reaps that at that age, whether infancy, youth or old age, at which he had sowed it in his previous birth. The Karma of a man draws him away from a foreign country and makes him feel its consequence even in spite of his will. A man gets in life what he is fated to get, and even a god cannot make it otherwise.

From the Bhagavad Gita

THE YOGA OF KNOWLEDGE

Arjuna said:

How, O Madhusūdana (Krishna), shall I attack, with arrows in battle, Bhīshma and Drona who are worthy of worship, O slayer of enemies?

It would be better (to live) in this world by begging than to slay these noble teachers. For by slaying these teachers who desire wealth, I would enjoy only blood-smeared delights.

We do not know which is better for us, whether we should conquer them or they should conquer us. There standing before us are the sons of Dhritarāshtra; if we were to slay them, we should not wish to live.

My being is afflicted with the defect of pity; my mind is confused about my *dharma*. I ask Thee: tell me decisively which is better. I am Thy pupil; teach me, who seeks refuge in Thee. . . .

The Blessed Lord said:

Thou grievest for those thou shouldst not grieve for, and yet thou speakest words that sound like wisdom. Wise men do not mourn for the dead or for the living.

Never was there a time when I did not exist, nor thou, nor these rulers of men; nor will there ever be a time hereafter when we shall all cease to be.

As the soul in this body passes through childhood and old age, so (after departure from this body) it passes on to another body. The sage is not bewildered by this.

Contacts with the objects of the senses, O son of Kuntī (Arjuna), give rise to cold and heat, pleasure and pain. They come and go, they are impermanent; endure them, O Bhārata (Arjuna).

The man who is not troubled by these (contacts), O bull among men (Arjuna), who treats alike pleasure and pain, who is wise; he is fit for immortality.

Of non-being there is no coming to be; of being there is no ceasing to be. The truth about both is seen by the seers of truth.

Know that by which all this is pervaded is indestructible, and that no one can cause the destruction of this immutable being.

It is said that (only) these bodies of the eternal embodied (soul), which is indestructible and incomprehensible, are perishable. Therefore fight, O Bhārata (Arjuna)!

He who thinks that this (soul) is a slayer, and he who thinks that this (soul) is slain; both of them are ignorant. This (soul) neither slays nor is slain. . . .

It is uncleavable, it cannot be burnt, it can be neither wetted nor dried. It is eternal, omnipresent, unchanging and immovable. It is everlasting. . . .

Even if thou thinkest that it is constantly born and constantly dies, even then, O mighty-armed (Arjuna), thou shouldst not grieve.

For death is certain for one that has been born, and birth is certain for one that has died. Therefore for what is unavoidable, thou shouldst not grieve. . . .

Further, having regard for thine own *dharma,* thou shouldst not tremble. There exists no greater good for a Kshatriya than a battle required by duty.

Happy are the Kshatriyas, O Pārtha (Arjuna), for whom such a battle comes by mere chance, opening the door to heaven.

But if thou wilt not wage this righteous battle, then having thrown away thy duty and glory, thou wilt incur sin. . . .

In action only hast thou a right and never in its fruits. Let not thy motive be the fruits of action; nor let thy attachment be to inaction.

Fixed in yoga, O winner of wealth, perform actions, abandoning attachment and remaining evenminded in success and failure; for serenity of mind is called yoga.

(Mere) action is far inferior to the discipline of intelligence, O winner of wealth. Seek refuge in intelligence; pitiful are those whose motive is the fruit (of action). . . .

When thy intelligence, which is now perplexed by the Vedic texts, shall stand immovable and be fixed in concentration, then shalt thou attain yoga.

Arjuna said:

What is the description of the man of steady mind who is fixed in concentration, O Keshava (Krishna)? How might the man of steady mind speak, how might he sit, how might he walk?

The Blessed Lord said:

When a man abandons all the desires of his mind, O Pārtha (Arjuna), and is satisfied in his self by the self alone, then he is called a man of steady mind.

He whose mind is not troubled in sorrow, and has no desire in pleasure, his passion, fear and anger departed, he is called a steady-minded sage.

He who is not attached to anything, who neither delights nor is upset when he obtains good or evil, his mind is firmly established (in wisdom).

And when he completely withdraws his senses from the objects of sense, as a tortoise draws in his limbs, his mind is firmly established.

The objects of sense, but not the taste for them, fall away from the embodied soul who abstains from food. Even the taste falls away from him when the Supreme is seen.

The excited senses of even a wise man who strives (for perfection), O son of Kuntī, violently carry away his mind.

Having restrained them all, he should sit disciplined, intent on Me; for his mind is firmly set whose senses are under control. . . .

THE YOGA OF ACTION

Arjuna said:

If it be thought by Thee, O Janārdana (Krishna), that (the path of) knowledge is superior to (the path of) action, then why dost Thou urge me, O Keshava (Krishna), in this terrible deed?

With these apparently equivocal words, Thou confusest my understanding. Therefore tell me decisively the one path by which I may attain to the good.

The Blessed Lord said:

In this world, O blameless one, a twofold path has been taught before by Me; the path of knowledge (*jñāna yoga*) for men of discrimination (*sānkhyas*) and the path of works (*karma yoga*) for men of action (*yogins*).

Not by abstention from actions does a man gain freedom, and not by mere renunciation does he attain perfection.

No one can remain, even for a moment, without performing some action. . . .

He who controls his organs of action, but dwells in his mind on the objects of the senses; that man is deluded and is called a hypocrite.

But he who controls the senses by the mind, O Arjuna, and, without attachment, engages the organs of action in *karma yoga,* he excels.

Perform thy allotted work, for action is superior to inaction; even the maintenance of thy body cannot be accomplished without action.

This world is in bondage to *karma,* unless *karma* is performed for the sake of sacrifice. For the sake of that, O son of Kuntī, perform thy action free from attachment.

In ancient times Prajāpati created men together with sacrifice and said: By this shall ye procreate, let this be the granter of your desires.

By this nourish ye the gods and may the gods nourish thee; thus nourishing each other, ye shall attain to the highest good. . . .

Whatsoever the best man does, other men do too. Whatever standard he sets, that the world follows.

There is nothing in the three worlds, O Pārtha, to be done by Me, nor anything unobtained that needs to be obtained; yet I continue in action.

For if I, unwearied, were not always in action, O Pārtha, men everywhere would follow my path (example).

If I did not perform action, these worlds would be destroyed, and I should be the author of confusion and would destroy these people.

As the ignorant act with attachment to their work, O Bhārata, so the wise man should act (but) without attachment, desiring to maintain the order of the world.

Let no wise man unsettle the minds of the ignorant who are attached to action. Acting with discipline, he should make all action attractive. . . .

Arjuna said:

Then by what is a man impelled to (commit) sin against his will, as if compelled by force, O *Vārshneya?*

The Blessed Lord said:

It is desire, it is wrath, born of the *guna* of passion (*rajas*), all-devouring and very sinful. Know that this is the enemy here. . . .

Therefore, O best of the Bharatas, having in the beginning controlled thy senses, slay this evil destroyer of spiritual (*jñāna*) and practical (*vijñāna*) knowledge.

The senses, they say, are great; greater than the senses is the mind (*manas*); greater than the mind is the reason (*buddhi*); and greater than the reason is He.

Thus having known that which is greater than the reason, steadying the self by the self, slay the enemy, O mighty-armed one, (that has) the form of desire, and that is so hard to approach.

From the Sayings of Sri Ramakrishna

MANY PATHS TO THE ONE GOD

You see many stars at night in the sky but find them not when the sun rises; can you say that there are no stars in the heaven of day? So, O man!

because you behold not God in the days of your ignorance, say not that there is no god.

As one and the same material, water, is called by different names by different peoples, one calling it water, another eau, a third aqua, and another pani, so the one Sat-chit-ananda, the everlasting-intelligent-bliss, is invoked by some as God, by some as Allah, by some as Jehovah, by some as Hari, and by others as Brahman.

As one can ascend to the top of a house by means of a ladder or a bamboo or a staircase or a rope, so diverse are the ways and means to approach God, and every religion in the world shows one of these ways.

Different creeds are but different paths to reach the Almighty. Various and different are the ways that lead to the temple of Mother Kali at Kalighat (Calcutta). Similarly, various are the ways that lead to the house of the Lord. Every religion is nothing but one of such paths that lead to God.

As the young wife in a family shows her love and respect to her father-in-law, mother-in-law, and every other member of the family, and at the same time loves her husband more than these; similarly, being firm in thy devotion to the deity of thy own choice (Ishta-Devata), do not despise other deities, but honour them all.

Bow down and worship where others kneel, for where so many have been paying the tribute of adoration the kind Lord must manifest himself, for he is all mercy.

The Sat-chit-ananda has many forms. The devotee who has seen God in one aspect only, knows him in that aspect alone. But he who has seen him in manifold aspects is alone in a position to say, "All these forms are of one god and God is multiform." He is formless and with form, and many are his forms which no one knows.

The Vedas, Tantras, and the Puranas and all the sacred scriptures of the world have become as if defiled (as food thrown out of the mouth becomes polluted), because they have been constantly repeated by and have come out of human mouths. But the Brahman or the Absolute has never been defiled, for no one as yet has been able to express it by human speech.

The magnetic needle always points towards the north, and hence it is that the sailing vessel does not lose her course. So long as the heart of man is directed towards God, he cannot be lost in the ocean of wordliness.

Verily, verily, I say unto thee, he who longs for him, finds him. Go and verify this in thine own life; try for three consecutive days with genuine earnestness and thou arc sure to succeed.

God cannot be seen so long as there is the slightest taint of desire; therefore have thy small desires satisfied, and renounce the big desires by right reasoning and discrimination.

Knowledge and love of God are ultimately one and the same. There is no difference between pure knowledge and pure love.

The master said, "Everything that exists is God." The pupil understood it literally, but not in the right spirit.

SELECTIONS FROM BUDDHIST WRITINGS*

The first selection is said to be part of the first sermon ascribed to Gautama Buddha (b. 563 B.C.) and along with the second selection sets the four noble truths and the eight-fold path accepted by all Buddhists. The last selection stresses the meditative practices of the Ch'an (Zen) Sect as set forth by the Chinese Buddhist, Hui-neng, Sixth Patriarch, 638–713.

THE FOUNDATION OF THE KINGDOM OF RIGHTEOUSNESS

(From the First Sermon Ascribed to Gautama Buddha)

"This, monks, is the middle path the knowledge of which the Tathagata has gained, which leads to insight, which leads to wisdom, which conduces to calm, to knowledge, to perfect enlightenment, to Nirvana.

"This, monks, is the noble truth of suffering: birth is suffering; decay is suffering; death is suffering; presence of objects we hate is suffering; separation from objects we love is suffering; not to obtain what we desire is suffering.

"In brief, the five aggregates which spring from grasping, they are painful.

"This monks, is the noble truth concerning the origin of suffering: verily it originates in that craving which causes the renewal of becomings, is accompanied by sensual delight, and seeks satisfaction now here, now there; that is to say, craving for pleasures, craving for becoming, craving for not becoming.

*"The Foundation of the Kingdom of Righteousness" (from the Mahavagga) is from *The Life of Gotama the Buddha,* E. H. Brewster (London: Kegan Paul, Trench Trubner; New York: Dutton, 1926). "The Aryan Eightfold Path" (from the Maha Satipatthana Sutra) is from *Dialogues of the Buddha,* trans. T. W. and C. A. F. Rhys-Davids (London: Henry Frowde, Oxford U. Press, 1938). Copyright vested in Pali Text Society. "Meditation and Calmness" (from the *Platform Scripture*) is from *A Source Book in Chinese Philosophy,* trans. and comp. Wing-tsit Chan (Princeton: Princeton U. Press, 1963), p. 436. Reprinted by permission of the Princeton University Press.

"This monks, is the noble truth concerning the cessation of suffering. Verily, it is passionlessness, cessation without remainder of this very craving; the laying aside of, the giving up, the being free from, the harbouring no longer of, this craving.

"This, monks, is the noble truth concerning the path which leads to the cessation of suffering. Verily, it is this noble eightfold path, that is to say, right views, right intent, right speech, right conduct, right means of livelihood, right endeavour, right mindfulness and right meditation."

THE ARYAN EIGHTFOLD PATH

The Exalted One said:

"And what, bhikkhus, is the Aryan truth concerning the way it leads to the cessation of ill?

"This is that Aryan eightfold path, to wit, right view, right aspiration, right speech, right doing, right livelihood, right effort, right mindfulness, right rapture [or meditation].

"And what, bhikkhus, is right view?

"Knowledge, bhikkhus, about ill, knowledge about the coming to be of ill, knowledge about the cessation of ill, knowledge about the way that leads to the cessation of ill. This is what is called right view.

"And what, bhikkhus, is right aspiration?

"The aspiration towards renunciation, the aspiration towards benevolence, the aspiration towards kindness. This is what is called right aspiration.

"And what, bhikkhus, is right speech?

"Abstaining from lying, slander, abuse and idle talk. This is what is called right speech.

"And what, bhikkhus, is right doing?

"Abstaining from taking life, from taking what is not given, from carnal indulgence. This is what is called right doing.

"And what, bhikkhus, is right livelihood?

"Herein, O bhikkhus, the Aryan disciple, having put away wrong livelihood, supports himself by right livelihood.

"And what, bhikkhus, is right effort?

"Herein, O bhikkhus, a brother makes effort in bringing forth will that evil and bad states that have not arisen within him may not arise; to that end he stirs up energy, he grips and forces his mind. That he may put away evil and bad states that have arisen within him he puts forth will, he makes effort, he stirs up energy, he grips and forces his mind. That good states which have not arisen may arise he puts forth will, he makes effort, he stirs up energy, he grips and forces his mind. That good states which have arisen may persist, may not grow blurred, may multiply, grow abundant, develop and come to perfection, he puts forth will, he makes effort, he stirs up energy, he grips and forces his mind. This is what is called right effort.

"And what, bhikkhus, is right mindfulness?

"Herein, O bhikkhus, a brother, as to the body, continues so to look upon the body, that he remains ardent, self-possessed and mindful, having overcome both the hankering and the dejection common in the world. And in the same way as to feelings, thoughts and ideas, he so looks upon each, that he remains ardent, self-possessed and mindful, having overcome the hankering and the dejection that is common in the world. This is what is called right mindfulness.

"And what, bhikkhus, is right rapture [or meditation]?

"Herein, O bhikkhus, a brother, aloof from sensuous appetites, aloof from evil ideas, enters into and abides in the first Jhana, wherein there is cogitation and deliberation, which is born of solitude and is full of joy and ease. Suppressing cogitation and deliberation, he enters into and abides in the second Jhana, which is self-evoked, born of concentration, full of joy and ease, in that, set free from cogitation and deliberation, the mind grows calm and sure, dwelling on high. And further, disenchanted with joy, he abides calmly contemplative while, mindful and self-possessed, he feels in his body that ease whereof Aryans declare: 'He that is calmly contemplative and aware, he dwelleth at ease.' So does he enter into and abide in the third Jhana. And further, by putting aside ease and by putting aside malaise, by the passing away of the happiness and of the melancholy he used to feel, he enters into and abides in the fourth Jhana, rapture of utter purity of mindfulness and equanimity, wherein neither ease is felt nor any ill. This is what is called right rapture.

"This, bhikkhus, is the Aryan truth concerning the way leading to the cessation of ill."

MEDITATION AND CALMNESS

"Now, this being the case, in this method, what is meant by sitting in meditation? In this method, to sit means to be free from all obstacles, and externally not to allow thoughts to rise from the mind over any sphere of objects. To meditate means to realize the imperturbability of one's original nature. What is meant by meditation and calmness? Meditation means to be free from all characters externally, calmness means to be unperturbed internally. If there are characters outside and the inner mind is not disturbed, one's original nature is naturally pure and calm. It is only because of the spheres of objects that there is contact, and contact leads to perturbation. There is calmness when one is free from characters and is not perturbed. There is meditation when one is externally free from characters, and there is calmness when one is internally undisturbed. Meditation and calmness mean that external meditation is attained and internal calmness is achieved. The *Wei-mo-chieh* [*so-shuo*] *ching* says, 'Immediately we become completely clear and recover our original mind.' The *P'u-sa chieh ching* (Scripture of Disciplines for Bodhisattvahood) says, 'We are originally pure in our self-nature.' Good and learned friends, realize that your self-nature is naturally pure. Cultivate and achieve for yourselves the Law-body of your self-nature. Follow the Way of the Buddha yourselves. Act and achieve Buddhahood for yourselves."

D. T. SUZUKI

*The Sense of Zen**

D. T. Suzuki (1870–1966) was a world-renowned Japanese scholar of Buddhism who graduated from the Literature Department of Tokyo University and lectured there for some years. He also studied in the United States around the turn of the century. For many years he was Professor of Zen Buddhism in Otani University, Kyoto, Japan. He was the author of many articles and books, including *Zen and Japanese Culture* and *Essays on Zen* (three volumes).

In this selection, Suzuki argues that Zen helps us open our "third eye" and leads us to a level of existence and meaningfulness to which our ordinary attitudes and presuppositions blind us. He tells us that Zen teaches us to seek to penetrate the "mysteries of life" not through book-learning but through the facts of personal experience. We possess a faculty higher than the intellect which can lead us to reality.

Zen in its essence is the art of seeing into the nature of one's own being, and it points the way from bondage to freedom. By making us drink right from the fountain of life, it liberates us from all the yokes under which we finite beings are usually suffering in this world. We can say that Zen liberates all the energies properly and naturally stored in each of us, which are in ordinary circumstances cramped and distorted so that they find no adequate channel for activity.

*Daisetz Teitaro Suzuki, from *Essays in Zen Buddhism* (First Series), published for the Buddhist Society, London (London: Rider & Company, 1949, 1958), pp. 13–20 with omissions. Used by permission of the publisher.

This body of ours is something like an electric battery in which a mysterious power latently lies. When this power is not properly brought into operation, it either grows mouldy and withers away or is warped and expresses itself abnormally. It is the object of Zen, therefore, to save us from going crazy or being crippled. This is what I mean by freedom, giving free play to all the creative and benevolent impulses inherently lying in our hearts. Generally, we are blind to this fact, that we are in possession of all the necessary faculties that will make us happy and loving towards one another. All the struggles that we see around us come from this ignorance. Zen, therefore, wants us to open a "third eye," as Buddhists call it, to the hitherto undreamed-of region shut away from us through our own ignorance. When the cloud of ignorance disappears, the infinity of the heavens is manifested, where we see for the first time into the nature of our own being. We now know the signification of life, we know that it is not blind striving, nor is it a mere display of brutal forces, but that while we know not definitely what the ultimate purport of life is, there is something in it that makes us feel infinitely blessed in the living of it and remain quite contented with it in all its evolution, without raising questions or entertaining pessimistic doubts.

When we are full of vitality and not yet awakened to the knowledge of life, we cannot comprehend the seriousness of all the conflicts involved in it which are apparently for the moment in a state of quiescence. But sooner or later the time will come when we have to face life squarely and solve its most perplexing and most pressing riddles. Says Confucius, "At fifteen my mind was directed to study, and at thirty I knew where to stand." This is one of the wisest sayings of the Chinese sage. Psychologists will all agree to this statement of his; for, generally speaking, fifteen is about the age youth begins to look around seriously and inquire into the meaning of life. All the spiritual powers until now securely hidden in the subconscious part of the mind break out almost simultaneously. And when this breaking out is too precipitous and violent, the mind may lose its balance more or less permanently; in fact, so many cases of nervous prostration reported during adolescence are chiefly due to this loss of the mental equilibrium. In most cases the effect is not very grave and the crisis may pass without leaving deep marks. But in some characters, either through their inherent tendencies or on account of the influence of environment upon their plastic constitution, the spiritual awakening stirs them up to the very depths of their personality. This is the time you will be asked to choose between the "Everlasting No" and the "Everlasting Yea". This choosing is what Confucius means by "study"; it is not studying the classics, but deeply delving into the mysteries of life. . . .

The Buddha was perfectly right when he propounded his "Fourfold Noble Truth", the first of which is that life is pain. Did not everyone of us come to this world screaming and in a way protesting? To come out into cold and prohibitive surroundings after a soft, warm motherly womb was surely a painful incident, to say the least. Growth is always attended with pain. Teething is more or less a painful process. Puberty is usually accompanied by a mental as well as a physical disturbance. The growth of the organism called society is also marked with painful cataclysms and we are at present witnessing one of its birth-throes. We may calmly reason and say that this is all inevitable, that inasmuch as every reconstruction means the destruction of the old regime, we cannot help going through a painful operation. But this cold intellectual analysis does not alleviate whatever harrowing feelings we have to undergo. The pain heartlessly inflicted on our nerves is ineradicable. Life is, after all arguing, a painful struggle.

This, however, is providential. For the more you suffer the deeper grows your character, and with the deepening of your character you read the more penetratingly into the secrets of life. All great artists, all great religious leaders, and all great social reformers have come out of the intensest struggles which they fought bravely, quite frequently in tears and with bleeding hearts. Unless you eat your bread in sorrow, you cannot taste of real life. Mencius is right when he says that when Heaven wants to perfect a great man it tries him in every possible way until he comes out triumphantly from all his painful experiences. . . .

We are too ego-centered. The ego-shell in which we live is the hardest thing to outgrow. We seem to carry it all the time from childhood up to the time we finally pass away. We are, however, given many chances to break through this shell, and the first and greatest of them is when we reach adolescence. This is the first time the ego really comes to recognize the "other." I mean the awakening of sexual love. An ego, entire and undivided, now begins to feel a sort of split in itself. Love hitherto dormant deep in his heart lifts its head and causes a great commotion in it. For the love now stirred demands at once the assertion of the ego and its annihilation. Love makes the ego lose itself in the object it loves, and yet at the same time it wants to have the object as its own. This is a contradiction, and a great tragedy of life. This elemental feeling must be one of the divine agencies whereby man is urged to advance in his upward walk. God gives tragedies to perfect man. The greatest bulk of literature ever produced in this world is but the harping on the same string of love, and we never seem to grow weary of it. But this is not the topic we are concerned with here. What I want to emphasize in this connection is this: that through the awakening of love we get a glimpse into the infinity of things, and that this glimpse urges youth to Romanticism or to Rationalism according to his temperament and environment and education.

When the ego-shell is broken and the "other" is taken into its own body, we can say that the ego has denied itself or that the ego has taken its first steps towards the infinite. Religiously, here ensues an intense struggle between the finite and the infinite, between the intellect and higher power, or, more plainly, between the flesh and the spirit. This is the problem of problems that has driven many a youth into the hands of Satan. When a grown-up man looks back to these youthful days he cannot but feel a sort of shudder going through his entire frame. The struggle to be fought in sincerity may go on up to the age of thirty, when Confucius states that he knew where to stand. The religious consciousness is now fully awakened, and all the possible ways of escaping from the struggle or bringing it to an end are most earnestly sought in every direction. Books are read, lectures are attended, sermons are greedily taken in, and various religious exercises or disciplines are tried. And naturally Zen too comes to be inquired into.

How does Zen solve the problem of problems?

In the first place, Zen proposes its solution by directly appealing to facts of personal experience and not to book-knowledge. The nature of one's own being where apparently rages the struggle between the finite and the infinite is to be grasped by a higher faculty than the intellect. For Zen says it is the latter that first made us raise the question which it could not answer by itself, and that therefore it is to be put aside to make room for something higher and more enlightening. For the intellect has a peculiarly disquieting quality in it. Though it raises questions enough to disturb the serenity of the mind, it is too frequently unable to give satisfactory answers to them. It upsets the blissful peace of ignorance and yet it does not restore the former state of things by offering something else. Because it points out ignorance, it is often considered illuminating, whereas the fact is that it disturbs, not necessarily always bringing light on its path. It is not final, it waits for something higher than itself for the solution of all the questions it will raise regardless of consequences. If it were able to bring a new order into the disturbance and settle it once for all, there would have been no need for philosophy after it had been first systematized by a great thinker, by an Aristotle or by a Hegel. But the history of thought proves that each new structure raised by a man of extraordinary intellect is sure to be pulled down by the succeeding ones. This constant pulling down and building up is all right as far as philosophy itself is concerned; for the inherent nature of the intellect, as I take it, demands it and we cannot put a stop to the progress of philosophical inquiries any more than to our breathing. But when it comes to the question of life itself we cannot wait for the ultimate solution to be offered by the intellect, even if it could do so. We cannot suspend even for a moment our life-activity for philosophy to unravel its mysteries. Let the mysteries remain as they are, but live we must. The hungry cannot wait until a complete analysis of food is obtained and the nourishing value of each element is determined. For the dead the scientific knowledge of food will be of no use whatever. Zen therefore does not rely on the intellect for the solution of its deepest problems.

By personal experience it is meant to get at the fact at first hand and not through any intermediary, whatever this may be. Its favourite analogy is: to point at the moon a finger is needed, but woe to those who take the finger for the moon; a basket is welcome to carry our fish home, but when the fish are safely on the table why should we eternally bother ourselves with the basket? Here stands the fact, and let us grasp it with the naked hands lest it should slip away—this is what Zen proposes to do. As nature abhors a vacuum, Zen abhors anything coming between the fact and ourselves. According to Zen there is no struggle in the fact itself such as between the finite and the infinite, between the flesh and the spirit. These are idle distinctions fictitiously designed by the intellect for its own interest. Those who take them too seriously or those who try to read them into the very fact of life are those who take the finger for the moon. When we are hungry we eat; when we are sleepy we lay ourselves down; and where does the infinite or the finite come in here? Are not we complete in ourselves and each in himself? Life as it is lived suffices. It is only when the disquieting intellect steps in and tries to murder it that we stop to live and imagine ourselves to be short of or in something. Let the intellect alone, it has its usefulness in its proper sphere, but let it not interfere with the flowing of the life-stream. If you are at all tempted to look into it, do so while letting it flow. The fact of flowing must under no circumstances be arrested or meddled with; for the moment your hands are dipped into it, its transparency is disturbed, it ceases to reflect your image which you have had from the very beginning and will continue to have to the end of time.

Almost corresponding to the "Four Maxims" of the Nichiren Sect, Zen has its own four statements:

> "A special transmission outside the Scriptures;
> No dependence upon words and letters;
> Direct pointing to the soul of man;
> Seeing into one's nature and the attainment of
> Buddhahood.

This sums up all that is claimed by Zen as religion.

SELECTIONS FROM CONFUCIAN WRITINGS*

(1) *Teachings of Confucius, from the* Analects

Confucius (551–479 B.C.) was without doubt one of the world's most influential teachers. He lived most of his life in the small Chinese state of Lu (now part of Shantung province) during a time of great social and political unrest. While he may at times have occupied various minor governmental posts, virtually the whole of his adult life was devoted to teaching. For more than a dozen years he traveled with some of his students to neighboring states, vainly hoping to discover a prince or ruler who would adopt his policies. Most scholars agree that the *Analects* (Selected Discourses), although set down some time after his death, is our most reliable source of what he believed and taught. His views had a profound influence upon Chinese civilization, and for the eight centuries preceding our own, the *Analects,* together with the *Chung Yung* (Doctrine of the Mean), the *Ta Hsüeh* (Great Learning), and the *Meng-Tzu* (Book of Mencius), was a required text in examinations for the Chinese civil service.

The philosopher Tsang said, "I daily examine myself on three points: whether, in transacting business for others, I may have been not faithful; whether, in intercourse with friends, I may have been not sincere; whether I may have not mastered and practiced the instructions of my teacher."

The Master said, "A youth, when at home, should be filial, and, abroad, respectful to his elders. He should be earnest and truthful. He should overflow in love to all, and cultivate the friendship of the good. When he has time and opportunity, after the performance of these things, he should employ them in polite studies."

The Master said, "It is virtuous manners which constitute the excellence of a neighborhood. If a man in selecting a residence, do not fix on one where such prevail, how can he be wise?"

The Master said, "The superior man thinks of virtue; the small man thinks of comfort. . . . The mind of the superior man is conversant with righteousness; the mind of the mean man is conversant with gain."

*The selections from the *Analects* and the *Chung Yung* are from *The Four Books,* trans. James Legge (Shanghai: The Commercial Press, n.d.). Selections from the *Meng-Tzu* and the *Ta Hsüeh* are translated by Maylon H. Hepp. The final selection is from Chang Tsai, "Hsi Ming" (The Western Inscription), in *A Sourcebook in Chinese Philosophy,* trans. and comp. Wing-tsit Chan (Princeton: Princeton U. Press, 1963), pp. 497–498. Reprinted by permission of the Princeton University Press.

The Master said of Tsze-ch'an that he had four of the characteristics of a superior man—"in his conduct of himself, he was humble; in serving his superior, he was respectful; in nourishing the people, he was kind; in ordering the people, he was just."

The philosopher Tsang said, "There are three principles of conduct which the man of high rank should consider especially important: that in his deportment and manner he keep from violence and heedlessness; that in regulating his countenance he keep near to sincerity; and that in his words and tones he keep from lowness and impropriety. . . .

Confucius said, "There are three things which the superior man guards against. In youth, when the physical powers are not yet settled, he guards against lust. When he is strong and the physical powers are in full vigor, he guards against quarrelsomeness. When he is old, and the animal powers are decayed, he guards against covetousness."

Confucius said, "There are three things of which the superior man stands in awe. He stands in awe of the ordinances of Heaven. He stands in awe of great men. He stands in awe of the words of sages."

Tsze-chang asked Confucius about perfect virtue. Confucius said, "To be able to practice five things everywhere under heaven constitutes perfect virtue." He begged to ask what they were, and was told, "Gravity, generosity of *soul,* sincerity, earnestness, and kindness. If you are grave, you will not be treated with disrespect. If you are generous, you will win all. If you are earnest, you will accomplish much. If you are kind, this will enable you to employ the services of others." . . .

Someone said, "What do you say concerning the principle that injury should be recompensed with kindness?" The Master said, "With what then will you recompense kindness? Recompense injury with justice and recompense kindness with kindness."

The Master said, "Alas! there is no one that knows me." Tsze-kung said, "What do you mean by thus saying—that no one knows you?" The Master replied, "I do not murmur against heaven. I do not grumble against men. My studies lie low, and my penetration rises high. But there is heaven;—that knows me!" . . .

From the Son of Heaven down to the mass of the people, all must consider the cultivation of the person the root of everything besides.

(2) *The Middle Way, from the* Chung Yung

Although the *Chung Yung* (The Doctrine of the Mean) is a central Confucian document, its stress on the attainment of a harmonious equilibrium which reflects the cosmic order appealed also to the Taoists and the Buddhists. Integrity (or sincerity) is lauded, not merely as a personal virtue and as a means to self-realization, but as "that by which all things are completed."

What heaven has conferred is called the nature; and accordance with this nature is called the Path of Duty; the regulation of this path is called instruction. The path may not be left for an instant. If it could be left it would not be the path. . . .

While there are no stirrings of pleasure, anger, sorrow, or joy, the mind may be said to be in the state of equilibrium. When those feelings have been stirred, and they act in their due degree, there ensues what may be called the state of harmony. This equilibrium is the great root from which grow all the human actings in the world, and this harmony is the universal path which they all should pursue. Let the states of equilibrium and harmony exist in perfection, and a happy order will prevail throughout heaven and earth, and all things will be nourished and flourish.

The Master said, "Perfect is the virtue which is according to the Mean! Rare have they long been among the people, who could practise it! . . .

The Master said, "The path is not far from man. When men try to pursue a course which is far from the common indications of consciousness, this course cannot be considered the path. When one cultivates to the utmost the principles of his nature, and exercises them on the principle of reciprocity, he is not far from the path. What you do not like when done to yourself, do not do to others.

"In the way of the superior man there are four things, to not one of which have I as yet attained.—To serve my father, as I would require my son to serve me: to this I have not attained; to serve my prince, as I would require my minister to serve me: to this I have not attained; to serve my elder brother, as I would require my younger brother to serve me: to this I have not attained; to set the example in behaving to a friend, as I would require him to behave to me: to this I have not attained."

The superior man does what is proper to the station in which he is; he does not desire to go beyond this.

In a position of wealth and honour, he does what is proper to a position of wealth and honour. In a poor and low position, he does what is proper to a poor and low position. Situated among barbarous tribes, he does what is proper to a situation among barbarous tribes. In a position of sorrow and difficulty, he does what is proper to a position of sorrow and difficulty. The superior man can find himself in no situation in which he is not himself. . . .

Sincerity is that whereby self-completion is effected, and its way is that by which man must direct himself. Sincerity is the end and beginning of things; without sincerity there would be nothing. On this account, the superior man regards the attainment of sincerity as the most excellent thing. The possessor of sincerity does not merely accomplish the self-completion of himself. With this quality he completes other men and things also. The completing himself shows his perfect virtue. The completing other men and things shows his knowledge. Both these are virtues belonging to the nature, and this is the way by which a union is effected of the external and internal. Therefore, whenever he, the entirely sincere man, employs these virtues, their action will be right.

(3) *The Four Beginnings, from the* Meng-Tzu

It was Mencius (371–289 B.C.?) rather than Confucius himself (551–479 B.C.) who first explicitly stated the view of human nature which was to become standard in Confucianism. Man's original nature is good, and if its innate tendencies (the Four Beginnings) are properly nurtured, men will develop the characteristic human excellences of humaneness, righteousness, propriety, and wisdom.

Mencius said, All men have a heart that cannot bear [to see] others [suffer, without feeling compassion for them.] The former kings had such a sense, and hence there was compassionate governing. By means of this sense of compassion, they practiced compassionate government, ruling the world as it were, as if rolling it around in their palm.

What I mean by all men having a sense of compassion is this: Suppose people were suddenly to see a child about to fall into a well. They would in every case have a feeling of apprehension and sympathetic concern, not in order to get on intimate terms with the child's parents, nor because they wanted praise from neighbors and friends, nor because they disliked a bad reputation. From this we see that one who lacked a sense of sympathetic concern would not be a man. [In a similar way, I could go on to show that] one who lacked a sense of shame and dislike would not be a man; one who lacked a sense of modesty and humility would not be a man; one who lacked a sense of right and wrong would not be a man.

The sense of sympathetic concern is the beginning of humaneness; the sense of shame and dislike, the beginning of righteousness; the sense of modesty and humility, the beginning of propriety; the sense of right and wrong, the beginning of wisdom. Men have these four beginnings just as they have four limbs. To have these four beginnings and yet to say that one is unable to do anything about the kind of person one becomes is to malign oneself, and to say this about one's ruler is to malign one's ruler.

Everyone who has these four beginnings within himself knows without exception what it takes to enlarge and develop them, just as a fire [knows how to start] burning or a spring to gush out. If one develops them fully, they will be sufficient to protect all within the four seas; if one does not develop them, they will not even suffice to serve one's parents.

(4) *The Way to Learn Greatness, from the* Ta Hsüeh

The *Ta Hsüeh* (The Great Learning) has exercised an influence upon Confucian thought out of all proportion to its brevity. Chu Hsi (1130–1200), the eminent Sung dynasty Neo-Confucian, followed the traditional practice of attributing the basic text, which we translate in full, to Confucius himself, and the appended chapters of commentary, omitted here, to Tseng Tzu, one of Confucius' leading disciples.

The way to learn greatness is to throw light on enlightened virtue, to love the people, and to rest in the highest good. Knowing where to rest, one's goal is determined; this being determined, one can be tranquil; being tranquil, one can be at peace; being at peace, one can plan carefully. Planning carefully, one can achieve one's goal.

Things have roots and branches; affairs have ends and beginnings. By knowing what comes before and what comes after, one keeps near the Way.

The men of old, desiring to throw light on enlightened virtue, first put their states in order. Desiring to put their states in order, they first regulated their families. Desiring to regulate their families, they first cultivated their own selves. Desiring to cultivate their own selves, they first set their hearts right. Desiring to set their hearts right, they first made their thoughts sincere. Desiring to make their thoughts sincere, they first extended their knowledge. Extending knowledge involves inquiring into things.

By inquiring into things, knowledge is achieved. By achieving knowledge, thoughts are made sincere. By making thoughts sincere, the heart is set right. By setting the heart right, the self is cultivated. By cultivating the self, the family is regulated. By regulating the family, states are put in order. By putting states in order, the world becomes peaceful.

From the Son of Heaven to the common people, in every case without exception, cultivating the self constitutes the root. If this root is in confusion, the branches will be in bad condition too. To treat the weighty lightly and the trivial weightily will never do.

(5) *Man and His Place in Nature, from "The Western Inscription"*

The "Hsi Ming" (The Western Inscription) of Chang Tsai (1020–1077) marks a high point in the expression of a mature Confucian view of man and his place in the universe.

Heaven is my father and Earth is my mother, and even such a small creature as I find an intimate place in their midst.

Therefore, that which fills the universe I regard as my body and that which directs the universe I consider as my nature.

All people are my brothers and sisters, and all things are my companions. . . .

Wealth, honor, blessing, and benefits are meant for the enrichment of my life, while poverty, humble station, and sorrow are meant to help me to fulfillment.

In life I follow and serve [Heaven and Earth]. In death I will be at peace.

SELECTIONS FROM TAOIST WRITINGS*

The two most basic documents of philosophical Taoism are the *Tao Te Ching* (Classic of the Way and Its Power), traditionally attributed to Lao Tzu, held to be an older contemporary of Confucius, and the *Nan Hua Chen Ching* by Chuang Tzu, who lived during the fourth century B.C.

While Confucianism, following the emphasis of Confucius himself, is primarily concerned with the relations of individuals within society, Taoism centers on the individual in his relation to the rest of nature. From our Western point of view, Taoism reveals from the outset a metaphysical dimension that was only gradually acquired by Confucianism. Our first selection sets forth the concept of the Tao (Way) as the underlying reality of the universe, manifesting itself in man and nature, but eluding our attempts to classify or categorize it. The second selection deals with the relation between man and nature in one of its most poignant forms: how is the death of the individual related to the ongoing processes of nature? In our third selection, Chuang Tzu faces the perennial philosophical problem of the basis for distinguishing between appearance and reality, between the seeming and the so. He does not solve the problem, but poses it in the concrete terms characteristic of this philosophizing.

TAO (THE WAY)

If you can talk about it, it is other than the Constant Tao;
If you can name it, it is other than the Constant Name.
Nameless, Tao is the beginning of Heaven and Earth.
Named, it is "Mother" of the ten thousand things.

There is a Thing undifferentiated, yet, complete,
Born before Heaven and Earth.
Silent and vast,
Standing alone, unchanging,
Extending everywhere and yet not in peril.
I do not know its name.
I dub it "Tao."
Pressed for its name, I call it "The Great."

*Translated by Maylon H. Hepp from Lao Tzu, *Tao Te Ching* (Classic of the Way and Its Power), Chapters 1, 25, 34, and 41; and from Chuang Tzu, *Nan Hua Chen Ching* (Pure Classic of Nan Hua), Chapter 18, "Perfect Happiness," and Chapter 2, "Discussion on Equalizing Things."

Man patterns himself after Earth;
Earth patterns itself after Heaven;
Heaven patterns itself after Tao;
Tao patterns itself after its own spontaneity.

The great Tao is like a flood;
It can go to left or right.
Since the ten thousand things depend upon it,
Having produced them, it does not abandon them.
Though its merit is complete, it lays no claim to fame.
Though it clothes and nourishes the ten thousand things,
It does not lord it over them.
Since it constantly lacks desires, it may be named "The Small."
Since the ten thousand things return to it, it may be
named "The Great."
Because it pursues its goal without aggrandizing itself,
It is able to fulfil its greatness.

When a superior person hears about Tao,
He diligently practices it.
When a middling person hears about Tao,
He wavers between keeping it and losing it.
When an inferior person hears about Tao,
He treats it as a big laugh.
If it were not just a big laugh to him,
It would fall short of being the Tao.

REFLECTIONS ON LIFE AND DEATH

When Chuang Tzu's wife died, Hui Tzu came to express his sympathy. There sat Chuang Tzu with legs spread out, drumming on a bowl and singing.

Hui Tzu said, "Not to weep at the death of someone who has lived with you, raised your children, and grown old would be bad enough. But to drum on a bowl and sing—isn't that just too much?"

Chuang Tzu replied, "Not at all. Right after she died, left alone like this, how could I not feel depressed? But then I reflected on how it all began: originally she lacked life, and not only life but form, and not only form but spirit. Within the confusion and vastness, something changed and there was spirit; spirit changed and there was form; form changed and there was life. Now another change and she is dead, just as the four seasons progress through spring, summer, fall, and winter.

Now that she has lain down to sleep in the Great Room, for me to go around weeping and wailing for her would show that I don't understand what's what. So I stopped."

CHUANG TZU'S DREAM

Once I, Chuang Chou, dreamed I was a butterfly, a butterfly flitting to and fro, aware of my pleasure and expressing myself, not knowing I was Chou. Suddenly I woke up, and there I was, sound and solid Chou. I didn't know whether it had been Chou dreaming he was a butterfly, or now a butterfly dreaming it was Chou. Chou or butterfly—there must be a difference. This is what is meant by "the transformation of things."

WING-TSIT CHAN

*The Meaning of Tao**

Wing-tsit Chan (b. 1901) was born in a country village southwest of Canton, China, attended Lingnan University in that city, and obtained his Ph.D. from Harvard University with his dissertation on the philosophy of Chuang Tzu, the Taoist philosopher dealt with in our preceding selections. He taught for many years at Dartmouth College and was recently the Anna Gillespie Professor of Philosophy at Chatham College.

Through his extensive publications and lucid translations of Chinese philosophical works into English, he has perhaps done more than any other living scholar to make the riches of Chinese philosophy available to the contemporary English-speaking world. In the short essay which follows, Chan explores the central concept of Tao, especially as it appears in the thought of Lao Tzu.

The far more important element in Lao Tzu's teachings is . . . the constructive one. This is his formulation of the philosophy of Tao. In this he evolved a concept that had never been known in China before, a concept that served not only as the standard for man but for all things as well.

*From *The Way of Lao Tzu,* translated by Wing-tsit Chan, Copyright © 1963, by The Bobbs-Merrill Company, Inc., reprinted by permission of the publisher. Pages 6–9.

The word *tao* consists of one element meaning a head and another meaning to run. It means that on which something or someone goes, a path, or road, later extended to mean "method," "principle," "truth," and finally "reality." All of this is well summed up in the common English translation, "the Way." It is a cardinal concept in practically all ancient Chinese philosophical schools. Hitherto the connotation had been social and moral, but in Lao Tzu it connotes for the first time the metaphysical. It is the "mother" and "ancestor" of all things. It exists before heaven and earth. It is the "storehouse" of things. It is at once their principle of being and their substance. "All things depend on it for life." In its substance it is "invisible," "inaudible," "vague and elusive," indescribable and above shape and form. It is one, a unity behind all multiplicity. It is single like an uncarved block that has not been split up into individual pieces or covered up with superficial adornment. It is everlasting and unchangeable. It is all-pervasive and "flows everywhere." "It operates everywhere and is free from danger." Use it and you "will never wear it out." "While vacuous, it is never exhausted." It depends on nothing. It is natural, for it comes into existence by itself and is its own principle for being. It is the "great form." It is nameless (*wu-ming*), and if one is forced to give it a name, he can only call it "great," that is, unlimited in space and time. It is nameless because it is not a concrete, individual thing or describable in particular terms. Above all, it is non-being (*wu*). "All things in the world come from being. And being comes from non-being."

This concept of non-being is basic in Lao Tzu's thought. As Chuang Tzu (between 399 and 295 B.C.) said, the system of Lao Tzu is "based on the principles of non-being and being." In a sense being and non-being are of equal importance. They complement and produce each other. "Let there always be non-being," Lao Tzu says, and "let there always be being." As Fung Yu-lan has said, by non-being is not meant that there was a time when nothing but non-being existed, but logically non-being must be prior because before beings come into existence, there must be something before them. In the final analysis, then, non-being is the ultimate, and in Chuang Tzu's statement it comes first.

On the surface non-being seems to be empty and devoid of everything. Actually, this is not the case. It is devoid of limitations but not devoid of definite characteristics. Han Fei Tzu (d. 233 B.C.), the first commentator on Lao Tzu, did not understand Tao in the negative sense of emptiness but in the positive sense of involving definite principles. He says:

> Tao is that by which all things become what they are. It is that with which all principles (*li*) are commensurable. Principles are patterns according to which all things come into being, and Tao is the cause of their being. Therefore it is said that Tao puts things in order (*li*). Everything has its own

> principle different from that of others, and Tao is commensurate with all of them. . . . According to definite principles, there are existence and destruction, life and death, and flourish and decline. . . . What is eternal has neither change nor any definite, particular principle itself. Since it has no definite principle itself, it is not bound in any particular locality. This is why it is said that it cannot be told.

Tao as non-being, then, is not negative but positive in character. This concept of non-being was absolutely new in Chinese thought and most radical. Other Chinese schools of thought conceived of non-being simply as the absence of something, but in Taoism it is not only positive; it is basic. This was epoch-making in the history of Chinese philosophy. According to Dubs, it is also new to Occidental thought. He says, "Here is a solution to the problem of creation which is new to Western philosophy: the universe can arise out of nothing because nonexistence itself is not characterless or negative." In his opinion, "here is a metaphysical system which starts, not with matter or with ideas, but with law (*Tao*), nonexistence, and existence as the three fundamental categories of reality." He found nothing similar in Occidental philosophy. "After Parmenides declared that nonexistence cannot exist," he says, "Western philosophers never attempted to challenge his dogma. The non-being of Plato and Plotinus, like the empty space of Greek atomists, was given no positive character. Only Einsteinian space-time—which is nothing, yet directs the motion of particles—comes at all close to the *Lao Tzu*'s concept of nonexistence."

This positive character can be seen not only in the substance of Tao. It can also be seen in its function. Just as its nature is characterized by having no name, so its activity is characterized by taking no action (*wu-wei*). Taking no action does not mean to be "dry wood and dead ashes," to use the metaphors of Chuang Tzu. Rather, it means taking no artificial action, noninterference, or letting things take their own course. Tao invariably "takes no action" but "supports all things in their natural state" and thus "all things will transform spontaneously." As things arise, Tao "does not turn away from them." "It produces them, but does not take possession of them," and "accomplishes its task, but does not claim credit for it." It "benefits all things and does not compete with them." At the same time, things are governed by it and cannot deviate from it. Following it, a thing will flourish and "return to its root and destiny." With it, heaven becomes clear, the earth becomes tranquil, spiritual beings become divine, the valley becomes full, and all things live and grow, but without it they will be exhausted, crumble, and wither away. In the production of things, it proceeds from the one to the many. "Tao produced the One. The One produced the two. The two produced the three. And the three produced the ten thousand things." In its own activities, it always returns to the root or the non-ultimate. It operates in cycles.

From the above, it is not an exaggeration to say that Tao operates according to certain laws which are constant and regular. One may even say there is an element of necessity in these laws, for Tao by its very nature behaves in this way and all things, in order to achieve their full realization, have to obey them. Tao, after all, is *the* Way. In the words of Han Fei Tzu, it is the way in which things are ordered. Needham is fundamentally correct in equating Tao with the Order of Nature and in saying that Tao "brought all things into existence and governs their every action, not so much by force as by a kind of natural curvature in space and time." When things obey its laws, all parts of the universe will form a harmonious whole and the universe will become an integrated organism. One is tempted to compare Taoism with the organicism of Whitehead, but that would be putting too much modern philosophy into ancient Chinese thought. One thing is sure, however. Because Tao operates in a regular pattern, it is nothing mysterious. It is deep and profound (*hsüan*), to be sure, and it is described as subtle and elusive. But it is neither chaotic nor unpredictable, for it is the "essence" which is "very real," and "in it are evidences." It is popular, especially in the West, to describe Tao as mysterious, and there seems to be a special attraction to translate *hsüan* as mystery. It is mysterious only in the sense of subtlety and depth, not in the sense of irrationality.

HUSTON C. SMITH

*Man's Religious Heritage**

Huston C. Smith (b. 1919), educator and philosopher, was born in Soochow, China, of American parents. He received the Ph.D. degree from the University of Chicago and has taught at the University of Denver, Washington University (St. Louis), Massachusetts Institute of Technology, and Syracuse University. His books include *The Purpose of Higher Education, The Search for America,* and *Condemned to Meaning.*

After presenting seven of the great religions of the world in his book *The Religions of Man,* Smith, in the selection below, asks a number of questions: "What have we gotten out of it?" "How do these religions fit together?" He states the three main answers that have been defended by religious leaders, then

*"The Final Examination" in *The Religions of Man* by Huston Smith. Copyright © 1958 by Huston Smith. By permission of Harper & Row, Publishers, Inc.

discusses them briefly. He concludes by examining the approach to the religions of man he believes we must take in the future.

The most obvious question that suggests itself at the close of this kind of inquiry is: What have we gotten out of it? Has it done us any good?

It would be surprising if we had not picked up some facts about man's religious heritage: what the *yogas* mean for the Hindus, Buddha's analysis of the cause of life's dislocation, Confucius' ideal of the Gentleman, who Lao Tzu was, Islam's Five Pillars, what the Exodus meant to the Jews, the substance of the Good News for the early Christians, and so on. These are not to be belittled. But are they all?

We may have caught some sense of what an important part in the human venture religion has played. It may have left us with dismay at how far short of its finest embodiments religion often falls. We may see how important the quality of religion is to the way civilization goes.

Perhaps, too, we have emerged with a new appreciation of faiths not our own. Not that we now agree with them all. There is nothing in the study of man's religions that requires that they cross the line of the reader's acceptance in a photo finish. But perhaps we are able to see them more as faiths of real people, people who are asking the same basic questions that we are, seekers like us of the illumined life.

These, however, are matters of personal attitude. We may leave them, therefore, for our second question. How do these religions fit together? In what relation do they stand to one another?

This is the most difficult question in the field of comparative religion today, and as such has no one answer that would be universally accepted as correct. Consequently at this stage of our understanding the worth of an answer depends more on the adequacy with which it is defended than on whether it is right or wrong in any objectively demonstrable sense.

There are today three main answers that can be defended enough to find advocates among knowledgeable scholars in the field. The first is that in the midst of all the religions of man there stands one so incomparably superior that no significant religious truth is to be found in any of the others which is not present in equal or clearer form within this religion itself. That this view is both held and challenged by so many truly learned men is clear evidence that it is impossible to prove, flatly, that it is either right or wrong. Evaluation turns, instead, on the adequacy with which it is maintained. Has the answerer, let us suppose him to be a Christian, faced up to the extent to which identical claims are made by equally knowing proponents of other faiths, Muslims and Jews for example? What does he do with this paradox? Is it clear that his answer has not been prompted by an unconscious fear that should he acknowledge the possibility of some unique and significant truth in other religions he may be mounting the slippery incline that slopes toward conversion? Fear is never an adequate base for faith; the man who is afraid of being converted to another religion does not really believe that his contains the truth about God. Above all, in comparing his faith with others does he really know what he is talking about? Has he genuinely tried to unite himself with others in spirit before making the judgment?

Laying aside condescension and contempt, and even that sort of "objectivity" which, while it may depict, never truly understands, has he learned to see and feel the world and God as others have seen and felt these? Grant that success in such an undertaking can only be proximate, has he really tried to find in other religions something besides what his preconceptions have unconsciously deposited there in advance? In the language of religion, has he sought to draw some of the water, tasting which man thirsts not again, from some well other than his own? If his answer acquits itself well before these cross-questions, it stands.

A second possible answer to the question of the relation between religions is that in all important respects they are the same. Does not each contain some version of the Golden Rule? Do they not all regard man's self-centeredness to be the source of his troubles and seek to help him in its conquest? Does not each acknowledge a universal Divine Ground from which man has sprung and in relation to which his true good is to be sought? If all truth essential to salvation can be found in one religion, it can also be found in each of the other great ones. Edward Steichen, the great photographer of *The Family of Man,* summarized his creed by saying, "I believe that in all the things that are important, in all of these we are alike." The words are tailor-made for this second hypothesis. Religion is important; in religion all the peoples of the world are fundamentally alike. The differences are but dialects of a single spiritual language that employs different words but expresses the same ideas. If it be true as Michael Scott has recently suggested that "humanity has never before stood so desperately in need of a universal religion, a living, cohesive force that will emancipate mankind, that will overcome the dangers of arrogant nationalism and the doctrines of self-interest, hatred and violence," we need only open our eyes to see this universal religion embedded in the heart of each of the world's great existing religions, the *philosophia perennis* of St. Augustine's "wisdom uncreated, the same now that it ever was, and the same to be forevermore."

It is an appealing doctrine, and, like the previous one, may be true. Everything depends on what is essential to salvation and what is husk and cultural accident. But before its advocate goes hiking off too quickly to Baha'i, the current syncretistic faith that is making the most serious attempt to institutionalize this conviction, several questions again must be raised. The main one, interestingly enough, is the same as that which challenged the previous hypothesis; namely, how seriously and fully have the various faiths of mankind been entered into before the judgment was reached? How fully has the proponent tried and succeeded in understanding Christianity's claim that Christ was the *only* begotten Son of God, or the Muslim's claim that Muhammed is the *Seal* of the Prophets, or the Jews' sense of their being the Chosen People? How does he propose to reconcile Hinduism's conviction that this will always remain a "middle world" with Judaism's promethean faith that it can be decidedly improved? How does Buddha's "*anatta* doctrine" of non-soul square with Christianity's belief in man's individual destiny in eternity? How does Theravada Buddhism's rejection of every form of personal God find echo in Christ's sense of relationship to his Heavenly Father? How does the Indian view of Nirguna Brahman, the God who stands completely aloof from time and history, fit with the Biblical view that the very essence of God is contained in his historical acts? Are these beliefs really only accretions, tangential to the main concern of spirit? The religions of man may fit together, but they do not do so easily....

A third possible answer to the question of the relation between religions is best defined in contrast to both preceding ones. It does not find all religions saying the same things, though the unity is in certain respects both striking and impressive. But neither, in the presence of differences, does it assume that all important truths can be found in any single tradition. If God is a God of love, it seems most unlikely that he would not have revealed himself to his other children as well. And it seems probable that his revelation would have taken different facets and different forms according to the differences in nature of individual souls and the differences in character of local traditions and civilizations. This is one possible contemporary meaning of Paul's statement about "one spirit, many gifts." One who holds this view will find many things in other religions that puzzle and disturb, but will see their light as deriving basically from the same source as his own. As they too come from God, God may in certain respects speak to him through them.

"Isn't it ironical," remarked G. K. Chesterton upon hearing of the first round-the-world wireless communication, "that we have learned to talk around the world at precisely that moment when no one has anything to say." For the advocate of this third hypothesis this is far from true of religion. Here the people of the world have a great deal to say to one another, and they have drawn close at precisely the time when man's spiritual life, facing severe threats from nationalism, materialism, and conformity, stands in desperate need of the stimulus that searching conversation can encourage.

Where this conversation will lead cannot be fully predicted, but it looks as though it will be less toward an amalgamated world religion than toward certain emendations and restored emphases while each religion continues to maintain its historic identity. Vision, genius, and the will and capacity to follow the light where it leads will be needed. And there will be risks, for some pioneers may, like Jawaharlal Nehru, "become a queer mixture of East and West, out of place everywhere, at home nowhere." The chief question anyone who presumes to pioneer in this direction must answer is whether his personal, autonomous reason is qualified to stand judgment on matters as important as these, picking and choosing what in other traditions is authentic and what is spurious? To the extent that he can satisfactorily meet this question, his answer too, in the present state of man's religious knowledge, may stand.

Our last question is: What should be our approach to the religions of man from this point on? Whereas the preceding question did not permit a single answer, this one seems to require it. The only defensible reply must be continued listening, for we have had little more than a brief glimpse of these faiths we have passed through so hurriedly. We must listen first to our own faith, for every heritage is inexhaustible and the ways of spirit, even as channeled through a single tradition, are beyond the wit of anyone to master completely. Though a man sink himself into his faith as deeply as he can, there will remain the persistent challenge of more to be experienced than has been known or told.

But we must also listen to the faiths of others. This holds however we may have answered the question of their relation to our own—even if we assume that they have no truth that cannot be found in our own.

We must listen to them, first, because as said at the outset of this book, our times require it. The community today can be no single tradition; it is the planet. Daily the world grows smaller, leaving understanding the only bridge on which peace can find its home. But the annihilation of distance has caught us unprepared. Who today stands ready to accept the solemn equality of nations? Who does not have to fight an unconscious tendency to equate foreign with inferior? We live in a great century, but if it is to rise to its full opportunity, the scientific achievements of its first half must be matched by comparable achievements in human relations in its second. Those who listen in the present world work for peace, a peace built not upon ecclesiastical or political empire, but upon understanding and the mutual involvement in the lives of others that this brings. For understanding, at least in realms as inherently noble as the great faiths of mankind, brings respect, and respect prepares the way for a higher power, love—the only power that can quench the flames of fear, suspicion, and prejudice, and provide the means by which the peoples of this great earth can become one to one another.

Understanding then can lead to love. But the reverse is equally true. Love brings understanding; the two are reciprocal. So we must listen in order to further the understanding the world so desperately needs, but we must also listen in order to practice the love which our own religion (whichever it be) enjoins, for it is impossible to love another without listening to him. If then, we are to be true to our own faith we must attend to others when they speak, as deeply and as alertly as we hope they will attend to us. We must have the graciousness to receive as well as to give. For there is no greater way to depersonalize another than to speak to him without also listening.

Said Jesus, blest be his name, "Do unto others as you would that they should do unto you." Said Buddha, blest be his name as well, "He who would, may reach the utmost height—but he must be anxious to learn." If we do not quote the other religions on these points it is because their words would be redundant.

Philosophical Outlooks

FORMS OF NATURALISM

ERNEST NAGEL

*Naturalism Reconsidered**

See the biographical note on p. 239.

In the selection below, we find a reconstructed naturalism that differs sharply from the old materialism and from the more optimistic idealism. The author points out that there is much skepticism about the claims of the traditional system-builders in the history of philosophy—a skepticism which he maintains is well founded. He states what he considers to be the central tenets of philosophical naturalism and expresses his own faith in the logical-empirical method of evaluating truth claims. Nature is man's home and man needs to rely on reason and scientific method for the achievement of "human goods" and the building of a humane civilization.

The past quarter century has been for philosophy in many parts of the world a period of acute self-questioning, engendered in no small measure by developments in scientific and logical thought, and in part no doubt by fundamental changes in the social order. In any event, there has come about a general loss of confidence in the competence of philosophy to provide by way of a distinctive intellectual method a basic ground-plan of the cosmos, or for that matter to contribute to knowledge of any primary

*Reprinted with permission of Macmillan Publishing Co., Inc. from *Logic Without Metaphysics* by Ernest Nagel. Copyright by The Free Press, A Corporation, 1956. From "Naturalism Reconsidered," pp. 3–18.

subject-matter except by becoming a specialized positive science and subjecting itself to the discipline of empirical inquiry. Although the abysses of human ignorance are undeniably profound, it has also become apparent that ignorance, like actual knowledge, is of many special and heterogeneous things; and we have come to think, like the fox and unlike the hedgehog of whom Mr. Isaiah Berlin has recently reminded us, that there are a great many things which are already known or remain to be discovered, but that there is no one "big thing" which, if known, would make everything else coherent and unlock the mystery of creation. In consequence, many of us have ceased to emulate the great system-builders in the history of philosophy. In partial imitation of the strategy of modern science, and in the hope of achieving responsibly held conclusions about matters concerning which we could acquire genuine competence, we have tended to become specialists in our professional activities. We have come to direct our best energies to the resolution of limited problems and puzzles that emerge in the analysis of scientific and ordinary discourse, in the evaluation of claims to knowledge, in the interpretation and validation of ethical and esthetic judgments, and in the assessment of types of human experience. . . .

Some of us, I know, are distressed by the widespread scepticism of the traditional claims for a *philosophia perennis,* and have dismissed as utterly trivial most if not all the products of various current forms of analytical philosophy. I do not share this distress, nor do I think the dismissal is uniformly perspicacious and warranted. For in my judgment, the scepticism which many deplore is well-founded. Even though a fair-sized portion of recent analytical literature seems inconsequential also to me, analytical philosophy in our own day is the continuation of a major philosophic tradition, and can count substantial feats of clarification among its assets. Concentration on limited and determinate problems has yielded valuable fruits, not least in the form of an increased and refreshing sensitivity to the demands of responsible discourse.

On the other hand, philosophers like other men conduct their lives within the framework of certain comprehensive if not always explicit assumptions about the world they inhabit. These assumptions color evaluations of major ideas and proposed policies. I also suspect that the directions taken by analyses of specific intellectual problems are frequently if subtly controlled by the expressed or tacit beliefs philosophers hold concerning the over-all nature of things, by their views on human destiny, and by their conceptions of the scope of human reason. But conversely, resolutions of special problems made plausible by recent philosophical analysis, as well as by the findings of various positive sciences, seem to me to support certain broad generalizations about the cosmos and to disconfirm others. It is clearly desirable that such basic intellectual commitments, which are at once the matrix and the outcome of inquiries into specific problems, be made as explicit as possible. A philosopher who is a reflective man by profession, certainly owes it to himself to articulate, if only occasionally, what sort of world he thinks he inhabits, and to make clear to himself where approximately lies the center of his convictions.

The discharge of the important obligation which is mine this evening, seems to me an appropriate occasion for stating as simply and as succinctly as I can the substance of those intellectual commitments I like to call "naturalism." The label itself is of no importance, but I use it partly because of its historical associations, and partly because it is a reminder that the doctrines for which it is a name are neither new nor untried. With Santayana, I prefer not to accept in philosophic debate what I do not believe when I am not arguing; and naturalism as I construe it merely formulates what centuries of human experience have repeatedly confirmed. At any rate, naturalism seems to me a sound generalized account of the world encountered in practice and in critical reflection, and a just perspective upon the human scene. I wish to state briefly and hence with little supporting argument what I take to be its major tenets, and to defend it against some recent criticisms.

Claims to knowledge cannot ultimately be divorced from an evaluation of the intellectual methods used to support those claims. It is nevertheless unfortunate that in recent years naturalists in philosophy have so frequently permitted their allegiance to a dependable method of inquiry to obscure their substantive views on things in general. For it is the inclusive intellectual image of nature and man which naturalism supplies that set it off from other comprehensive philosophies. In my conception of it, at any rate, naturalism embraces a generalized account of the cosmic scheme and of man's place in it, as well as a logic of inquiry.

I hasten to add, however, that naturalism does not offer a theory of nature in the sense that Newtonian mechanics, for example, provides a theory of motion. Naturalism does not, like the latter, specify a set of substantive principles with the help of which the detailed course of concrete happenings can be explained or understood. Moreover, the principles affirmed by naturalism are not proposed as competitors or underpinnings for any of the special theories which the positive sciences assert. Nor, finally, does naturalism offer its general view of nature and man as the product of some special philosophical mode of knowing. The account of things proposed by naturalism is a distillation from knowledge acquired in the usual way in daily encounters with the world or in specialized scientific inquiry. Naturalism articulates features of the world which, because they have become so obvious, are rarely mentioned in discussions of special subject-matter, but which distinguish our actual world from other conceivable worlds. The major affirmations of naturalism are accordingly meager in content; but the principles affirmed are nevertheless effective guides in responsible criticism and evaluation.

Two theses seem to me central to naturalism as I conceive it. The first is the existential and causal primacy of organized matter in the executive order of nature. This is the assumption that the occurrence of events, qualities and processes, and the characteristic behaviors of various individuals, are contingent on the organization of spatio-temporally located bodies, whose internal structures and external relations determine and limit the appearance and disappearance of everything that happens. That this is so, is one of the best-tested conclusions of experience. We are frequently ignorant of the special conditions under which things come into being or pass away; but we have also found repeatedly that when we look closely, we eventually ascertain at least the approximate and gross conditions under which events occur, and we discover that those conditions invariably consist of some more or less complex organization of material substances. Naturalism does not maintain that only what is material exists, since many things noted in experience, for example, modes of action, relations of meaning, dreams, joys, plans, aspirations, are not as such material bodies or organizations of material bodies. What naturalism does assert as a truth about nature is that though *forms* of behavior or *functions* of material systems are indefeasibly parts of nature, forms and functions are not themselves agents in their own realization or in the realization of anything else. In the conception of nature's processes which naturalism affirms, there is no place for the operation of disembodied forces, no place for an immaterial spirit directing the course of events, no place for the survival of personality after the corruption of the body which exhibits it.

The second major contention of naturalism is that the manifest plurality and variety of things, of their qualities and their functions, are an irreducible feature of the cosmos, not a deceptive appearance cloaking some more homogeneous "ultimate reality" or transempirical substance, and that the sequential orders in which events occur or the manifold relations of dependence in which things exist are *contingent* connections, not the embodiments of a fixed and unified pattern of logically necessary links. The existential primacy of organized matter does not make illusory either the relatively permanent or the comparatively transient characters and forms which special configurations of bodies may possess. In particular, although the continued existence of the human scene is precarious and is dependent on a balance of forces that doubtless will not endure indefinitely, and even though its distinctive traits are not pervasive throughout space, it is nonetheless as much a part of the "ultimate" furniture of the world, and is as genuine a sample of what "really" exists, as are atoms and stars. There undoubtedly occur integrated systems of bodies, such as biological organisms, which have the capacity because of their material organization to maintain themselves and the direction of their characteristic activities. But there is no positive evidence, and much negative evidence, for the supposition that all existential structures are teleological systems in this sense, or for the view that whatever occurs is a phase in a unitary, teleologically organized, and all-inclusive process or system. Modern physical cosmology does indeed supply some evidence for definite patterns of evolutionary development of stars, galactic systems, and even of the entire physical universe; and it is quite possible that the stage of cosmic evolution reached at any given time causally limits the types of things which can occur during that period. On the other hand, the patterns of change investigated in physical cosmogony are not patterns that are exhaustive of everything that happens; and nothing in these current physical speculations requires the conclusion that changes in one star or galaxy are related by inherent necessity to every action of biological organisms in some remote planet. Even admittedly teleological systems contain parts and processes which are causally irrelevant to some of the activities maintained by those systems; and the causal dependencies known to hold between the parts of any system, teleological or not, have never been successfully established as forms of logically necessary relations. In brief, if naturalism is true, irreducible variety and logical contingency are fundamental traits of the world we actually inhabit. The orders and connections of things are all accessible to rational inquiry; but these orders and connections are not all derivable by deductive methods from any set of premises that deductive reason can certify.

It is in this framework of general ideas that naturalism envisages the career and destiny of man. Naturalism views the emergence and the continuance of human society as dependent on physical and physiological conditions that have not always obtained, and that will not permanently endure. But it does not in consequence regard man and his works as intrusions into nature, any more than it construes as intrusions the presence of heavenly bodies or of terrestrial protozoa. The stars are no more foreign to the cosmos than are men, even if the conditions for the existence of both stars and men are realized only occasionally or only in a few regions. Indeed, the conception of human life as a war with nature, as a struggle with an implacable foe that has doomed man to extinction, is but an inverted theology, with a malicious Devil in the seat of Omnipotence. It is a conception that is immodest as well as anthropomorphic in the importance it imputes to man in the scheme of things.

On the other hand, the affirmation that nature is man's "home" as much as it is the "home" of anything else, and the denial that cosmic forces are *intent* on destroying the human scene, do not warrant the interpretation that every sector of nature is explicable in terms of traits known to characterize only human individuals and human actions. Man undoubtedly possesses characteristics which are shared by everything that exists; but he also manifests traits and capacities that appear to be distinctive of him. Is anything gained but confusion when all forms of dependence between things, whether animate or inanimate, and all types of behaviors they display, are subsumed under distinctions that have an identifiable content only in reference to the human psyche? Measured by the illumination they bring, there is nothing to differentiate the thesis that human traits are nothing but the properties of bodies which can be formulated exclusively in the language of current physical theory, from the view that every change and every mode of operation, in whatever sector of the cosmos it may be encountered, is simply an illustration of some category pertinent to the description of human behavior.

Indeed, even some professed naturalists sometimes appear to promote the confusion when they make a fetish of continuity. Naturalists usually stress the emergence of novel forms in physical and biological evolution, thereby emphasizing the fact that human traits are not identical with the traits from which they emerge. Nevertheless, some distinguished contemporary naturalists also insist, occasionally with overtones of anxiety, that there is a "continuity" between the typically human on the one hand, and the physical and biological on the other. But is man's foothold in the scheme of things really made more secure by showing that his distinctive traits are in some sense "continuous" with features pervasive in nature, and would man's place in nature be less secure if such continuity did not obtain? The actual evidence for a continuity of development is conclusive in some instances of human traits, however it may be in others. But I sometimes suspect that the cardinal importance philosophers assign to the alleged universality of such continuity is a lingering survival of that ancient conception, according to which things are intelligible only when seen as teleological systems producing definite ends, so that nature itself is properly understood only when construed as the habitat of human society. In any event, a naturalism that is not provincial in its outlook will not accept the intellectual incorporation of man into nature at the price of reading into all the processes of the cosmos the passions, the strivings, the defeats and the glories of human life, and then exhibiting man as the most adequate, because most representative, expression of nature's inherent constitution. No, a mature naturalism seeks to understand what man is, not in terms of a discovered or postulated continuity between what is distinctive of him and what is pervasive in all things. Without denying that even the most distinctive human traits are dependent on things which are non-human, a mature naturalism attempts to assess man's nature in the light of *his* actions and achievements, *his* aspirations and capacities, *his* limitations and tragic failures, and *his* splendid works of ingenuity and imagination.

Human nature and history, in short, are *human* nature and history, not the history and nature of anything else, however much knowledge of other things contributes to a just appraisal of what man is. In particular, the adequacy of proposed ideals for human life must be judged, not in terms of their causes and origins, but in reference to how the pursuit and possible realization of ideals contribute to the organization and release of *human* energies. Men are animated by many springs of action, no one of which is intrinsically good or evil; and a moral ideal is the imagined satisfaction of some complex of impulses, desires, and needs. When ideals are handled responsibly, they therefore function as hypotheses for achieving a balanced exercise of human powers. Moral ideals are not self-certifying, any more than are the theories of the physical sciences; and evidence drawn from experienced satisfactions is required to validate them, however difficult may be the process of sifting and weighing the available data. Moral problems arise from a conflict of specific impulses and interests. They cannot, however, be effectively resolved by invoking standards derived from the study of non-human nature, or of what is allegedly beyond nature. If moral problems can be resolved at all, they can be resolved only in the light of specific human capacities, historical circumstance and acquired skills, and the opportunities (revealed by an imagination disciplined by knowledge) for altering the physical and social environment and for redirecting habitual behaviors. Moreover, since human virtues are in part the products of the society in which human powers are matured, a naturalistic moral theory is at the same time a critique of civilization, that is, a critique of the institutions that channel human energies, so as to exhibit the possibilities and limitations of various forms and arrangements of society for bringing enduring satisfactions to individual human careers.

These are the central tenets of what I take to be philosophical naturalism. They are tenets which are supported by compelling empirical evidence, rather than dicta based on dogmatic preference. In my view of it, naturalism does not dismiss every other differing conception of the scheme of things as logically impossible; and it does not rule out all alternatives to itself on a priori grounds. It is possible, I think, to conceive without logical inconsistency a world in which disembodied forces are dynamic agents, or in which whatever happens is a manifestation of an unfolding logical pattern. In such possible worlds it would be an error to be a naturalist. But philosophy is not identical with pure mathematics, and its ultimate concern is with the actual world, even though philosophy must take cognizance of the fact that the actual world contains creatures who can envisage possible worlds and who employ different logical procedures for deciding which hypothetical world is the actual one. It is partly for this reason that contemporary naturalists devote so much attention to methods of evaluating evidence. When naturalists give their allegiance to the method of intelligence commonly designated as the method of modern empirical science, they do so because that method appears to be the most assured way of achieving reliable knowledge.

As judged by that method, the evidence in my opinion is at present conclusive for the truth of naturalism, and it is tempting to suppose that no one familiar with the evidence can fail to acknowledge that philosophy. Indeed, some commentators there are who assert that all philosophies are at bottom only expressions in different idioms of the same conceptions about the nature of things, so that the strife of philosophic systems is mainly a conflict over essentially linguistic matters. Yet many thinkers for whom I have a profound respect explicitly reject naturalism, and their espousal of contrary views seems to me incompatible with the irenic claim that we really are in agreement on fundamentals.

MAO TSE-TUNG

*Dialectical Materialism Restated**

Mao Tse-tung, (b. 1893), born in Hunan province of peasant background, became the leader of Communist China. He was a student at the National University in Peking, attended in 1921 the first Congress of the Chinese Communist Party in Shanghai, and in 1934 led the Communists in what is called The Long March through Southwest China to escape the forces under Chiang Kai-shek (the Kuomintang). "Half scholar, half warrior," he has ruled China with a strong hand and controlled the cultural life of the country. Mao's writings range from the role of peasants to guerilla warfare. He considers himself the true interpreter of Marx, Lenin, and Stalin.

In the selection that follows, Mao Tse-tung discusses the relation between knowledge and practice, between knowing and doing. The perceptual and the rational, while qualitatively different, are unified on the basis of man's activity and the development of society. The Marxist-Leninist outlook opposes both idealism and mechanical materialism since they separate the subjective and the objective. The law of the unity of opposites is basic in society and in thought. Correct ideas are not inborn, they come from social practice in the struggle for production, from class struggle, and from scientific experiment.

*Mao Tse-tung, from *Four Essays on Philosophy* (Peking: Foreign Language Press, 1968). Our selections are drawn from the essays "Where Do Correct Ideas Come From?"; "On Practice"; and "On Contradiction."

Where do correct ideas come from? Do they drop from the skies? No. Are they innate in the mind? No. They come from social practice, and from it alone; they come from three kinds of social practice, the struggle for production, the class struggle and scientific experiment. It is man's social being that determines his thinking. Once the correct ideas characteristic of the advanced class are grasped by the masses, these ideas turn into a material force which changes society and changes the world. In their social practice, men engage in various kinds of struggle and gain rich experience, both from their successes and from their failures. Countless phenomena of the objective external world are reflected in a man's brain through his five sense organs—the organs of sight, hearing, smell, taste and touch. At first, knowledge is perceptual. The leap to conceptual knowledge, *i.e.,* to ideas, occurs when sufficient perceptual knowledge is accumulated. This is one process in cognition. It is the first stage in the whole process of cognition, the stage leading from objective matter to subjective consciousness, from existence to ideas. Whether or not one's consciousness or ideas (including theories, policies, plans or measures) do correctly reflect the laws of the objective external world is not yet proved at this stage, in which it is not yet possible to ascertain whether they are correct or not. Then comes the second stage in the process of cognition, the stage leading from consciousness back to matter, from ideas back to existence, in which the knowledge gained in the first stage is applied in social practice to ascertain whether the theories, policies, plans or measures meet with the anticipated success. Generally speaking, those that succeed are correct and those that fail are incorrect, and this is especially true of man's struggle with nature. In social struggle, the forces representing the advanced class sometimes suffer defeat not because their ideas are incorrect but because, in the balance of forces engaged in struggle, they are not as powerful for the time being as the forces of reaction; they are therefore temporarily defeated, but they are bound to triumph sooner or later. Man's knowledge makes another leap through the test of practice. This leap is more important than the previous one. For it is this leap alone than can prove the correctness or incorrectness of the first leap, *i.e.,* of the ideas, theories, policies, plans or measures formulated in the course of reflecting the objective external world. There is no other way of testing truth. Furthermore, the one and only purpose of the proletariat in knowing the world is to change it. Often, a correct idea can be arrived at only after many repetitions of the process leading from matter to consciousness and then back to matter, that is, leading from practice to knowledge and then back to practice. Such is the Marxist theory of knowledge, the dialectical materialist theory of knowledge. Among our comrades there are many who do not yet understand this theory of knowledge. When asked the source of their ideas, opinions, policies, methods, plans and conclusions, eloquent speeches and long articles, they consider the question strange and cannot answer it. Nor do they comprehend that matter can be transformed into consciousness and consciousness into matter, although such leaps are phenomena of everyday life. It is therefore necessary to educate our comrades in the dialectical materialist theory of knowledge, so that they can orientate their thinking correctly, become good at investigation and study and at summing up experience, overcome difficulties, commit fewer mistakes, do their work better, and struggle hard so as to build China into a great and powerful socialist country and help the broad masses of the oppressed and exploited throughout the world in fulfilment of our great internationalist duty....

Before Marx, materialism examined the problem of knowledge apart from the social nature of man and apart from his historical development, and was therefore incapable of understanding the dependence of knowledge on social practice, that is, the dependence of knowledge on production and the class struggle.

Above all, Marxists regard man's activity in production as the most fundamental practical activity, the determinant of all his other activities. Man's knowledge depends mainly on his activity in material production, through which he comes gradually to understand the phenomena, the properties and the laws of nature, and the relations between himself and nature; and through his activity in production he also gradually comes to understand, in varying degrees, certain relations that exist between man and man. None of this knowledge can be acquired apart from activity in production. In a classless society every person, as a member of society, joins in common effort with the other members, enters into definite relations of production with them and engages in production to meet man's material needs. In all class societies, the members of the different social classes also enter, in different ways, into definite relations of production and engage in production to meet their material needs. This is the primary source from which human knowledge develops.

Man's social practice is not confined to activity in production, but takes many other forms—class struggle, political life, scientific and artistic pursuits; in short, as a social being, man participates in all spheres of the practical life of society. Thus man, in varying degrees, comes to know the different relations between man and man, not only through his material life but also through his political and cultural life (both of which are intimately bound up with material life). Of these other types of social practice, class struggle in particular, in all its various forms, exerts a profound influence on the development of man's knowledge. In class society everyone lives as a member of a particular class, and every kind of thinking, without exception, is stamped with the brand of a class.

Marxists hold that in human society activity in production develops step by step from a lower to a higher level and that consequently man's knowledge, whether of nature or of society, also develops step by step from a lower to a higher level, that is, from the shallower to the deeper, from the one-sided to the many-sided. For a very long period in history, men were necessarily confined to a one-sided understanding of the history of society because, for one thing, the bias of the exploiting classes always distorted history and, for another, the small scale of production limited man's outlook. It was not until the modern proletariat emerged along with immense forces of production (large-scale industry) that man was able to acquire a comprehensive, historical understanding of the development of society and turn this knowledge into a science, the science of Marxism.

Marxists hold that man's social practice alone is the criterion of the truth of his knowledge of the external world. What actually happens is that man's knowledge is verified only when he achieves the anticipated results in the process of social practice (material production, class struggle or scientific experiment). If a man wants to succeed in his work, that is, to achieve the anticipated results, he must bring his ideas into correspondence with the laws of the objective external world; if they do not correspond, he will fail in his practice. After he fails, he draws his lessons, corrects his ideas to make them correspond to the laws of the external world, and can thus turn failure into success; this is what is meant by "failure is the mother of success" and "a fall into the pit, a gain in your wit." The dialectical-materialist theory of knowledge places practice in the primary position, holding that human knowledge can in no way be separated from practice and repudiating all the erroneous theories which deny the importance of practice or separate knowledge from practice. Thus Lenin said, "*Practice is higher than (theoretical) knowledge,* for it has not only the dignity of universality, but also of immediate actuality." The Marxist philosophy of dialectical materialism has two outstanding characteristics. One is its class nature: it openly avows that dialectical materialism is in the service of the proletariat. The other is its practicality: it emphasizes the dependence of theory on practice, emphasizes that theory is based on practice and in turn serves practice. The truth of any knowledge or theory is determined not by subjective feelings, but by objective results in social practice. Only social practice can be the criterion of truth. The standpoint of practice is the primary and basic standpoint in the dialectical-materialist theory of knowledge.

But how then does human knowledge arise from practice and in turn serve practice? This will become clear if we look at the process of development of knowledge.

In the process of practice, man at first sees only the phenomenal side, the separate aspects, the external relations of things....

As social practice continues, things that give rise to man's sense perceptions and impressions in the course of his practice are repeated many times; then a sudden change (leap) takes place in the brain in the process of cognition, and concepts are formed. Concepts are no longer the phenomena, the separate aspects and the external relations of things; they grasp the essence, the totality and the internal relations of things. Between concepts and sense perceptions there is not only a quantitative but also a qualitative difference. Proceeding further, by means of judgment and inference one is able to draw logical conclusions. The expression in *San Kuo Yen Yi, [Tales of the Three Kingdoms]* "knit the brows and a stratagem comes to mind," or in everyday language, "let me think it over," refers to man's use of concepts in the brain to form judgments and inferences. This is the second stage of cognition. . . . This stage of conception, judgment and inference is the more important stage in the entire process of knowing a thing; it is the stage of rational knowledge. The real task of knowing is, through perception, to arrive at thought, to arrive step by step at the comprehension of the internal contradictions of objective things, of their laws and of the internal relations between one process and another, that is, to arrive at logical knowledge. To repeat, logical knowledge differs from perceptual knowledge in that perceptual knowledge pertains to the separate aspects, the phenomena and the external relations of things, whereas logical knowledge takes a big stride forward to reach the totality, the essence and the internal relations of things and discloses the inner contradictions in the surrounding world. Therefore, logical knowledge is capable of grasping the development of the surrounding world in its totality, in the internal relations of all its aspects.

This dialectical-materialist theory of the process of development of knowledge, basing itself on practice and proceeding from the shallower to the deeper, was never worked out by anybody before the rise of Marxism. Marxist materialism solved this problem correctly for the first time, pointing out both materialistically and dialectically the deepening movement of cognition, the movement by which man in society progresses from perceptual knowledge to logical knowledge in his complex, constantly recurring practice of production and class struggle. Lenin said, "The abstraction of *matter,* of a *law* of nature, the abstraction of *value,* etc., in short, *all* scientific (correct, serious, not absurd) abstractions reflect nature more deeply, truly and *completely.*" Marxism-Leninism holds that each of the two stages in the process of cognition has its own characteristics, with knowledge manifesting itself as perceptual at the lower stage and logical at the higher stage, but that both are stages in an integrated process of cognition. The perceptual and the rational are qualitatively different, but are not divorced from each other; they are unified on the basis of practice. Our practice proves that what is perceived cannot at once be comprehended and that only what is comprehended can be more deeply perceived. Perception only solves the problem of phenomena; theory alone can solve the problem of essence. The solving of both these problems is not separable in the slightest degree from practice.

Whoever wants to know a thing has no way of doing so except by coming into contact with it, that is, by living (practising) in its environment. In feudal society it was impossible to know the laws of capitalist society in advance because capitalism had not yet emerged, the relevant practice was lacking. Marxism could be the product only of capitalist society. Marx, in the era of laissez-faire capitalism, could not concretely know certain laws peculiar to the era of imperialism beforehand, because imperialism, the last stage of capitalism, had not yet emerged and the relevant practice was lacking; only Lenin and Stalin could undertake this task. Leaving aside their genius, the reason why Marx, Engels, Lenin and Stalin could work out their theories was mainly that they personally took part in the practice of the class struggle and the scientific experimentation of their time; lacking this condition, no genius could have succeeded. The saying, "without stepping outside his gate the scholar knows all the wide world's affairs," was mere empty talk in past times when technology was undeveloped. Even though this saying can be valid in the present age of developed technology, the people with real personal knowledge are those engaged in practice the wide world over. And it is only when these people have come to "know" through their practice and when their knowledge has reached him through writing and technical media that the "scholar" can indirectly "know all the wide world's affairs." If you want to know a certain thing or a certain class of things directly, you must personally participate in the practical struggle to change reality, to change that thing or class of things, for only thus can you come into contact with them as phenomena; only through personal participation in the practical struggle to change reality can you uncover the essence of that thing or class of things and comprehend them. This is the path to knowledge which every man actually travels, though some people, deliberately distorting matters, argue to the contrary. The most ridiculous person in the world is the "know-all" who picks up a smattering of hearsay knowledge and proclaims himself "the world's Number One authority"; this merely shows that he has not taken a proper measure of himself. Knowledge is a matter of science, and no dishonesty or conceit whatsoever is permissible. What is required is definitely the reverse—honesty and modesty. If you want knowledge, you must take part in the practice of changing reality. If you want to know the taste of a pear, you must change the pear by eating it yourself. If you want to know the structure and properties of the atom, you must make physical and chemical experiments to change the state of the atom. If you want to know the theory and methods of revolution, you must take part in revolution. All genuine knowledge originates in direct experience. But one cannot have direct experience of everything; as a matter of fact, most of our knowledge comes from indirect experience, for example, all knowledge from past times and foreign lands. To our ancestors and to foreigners, such knowledge was—or is—a matter of direct experience, and this knowledge is reliable if in the course of their direct experience the requirement of "scientific abstraction," spoken of by Lenin, was—or is—fulfilled and objective reality scientifically reflected; otherwise it is not reliable. Hence a man's knowledge consists only of two parts, that which comes from direct experience and that which comes from indirect experience. Moreover, what is indirect experience for me is direct experience for other people. Consequently, considered as a whole, knowledge of any kind is inseparable from direct experience. All knowledge originates in perception of the objective external world through man's physical sense organs. Anyone who denies such perception, denies direct experience, or denies personal participation in the practice that changes reality, is not a materialist. That is why the "know-all" is ridiculous. There is an old Chinese saying, "How can you catch tiger cubs without entering the tiger's lair?" This saying holds true for man's practice and it also holds true for the theory of knowledge. There can be no knowledge apart from practice....

Idealism and mechanical materialism, opportunism and adventurism, are all characterized by the breach between the subjective and the objective, by the separation of knowledge from practice. The Marxist-Leninist theory of knowledge, characterized as it is by scientific social practice, cannot but resolutely oppose these wrong ideologies. Marxists recognize that in the absolute and general process of development of the universe, the development of each particular process is relative, and that hence, in the endless flow of absolute truth, man's knowledge of a particular process at any given stage of development is only relative truth. The sum total of innumerable relative truths constitutes absolute truth. The development of an objective process is full of contradictions and struggles, and so is the development of the movement of human knowledge. All the dialectical movements of the objective world can sooner or later be reflected in human knowledge. In social practice, the process of coming into being, developing and passing away is infinite, and so is the process of coming into being, developing and passing away in human knowledge. As man's practice which changes objective reality in accordance with given ideas, theories, plans or programmes, advances further and further, his knowledge of objective reality likewise becomes deeper and deeper. The movement of change in the world of objective reality is never-ending and so is man's cognition of truth through practice. Marxism-Leninism has in no way exhausted truth but ceaselessly opens up roads to the knowledge of truth in the course of practice. Our conclusion is the concrete, historical unity of the subjective and the objective, of theory and practice, of knowing and doing, and we are opposed to all erroneous ideologies, whether "Left" or Right, which depart from concrete history.

In the present epoch of the development of society, the responsibility of correctly knowing and changing the world has been placed by history upon the shoulders of the proletariat and its party. This process, the practice of changing the world, which is determined in accordance with scientific knowledge, has already reached a historic moment in the world and in China, a great moment unprecedented in human history, that is, the moment for completely banishing darkness from the world and from China and for changing the world into a world of light such as never previously existed. The struggle of the proletariat and the revolutionary people to change the world comprises the fulfilment of the following tasks: to change the objective world and, at the same time, their own subjective world—to change their cognitive ability and change the relations between the subjective and the objective world. Such a change has already come about in one part of the globe, in the Soviet Union. There the people are pushing forward this process of change. The people of China and the rest of the world either are going through, or will go through, such a process. And the objective world which is to be changed also includes all the opponents of change, who, in order to be changed, must go through a stage of compulsion before they can enter the stage of voluntary, conscious change. The epoch of world communism will be reached when all mankind voluntarily and consciously changes itself and the world.

Discover the truth through practice, and again through practice verify and develop the truth. Start from perceptual knowledge and actively develop it into rational knowledge; then start from rational knowledge and actively guide revolutionary practice to change both the subjective and the objective world. Practice, knowledge, again practice, and again knowledge. This form repeats itself in endless cycles, and with each cycle the content of practice and knowledge rises to a higher level. Such is the whole of the dialectical-materialist theory of knowledge, and such is the dialectical-materialist theory of the unity of knowing and doing. . . .

We may now say a few words to sum up. The law of contradiction in things, that is, the law of the unity of opposites, is the fundamental law of nature and of society and therefore also the fundamental law of thought. It stands opposed to the metaphysical world outlook. It represents a great revolution in the history of human knowledge. According to dialectical materialism, contradiction is present in all processes of objectively existing things and of subjective thought and permeates all these processes from beginning to end; this is the universality and absoluteness of contradiction. Each contradiction and each of its aspects have their respective characteristics; this is the particularity and relativity of contradiction. In given conditions, opposites possess identity, and consequently can coexist in a single entity and can transform themselves into each other; this again is the particularity and relativity of contradiction. But the struggle of opposites is ceaseless, it goes on both when the opposites are coexisting and when they are transforming themselves into each other, and becomes especially conspicuous when they are transforming themselves into one another; this again is the universality and absoluteness of contradiction. In studying the particularity and relativity of contradiction, we must give attention to the distinction between the principal contradiction and the non-principal contradictions and to the distinction between the principal aspect and the non-principal aspect of a contradiction; in studying the universality of contradiction and the struggle of opposites in contradiction, we must give attention to the distinction between the different forms of struggle. Otherwise we shall make mistakes. If, through study, we achieve a real understanding of the essentials explained above, we shall be able to demolish dogmatist ideas which are contrary to the basic principles of Marxism-Leninism and detrimental to our revolutionary cause, and our comrades with practical experience will be able to organize their experience into principles and avoid repeating empiricist errors. These are a few simple conclusions from our study of the law of contradiction.

HUMANIST MANIFESTO II*

Humanist Manifesto II was published in 1973. Forty years before, *Humanist Manifesto I* appeared, signed by thirty-four persons. The earlier Manifesto set forth humanist ideals in very general terms in fifteen brief statements; the second manifesto, signed by more than one hundred persons including philosophers, scientists, and religious leaders, is much more specific. It was edited by Paul Kurtz, Editor of *The Humanist,* and by Edwin H. Wilson, Editor Emeritus of *The Humanist.* The original draft was prepared by Kurtz, who since 1965 has been Professor of Philosophy at the State University of New York at Buffalo.

The following manifesto is not a binding credo, but it expresses the convictions of humanists on: the next century, religion, ethics, the individual, society, the world community, and the prospects or hope for humanity.

The next century can be and should be the humanistic century. Dramatic scientific, technological, and ever-accelerating social and political changes crowd our awareness. We have virtually conquered the planet,

*From "Humanist Manifesto II," ed. Paul Kurtz, in *The Humanist,* 33:5 (September/October 1973), pp. 4–8 with omissions. Used by permission.

explored the moon, overcome the natural limits of travel and communication; we stand at the dawn of a new age, ready to move farther into space and perhaps inhabit other planets. Using technology wisely, we can control our environment, conquer poverty, markedly reduce disease, extend our life-span, significantly modify our behavior, alter the course of human evolution and cultural development, unlock vast new powers, and provide humankind with unparalleled opportunity for achieving an abundant and meaningful life. . . .

We affirm a set of common principles that can serve as a basis for united action—positive principles relevant to the present human condition. They are a design for a secular society on a planetary scale.

For these reasons, we submit this new *Humanist Manifesto* for the future of humankind; for us, it is a vision of hope, a direction for satisfying survival.

RELIGION

First: In the best sense, religion may inspire dedication to the highest ethical ideals. The cultivation of moral devotion and creative imagination is an expression of genuine "spiritual" experience and aspiration.

We believe, however, that traditional dogmatic or authoritarian religions that place revelation, God, ritual, or creed above human needs and experience do a disservice to the human species. Any account of nature should pass the tests of scientific evidence; in our judgment, the dogmas and myths of traditional religions do not do so. Even at this late date in human history, certain elementary facts based upon the critical use of scientific reason have to be restated. We find insufficient evidence for belief in the existence of a supernatural; it is either meaningless or irrelevant to the question of the survival and fulfillment of the human race. As nontheists, we begin with humans not God, nature not deity. Nature may indeed be broader and deeper than we now know; any new discoveries, however, will but enlarge our knowledge of the natural. . . .

Second: Promises of immortal salvation or fear of eternal damnation are both illusory and harmful. They distract humans from present concerns, from self-actualization, and from rectifying social injustices. Modern science discredits such historic concepts as the "ghost in the machine" and the "separable soul." Rather, science affirms that the human species is an emergence from natural evolutionary forces. As far as we know, the total personality is a function of the biological organism transacting in a social and cultural context. There is no credible evidence that life survives the death of the body. We continue to exist in our progeny and in the way that our lives have influenced others in our culture.

ETHICS

Third: We affirm that moral values derive their source from human experience. Ethics is *autonomous* and *situational,* needing no theological or ideological sanction. Ethics stems from human need and interest. To deny this distorts the whole basis of life. Human life has meaning because we create and develop our futures. Happiness and the creative realization of human needs and desires, individually and in shared enjoyment, are continuous themes of humanism. We strive for the good life, here and now. The goal is to pursue life's enrichment despite debasing forces of vulgarization, commercialization, bureaucratization, and dehumanization.

Fourth: Reason and intelligence are the most effective instruments that humankind possesses. There is no substitute: neither faith nor passion suffices in itself. The controlled use of scientific methods, which have transformed the natural and social sciences since the Renaissance, must be extended further in the solution of human problems. But reason must be tempered by humility, since no group has a monopoly of wisdom or virtue. Nor is there any guarantee that all problems can be solved or all questions answered. Yet critical intelligence, infused by a sense of human caring, is the best method that humanity has for resolving problems. Reason should be balanced with compassion and empathy and the whole person fulfilled. Thus, we are not advocating the use of scientific intelligence independent of or in opposition to emotion, for we believe in the cultivation of feeling and love. As science pushes back the boundary of the known, man's sense of wonder is continually renewed, and art, poetry, and music find their places, along with religion and ethics.

THE INDIVIDUAL

Fifth: The preciousness and dignity of the individual person is a central humanist value. Individuals should be encouraged to realize their own creative talents and desires. We reject all religious, ideological, or moral codes that denigrate the individual, suppress freedom, dull intellect, dehumanize personality. We believe in maximum individual autonomy consonant with social responsibility. Although science can account for the causes of behavior, the possibilities of individual *freedom of choice* exist in human life and should be increased.

Sixth: In the area of sexuality, we believe that intolerant attitudes, often cultivated by orthodox religions and puritanical cultures, unduly repress sexual conduct. The right to birth control, abortion, and divorce should be recognized. While we do not approve of exploitive, denigrating forms of sexual expression, neither do we wish to prohibit, by law or social sanction, sexual behavior between consenting adults. The many varieties of sexual exploration should not in themselves be considered "evil." Without countenancing mindless permissiveness or unbridled promiscuity, a civilized society should be a *tolerant* one. Short of harming others or compelling them to do likewise, individuals should be permitted to express their sexual proclivities and pursue their life-styles as they desire. We wish to cultivate the development of a responsible attitude toward sexuality, in which humans are not exploited as sexual objects, and in which intimacy, sensitivity, respect, and honesty in interpersonal relations are encouraged. Moral education for children and adults is an important way of developing awareness and sexual maturity.

DEMOCRATIC SOCIETY

Seventh: To enhance freedom and dignity the individual must experience a full range of *civil liberties* in all societies. This includes freedom of speech and the press, political democracy, the legal right of opposition to governmental policies, fair judicial process, religious liberty, freedom of association, and artistic, scientific, and cultural freedom. It also includes a recognition of an individual's right to die with dignity, euthanasia, and the right to suicide. We oppose the increasing invasion of privacy, by whatever means, in both totalitarian and democratic societies. We would safeguard, extend, and implement the principles of human freedom evolved from the *Magna Carta* to the *Bill of Rights,* the *Rights of Man,* and the *Universal Declaration of Human Rights.*

Eighth: We are committed to an open and democratic society. We must extend *participatory democracy* in its true sense to the economy, the school, the family, the workplace, and voluntary associations. Decision-making must be decentralized to include widespread involvement of people at all levels—social, political, and economic. All persons should have a voice in developing the values and goals that determine their lives. Institutions should be responsive to expressed desires and needs. The conditions of work, education, devotion, and play should be humanized. Alienating forces should be modified or eradicated and bureaucratic structures should be held to a minimum. People are more important than decalogues, rules, proscriptions, or regulations.

Ninth: The separation of church and state and the separation of ideology and state are imperatives. The state should encourage maximum freedom for different moral, political, religious, and social values in society. It should not favor any particular religious bodies through the use of public monies, nor espouse a single ideology and function thereby as an instrument of propaganda or oppression, particularly against dissenters.

Tenth: Humane societies should evaluate economic systems not by rhetoric or ideology, but by whether or not they *increase economic well-being* for all individuals and groups, minimize poverty and hardship, increase the sum of human satisfaction, and enhance the quality of life. Hence the door is open to alternative economic systems. We need to democratize the economy and judge it by its responsiveness to human needs, testing results in terms of the common good.

Eleventh: The principle of moral equality must be furthered through elimination of all discrimination based upon race, religion, sex, age or national origin. This means equality of opportunity and recognition of talent and merit. Individuals should be encouraged to contribute to their own betterment. If unable, then society should provide means to satisfy their basic economic, health, and cultural needs, including, wherever resources make possible, a minimum guaranteed annual income. We are concerned for the welfare of the aged, the infirm, the disadvantaged, and also for the outcasts—the mentally retarded, abandoned or abused children, the handicapped, prisoners, and addicts—for *all* who are neglected or ignored by society. Practicing humanists should make it their vocation to humanize personal relations....

WORLD COMMUNITY

Twelfth: We deplore the division of humankind on nationalistic grounds. We have reached a turning point in human history where the best option is to *transcend the limits of national sovereignty* and to move toward the building of a world community in which all sectors of the human family can participate. Thus we look to the development of a system of world law and a world order based upon transnational federal government. This would appreciate cultural pluralism and diversity. It would not exclude pride in national origins and accomplishments nor the handling of regional problems on a regional basis. Human progress, however, can no longer be achieved by focusing on one section of the world, Western or Eastern, developed or underdeveloped. For the first time in human history, no part of humankind can be isolated from any other. Each person's future is in some way linked to all. We thus reaffirm a commitment to the building of world community, at the same time recognizing that this commits us to some hard choices.

Thirteenth: This world community must *renounce the resort to violence and force* as a method of solving international disputes. We believe in the peaceful adjudication of differences by international courts and by the development of the arts of negotiation and compromise. War is obsolete. So is the use of nuclear, biological, and chemical weapons. It is a planetary imperative to reduce the level of military expenditures and turn these savings to peaceful and people-oriented uses.

Fourteenth: The world community must engage in *cooperative planning* concerning the use of rapidly depleting resources. The planet earth must be considered a single *ecosystem.* Ecological damage, resource depletion, and excessive population growth must be checked by international concord. The cultivation and conservation of nature is a moral value; we should perceive ourselves as integral to the sources of our being in nature. We must free our world from needless pollution and waste, responsibly guarding and creating wealth, both natural and human. Exploitation of natural resources, uncurbed by social conscience, must end.

Fifteenth: The problems of *economic growth and development* can no longer be resolved by one nation alone; they are worldwide in scope. It is the moral obligation of the developed nations to provide—through an international authority that safeguards human rights—massive technical, agricultural, medical, and economic assistance, including birth control techniques, to the developing portions of the globe. World poverty must cease. Hence extreme disproportions in wealth, income, and economic growth should be reduced on a worldwide basis.

Sixteenth: Technology is a vital key to human progress and development. We deplore any neo-romantic efforts to condemn indiscriminately all technology and science or to counsel retreat from its further extension and use for the good of humankind. We would resist any moves to censor basic scientific research on moral, political, or social grounds. Technology must, however, be carefully judged by the consequences of its use; harmful and destructive changes should be avoided. We are particularly disturbed when technology and bureaucracy control, manipulate, or modify human beings without their consent. Technological feasibility does not imply social or cultural desirability.

Seventeenth: We must expand communication and transportation across frontiers. Travel restrictions must cease. The world must be open to diverse political, ideological, and moral viewpoints and evolve a worldwide system of television and radio for information and education. We thus call for full international cooperation in culture, science, the arts, and technology *across ideological borders.* We must learn to live openly together or we shall perish together.

HUMANITY AS A WHOLE

In closing: The world cannot wait for a reconciliation of competing political or economic systems to solve its problems. These are the times for men and women of good will to further the building of a peaceful and prosperous world. We urge that parochial loyalties and inflexible moral and religious ideologies be transcended. We urge recognition of the common humanity of all people. We further urge the use of reason and compassion to produce the kind of world we want—a world in which peace, prosperity, freedom, and happiness are widely shared.... Humanism thus interpreted is a moral force that has time on its side. We believe that humankind has the potential intelligence, good will, and cooperative skill to implement this commitment in the decades ahead.

THE TENSION BETWEEN IDEALISM AND REALISM

GEORGE BERKELEY

*Immaterialism**

George Berkeley (1685–1753), Irish philosopher and Anglican bishop, was a deeply religious man who desired to reconcile the emerging science of his time with the doctrines of Christianity. His practical interest in education and humanity is exhibited in his attempt to found a college in Bermuda and to build an ideal state in the New World. His best-known writings are *An Essay Towards a New Theory of Vision, A Treatise Concerning the Principles of Human Nature,* and *Three Dialogues Between Hylas and Philonous.*

Berkeley is called a philosophical "idealist" and an "immaterialist" since he claimed that things are mind-dependent. According to Berkeley, there exist only minds and their ideas; he tells us that "to be is to be perceived" (ideas) or to be a perceiver (mind). The order and consistency of the external world are due to active mind, not my mind or yours, but to a supreme mind or spirit, the mind of God. Things do not exist apart from minds; things are ideas imprinted on the senses by the Author of Nature.

It is evident to anyone who takes a survey of the *objects* of human knowledge that they are either ideas actually imprinted on the senses, or else such as are perceived by attending to the passions and operations of the mind, or lastly, ideas formed by help of memory and imagination—either compounding, dividing, or barely representing those originally perceived in the afore-

*George Berkeley, from *A Treatise Concerning the Principles of Human Knowledge* (1710), Secs. 1–4, 6–8, 9, 15, 25–30, 33.

said ways. By sight I have the ideas of light and colors, with their several degrees and variations. By touch I perceive, for example, hard and soft, heat and cold, motion and resistance, and of all these more and less either as to quantity or degree. Smelling furnishes me with odors, the palate with tastes, and hearing conveys sounds to the mind in all their variety of tone and composition. And as several of these are observed to accompany each other, they come to be marked by one name, and so to be reputed as one thing. Thus, for example, a certain color, taste, smell, figure, and consistence having been observed to go together, are accounted one distinct thing signified by the name "*apple*"; other collections of ideas constitute a stone, a tree, a book, and the like sensible things—which as they are pleasing or disagreeable excite the passions of love, hatred, joy, grief, and so forth.

2. But, besides all that endless variety of ideas or objects of knowledge, there is likewise something which knows or perceives them and exercises divers operations, as willing, imagining, remembering, about them. This perceiving, active being is what I call *mind, spirit, soul,* or *myself*. By which words I do not denote any one of my ideas, but a thing entirely distinct from them, wherein they exist or, which is the same thing, whereby they are perceived—for the existence of an idea consists in being perceived.

3. That neither our thoughts, nor passions, nor ideas formed by the imagination exist without the mind is what everybody will allow. And it seems no less evident that the various sensations or ideas imprinted on the sense, however blended or combined together (that is, whatever objects they compose), cannot exist otherwise than in a mind perceiving them.—I think an intuitive knowledge may be obtained of this by anyone that shall attend to what is meant by the term *exist* when applied to sensible things. The table I write on I say exists, that is, I see and feel it; and if I were out of my study I should say it existed—meaning thereby that if I was in my study I might perceive it, or that some other spirit actually does perceive it. There was an odor, that is, it was smelled; there was a sound, that is to say, it was heard; a color or figure, and it was perceived by sight or touch. This is all that I can understand by these and the like expressions. For as to what is said of the absolute existence of unthinking things without any relation to their being perceived, that seems perfectly unintelligible. Their *esse* is *percipi,* nor is it possible they should have any existence out of the minds or thinking things which perceive them.

4. It is indeed an opinion strangely prevailing amongst men that houses, mountains, rivers, and, in a word, all sensible objects have an existence, natural or real, distinct from their being perceived by the understanding. But with how great an assurance and acquiescence soever this principle may be entertained in the world, yet whoever shall find in his heart to call it in question may, if I mistake not, perceive it to involve a manifest con-

tradiction. For what are the forementioned objects but the things we perceive by sense? And what do we perceive besides our own ideas or sensations? And is it not plainly repugnant that any one of these, or any combination of them, should exist unperceived? . . .

6. Some truths then are so near and obvious to the mind that a man need only open his eyes to see them. Such I take this important one to be, to wit, that all the choir of heaven and furniture of the earth, in a word, all those bodies which compose the mighty frame of the world, have not any subsistence without a mind—that their *being* is to be perceived or known, that, consequently, so long as they are not actually perceived by me or do not exist in my mind or that of any other created spirit, they must either have no existence at all or else subsist in the mind of some eternal spirit—it being perfectly unintelligible, and involving all the absurdity of abstraction, to attribute to any single part of them an existence independent of a spirit. [To be convinced of which, the reader need only reflect, and try to separate in his own thoughts, the *being* of a sensible thing from its *being perceived*.]

7. From what has been said it follows there is not any other substance than *Spirit,* or that which perceives. But, for the fuller proof of this point, let it be considered the sensible qualities are color, figure, motion, smell, taste, and such like—that is, the ideas perceived by sense. Now, for an idea to exist in an unperceiving thing is a manifest contradiction, for to have an idea is all one as to perceive; that, therefore, wherein color, figure, and the like qualities exist must perceive them; hence it is clear there can be no unthinking substance or *substratum* of those ideas.

8. But, say you, though the ideas themselves do not exist without the mind, yet there may be things like them, whereof they are copies or resemblances, which things exist without the mind in an unthinking substance. I answer, an idea can be like nothing but an idea; a color or figure can be like nothing but another color or figure. If we look but ever so little into our thoughts, we shall find it impossible for us to conceive a likeness except only between our ideas. Again, I ask whether those supposed originals or external things, of which our ideas are the pictures or representations, be themselves perceivable or no? If they are, then they are ideas and we have gained our point; but if you say they are not, I appeal to anyone whether it be sense to assert a color is like something which is invisible; hard or soft, like something which is intangible; and so of the rest.

9. Some there are who make a distinction betwixt *primary* and *secondary* qualities. By the former they mean extension, figure, motion, rest, solidity or impenetrability, and number; by the latter they denote all other sensible qualities, as colors, sounds, tastes, and so forth. The ideas we have of these they acknowledge not to be the resemblances of anything existing

without the mind, or unperceived, but they will have our ideas of the primary qualities to be patterns or images of things which exist without the mind, in an unthinking substance which they call "matter." By "matter," therefore, we are to understand an inert, senseless substance, in which extension, figure, and motion do actually subsist. But it is evident from what we have already shown that extension, figure, and motion are only ideas existing in the mind, and that an idea can be like nothing but another idea, and that consequently neither they nor their archetypes can exist in an unperceiving substance. Hence it is plain that the very notion of what is called *matter* or *corporeal substance* involves a contradiction in it....

15. In short, let anyone consider those arguments which are thought manifestly to prove that colors and taste exist only in the mind, and he shall find they may with equal force be brought to prove the same thing of extension, figure, and motion. Though it must be confessed this method of arguing does not so much prove that there is no extension or color in an outward object as that we do not know by sense which is the true extension or color of the object. But the arguments foregoing plainly show it to be impossible that any color or extension at all, or other sensible quality whatsoever, should exist in an unthinking subject without the mind, or, in truth, that there should be any such thing as an outward object....

25. All our ideas, sensations, or the things which we perceive, by whatsoever names they may be distinguished, are visibly inactive—there is nothing of power or agency included in them. So that one idea or object of thought cannot produce or make any alteration in another. To be satisfied of the truth of this, there is nothing else requisite but a bare observation of our ideas. For since they and every part of them exists only in the mind, it follows that there is nothing in them but what is perceived; but whoever shall attend to his ideas, whether of sense or reflection, will not perceive in them any power or activity; there is, therefore, no such thing contained in them. A little attention will discover to us that the very being of an idea implies passiveness and inertness in it, insomuch that it is impossible for an idea to do anything or, strictly speaking, to be the cause of anything; neither can it be the resemblance or pattern of any active being.... Whence it plainly follows that extension, figure, and motion cannot be the cause of our sensations. To say, therefore, that these are the effects of powers resulting from the configuration, number, motion, and size of corpuscles must certainly be false.

26. We perceive a continual succession of ideas, some are anew excited, others are changed or totally disappear. There is, therefore, some cause of these ideas, whereon they depend and which produces and changes them. That this cause cannot be any quality or idea or combination of ideas is clear from the preceding section. It must therefore be a substance; but it

has been shown that there is no corporeal or material substance: it remains, therefore, that the cause of ideas is an incorporeal, active substance or spirit.

27. A spirit is one simple, undivided, active being—as it perceives ideas it is called the *understanding,* and as it produces or otherwise operates about them it is called the *will.* Hence there can be no *idea* formed of a soul or spirit; for all ideas whatever, being passive and inert (*vide* sect. 25), they cannot represent unto us, by way of image or likeness, that which acts. A little attention will make it plain to anyone that to have an idea which shall be like that active principle of motion and change of ideas is absolutely impossible. Such is the nature of *spirit,* or that which acts, that it cannot be of itself perceived, but only by the effects which it produces. If any man shall doubt of the truth of what is here delivered, let him but reflect and try if he can frame the idea of any power or active being and whether he has ideas of two principal powers marked by the names *will* and *understanding,* distinct from each other as well as from a third idea of substance or being in general, with a relative notion of its supporting or being the subject of the aforesaid powers—which is signified by the name *soul* or *spirit.* This is what some hold; but, so far as I can see, the words *will, soul, spirit* do not stand for different ideas or, in truth, for any idea at all, but for something which is very different from ideas, and which, being an agent, cannot be like unto, or represented by, any idea whatsoever. [Though it must be owned at the same time that we have some notion of soul, spirit, and the operations of the mind, such as willing, loving, hating—in as much as we know or understand the meaning of those words.]

28. I find I can excite ideas in my mind at pleasure, and vary and shift the scene as oft as I think fit. It is no more than willing, and straightway this or that idea arises in my fancy; and by the same power it is obliterated and makes way for another. This making and unmaking of ideas does very properly denominate the mind active. Thus much is certain and grounded on experience; but when we talk of unthinking agents or of exciting ideas exclusive of volition, we only amuse ourselves with words.

29. But, whatever power I may have over my own thoughts, I find the ideas actually perceived by sense have not a like dependence on my will. When in broad daylight I open my eyes, it is not in my power to choose whether I shall see or no, or to determine what particular objects shall present themselves to my view; and so likewise as to the hearing and other senses; the ideas imprinted on them are not creatures of my will. There is therefore some *other* will or spirit that produces them.

30. The ideas of sense are more strong, lively, and distinct than those of the imagination; they have likewise a steadiness, order, and coherence, and are not excited at random, as those which are the effects of human wills often are, but in a regular train or series, the admirable connection whereof

sufficiently testifies the wisdom and benevolence of its Author. Now the set rules or established methods wherein the mind we depend on excites in us the ideas of sense are called the *laws of nature;* and these we learn by experience, which teaches us that such and such ideas are attended with such and such other ideas in the ordinary course of things....

33. The ideas imprinted on the senses by the Author of Nature are called *real things;* and those excited in the imagination, being less regular, vivid, and constant, are more properly termed *ideas* or *images of things* which they copy and represent. But then our sensations, be they never so vivid and distinct, are nevertheless ideas, that is, they exist in the mind, or are perceived by it, as truly as the ideas of its own framing. The ideas of sense are allowed to have more reality in them, that is, to be more strong, orderly, and coherent than the creatures of the mind; but this is no argument that they exist without the mind. They are also less dependent on the spirit, or thinking substance which perceives them, in that they are excited by the will of another and more powerful spirit; yet still they are *ideas;* and certainly no idea, whether faint or strong, can exist otherwise than in a mind perceiving it.

JOSIAH ROYCE

*Reality and Idealism**

Josiah Royce (1855–1916) graduated from the University of California, received his doctorate from Johns Hopkins University, and spent some time studying in Germany. From 1882 until his death he taught at Harvard, where he carried on friendly debate with such men as William James and George Santayana. He was a prolific writer and much in demand as a public speaker. He is one of the best American representatives of absolute idealism. His writings include *The World and the Individual, The Philosophy of Loyalty,* and *The Problem of Christianity.*

In the following selection, Royce leads his reader to view the world beyond as "such stuff as ideas are made of." While there appear to be stubborn material facts, and many sorts of reality, yet, if this world beyond is knowable, it must be in and for itself essentially a mental world. The whole world of ideas is basically one world that exists in and for a universal mind—an Infinite Self.

*Josiah Royce, from "Reality and Idealism," in *The Spirit of Modern Philosophy* (Boston: Houghton Mifflin, 1892), pp. 350–361, 364, 366–368, 370, 373, 379.

... I must remind you that idealism has two aspects. It is, for the first, a kind of analysis of the world, an analysis which so far has no absolute character about it, but which undertakes, in a fashion that might be acceptable to any skeptic, to examine what you mean by all the things, whatever they are, that you believe in or experience. This idealistic analysis consists merely in a pointing out, by various devices, that the world of your knowledge, whatever it contains, is through and through such stuff as ideas are made of, that you never in your life believed in anything definable *but* ideas, that, as Berkeley put it, "this whole choir of heaven and furniture of earth" is nothing for any of us but a system of ideas which govern our belief and our conduct. Such idealism has numerous statements, interpretations, embodiments: forms part of the most various systems and experiences, is consistent with Berkeley's theism, with Fichte's ethical absolutism, with Professor Huxley's agnostic empiricism, with Clifford's mind-stuff theory, with countless other theories that have used such idealism as a part of their scheme. In this aspect idealism is already a little puzzling to our natural consciousness, but it becomes quickly familiar, in fact almost commonplace, and seems after all to alter our practical faith or to solve our deeper problems very little.

The other aspect of idealism is the one which gives us our notion of the absolute Self. To it the first is only preparatory. This second aspect is the one which from Kant, until the present time, has formed the deeper problem of thought. Whenever the world has become more conscious of its significance, the work of human philosophy will be, not nearly ended (Heaven forbid an end!), but for the first time fairly begun. For then, in critically estimating our passions, we shall have some truer sense of whose passions they are.

I begin with the first and the less significant aspect of idealism. Our world, I say, whatever it may contain, is such stuff as ideas are made of. This preparatory sort of idealism is the one that, as I just suggested, Berkeley made prominent, and after a fashion familiar. I must state it in my own way, although one in vain seeks to attain novelty in illustrating so frequently described a view.

Here, then, is our so real world of the senses, full of light and warmth and sound. If anything could be solid and external, surely, one at first will say, it is this world. Hard facts, not mere ideas, meet us on every hand. Ideas any one can mould as he wishes. Not so facts. In idea socialists can dream out Utopias, disappointed lovers can imagine themselves successful, beggars can ride horses, wanderers can enjoy the fireside at home. In the realm of facts, society organizes itself as it must, rejected lovers stand for the time defeated, beggars are alone with their wishes, oceans roll drearily between home and the wanderer. Yet this world of fact is, after all, not entirely stubborn, not merely hard. The strenuous will can mould facts.

We can form our world, in part, according to our ideas. Statesmen influence the social order, lovers woo afresh, wanderers find the way home. But thus to alter the world we must work, and just because the laborer is worthy of his hire, it is well that the real world should thus have such fixity of things as enables us to anticipate what facts will prove lasting, and to see of the travail of our souls when it is once done. This, then, is the presupposition of life, that we work in a real world, where house-walls do not melt away as in dreams, but stand firm against the winds of many winters, and can be felt as real. We do not wish to find facts wholly plastic; we want them to be stubborn, if only the stubbornness be not altogether unmerciful. Our will makes constantly a sort of agreement with the world, whereby, if the world will continually show some respect to the will, the will shall consent to be strenuous in its industry. Interfere with the reality of my world, and you therefore take the very life and heart out of my will.

The reality of the world, however, when thus defined in terms of its stubbornness, its firmness as against the will that has not conformed to its laws, its kindly rigidity in preserving for us the fruits of our labors,—such reality, I can say, is still something wholly unanalyzed. In what does this stubbornness consist? Surely, many different sorts of reality, as it would seem, may be stubborn. Matter is stubborn when it stands in hard walls against us, or rises in vast mountain ranges before the path-finding explorer. But minds can be stubborn also. The lonely wanderer, who watches by the seashore the waves that roll between him and his home, talks of cruel facts, material barriers that, just because they *are* material, and not ideal, shall be the irresistible foes of his longing heart. "In wish," he says, "I am with my dear ones, but alas, wishes cannot cross oceans! Oceans are material facts, in the cold outer world. Would that the world of the heart were all!" But alas! to the rejected lover the world of the heart *is* all, and that is just his woe. Were the barrier between him and his beloved only made of those stubborn material facts, only of walls or of oceans, how lightly might his will erelong transcend them all! Matter stubborn! Outer nature cruelly the foe of ideas! Nay, it is just an idea that now opposes him,—just an idea, and that, too, in the mind of the maiden he loves. But in vain does he call this stubborn bit of disdain a merely ideal fact. No flint was ever more definite in preserving its identity and its edge than this disdain may be. Place me for a moment, then, in an external world that shall consist wholly of ideas,—the ideas, namely, of other people about me, a world of maidens who shall scorn me, of old friends who shall have learned to hate me, of angels who shall condemn me, of God who shall judge me. In what piercing north winds, amidst what fields of ice, in the labyrinths of what tangled forests, in the depths of what thick-walled dungeons, on the edges of what tremendous precipices, should I be more genuinely in the presence of stubborn and unyielding facts than in that conceived world of ideas! So, as one sees, I by no means deprive my world of stubborn reality, if I merely call it a world of ideas. On the contrary, as every teacher knows, the ideas of the people are often the most difficult of facts to influence. We were wrong, then, when we said that whilst matter was stubborn, ideas could be moulded at pleasure. Ideas are often the most implacable of facts. Even my own ideas, the facts of my own inner life, may cruelly decline to be plastic to my wish. . . .

No, here are barriers worse than any material chains. The world of ideas has its own horrible dungeons and chasms. Let those who have refuted Bishop Berkeley's idealism by the wonder why he did not walk over every precipice or into every fire if these things existed only in his idea, let such, I say, first try some of the fires and the precipices of the inner life, ere they decide that dangers cease to be dangers as soon as they are called ideal, or even subjectively ideal in me.

Many sorts of reality, then, may be existent at the heart of any world of facts. But this bright and beautiful sense-world of ours,—what, amongst these many possible sorts of reality, does that embody? . . . Evidently here we shall have no question. So far as the sense-world is beautiful, is majestic, is sublime, this beauty and dignity exist only for the appreciative observer. If they exist beyond him, they exist only for some other mind, or as the thought and embodied purpose of some universal soul of nature. . . . But let us look a little deeper. Surely, if the objects yonder are unideal and outer, odors and tastes and temperatures do not exist in these objects in just the way in which they exist in us. Part of the being of these properties, at least, if not all of it, is ideal and exists for us, or at best is once more the embodiment of the thought or purpose of some world-mind. About tastes you cannot dispute, because they are not only ideal but personal. For the benumbed tongue and palate of diseased bodily conditions, all things are tasteless. As for temperatures, a well-known experiment will show how the same water may seem cold to one hand and warm to the other. But even so, colors and sounds are at least in part ideal. Their causes may have some sort of reality; but colors themselves are not in the things, since they change with the light that falls on the things, vanish in the dark (whilst the things remained unchanged), and differ for different eyes. And as for sounds, both the pitch and the quality of tones depend for us upon certain interesting peculiarities of our hearing organs, and exist in nature only as voiceless sound-waves trembling through the air. All such sense qualities, then, are ideal. . . .

. . . [T]hat real world (to repeat one of the commonplaces of modern popular science) is in itself, apart from somebody's eyes and tongue and ears and touch, neither colored nor tasteful, neither cool nor warm, neither light nor dark, neither musical nor silent. All these qualities belong to our ideas, being indeed none the less genuine facts for that, but being in so far ideal facts. . . .

But now, at this point, the Berkeleyan idealist goes one step further. The real outside world that is still left unexplained and unanalyzed after its beauty, its warmth, its odors, its tastes, its colors, and its tones, have been relegated to the realm of ideal truths, what do you now *mean* by calling it real? No doubt it *is* known as somehow real, but *what* is this reality *known as* being? . . . What I mean by saying that the things yonder have shape and size and trembling molecules, and that there is air with sound-waves, and ether with light-waves in it,—what I *mean* by all this is that experience forces upon me, directly or indirectly, a vast system of ideas, which may indeed be founded in truth beyond me, which in fact *must* be founded in such truth if my experience has any sense, but which, like my ideas of color and of warmth, are simply expressions of how the world's order must appear to me, and to anybody constituted like me. . . .

Thus, all the reality that *we* attribute to our world, in so far as *we* know and can tell what we mean thereby, becomes ideal. There is, in fact, a certain system of ideas, forced upon us by experience, which we have to use as the guide of our conduct. This system of ideas we can't change by our wish; it is for us as overwhelming a fact as guilt, or as the bearing of our fellows towards us, but we know it only *as* such a system of ideas. And we call it the world of matter. John Stuart Mill very well expressed the puzzle of the whole thing, as we have now reached the statement of this puzzle, when he called matter a mass of "permanent possibilities of experience" for each of us. Mill's definition has its faults, but it is a very fair beginning. You know matter as something that either now gives you this idea or experience, or that would give you some other idea or experience under other circumstances. . . .

. . . The closer I come to the truth about the things, the more ideas I get. Isn't it plain, then, that *if* my world yonder is anything knowable at all, it must be in and for itself essentially a mental world? Are my ideas to *resemble* in any way the world? Is the truth of my thought to consist in its *agreement* with reality? And am I thus capable, as common sense supposes, of *conforming* my ideas to things? Then reflect. What can, after all, so well agree with an idea as another idea? To what can things that go on in my mind conform unless it be to another mind? If the more my mind grows in mental clearness, the nearer it gets to the nature of reality, then surely the reality that my mind thus resembles must be in itself mental.

After all, then, would it deprive the world here about me of reality, nay, would it not rather save and assure the reality and the knowableness of my world of experience, if I said that this world, as it exists outside of my mind, and of any other human minds, exists in and for a standard, an universal mind, whose system of ideas simply constitutes the world? Even if I fail to prove that there is such a mind, do I not at least thus make plausible that, as I said, our world of common sense has no fact in it which we cannot interpret in terms of ideas, so that this world is throughout such stuff as ideas are made of ?...

Note the point we have reached. *Either,* as you see, your real world yonder is through and through a world of ideas, an outer mind that you are more or less comprehending through your experience, or *else,* in so far as it is real and outer it is unknowable, an inscrutable *x,* an absolute mystery. The dilemma is perfect. There is no third alternative. Either a mind yonder, or else the unknowable; that is your choice. . . . Surely one must choose the former alternative. The real world may be unknown; it can't be essentially unknowable. . . .

. . . For any fair and statable problem admits of an answer. *If* the world exists yonder, its essence is then already capable of being known by some mind. If capable of being known by a mind, this essence is then already essentially ideal and mental. A mind that knew the real world would, for instance, find it a something possessing qualities. But qualities are ideal existences, just as much as are the particular qualities called odors or tones or colors. A mind knowing the real world would again find in it relations, such as equality and inequality, attraction and repulsion, likeness and unlikeness. But such relations have no meaning except as objects of a mind. In brief, then, the world as known would be found to be a world that had all the while been ideal and mental, even before it became known to the particular mind that we are to conceive as coming into connection with it. . . . The real world must be a mind, or else a group of minds.

But with this result we come in presence of a final problem. All this, you say, depends upon my assurance that there is after all a real and therefore an essentially knowable and rational world yonder. Such a world would have to be in essence a mind, or a world of minds. But after all, how does one ever escape from the prison of the inner life? Am I not in all this merely wandering amidst the realm of my own ideas?. . . My world is thus a world of ideas, but alas! how do I then ever reach those ideas of the minds beyond me?

The answer is a simple, but in one sense a very problematic one. You, in one sense, namely, never *do* or can get beyond your own ideas, nor ought you to wish to do so, because in truth all those other minds that constitute your outer and real world are in essence one with your own self. This whole world of ideas is essentially *one* world, and so it is essentially the world of one self and *That art Thou*. . . .

. . . In order to think *about* a thing, it is *not* enough that I should have an idea in me that merely resembles that thing. This last is a very important observation. I repeat, it is *not* enough that I should merely have an idea in me that resembles the thing whereof I think. I have, for instance, in me the idea of a pain. Another man has a pain just like mine. Say we both have toothache; or have both burned our finger-tips in the same way.

Now my idea of pain is just like the pain in him, but I am not on that account necessarily thinking about *his* pain, merely because what I am thinking about, namely my own pain, resembles his pain. No; to think about an object you must not merely have an idea that resembles the object, but you must *mean* to have your idea resemble that object. Stated in other form, to think of an object you must consciously aim at that object, you must pick out that object, you must already in some measure possess that object enough, namely, to identify it as what you mean. But how can you *mean,* how can you *aim at,* how can you *possess,* how can you *pick out,* how can you *identify* what is not already present in essence to your own hidden self? Here is surely a deep question. When you aim at yonder object, be it the mountains in the moon or the day of your death, you really say, "I, as my real self, as my larger self, as my complete consciousness, already in deepest truth possess that object, have it, own it, identify it. And that, and that alone, makes it possible for me in my transient, my individual, my momentary personality, to mean yonder object, to inquire about it, to be partly aware of it and partly ignorant of it." You can't mean what is utterly foreign to you. You mean an object, you assert about it, you talk about it, yes, you doubt or wonder about it, you admit your private and individual ignorance about it, only in so far as your larger self, your deeper personality, your total of normal consciousness already *has* that object....

...The relation of my thought to its object has, I insist, this curious character, that *unless* the thought and its object are parts of one larger thought, I can't even be *meaning* that object yonder, can't even be in error about it, can't even doubt its existence. You, for instance, are part of one larger self with me, or else I can't even be meaning to address you as outer beings. You are part of one larger self along with the most mysterious or most remote fact of nature, along with the moon, and all the hosts of heaven, along with all truth and all beauty. Else could you not even intend to speak of such objects beyond you. For whatever you speak of you will find that your world is meant by you as just your world. Talk of the unknowable, and it forthwith becomes your unknowable, your problem, whose solution, unless the problem be a mere nonsense question, your larger self must own and be aware of. The deepest problem of life is, "What is this deeper self?" And the only answer is, *It is the self that knows in unity all truth.* This, I insist, is no hypothesis. It is actually the presupposition of your deepest doubt. And that is why I say: Everything finite is more or less obscure, dark, doubtful. Only the Infinite Self, the problem-solver, the complete thinker, the one who knows what we mean even when we are most confused and ignorant, the one who includes us, who has the world present to himself in unity, before whom all past and future truth, all distant and dark truth is clear in one eternal moment, to whom far and forgot is near, who thinks the whole of nature, and in whom are all things, the Logos, the world-possessor,—only his existence, I say, is perfectly sure....

Flee where we will, then, the net of the larger Self ensnares us. We are lost and imprisoned in the thickets of its tangled labyrinth. The moments are not at all in themselves, for as moments they have no meaning; they exist only in relation to the beyond. The larger Self alone is, and they are by reason of it, organic parts of it. They perish, but it remains; they have truth or error only in its overshadowing presence.

And now, as to the unity of this Self. Can there be many such organic selves, mutually separate unities of moments and of the objects that these moments mean? Nay, were there *many* such, would not their manifoldness be a truth? Their relations, would not these be real? Their distinct places in the world-order, would not these things be objects of possible true or false thoughts? If so, must not there be once more the inclusive real Self for whom these truths were true, these separate selves interrelated, and their variety absorbed in the organism of its rational meaning?

There is, then, at last, but one Self, organically, reflectively, consciously inclusive of all the selves, and so of all truth....

DURANT DRAKE

*The Grounds of Realism**

Durant Drake (1878–1933) graduated from Harvard and received his Ph.D. from Columbia. He was professor of philosophy and education at Vassar College, 1915–1933. He was the author of various books, including *Problems of Conduct, Problems of Religion, Mind and Its Place in Nature, The New Morality,* and, with others, *Essays in Critical Realism.*

In the following essay, Drake seeks to show that the most notable features of our experience furnish evidence for philosophical realism. The sense data (sensa) of our everyday experience are clearly to be distinguished from our dreaming, imagining, and thinking. They point to realities beyond our minds, to an independent outer world that is supported by the testimony of different senses.

*Durant Drake, from "The Grounds of Realism," in *Invitation to Philosophy* (Boston: Houghton Mifflin, 1933), pp. 152–160. Used by permission of the publisher.

Our sense experiences are in large part at the mercy of an external world. The facts of our experience and the events of history lead us to the realistic hypothesis.

Everyone, except a few philosophers and their disciples, believes in the realistic world; the belief is implied in all our science and all our ordinary discourse. There is considerable variation of opinion among reflective thinkers as to the fundamental stuff of which things consist, but there is an almost complete agreement that the physical world is made up of electrons and protons (whatever they may be) combining in complicated structures to form atoms, chemical compounds, biological organisms, and astronomical bodies. Causal interactions are going on in this intricately patterned world, quite independently of our experience; indeed, to a great extent, these processes are not yet known by any human observer, or even imagined. External as these physical things are to our bodies, and to our minds, we can, somehow, know a good deal *about* them. And other people can know about them; they are objects of common, public knowledge. We can also know a good deal about one another's *minds*. And we can see that these things which physics studies are *different* from minds, that minds (i.e., such minds as we quite definitely discover about us) are immersed, so to speak, in a great sea of what is quite different from mind. Such is the world of common sense, the familiar world of mind *and* matter.

The subjectivist is right, however, in protesting that we have no *guaranty* of the existence of this world. It is conceivable that our supposed knowledge of it is illusion and our experience but a coherent dream. As cautious thinkers we must beware of trusting common sense; we must see whether we can *justify* our instinctive realism—just as we have insisted that the idealist justify his idealism. Belief in *any* sort of universe, belief, for that matter, in anything whatever beyond the passing data of experience, is, in the nature of the case, *hypothesis,* and not unquestionable *datum*.

Well, how do we set out to justify any hypothesis? If we use the empirical method, we accept an hypothesis when it seems to cover the facts of experience more adequately than any other hypothesis that we can frame. And our belief in realism rests, in the end, upon our discovery that it fits, it explains, the peculiarities of experience better than any form of idealism. In fact, there is no scientific hypothesis which serves to tie together and explain so many otherwise inexplicable facts as this hypothesis of realism. The following paragraphs will summarize the most notable peculiarities of our experience which serve in this way as the *evidence* for realism—in the same sense as that in which the sense-data accumulated by the astronomer are evidence for the truth of the Copernican hypothesis, which covers and explains them.

1. THE DIFFERENCE BETWEEN PERCEPTUAL AND NON-PERCEPTUAL EXPERIENCE

Within our experience itself there is an observable difference between our sensa and the images which appear to us in our dreaming, thinking, imagining. There is, indeed, a borderland where it is difficult to distinguish the two types of data, but in general they are clearly distinguishable. Sensa are relatively vivid, clear, steady, coherent, whereas these other images are, by contrast, faint, blurred, flickering. If realism is true, this difference is easily intelligible. Sensa are produced in our experience by causal processes coming from the outer world, they are sharply defined by the definite nature of the messages that reach us from without, and are as stable as those processes—which, in turn, reflect the stability of the outer objects which initiate them. Our non-perceptual experience is engendered from within the organism, lacks the shock-effect of the experience provoked from without, and lacks its steadiness, since it is not subject to this outer control. This suggests, with force, that physical things are not mere "potentialities of perception," but are *realities,* of a very definite nature, capable of affecting our experience in definite ways, pretty clearly distinguishable from the ways in which our non-perceptual experience develops.

2. THE MECHANISM OF PERCEPTION

Sensa are obtained in a different way from that in which non-perceptual experience is obtained. The latter can be had with eyes shut and all the other sense-organs slumbering. To get sensa we have to have sense-organs functioning, and a whole series of events proceeding from the outer object to the brain. If any link in this chain of events is broken, the perceptual experience will not be had. Now it is conceivable that our experience of this complicated series of events is merely one kind of *experience,* not actually revealing a series of real events *preceding* the appearance of our sensa. But if so, the question insistently arises, Why do we find, so regularly, this particular series of experiences obtainable, whenever we have sensa of each particular sort? The whole business *looks* as if these experiences (our knowledge of light-waves, eye-events, and optical-nerve-events, for example) reveal to us a real series of events going on outside our minds and necessarily preceding the appearance in our field of consciousness of each definite sort of sensum. If there *are* no physical things, if there are only minds, why this constant illusion of a complicated inter-mental medium? If there is, in reality, only One Mind, why should one part of it affect another part in this roundabout way, instead of in the way one part of my mind affects another part, without the complicated mechanism of sense-perception? Is not realism the most sensible hypothesis to cover these facts?

3. THE CONTINUITY OF THE PHYSICAL ORDER

Our sense-experience is very fragmentary. But the pieces strongly suggest a continuous, coherent set of processes back of them, giving them their precise nature. For example, I start a fire on the hearth and then leave the room. Ten minutes later I return and find the wood partly consumed. An hour later I return and find nothing but hot ashes. It *looks* as if a continuous process was going on during that hour of which my sensa reveal definite phases, whenever I put myself in a position to receive effects from it. I can construct in my imagination such a series of physical events, external to me, the events making up the fire itself. My sensa invariably report the stage due at each moment of that series of events. When I enter the room they jump into my conscious field, unrelated to anything antecedently there; they apparently obey, not laws of my mind, primarily, but the laws of that external series of events which I have imagined. That external order is a changing order. Relatively few of its changes are reflected in my direct experience, but they serve nevertheless as controls of the experience which I actually have. After dreamless sleep, my experience picks up the pattern, so to speak—the pattern of processes which apparently have been going on while I slept. Are not these facts *explicanda?* And what explanation of them can we give half as plausible as the explanation that the processes we have imagined really *are* going on in the world about us, even when we are not aware of them?

4. THE CONVERGING TESTIMONY OF DIFFERING SENSES

Physical objects are usually perceived by several senses. I can see my table, I can feel of it, push against it, lift it, hear the sound I make when I hit it. In subjectivistic language, I have groups of very different sorts of sensa, which, in spite of their differences, fit together to form my concept of this table. Why should our experience be thus analyzable into groups of sensa which combine to form the picture of a physical *thing?* Various other people have somewhat similar groups of sensa, which seem, as we describe and utilize them, to reveal this same table. What meaning can these facts have, if not that there *is* a single physical table, which affects several of my senses, thus producing several differing groups of sensa, and similarly affects other people's senses, producing in their experience more or less similar groups of sensa?

5. THE TIME-GAP WHEN MIND AFFECTS MIND

When I speak to you, *my* experience-of-speaking occurs at a certain time. Then an interval of time elapses. Then you hear my voice. The time-gap varies exactly with our distance apart. Now, if only minds exist, why should there be this interval between the event-in-me, the cause, and the event-in-you, the effect? What happens during that interval? And what is the real meaning of what we call distance? If Space is only a form of experience, something *within* minds, not something existing *between* minds, and separating them, why should it take longer for my mind to influence yours when we are, as we commonly say, farther apart than when we are nearer? If the reality is One Mind, and nothing else, the matter becomes, if possible, still stranger. Why should one part of the Divine Mind require half a second to influence another part, and two seconds to influence another part? And what happens during the interval, when neither part is conscious of speaking or hearing, when apparently *no* (relevant) conscious experience is taking place? Surely it *looks* as if distance were real, and a real series of events were taking place *between* the two minds, requiring time to occur, in proportion to the distance.

6. THE DEPENDENCE OF MINDS UPON MATTER

Our ideational-volitional life—our thinking, dreaming, planning, willing —is, to some degree, self-contained. Our ideas follow one another along the lines of traceable associations; they are, in part, modifiable at will, and depend upon the state of our mind at a given time. But with sensa it is quite different. We are *confronted* by them. They appear suddenly in our field of experience, often quite unrelated to anything antecedently there. We cannot banish them by effort of will. They evidently obey other laws than those of our minds. And we are at their mercy. A cold wind blows on me (i.e., I have sensa thus described in realistic language), and I suffer, perhaps become ill. The sensa implied by saying that a bullet has hit me are followed, perhaps, by the complete and permanent cessation of my consciousness. Is it not clear that we are in the grip of a world of realities vastly greater than ourselves? To see a man freezing to death, or dying of a bullet wound, is, inevitably, to be a realist, at least *pro tem.*

These extreme experiences—which come to us all, in some form sooner or later—make us realize that even our ideational and volitional experience is at the mercy of this environing world. A bottle of whisky alters the whole tone of my mental life, a whiff of chloroform brings it to an abrupt end for the time being, a clotting of blood may drive me insane. Specifically, . . . our whole mental life is dependent, point by point, upon the functioning of our *brains.* But if our brains are but a name for a certain group of potentialities of experience, or even if they are a certain specific group of images in a Universal Mind, it seems curious that our whole mental life should be dependent upon them.

7. THE FACTS OF COSMIC HISTORY

It is generally agreed that the universe existed for long ages before any minds appeared on this earth, or, so far as we know, anywhere. The events of this cosmic history are known by astronomers and geologists, in considerable detail. But what *meaning* is there in this long story, on idealistic premises, if there were no experiencers present to experience these events? It will be said that we have here the story of the unfolding of the Divine Experience. And this is conceivable. But when one reads the story in detail —the evolution of stars from nebulae (a monotonous process consuming trillions of years), the (apparently accidental) formation of our solar system, the laborious laying-down of rocks, the slow development of chemical compounds, the seething of currents of wind and water, the breeding of endless varieties of microbes, worms, reptiles, and all the strange profusion of vegetable and animal life, one creature warring upon and devouring another creature, with volcanic eruptions, floods, droughts wiping out countless millions at a sweep—the story surely sounds far more like a realistic story of separate *things* and organisms, than like the unfolding of the story of a Divine consciousness.

It is quite evident that our fragmentary and evanescent data of experience can never be *understood* except as an *enclave* within a far greater, independent reality, which we call Nature; and that this Nature is, in detail, just what the sciences report it to be. Our experience is not only fragmentary, it is, by itself, a jumble, a chaos. Only by constructing, with infinite patience, this picture of a vast environing Nature, can we replace this chaos with order, predict future experiences, and learn, in increasing measure, to control them. The belief in a Universal Mind inspires and consoles some people; but it does not help us to predict and control experience. Thus realism is, at least, pragmatically justified.

And what more *could* we have in the way of proof? As we saw in studying the empirical method, there is no such thing as guaranteed proof, of the Q.E.D. sort, except in the purely hypothetical realms of logic and mathematics. An independently existing physical world is proved to exist in the same sense, and with as great certainty, as *anything* can be proved to exist. The idealist accepts as proved the facts of human history. But these facts, and indeed the facts of the idealist's own earlier life, can be proved to be actual facts by no other method, and with no greater certainty, than the facts of the life of the physical world.

ATTACKS ON TRADITIONAL METAPHYSICS

WILLIAM JAMES

*What Pragmatism Means**

See the biographical note on p. 84.

James offers his pragmatic method as a way of settling issues—even metaphysical disputes—by asking what difference it makes or what the consequences are of accepting this or that as true. Pragmatism, he says, turns away from abstractions and makes its appeal to particular consequences and to facts. The method, we are told, goes back as far as Socrates in its practical emphasis and usefulness.

Some years ago, being with a camping party in the mountains, I returned from a solitary ramble to find every one engaged in a ferocious metaphysical dispute. The *corpus* of the dispute was a squirrel—a live squirrel supposed to be clinging to one side of a tree-trunk; while over against the tree's opposite side a human being was imagined to stand. This human witness tries to get sight of the squirrel by moving rapidly round the tree, but no matter how fast he goes, the squirrel moves as fast in the opposite direction, and always keeps the tree between himself and the man, so that never a glimpse of him is caught. The resultant metaphysical problem now is this: *Does the man go round the squirrel or not?* He goes round the tree, sure enough, and the squirrel is on the tree; but does he go round the squirrel? In the unlimited leisure of the wilderness, discussion had been worn threadbare. Everyone had taken sides, and was obstinate; and the numbers on both sides were even. Each side, when I appeared therefore appealed to me to make it a majority. Mindful of the scholastic adage that whenever you meet a contradiction you must make a distinction, I immediately sought and found one, as follows: "Which party is right," I said,

*William James, from "What Pragmatism Means," in *Pragmatism* (New York: Longmans, Green, 1907), pp. 43–47, 49–55.

"depends on what you *practically mean* by 'going round' the squirrel. If you mean passing from the north of him to the east, then to the south, then to the west, and then to the north of him again, obviously the man does go round him, for he occupies these successive positions. But if on the contrary you mean being first in front of him, then on the right of him, then behind him, then on his left, and finally in front again, it is quite as obvious that the man fails to go round him, for by the compensating movements the squirrel makes, he keeps his belly turned towards the man all the time, and his back turned away. Make the distinction, and there is no occasion for any further dispute. You are both right and both wrong according as you conceive the verb 'to go round' in one practical fashion or the other."

Although one or two of the hotter disputants called my speech a shuffling evasion, saying they wanted no quibbling or scholastic hair-splitting, but meant just plain honest English "round," the majority seemed to think that the distinction has assuaged the dispute.

I tell this trivial anecdote because it is a peculiarly simple example of what I wish now to speak of as *the pragmatic method*. The pragmatic method is primarily a method of settling metaphysical disputes that otherwise might be interminable. Is the world one or many?—fated or free?—material or spiritual?—here are notions either of which may or may not hold good of the world; and disputes over such notions are unending. The pragmatic method in such cases is to try to interpret each notion by tracing its respective practical consequences. What difference would it practically make to any one if this notion rather than that notion were true? If no practical difference whatever can be traced, then the alternatives mean practically the same thing, and all dispute is idle. Whenever a dispute is serious, we ought to be able to show some practical difference that must follow from one side or the other's being right.

A glance at the history of the idea will show you still better what pragmatism means. The term is derived from the same Greek word πράγμα, meaning action, from which our words "practice" and "practical" come. It was first introduced into philosophy by Mr. Charles Peirce in 1878. In an article entitled "How to Make Our Ideas Clear," in the "Popular Science Monthly" for January of that year Mr. Peirce, after pointing out that our beliefs are really rules for action, said that, to develop a thought's meaning, we need only determine what conduct it is fitted to produce: that conduct is for us its sole significance. And the tangible fact at the root of all our thought-distinctions, however subtle, is that there is no one of them so fine as to consist in anything but a possible difference of practice. To attain perfect clearness in our thoughts of an object, then, we need only consider what conceivable effects of a practical kind the object may involve—what sensations we are to expect from it, and what reactions we must prepare.

Our conception of these effects, whether immediate or remote, is then for us the whole of our conception of the object, so far as that conception has "come to stay."...

This is the principle of Peirce, the principle of pragmatism. It lay entirely unnoticed by any one for twenty years, until I, in an address before Professor Howison's philosophical union at the University of California, brought it forward again and made a special application of it to religion. By that date (1898) the times seemed ripe for its reception. The word "pragmatism" spread, and at present it fairly spots the pages of the philosophic journals. On all hands we find the "pragmatic movement" spoken of, sometimes with respect, sometimes with contumely, seldom with clear understanding. It is evident that the term applies itself conveniently to a number of tendencies that hitherto have lacked a collective name, and that it has "come to stay."....

It is astonishing to see how many philosophical disputes collapse into insignificance the moment you subject them to this simple test of tracing a concrete consequence. There can *be* no difference anywhere that doesn't *make* a difference elsewhere—no difference in abstract truth that doesn't express itself in a difference in concrete fact and in conduct consequent upon that fact, imposed on somebody, somehow, somewhere, and somewhen. The whole function of philosophy ought to be to find out what definite difference it will make to you and me, at definite instants of our life, if this world-formula or that world-formula be the true one.

There is absolutely nothing new in the pragmatic method. Socrates was an adept at it. Aristotle used it methodically. Locke, Berkeley, and Hume made momentous contributions to truth by its means. Shadworth Hodgson keeps insisting that realities are only what they are "known as." But these forerunners of pragmatism used it in fragments: they were preluders only. Not until in our time has it generalized itself, become conscious of a universal mission, pretended to a conquering destiny. I believe in that destiny, and I hope I may end by inspiring you with my belief.

Pragmatism represents a perfectly familiar attitude in philosophy, the empiricist attitude, but it represents it, as it seems to me, both in a more radical and in a less objectionable form than it has ever yet assumed. A pragmatist turns his back resolutely and once for all upon a lot of inveterate habits dear to professional philosophers. He turns away from abstraction and insufficiency, from verbal solutions, from bad *a priori* reasons, from fixed principles, closed systems, and pretended absolutes and origins. He turns towards concreteness and adequacy, towards facts, towards action and towards power. That means the empiricist temper regnant and the rationalist temper sincerely given up. It means the open air and possibilities of nature, as against dogma, artificiality, and the pretence of finality in truth.

At the same time it does not stand for any special results. It is a method only. But the general triumph of that method would mean an enormous change in what I called in my last lecture the "temperament" of philosophy. Teachers of the ultra-rationalistic type would be frozen out, much as the courtier type is frozen out in republics, as the ultramontane type of priest is frozen out in protestant lands. Science and metaphysics would come much nearer together, would in fact work absolutely hand in hand.

Metaphysics has usually followed a very primitive kind of quest. You know how men have always hankered after unlawful magic, and you know what a great part in magic *words* have always played. If you have his name, or the formula of incantation that binds him, you can control the spirit, genie, afrite, or whatever the power may be. Solomon knew the names of all the spirits, and having their names, he held them subject to his will. So the universe has always appeared to the natural mind as a kind of enigma, of which the key must be sought in the shape of some illuminating or power-bringing word or name. That word names the universe's *principle,* and to possess it is after a fashion to possess the universe itself. "God," "Matter," "Reason," "the Absolute," "Energy," are so many solving names. You can rest when you have them. You are at the end of your metaphysical quest.

But if you follow the pragmatic method, you cannot look on any such word as closing your quest. You must bring out of each word its practical cash-value, set it at work within the stream of your experience. It appears less as a solution, then, than as a program for more work, and more particularly as an indication of the ways in which existing realities may be *changed.*

Theories thus become instruments, not answers to enigmas, in which we can rest. We don't lie back upon them, we move forward, and, on occasion, make nature over again by their aid. Pragmatism unstiffens all our theories, limbers them up and sets each one at work. Being nothing essentially new, it harmonizes with many ancient philosophic tendencies. It agrees with nominalism for instance, in always appealing to particulars; with utilitarianism in emphasizing practical aspects; with positivism in its disdain for verbal solutions, useless questions and metaphysical abstractions. . . .

No particular results then, so far, but only an attitude of orientation, is what the pragmatic method means. *The attitude of looking away from first things, principles, "categories," supposed necessities; and of looking towards last things, fruits, consequences, facts.*

So much for the pragmatic method! . . . Meanwhile the word pragmatism has come to be used in a still wider sense, as meaning also a certain *theory of truth.*

ALFRED JULES AYER

*The Elimination of Metaphysics**

Alfred Jules Ayer (b. 1910) graduated from Eton and Oxford in England, then spent some time studying logical positivism at the University of Vienna. He became a lecturer in philosophy at the University of Oxford. In *Language, Truth and Logic* (published in 1936 and revised 1946), he acknowledges his debt to Bertrand Russell, Ludwig Wittgenstein, and the Vienna Circle, as well as to the empiricism of Berkeley and Hume. His writings combine British philosophical analysis and logical positivism.

In the following selection, Ayer makes a vigorous attack on metaphysics from the approach of logical positivism. Before reading this selection, the reader may find it helpful to review the distinction between "matters-of-fact statements" and "matters-of-logic statements" made in the selection from Elmer Sprague. Following the more technical terminology current among philosophers, Ayer refers to the first type as "empirical statements" or "empirical hypotheses" and to the latter as "tautologies" or "*a priori* statements." Note what he calls the "criterion of verifiability" and the "verification principle" by which he seeks to show that metaphysicians are deceived by grammar and errors of reasoning. The reader may wish to ask himself, What is the nature of Ayer's own statement that metaphysics is nonsense? Is it an empirical statement, a tautology, an *a priori* statement, or what?

The traditional disputes of philosophers are, for the most part, as unwarranted as they are unfruitful. The surest way to end them is to establish beyond question what should be the purpose and method of a philosophical enquiry. And this is by no means so difficult a task as the history of philosophy would lead one to suppose. For if there are any questions which science leaves it to philosophy to answer, a straightforward process of elimination must lead to their discovery.

We may begin by criticising the metaphysical thesis that philosophy affords us knowledge of a reality transcending the world of science and common sense. Later on, when we come to define metaphysics and account for its existence, we shall find that it is possible to be a metaphysician without believing in a transcendent reality; for we shall see that many

*Alfred Jules Ayer, from "The Elimination of Metaphysics," in *Language, Truth, and Logic* (New York: Dover, 1952; London: Gollancz, 1946), pp. 33–35, 38–42, 44–45. Used by permission of the publishers.

metaphysical utterances are due to the commission of logical errors, rather than to a conscious desire on the part of their authors to go beyond the limits of experience. But it is convenient for us to take the case of those who believe that it is possible to have knowledge of a transcendent reality as a starting-point for our discussion. The arguments which we use to refute them will subsequently be found to apply to the whole of metaphysics.

One way of attacking a metaphysician who claimed to have knowledge of a reality which transcended the phenomenal world would be to enquire from what premises his propositions were deduced. Must he not begin, as other men do, with the evidence of his senses? And if so, what valid process of reasoning can possibly lead him to the conception of a transcendent reality? Surely from empirical premises nothing whatsoever concerning the properties, or even the existence, of anything super-empirical can legitimately be inferred. But this objection would be met by a denial on the part of the metaphysician that his assertions were ultimately based on the evidence of his senses. He would say that he was endowed with a faculty of intellectual intuition which enabled him to know facts that could not be known through sense-experience. And even if it could be shown that he was relying on empirical premises, and that his venture into a nonempirical world was therefore logically unjustified, it would not follow that the assertions which he made concerning this nonempirical world could not be true. For the fact that a conclusion does not follow from its putative premise is not sufficient to show that it is false. Consequently one cannot overthrow a system of transcendent metaphysics merely by criticising the way in which it comes into being. What is required is rather a criticism of the nature of the actual statements which comprise it. And this is the line of argument which we shall, in fact, pursue. For we shall maintain that no statement which refers to a "reality" transcending the limits of all possible sense-experience can possibly have any literal significance; from which it must follow that the labours of those who have striven to describe such a reality have all been devoted to the production of nonsense....

...It cannot here be said that the author is himself overstepping the barrier he maintains to be impassable. For the fruitlessness of attempting to transcend the limits of possible sense-experience will be deduced, not from a psychological hypothesis concerning the actual constitution of the human mind, but from the rule which determines the literal significance of language. Our charge against the metaphysician is not that he attempts to employ the understanding in a field where it cannot profitably venture, but that he produces sentences which fail to conform to the conditions under which alone a sentence can be literally significant. Nor are we ourselves obliged to talk nonsense in order to show that all sentences of a certain type are necessarily devoid of literal significance. We need only formulate the criterion which enables us to test whether a sentence expresses a genuine proposition about a matter of fact, and then point out that the sentences under consideration fail to satisfy it....

The criterion which we use to test the genuineness of apparent statements of fact is the criterion of verifiability. We say that a sentence is factually significant to any given person, if, and only if, he knows how to verify the proposition which it purports to express—that is, if he knows what observations would lead him, under certain conditions, to accept the proposition as being true, or reject it as being false. If, on the other hand, the putative proposition is of such a character that the assumption of its truth, or falsehood, is consistent with any assumption whatsoever concerning the nature of his future experience, then, as far as he is concerned, it is, if not a tautology, a mere pseudo-proposition. The sentence expressing it may be emotionally significant to him; but it is not literally significant. And with regard to questions the procedure is the same. We enquire in every case what observations would lead us to answer the question, one way or the other; and, if none can be discovered, we must conclude that the sentence under consideration does not, as far as we are concerned, express a genuine question, however strongly its grammatical appearance may suggest that it does....

...We say that the question that must be asked about any putative statement of fact is not, Would any observations make its truth or falsehood logically certain? but simply, Would any observations be relevant to the determination of its truth or falsehood? And it is only if a negative answer is given to this second question that we conclude that the statement under consideration is nonsensical.

To make our position clearer, we may formulate it in another way. Let us call a proposition which records an actual or possible observation an experiential proposition. Then we may say that it is the mark of a genuine factual proposition, not that it should be equivalent to an experiential proposition, or any finite number of experiential propositions, but simply that some experiential propositions can be deduced from it in conjunction with certain other premises without being deducible from those other premises alone.

This criterion seems liberal enough. In contrast to the principle of conclusive verifiability, it clearly does not deny significance to general propositions or to propositions about the past. Let us see what kinds of assertion it rules out.

A good example of the kind of utterance that is condemned by our criterion as being not even false but nonsensical would be the assertion that the world of sense-experience was altogether unreal. It must, of course, be admitted that our senses do sometimes deceive us. We may, as the result of having certain sensations, expect certain other sensations to be obtainable which are, in fact, not obtainable. But, in all such cases, it is further sense-experience that informs us of the mistakes that arise out of sense-experience. We say that the senses sometimes deceive us, just because the expectations to which our sense-experiences give rise do not always accord with what we subsequently experience. That is, we rely on our senses to substantiate or confute the judgments which are based on our sensations. And therefore the fact that our perceptual judgments are sometimes found to be erroneous has not the slightest tendency to show that the world of sense-experience is unreal. And, indeed, it is plain that no conceivable observation, or series of observations, could have any tendency to show that the world revealed to us by sense-experience was unreal. Consequently, anyone who condemns the sensible world as a world of mere appearance, as opposed to reality, is saying something which, according to our criterion of significance, is literally nonsensical.

An example of a controversy which the application of our criterion obliges us to condemn as fictitious is provided by those who dispute concerning the number of substances that there are in the world. For it is admitted both by monists, who maintain that reality is one substance, and by pluralists, who maintain that reality is many, that it is impossible to imagine any empirical situation which would be relevant to the solution of their dispute. But if we are told that no possible observation could give any probability either to the assertion that reality was one substance or to the assertion that it was many, then we must conclude that neither assertion is significant.... [T]here are genuine logical and empirical questions involved in the dispute between monists and pluralists. But the metaphysical question concerning "substance" is ruled out by our criterion as spurious....

As to the validity of the verification principle, in the form in which we have stated it, a demonstration will be given in the course of this book. For it will be shown that all propositions which have factual content are empirical hypotheses; and that the function of an empirical hypothesis is to provide a rule for the anticipation of experience. And this means that every empirical hypothesis must be relevant to some actual, or possible, experience, so that a statement which is not relevant to any experience is not an empirical hypothesis, and accordingly has no factual content. But this is precisely what the principle of verifiability asserts.

It should be mentioned here that the fact that the utterances of the metaphysician are nonsensical does not follow simply from the fact that they are devoid of factual content. It follows from that fact, together with the fact that they are not *a priori* propositions. And in assuming that they are not *a priori* propositions, we are once again anticipating the conclusions of a later chapter in this book. For it will be shown there that *a priori* propositions, which have always been attractive to philosophers on account of their certainty, owe this certainty to the fact that they are tautologies. We may accordingly define a metaphysical sentence as a sentence which purports to express a genuine proposition, but does, in fact, express neither a tautology nor an empirical hypothesis. And as tautologies and empirical hypotheses form the entire class of significant propositions, we are justified in concluding that all metaphysical assertions are nonsensical. Our next task is to show how they come to be made.

The use of the term "substance," to which we have already referred, provides us with a good example of the way in which metaphysics mostly comes to be written. It happens to be the case that we cannot, in our language, refer to the sensible properties of a thing without introducing a word or phrase which appears to stand for the thing itself as opposed to anything which may be said about it. And, as a result of this, those who are infected by the primitive superstition that to every name a single real entity must correspond assume that it is necessary to distinguish logically between the thing itself and any, or all, of its sensible properties. And so they employ the term "substance" to refer to the thing itself. But from the fact that we happen to employ a single word to refer to a thing, and make that word the grammatical subject of the sentences in which we refer to the sensible appearances of the thing, it does not by any means follow that the thing itself is a "simple entity," or that it cannot be defined in terms of the totality of its appearances. It is true that in talking of "its" appearances we appear to distinguish the thing from the appearances, but that is simply an accident of linguistic usage. Logical analysis shows that what makes these "appearances" the "appearances of" the same thing is not their relationship to an entity other than themselves, but their relationship to one another. The metaphysician fails to see this because he is misled by a superficial grammatical feature of his language....

Among those who recognize that if philosophy is to be accounted a genuine branch of knowledge it must be defined in such a way as to distinguish it from metaphysics, it is fashionable to speak of the metaphysician as a kind of misplaced poet. As his statements have no literal meaning, they are not subject to any criteria of truth or falsehood: but they may still serve to express, or arouse, emotion, and thus be subject to ethical or aesthetic standards. And it is suggested that they may have considerable value, as means of moral inspiration, or even as works of art. In this way, an attempt is made to compensate the metaphysician for his extrusion from philosophy.

I am afraid that this compensation is hardly in accordance with his deserts. The view that the metaphysician is to be reckoned among the poets appears to rest on the assumption that both talk nonsense. But this assumption is false. In the vast majority of cases the sentences which are produced by poets do have literal meaning. The difference between the man who uses language scientifically and the man who uses it emotively is not that one produces sentences which are incapable of arousing emotion, and the other sentences which have no sense, but that the one is primarily concerned with the expression of true propositions, the other with the creation of a work of art. Thus, if a work of science contains true and important propositions, its value as a work of science will hardly be diminished by the fact that they are inelegantly expressed. And similarly, a work of art is not necessarily the worse for the fact that all the propositions comprising it are literally false. But to say that many literary works are largely composed of falsehoods, is not to say that they are composed of pseudo-propositions. It is, in fact, very rare for a literary artist to produce sentences which have no literal meaning. And where this does occur, the sentences are carefully chosen for their rhythm and balance. If the author writes nonsense, it is because he considers it most suitable for bringing about the effects for which his writing is designed.

The metaphysician, on the other hand, does not intend to write nonsense. He lapses into it through being deceived by grammar, or through committing errors of reasoning, such as that which leads to the view that the sensible world is unreal. But it is not the mark of a poet simply to make mistakes of this sort. There are some, indeed, who would see in the fact that the metaphysician's utterances are senseless a reason against the view that they have aesthetic value. And, without going so far as this, we may safely say that it does not constitute a reason for it.

It is true, however, that although the greater part of metaphysics is merely the embodiment of humdrum errors, there remain a number of metaphysical passages which are the work of genuine mystical feeling; and they may more plausibly be held to have moral or aesthetic value. But, as far as we are concerned, the distinction between the kind of metaphysics that is produced by a philosopher who has been duped by grammar, and the kind that is produced by a mystic who is trying to express the inexpressible, is of no great importance: what is important to us is to realise that even the utterances of the metaphysician who is attempting to expound a vision are literally senseless; so that henceforth we may pursue our philosophical researches with as little regard for them as for the more inglorious kind of metaphysics which comes from a failure to understand the workings of our language.

J. L. AUSTIN

*Logical Analysis and the Word "Real"**

J. L. Austin (1911–1960) was educated at Oxford University where he later became Professor of Moral Philosophy. He came to philosophy as a highly accomplished classical scholar and linguist, and his emphasis was on the philosophy of language and on rigorous analysis. He has been called a "philosopher's philosopher" and the "most linguistic minded" of all the Oxford philosophers. His lectures and classes attracted scholars from many areas of the world. Since his untimely death, his colleagues have published several volumes of his essays and papers which deal with how to do philosophy.

The following essay, one of his more easily understood papers, is a good example of his analytic method applied to the word "real." While this term has long been an important one in the vocabulary of traditional metaphysics, note that Austin prefers not to talk about "the nature of reality," but instead examines the ways in which the word "real" is actually used in everyday discourse.

...I propose, if you like, to discuss the Nature of Reality—a genuinely important topic, though in general I don't much like making this claim.

There are two things, first of all, which it is immensely important to understand here.

1. "Real" is an absolutely *normal* word, with nothing new-fangled or technical or highly specialized about it. It is, that is to say, already firmly established in, and very frequently used in, the ordinary language we all use every day. Thus *in this sense* it is a word which has a fixed meaning, and so can't, any more than can any other word which is firmly established, be fooled around with *ad lib.* Philosophers often seem to think that they can just "assign" any meaning whatever to any word; and so no doubt, in an absolutely trivial sense, they can (like Humpty-Dumpty). There are some expressions, of course, "material thing" for example, which only philosophers use, and in such cases they can, within reason, please themselves; but most words are *in fact* used in a particular way already, and this fact can't be just disregarded. (For example, some meanings that have been assigned to "know" and "certain" have made it seem outrageous that we

*J. L. Austin, from *Sense and Sensibilia,* reconstructed from the Manuscript Notes by G. J. Warnock, pp. 62–77, © 1964 Oxford University Press. Used by permission of The Clarendon Press, Oxford.

should use these terms as we actually do; but what this shows is that the meanings assigned by some philosophers are *wrong*.) Certainly, when we have discovered how a word is in fact used, that may not be the end of the matter; there is certainly no reason why, in general, things should be left exactly as we find them; we may wish to tidy the situation up a bit, revise the map here and there, draw the boundaries and distinctions rather differently. But still, it is advisable always to bear in mind (*a*) that the distinctions embodied in our vast and, for the most part, relatively ancient stock of ordinary words are neither few nor always very obvious, and almost never just arbitrary; (*b*) that in any case, before indulging in any tampering on our own account, we need to find out what it is that we have to deal with; and (*c*) that tampering with words in what we take to be one little corner of the field is always *liable* to have unforeseen repercussions in the adjoining territory. Tampering, in fact, is not so easy as is often supposed, is not justified or needed so often as is often supposed, and is often thought to be necessary just because what we've got already has been misrepresented. And we must always be particularly wary of the philosophical habit of dismissing some (if not all) the ordinary uses of a word as "unimportant," a habit which makes distortion practically unavoidable. For instance, if we are going to talk about "real," we must not dismiss as beneath contempt such humble but familiar expressions as "not real cream"; this may save us from saying, for example, or seeming to say that what is not real cream must be a fleeting product of our cerebral processes.

2. The other immensely important point to grasp is that "real" is *not* a normal word at all, but highly exceptional; exceptional in this respect that, unlike "yellow" or "horse" or "walk," it does not have one single, specifiable, always-the-same *meaning*. (Even Aristotle saw through this idea.) *Nor* does it have a large number of different meanings—it is not *ambiguous,* even "systematically." Now words of this sort have been responsible for a great deal of perplexity. Consider the expressions "cricket ball," "cricket bat," "cricket pavilion," "cricket weather." If someone did not know about cricket and were obsessed with the use of such "normal" words as "yellow," he might gaze at the ball, the bat, the building, the weather, trying to detect the "common quality" which (he assumes) is attributed to these things by the prefix "cricket." But no such quality meets his eye; and so perhaps he concludes that "cricket" must designate a *non-natural* quality, a quality to be detected not in any ordinary way but by *intuition*. If this story strikes you as too absurd, remember what philosophers have said about the word "good"; and reflect that many philosophers, failing to detect any ordinary quality common to real ducks, real cream, and real progress, have decided that Reality must be an *a priori* concept apprehended by reason alone.

Let us begin, then, with a preliminary, no doubt rather haphazard, survey of some of the complexities in the use of "real." Consider, for instance, a case which at first sight one might think was pretty straightforward—the case of "real colour." What is meant by the "real" colour of a thing? Well, one may say with some confidence, that's easy enough: the *real* colour of the thing is the colour that it looks to a normal observer in conditions of normal or standard illumination; and to find out what a thing's colour is, we just need to be normal and to observe it in those conditions.

But suppose (*a*) that I remark to you of a third party, "That isn't the real colour of her hair." Do I mean by this that, if you were to observe her in conditions of standard illumination, you would find that her hair did not look that colour? Plainly not—thc conditions of illumination may be standard already. I mean, of course, that her hair has been *dyed,* and normal illumination just doesn't come into it at all. Or suppose that you are looking at a ball of wool in a shop, and I say, "That's not its real colour." Here I *may* mean that it won't look that colour in ordinary daylight; but I *may* mean that wool isn't that colour before it's dyed. As so often, you can't tell what I mean just from the words that I use; it makes a difference, for instance, whether the thing under discussion is or is not of a type which is *customarily* dyed.

Suppose (*b*) that there is a species of fish which looks vividly multicoloured, slightly glowing perhaps, at a depth of a thousand feet. I ask you what its real colour is. So you catch a specimen and lay it out on deck, making sure the condition of the light is just about normal, and you find that it looks a muddy sort of greyish white. Well, is *that* its real colour? It's clear enough at any rate that we don't have to say so. In fact, is there any right answer in such a case?

Compare: "What is the real taste of saccharine?" We dissolve a tablet in a cup of tea and we find that it makes the tea taste sweet; we then take a tablet neat, and we find that it tastes bitter. Is it *really* bitter, or *really* sweet?

(*c*) What is the real colour of the sky? Of the sun? Of the moon? Of a chameleon? We say that the sun in the evening sometimes looks red—well, what colour is it *really?* (What are the "conditions of standard illumination" for the sun?)

(*d*) Consider a *pointilliste* painting of a meadow, say; if the general effect is of green, the painting may be composed of predominantly blue and yellow dots: What is the real colour of the painting?

(*e*) What is the real colour of an after-image? The trouble with this one is that we have no idea what an alternative to its "real colour" might be. Its apparent colour, the colour that it looks, the colour that it appears to be?—but these phrases have no application here. (You might ask me, "What colour is it really?" if you suspected that I had lied in telling you its colour. But "What colour is it really?" is not quite the same as "What is its real colour?")

Or consider "real shape" for a moment. This notion cropped up, you may remember, seeming quite unproblematic, when we were considering the coin which was said to "look elliptical" from some points of view; it had a real shape, we insisted, which remained unchanged. But coins in fact are rather special cases. For one thing their outlines are well defined and very highly stable, and for another they have a *known* and a *nameable* shape. But there are plenty of things of which this is not true. What is the real shape of a cloud? And if it be objected, as I dare say it could be, that a cloud is not a "material thing" and so not the kind of thing which has to have a real shape, consider this case: what is the real shape of a cat? Does its real shape change whenever it moves? If not, in what posture *is* its real shape on display? Furthermore, is its real shape such as to be fairly smooth-outlined, or must it be finely enough serrated to take account of each hair? It is pretty obvious that there is *no* answer to these questions—no rules according to which, no procedure by which, answers are to be determined. Of course, there are plenty of shapes which the cat definitely is not—cylindrical, for instance. But only a desperate man would toy with the idea of ascertaining the cat's real shape "by elimination."

Contrast this with cases in which we *do* know how to proceed: "Are those real diamonds?", "Is that a real duck?" Items of jewellery that more or less closely resemble diamonds may not be real diamonds because they are paste or glass; that may not be a real duck because it is a decoy, or a toy duck, or a species of goose closely resembling a duck, or because I am having a hallucination. These are all of course quite different cases. And notice in particular (*a*) that, in most of them "observation by a normal observer in standard conditions" is completely irrelevant; (*b*) that something which is not a real duck is not a *non-existent* duck, or indeed a non-existent anything; and (*c*) that something existent, e.g. a toy, may perfectly well not be real, e.g. not a real duck.

Perhaps by now we have said enough to establish that there is more in the use of "real" than meets the cursory eye; it has many and diverse uses in many diverse contexts. We must next, then, try to tidy things up a little; and I shall now mention under four headings what might be called the salient features of the use of "real"—though not *all* these features are equally conspicuous in all its uses.

1. First, "real" is a word that we may call *substantive-hungry*. Consider:

> "These diamonds are real";
> "These are real diamonds."

This pair of sentences looks like, in an obvious grammatical respect, this other pair:

"These diamonds are pink";
"These are pink diamonds."

But whereas we can *just* say of something "This is pink," we can't *just* say of something "This is real." And it is not very difficult to see why. We can perfectly well say of something that it is pink without knowing, without any reference to, what it *is*. But not so with "real." For one and the same object may be both a real *x* and not a real *y*; an object looking rather like a duck may be a real decoy duck (not just a toy) but not a real duck. When it isn't a real duck but a hallucination, it may still be a real hallucination—as opposed, for instance, to a passing quirk of a vivid imagination. That is, we must have an answer to the question "A real *what*?", if the question "Real or not?" is to have a definite sense, to get any foothold. And perhaps we should also mention here another point—that the question "Real or not?" does not always come up, can't always be raised. We *do* raise this question only when, to speak rather roughly, suspicion assails us—in some way or other things may be not what they seem; and we *can* raise this question only if there *is* a way, or ways, in which things may be not what they seem. What alternative is there to being a "real" after-image?

"Real" is not, of course, the only word we have that is substantive-hungry. Other examples, perhaps better known ones, are "the same" and "one." The same *team* may not be the same *collection of players*; a body of troops may be one *company* and also three *platoons*. Then what about "good"? We have here a variety of gaps crying out for substantives—"A good *what*?", "Good *at* what?"—a good book, perhaps, but not a good novel; good at pruning roses, but not good at mending cars.

2. Next, "real" is what we may call a *trouser-word*. It is usually thought, and I dare say usually rightly thought, that what one might call the affirmative use of a term is basic—that, to understand "*x*," we need to know what it is to be *x*, or to be an *x*, and that knowing this apprises us of what it is *not* to be *x*, not to be an *x*. But with "real" (as we briefly noted earlier) it is the *negative* use that wears the trousers. That is, a definite sense attaches to the assertion that something is real, a real such-and-such, only in the light of a specific way in which it might be, or might have been, *not* real. "A real duck" differs from the simple "a duck" only in that it is used to exclude various ways of being not a real duck—but a dummy, a toy, a picture, a decoy, &c.; and moreover I don't know *just* how to take the assertion that it's a real duck unless I know *just* what, on that particular occasion, the speaker has it in mind to exclude. This, of course, is why the attempt to find a characteristic common to all things that are or could be called "real" is doomed to failure; the function of "real" is not to contribute positively to the characterization of anything, but to exclude possible ways of being *not* real—and these ways are both numerous for particular kinds of things, and liable to be quite different for things of different kinds.

It is this identity of general function combined with immense diversity in specific applications which gives to the word "real" the, at first sight, baffling feature of having neither one single "meaning," nor yet ambiguity, a number of different meanings.

3. Thirdly, "real" is (like "good") a *dimension-word*. I mean by this that it is the most general and comprehensive term in a whole group of terms of the same kind, terms that fulfil the same function. Other members of this group, on the affirmative side, are, for example, "proper," "genuine," "live," "true," "authentic," "natural"; and on the negative side, "artificial," "fake," "false," "bogus," "makeshift," "dummy," "synthetic," "toy"—and such nouns as "dream," "illusion," "mirage," "hallucination" belong here as well. It is worth noticing here that, naturally enough, the *less* general terms on the affirmative side have the merit, in many cases, of suggesting more or less definitely what it is that is being excluded; they tend to pair off, that is, with particular terms on the negative side and thus, so to speak, to narrow the range of possibilities. If I say that I wish the university had a proper theatre, this suggests that it has at present a *makeshift* theatre; pictures are genuine as opposed to *fake*, silk is natural as opposed to *artificial*, ammunition is live as opposed to *dummy*, and so on. In practice, of course, we often get a clue to what it is that is in question from the substantive in the case, since we frequently have a well-founded antecedent idea in what respects the kind of thing mentioned could (and could not) be "not real." For instance, if you ask me "Is this real silk?" I shall tend to supply "as opposed to artificial," since I already know that silk is the kind of thing which can be very closely simulated by an artificial product. The notion of its being *toy* silk, for instance, will not occur to me.

A large number of questions arises here—which I shall not go into—concerning both the composition of these families of "reality"-words and "unreality"-words, and also the distinctions to be drawn between their individual members. Why, for instance, is being a *proper* carving-knife one way of being a real carving-knife, whereas being *pure* cream seems not to be one way of being *real* cream? Or to put it differently: how does the distinction between real cream and synthetic cream differ from the distinction between pure cream and adulterated cream? Is it just that adulterated cream still is, after all, *cream*? And why are false teeth called "false" rather than, say, "artificial"? Why are artificial limbs so-called, in *preference* to "false"? Is it that false teeth, besides doing much the same job as real teeth, look, and are meant to look, *deceptively* like real teeth? Whereas an artificial limb, perhaps, is meant to do the same job, but is neither intended, nor likely, to be *passed off* as a real limb.

Another philosophically notorious dimension-word, which has already been mentioned in another connexion as closely comparable with "real," is "good." "Good" is the most general of a very large and diverse list of more specific words, which share with it the general function of expressing commendation, but differ among themselves in their aptness to, and implications in, particular contexts. It is a curious point, of which Idealist philosophers used to make much at one time, that "real" itself, in certain uses, may belong to this family. "Now this is a *real* carving-knife!" may be one way of saying that this is a good carving-knife. And it is sometimes said of a bad poem, for instance, that it isn't really a poem at all; a certain standard must be reached, as it were, even to *qualify*.

4. Lastly, "real" also belongs to a large and important family of words that we may call *adjuster-words*—words, that is, by the use of which other words are adjusted to meet the innumerable and unforeseeable demands of the world upon language. The position, considerably oversimplified no doubt, is that at a given time our language contains words that enable us (more or less) to say what we want to say in most situations that (we think) are liable to turn up. But vocabularies are finite; and the variety of possible situations that may confront us is neither finite nor precisely foreseeable. So situations are practically bound to crop up sometimes with which our vocabulary is not already fitted to cope in any tidy, straightforward style. We have the word "pig," for instance, and a pretty clear idea which animals, among those that we fairly commonly encounter, are and are not to be so called. But one day we come across a new kind of animal, which looks and behaves very much as pigs do, but not *quite* as pigs do; it is somehow different. Well, we might just keep silent, not knowing what to say; we don't want to say positively that it *is* a pig, or that it is *not*. Or we might, if for instance we expected to want to refer to these new creatures pretty often, invent a quite new word for them. But what we could do, and probably would do first of all, is to say, "It's *like* a pig." ("*Like*" is *the* great adjuster-word, or, alternatively put, the main flexibility-device by whose aid, in spite of the limited scope of our vocabulary, we can always avoid being left completely speechless.) And then, having said of this animal that it's *like* a pig, we may proceed with the remark, "But it isn't a *real* pig"—or more specifically, and using a term that naturalists favour, "not a *true* pig." If we think of words as being shot like arrows at the world, the function of these adjuster-words is to free us from the disability of being able to shoot only straight ahead; by their use on occasion, such words as "pig" can be, so to speak, brought into connexion with targets lying slightly off the simple, straightforward line on which they are ordinarily aimed. And in this way we gain, besides flexibility, precision; for if I can say, "Not a real pig, but like a pig," I don't have to tamper with the meaning of "pig" itself.

But, one might ask, do we *have* to have "like" to serve this purpose? We have, after all, other flexibility-devices. For instance, I might say that animals of this new species are "piggish"; I might perhaps call them "quasi-pigs," or describe them (in the style of vendors of peculiar wines) as "pig-type" creatures. But these devices, excellent no doubt in their way, can't be regarded as substitutes for "like," for this reason: they equip us simply with new expressions on the same level as, functioning in the same way as, the word "pig" itself; and thus, though they may perhaps help us out of our immediate difficulty, they themselves may land us in exactly the same *kind* of difficulty at any time. We have this kind of wine, not real port, but a tolerably close approximation to port, and we call it "port type." But then someone produces a new kind of wine, not port exactly, but also not quite the same as what we now call "port type." So what are we to say? Is it port-type type? It would be tedious to have to say so, and besides there would clearly be no future in it. But as it is we can say that it is *like* port-type wine (and for that matter rather like port, too); and in saying this we don't saddle ourselves with a *new word*, whose application may itself prove problematic if the vintners spring yet another surprise on us. The word "like" equips us *generally* to handle the unforeseen, in a way in which new words invented *ad hoc* don't, and can't.

(Why then do we need "real" as an adjuster-word as well as "like"? Why exactly do we want to say, sometimes "It is like a pig," sometimes "It is not a real pig"? To answer these questions properly would be to go a long way towards making really clear the use, the "meaning," of "real.")

It should be quite clear, then, that there are no criteria to be laid down *in general* for distinguishing the real from the not real. How this is to be done must depend on *what* it is with respect to which the problem arises in particular cases. Furthermore, even for particular kinds of things, there may be many different ways in which the distinction may be made (there is not just *one* way of being "not a real pig")—this depends on the number and variety of the surprises and dilemmas nature and our fellow men may spring on us, and on the surprises and dilemmas we have been faced with hitherto. And of course, if there is *never* any dilemma or surprise, the question simply doesn't come up; if we had simply never had occasion to distinguish anything as being in any way like a pig but not a *real* pig, then the words "real pig" themselves would have no application—as perhaps the words "real after-image" have no application.

Again, the criteria we employ at a given time can't be taken as *final*, not liable to change. Suppose that one day a creature of the kind we now call a cat takes to talking. Well, we say to begin with, I suppose, "This cat can talk." But then other cats, not all, take to talking as well; we now have to say that some cats talk, we distinguish between talking and non-talking cats. But again we may, if talking becomes prevalent and the distinction between talking and not talking seems to us to be really important, come to insist that a *real cat* be a creature that can talk. And this will give us a new case of being "not a real cat," i.e. being a creature just like a cat except for not talking.

Of course—this may seem perhaps hardly worth saying, but in philosophy it seems it does need to be said—we make a distinction between "a real *x*" and "not a real *x*" only if there is a way of telling the difference between what is a real *x* and what is not. A distinction which we are not in fact able to draw is—to put it politely—not worth making.

EXISTENTIALISM AND PHENOMENOLOGY

JEAN-PAUL SARTRE

*What Is Existentialism?**

Jean-Paul Sartre (b. 1905) was born and educated in Paris. During World War II he fought with the French army and with the resistance movement. He is known most widely through his novels, plays, and short stories, and for his defense of human freedom and support of various left-wing movements. His chief philosophical works are *Being and Nothingness,* which deals with the nature and forms of existence or being, *Critique of Dialectical Reason,* and *Existentialism and Humanism,* which is concerned with man and his fate.

In the selection below, after defining existentialism Sartre distinguishes the different forms of it and explains the conditions and periods in which they emerge. In the course of the discussion he introduces a few of the leading existentialists and makes clear his own conviction.

...What is meant by the term existentialism?

Most people who use the word would be rather embarrassed if they had to explain it, since, now that the word is all the rage, even the work of a musician or painter is being called existentialist. A gossip columnist in *Clartés* signs himself *The Existentialist,* so that by this time the word has been so stretched and has taken on so broad a meaning, that it no longer means anything at all. It seems that for want of an advance-guard doctrine

*Jean-Paul Sartre, from *Existentialism,* trans. Bernard Frechtman (New York: Philosophical Library, 1947), pp. 14–19, 20–24, 25–27, 34–35, 42–44. Used by permission of the publisher.

analogous to surrealism, the kind of people who are eager for scandal and flurry turn to this philosophy which in other respects does not at all serve their purposes in this sphere.

Actually, it is the least scandalous, the most austere of doctrines. It is intended strictly for specialists and philosophers. Yet it can be defined easily. What complicates matters is that there are two kinds of existentialist; first, those who are Christian, among whom I would include Jaspers and Gabriel Marcel, both Catholic; and on the other hand the atheistic existentialists, among whom I class Heidegger, and then the French existentialists and myself. What they have in common is that they think that existence precedes essence, or, if you prefer, that subjectivity must be the starting point.

Just what does that mean? Let us consider some object that is manufactured, for example, a book or a paper-cutter: here is an object which has been made by an artisan whose inspiration came from a concept. He referred to the concept of what a paper-cutter is and likewise to a known method of production, which is part of the concept, something which is, by and large, a routine. Thus, the paper-cutter is at once an object produced in a certain way and, on the other hand, one having a specific use; and one can not postulate a man who produces a paper-cutter but does not know what it is used for. Therefore, let us say that, for the paper-cutter, essence—that is, the ensemble of both the production routines and the properties which enable it to be both produced and defined—precedes existence. Thus, the presence of the paper-cutter or book in front of me is determined. Therefore, we have here a technical view of the world whereby it can be said that production precedes existence.

When we conceive God as the Creator, He is generally thought of as a superior sort of artisan. Whatever doctrine we may be considering, whether one like that of Descartes or that of Leibnitz, we always grant that will more or less follows understanding or, at the very least, accompanies it, and that when God creates He knows exactly what He is creating. Thus, the concept of man in the mind of God is comparable to the concept of paper-cutter in the mind of the manufacturer, and, following certain techniques and a conception, God produces man, just as the artisan, following a definition and a technique, makes a paper-cutter. Thus, the individual man is the realisation of a certain concept in the divine intelligence.

In the eighteenth century, the atheism of the *philosophes* discarded the idea of God, but not the [related] notion that essence precedes existence. To a certain extent, this idea is found everywhere; we find it in Diderot, in Voltaire, and even in Kant. Man has a human nature; this human nature, which is the concept of the human, is found in all men, which means that each man is a particular example of a universal concept, man. In Kant, the result of this universality is that the wild-man, the natural man, as well as the bourgeois, are circumscribed by the same definition and have the same basic qualities. Thus, here too the essence of man precedes the historical existence that we find in nature.

Atheistic existentialism, which I represent, is more coherent. It states that if God does not exist, there is at least one being in whom existence precedes essence, a being who exists before he can be defined by any concept, and that this being is man, or, as Heidegger says, human reality. What is meant here by saying that existence precedes essence? It means that, first of all, man exists, turns up, appears on the scene, and, only afterwards, defines himself. If man, as the existentialist conceives him, is indefinable, it is because at first he is nothing. Only afterward will he be something, and he himself will have made what he will be. Thus, there is no human nature, since there is no God to conceive it. Not only is man what he conceives himself to be, but he is also only what he wills himself to be after this thrust toward existence.

Man is nothing else but what he makes of himself. Such is the first principle of existentialism. It is also what is called subjectivity, the name we are labeled with when charges are brought against us. But what do we mean by this, if not that man has a greater dignity than a stone or table? For we mean that man first exists, that is, the man first of all is the being who hurls himself toward a future and who is conscious of imagining himself as being in the future....

...When we say that man chooses his own self, we mean that every one of us does likewise; but we also mean by that that in making this choice he also chooses all men. In fact, in creating the man that we want to be, there is not a single one of our acts which does not at the same time create an image of man as we think he ought to be. To choose to be this or that is to affirm at the same time the value of what we choose, because we can never choose evil. We always choose the good, and nothing can be good for us without being good for all.

If,... [furthermore], existence precedes essence, and if we grant that we exist and fashion our image at one and the same time, the image is valid for everybody and for our whole age. Thus, our responsibility is much greater than we might have supposed, because it involves all mankind. ...Therefore, I am responsible for myself and for everyone else. I am creating a certain image of man of my own choosing. In choosing myself, I choose man.

This helps us understand what the actual content is of such rather grandiloquent words as anguish, forlornness, despair. As you will see, it's all quite simple.

First, what is meant by anguish? The existentialists say at once that man is anguish. What that means is this: the man who involves himself and who realizes that he is not only the person he chooses to be, but also a lawmaker who is, at the same time, choosing all mankind as well as himself, can not . . . escape the feeling of his total and deep responsibility. Of course, there are many people who are not anxious; but we claim that they are hiding their anxiety, that they are fleeing from it. Certainly, many people believe that when they do something, they themselves are the only ones involved, and when someone says to them, "What if everyone acted that way?" they shrug their shoulders and answer, "Everyone doesn't act that way." But really, one should always ask himself, "What would happen if everybody looked at things that way?" There is no escaping this disturbing thought except by a kind of double-dealing. A man who lies and makes excuses for himself by saying "not everybody does that," is someone with an uneasy conscience, because the act of lying implies that a universal value is conferred upon the lie.

Anguish is evident even when it conceals itself. This is the anguish that Kierkegaard called the anguish of Abraham. You know the story: an angel has ordered Abraham to sacrifice his son; if it really were an angel who has come and said, "You are Abraham, you shall sacrifice your son," everything would be all right. But everyone might first wonder, "Is it really an angel, and am I really Abraham? What proof do I have?"

There was a madwoman who had hallucinations; someone used to speak to her on the telephone and give her orders. Her doctor asked her, "Who is it who talks to you?" She answered, "He says it's God." What proof did she really have that it was God? If an angel comes to me, what proof is there that it's an angel? And if I hear voices, what proof is there that they come from heaven and not from hell, or from the subconscious, or a pathological condition? What proves that they are addressed to me? What proof is there that I have been appointed to impose my choice and my conception of man on humanity? I'll never find any proof or sign to convince me of that. If a voice addresses me, it is always for me to decide that this is the angel's voice; if I consider that such an act is a good one, it is I who will choose to say that it is good rather than bad.

Now, I'm not being singled out as an Abraham, and yet at every moment I'm obliged to perform exemplary acts. For every man, everything happens as if all mankind had its eyes fixed on him and were guiding itself by what he does. And every man ought to say to himself, "Am I really the kind of man who has the right to act in such a way that humanity might guide itself by my actions?" And if he does not say that to himself, he is masking his anguish.

There is no question here of the kind of anguish which would lead to quietism, to inaction. It is a matter of a simple sort of anguish that anybody who has had responsibilities is familiar with. . . .

When we speak of forlornness, a term Heidegger was fond of, we mean only that God does not exist and that we have to face all the consequences of this. The existentialist is strongly opposed to a certain kind of secular ethics which would like to abolish God with the least possible expense. About 1880, some French teachers tried to set up a secular ethics which went something like this: God is a useless and costly hypothesis; we are discarding it; but, meanwhile, in order for there to be an ethics, a society, a civilization, it is essential that certain values be taken seriously and that they be considered as having an *a priori* existence. It must be obligatory, *a priori,* to be honest, not to lie, not to beat your wife, to have children, etc., etc. So we're going to try a little device which will make it possible to show that values exist all the same, inscribed in a heaven of ideas, though otherwise God does not exist. In other words—and this, I believe, is the tendency of everything called reformism in France—nothing will be changed if God does not exist. We shall find ourselves with the same norms of honesty, progress, and humanism, and we shall have made of God an outdated hypothesis which will peacefully die off by itself.

The existentialist, on the contrary, thinks it very distressing that God does not exist, because all possibility of finding values in a heaven of ideas disappears along with Him; there can no longer be an *a priori* Good, since there is no infinite and perfect consciousness to think it. Nowhere is it written that the Good exists, that we must be honest, that we must not lie; because the fact is we are on a plane where there are only men. Dostoievsky said, "If God didn't exist, everything would be possible." That is the very starting point of existentialism. Indeed, everything is permissible if God does not exist, and as a result man is forlorn, because neither within him nor without does he find anything to cling to. He can't start making excuses for himself.

If existence really does precede essence, there is no explaining things away by reference to a fixed and given human nature. In other words, there is no determinism, man is free, man is freedom. On the other hand, if God does not exist, we find no values or commands to turn to which legitimize our conduct. So, in the bright realm of values, we have no excuse behind us, nor justification before us. We are alone, with no excuses.

That is the idea I shall try to convey when I say that man is condemned to be free. Condemned, because he did not create himself, yet, in other respects is free; because, once thrown into the world, he is responsible for everything he does....

As for despair, the term has a very simple meaning. It means that we shall confine ourselves to reckoning only with what depends upon our will, or on the ensemble of probabilities which make our action possible. When we want something, we always have to reckon with probabilities. I may be counting on the arrival of a friend. The friend is coming by rail or streetcar; this supposes that the train will arrive on schedule, or that the streetcar will not jump the track. I am left in the realm of possibility; but possibilities are to be reckoned with only to the point where my action comports with the ensemble of these possibilities, and no further. The moment the possibilities I am considering are not rigorously involved by my action, I ought to disengage myself from them, because no God, no scheme, can adapt the world and its possibilities to my will. When Descartes said, "Conquer yourself rather than the world," he meant essentially the same thing....

...You see that it [existentialism] can not be taken for a philosophy of quietism, since it defines man in terms of action; nor for a pessimistic description of man—there is no doctrine more optimistic, since man's destiny is within himself; nor for an attempt to discourage man from acting, since it tells him that the only hope is in his acting and that action is the only thing that enables a man to live. Consequently, we are dealing here with an ethics of action and involvement.

Nevertheless, on the basis of a few notions like these, we are still charged with immuring man in his private subjectivity. There again we're very much misunderstood. Subjectivity of the individual is indeed our point of departure, and this for strictly philosophic reasons. Not because we are bourgeois, but because we want a doctrine based on truth and not a lot of fine theories, full of hope but with no real basis. There can be no other truth to take off from than this: *I think; therefore, I exist.* There we have the absolute truth of consciousness becoming aware of itself. Every theory which takes man out of the moment in which he becomes aware of himself is, at its very beginning, a theory which confounds truth, for outside the Cartesian *cogito,* all views are only probable, and a doctrine of probability which is not bound to a truth dissolves into thin air. In order to describe the probable, you must have a firm hold on the true. Therefore, before there can be any truth whatsoever, there must be an absolute truth; and this one is simple and easily arrived at; it's on everyone's doorstep; it's a matter of grasping it directly.

Secondly, this theory is the only one which gives man dignity, the only one which does not reduce him to an object. The effect of all materialism is to treat all men, including the one philosophizing, as objects, that is, as an ensemble of determined reactions in no way distinguished from the ensemble of qualities and phenomena which constitute a table or a chair or a stone. We definitely wish to establish the human realm as an ensemble of values distinct from the material realm. But the subjectivity that we have thus arrived at, and which we have claimed to be truth, is not a strictly individual subjectivity, for we have demonstrated that one discovers in the *cogito* not only himself, but others as well.

QUENTIN LAUER

*What Is Phenomenology?**

Quentin Lauer (b. 1917), an educator, was born in Brooklyn, New York, and received the degree of Doctor of Letters from the University of Paris. A member of the Society of Jesus, he has taught philosophy at Fordham University since 1954 and has been chairman of the department. His publications in France and in the United States include *The Phenomenology of Husserl, The Problem of Unbelief,* and *Hegel's Idea of Philosophy.*

The selection below discusses the relation between phenomenology and existentialism and the sources of the former which go back as far as Kant in the eighteenth century. The term "phenomenology" today usually refers to the philosophy of Edmund Husserl and his colleagues and followers. Husserl attempted to penetrate the mystery of consciousness and reality and to get back to pure consciousness and to an "intuition" of value essences.

With the passage of time it becomes more and more difficult to determine what the words "phenomenology" and "phenomenological" are supposed to mean in the contexts in which they are used. Like the terms "existentialism" and "existential" it has become fashionable to designate thereby some sort of profound, recondite, and very up-to-date approach to philosophy or science, without it being entirely clear in what sense the terms are being applied. There is a sense, of course, in which this vague use is justified, since every attempt to get away from speculative constructionism and to limit oneself to the data which are presented in consciousness —describing rather than explaining them—is to that extent phenomenological, at least in method. Still, the sort of vagueness which goes with modishness leads to confusion and makes for a terminology almost empty of meaning. In recent years, for example, phenomenology has in some minds become so intimately bound up with existentialism that the two terms are used almost indiscriminately, despite significant differences in the attitudes represented by the two titles. The reason for this may be that the thought of Jean-Paul Sartre, which is both phenomenological and existential, it taken as typical. Many thinkers, such as Martin Heidegger and Gabriel Marcel, who consider their own approach to philosophy as phenomenological, have

*Reprinted by permission of the publisher from Quentin Lauer, S. J., *The Triumph of Subjectivity* (also Harper Torchbook *Phenomenology: Its Genesis and Prospect*) (New York: Fordham University Press, 1958), Copyright © 1958 by Fordham University Press, pp. 1–2, 3–4, 5–10.

expressly indicated their desire not to be identified with the direction represented by Sartre. Others, such as Jean Hering or Dietrich von Hildebrand, would see no sense in referring to their thought as in any way "existential."

In whatever context the term phenomenology is used, however, it refers back to the distinction introduced by Kant between the *phenomenon* or appearance of reality in consciousness, and the *noumenon,* or being of reality in itself. Kant himself did not develop a phenomenolgy as such, but since his *Critique of Pure Reason* recognizes scientific knowledge only of *phenomena* and not at all of *noumena,* his critique can be considered a sort of phenomenology. According to this position whatever is known is phenomenon, precisely because to be known means to appear to consciousness in a special way, so that what does not in any way appear is not known—at least not by speculative reason. Still, according to Kant, it is possible to *think* what is not *known,* and this we think of as a "thing-in-itself" or *noumenon,* of which the *phenomenon* is the known aspect. This sort of phenomenology, which will restrict scientific knowledge to appearances, is directed both against the rationalism of Descartes, which seeks a rational knowledge of all reality, and against the phenomenism of Hume, which will accept no scientific knowledge at all except that of mathematics. Kant insists that there can be true scientific knowledge which is not mathematical, but he denies that there can be such a knowledge in metaphysics....

When the term "phenomenology" is used today it usually refers to the philosophy of Edmund Husserl or of someone of those who have drawn their inspiration from him. From the beginning of his philosophical career, Husserl was opposed to what he called the "dualism" of Kant, the "constructionism" of Hegel, and the "naturalism" or "psychologism" of the positivists. He agrees with them in asserting that only phenomena are *given,* but he will claim that *in* them is given the very *essence* of that which is. Here there is no concern with reality as existing, since existence is at best contingent and as such can add to reality nothing which would be the object of scientific knowledge. If one has described phenomena, one has described all that can be described, but in the very constant elements of that description is revealed the *essence* of what is described. Such a description can say nothing regarding the existence of what is described, but the phenomenological "intuition" in which the description terminates tells us *what* its object *necessarily* is. To know this is to have an "essential" and hence a "scientific" knowledge of being. Contemporary phenomenologists usually follow the development elaborated by Husserl—at least in its methodological aspects—though many of them have rejected the idealistic and metaphysical implications of Husserl's own position. They consider as phenomenology's distinctive mark its capacity to reveal essences, not its refusal to come to terms with "existing" reality. Unlike the investigations of Husserl, those of his followers range over a very wide field, so that there is scarcely an aspect of philosophy or of science which has not been investigated phenomenologically.... The problem of reconciling reality and thought about reality is as old as philosophy—we might say, as old as thought itself. The problem is complicated by the obvious fact that we cannot know reality independently of consciousness, and we cannot know consciousness independently of reality—to do so would be to meet the one and the other in isolation, which is an impossibility. We meet consciousness only as consciousness of something; and we meet reality only as a reality of which we are conscious. It seems reasonable to assume that the normal individual will, without reflection, see a certain duality in his experiences of the world about him: in them there is a world which he experiences, and which he assumes to be indepedently of himself pretty much as he experiences it; and there is also the experience wherein he grasps this world, which he assumes to be distinct from the world. It is also reasonable to assume that he has never been able to analyze his experiences to such an extent that he can isolate—the way one does in analyzing water into hydrogen and oxygen (if even that is possible)—the "elements" which belong to the "independent" world of reality and those which have been contributed by the very act of experiencing this reality. Finally, it seems reasonable to assume that he will not be too much concerned.

The philosopher, however, is committed to penetrating this mystery—for mystery it is—and to coming up with some sort of consistent reconciliation of the two worlds, if he is to continue plying his trade. In a certain sense, the history of philosophy is the record of a series of attempts to make this reconciliation. The problem as it faces us, and it has faced philosophers from the beginning of philosophizing—apart from the accuracy of the original judgment which the "normal" individual makes—offers a limited number of approaches to a solution. One can approach it from the side of the reality of which we are conscious, from that of the consciousness we have of reality, or from the point of view of a contact between the two. Despite the limited number of approaches, however, there seems to be no limit to the explanations which have been and will continue to be attempted.

The phenomenologist is no exception in this almost universal quest for a solution. Whatever may be his particular position, he seeks to reduce the problem to its simplest terms and *in* them, rather than *from* them, to find a solution, or at least, the approach to a solution. According to the phenomenologist, if there is a solution at all, it must be contained in the *data* of the problem—although, of course, there is a disagreement as to what the data are. The point of agreement, however—and this is what makes each a phenomenologist—is that only phenomena are *given* and that therefore, if an answer is to be found, it must be sought in phenomena. There will be a disagreement as to just what are to be considered as phenomena and as to what can be discovered in them, but there will be agreement that we cannot enlist the aid of the non-phenomenal in seeking our solution. As Maurice Merleau-Ponty, one of the most coherent of the phenomenologists, has expressed it, "Phenomenology is an inventory of consciousness as of that wherein a universe resides." If we are to know what anything is—and this the phenomenologist will do—we must examine the consciousness we have of it; if this does not give us an answer, nothing will.

The consciousness with which the phenomenologist is here concerned, is not consciousness as a psychic function, in the way it is, for example, to the experimental psychologist. He is concerned with consciousness as a kind of being which things exercise, the only kind of being directly available to the investigator. Thus, for him, consciousness is best expressed by the German word *Bewusstsein,* which means the kind of being an object of knowledge has in being known. This is not necessarily an identification of being and being-known, but it is an assertion that the only key we have to being is in examining its being-known. Now, even a superficial examination of any act of consciousness will reveal two inescapable facts: (1) it cannot be isolated from other acts of consciousness, but belongs to a whole life of consciousness, is conditioned by all the dispositions of which a subject is capable, is prepared for and colored by the whole series of conscious acts which have preceded it; (2) it is never completely arbitrary, in the sense of being conditioned only subjectively; it is what it is because it is consciousness of this or that object, which, precisely as an object, is in some sense independent of the individual act wherein it is grasped; there is some similarity between the experiences of one subject and another when faced with a similar situation, no matter what the previous experiences of the two may have been.

The attempts to reduce the problem to its simplest terms, however, is not so simple after all. If the only approach we have is through consciousness, and if every act of consciousness is a complex of inseparable elements, some objective and some subjective, the analysis of consciousness which will reveal to us the very meaning of being is a complex affair. The phenomenologist, however, is convinced that this analysis can be made and that in making it he can return to the very origin of consciousness, distinguishing what is pure consciousness from all the accretions which custom, prejudice, assumption, and tradition have built around it. When he has uncovered consciousness in this pure form, he is convinced that he will have arrived at an understanding of the only being which can have significance for him.

In speaking thus of phenomenology we have admittedly come to treat exclusively of the kind of phenomenology advocated by Edmund Husserl and by those who follow him more or less closely. In this sense phenomenology is both a method and a philosophy. As a method it outlines the steps which must be taken in order to arrive at the pure phenomenon, wherein is revealed the very essence not only of appearances but also of that which appears.[1] As a philosophy it claims to give necessary, essential knowledge of that which is,[2] since contingent existence cannot change what reason has recognized as the very essence of its object. In the course of its investigations, therefore, it discovers (or claims to discover) that the quasi infinity of objects which go to make up an experienced world can be described in terms of the consciousness wherein they are experienced. Phenomenology is conceived as a return to "things," as opposed to illusions, verbalisms, or mental constructions, precisely because a "thing" *is* the direct object of consciousness in its purified form. The color "red" is no less a thing than is a horse, since each has an "essence" which is entirely independent of any concrete, contingent existence it may have. It is sufficient that the experience of red can be as clearly distinguished from the experience of green as can the experience of horse from that of man. The dispute as to whether colors are "primary" or "secondary" qualities is entirely without significance; each color has an essence which can be grapsed in consciousness, precisely because the essence of any color is contained in the experience of that color. The fact that the content of this experience is an essence is manifest from the fact that it can be clearly distinguished from whatever is essentially something else. In this sense an imaginary object has its distinct *essence* just as truly as does a "real" object. Whether an object is *real* or *fictitious* can be determined by an analysis of the act of which it is object.

All this, however, would be without significance if it were not aimed at discovering "objective" essences, which are what they are not only independently of contingent existence but also independently of any arbitrary meaning which a subject *wants* to give them. Though it is of the essence of an object to be related to a subject, the phenomenologist will deny that "things" act upon subjects in such a way as to engender this relation or that subjects simply "produce" objects. He will insist that by investigating pure consciousness he can discover a relationship which is truly objective, in the sense that its validity is not derived from the conscious act wherein the relationship resides, and is necessary, in the sense that it could not be

[1.] According to Husserl, there is no essence other than that discoverable in appearances.

[2.] "Phenomenology, which will be nothing less than a theory of essence contained in pure intuition," from *Ideen I*. . . . "With regard to phenomenology, it wants to be a *descriptive* theory of essences." . . . Among the followers of Husserl there is considerable divergence of emphasis, some stressing the *description* of phenomena, others stressing the discovery of *essences* in phenomena. As is so frequently the case, the differences seem to be traceable to the predispositions which each has brought with him in his approach to phenomenology.

otherwise, no matter who the subject grasping the object may be. Husserl's own phenomenological investigations were, it is true, chiefly logical, epistemological, and to a certain extent ontological. Still, phenomenology even as he conceived it is at its persuasive best in the realm of values.

Realistic systems of philosophy have always found the question of moral, religious, esthetic, and social values a particularly difficult hurdle to clear since the subjective elements in all value judgments are too obvious to be ignored. One can, of course, explain evaluations in terms of the objective values which are being judged, and then describe objective values in terms of their relationship to an evaluating subject; but this sort of thing looks suspiciously like going around in a circle. It is perhaps for this reason that there were no consistent attempts to evolve theories of value, until the days when idealism was enjoying widespread triumph. Idealistic theories, however, have always run the risk of becoming so subjective that the very concept of value loses any communicable significance. Husserl himself was not particularly successful—we might even say that he was eminently unsuccessful—in coming to terms with the complicated problems of value, but his theories, particularly in their ontological aspects, inspired others to look for a world of values which are *what* they are independently of any particular or general judgments regarding them. According to Scheler, Hartmann, Von Hildebrand, and others such values are to be *discovered in* things and not to be *imposed on* things by an observing—and evaluating—subject. And the techniques for discovering them are to be the phenomenological techniques of objective analysis and description, resulting in an *"intuition"* of value essences (essential values).

Is a Comprehensive Vision Possible?

PLATO

*The Vision of the Good**

Plato (427–347 B.C.) was born in Athens in a wealthy family and became a student and devoted follower of Socrates. After the death of Socrates, he left Athens and traveled until 387 B.C. when he returned and founded a school, known as the Academy, where he taught for forty years. Along with his brilliant student Aristotle, he was one of the most influential intellectual leaders in Western civilization. His writings, of which we have more than thirty, use the literary form of dialogue in which Socrates and others represent various points of view. His writings include the *Apology* and *Crito,* dealing with the trial and last days of Socrates; *Euthyphro,* discussing piety or reverence; *Phaedo,* treating the "Idea of the Good"; *Symposium,* dealing with love, including the love of the good; and his great masterpiece, *The Republic,* concerned with justice and the ideal state.

In the following selection from *The Republic,* Plato, by picturing prisoners chained in a cave, creates an allegory of the development of the soul from a state of ignorance and illusion through various stages of enlightenment until it achieves understanding, wisdom, and the vision of the good. Plato applies his allegory to the world of education and government.

SOCRATES, GLAUCON

And now, I said, let me show in a figure how far our nature is enlightened or unenlightened: Behold! human beings living in an underground den, which has a mouth open toward the light and reaching all

*From *The Republic of Plato,* trans. Benjamin Jowett (New York: Willey Book Co., 1901), Book VII with omissions.

along the den; here they have been from their childhood, and have their legs and necks chained so that they cannot move, and can only see before them, being prevented by the chains from turning round their heads. Above and behind them a fire is blazing at a distance, and between the fire and the prisoners there is a raised way; and you will see, if you look, a low wall built along the way, like the screen which marionette-players have in front of them, over which they show the puppets.

I see.

And do you see, I said, men passing along the wall carrying all sorts of vessels, and statues and figures of animals made of wood and stone and various materials, which appear over the wall? Some of them are talking, others silent.

You have shown me a strange image, and they are strange prisoners.

Like ourselves, I replied; and they see only their own shadows, or the shadows of one another, which the fire throws on the opposite wall of the cave?

True, he said; how could they see anything but the shadows if they were never allowed to move their heads?

And of the objects which are being carried in like manner they would only see the shadows?

Yes, he said.

And if they were able to converse with one another, would they not suppose that they were naming what was actually before them?

Very true.

And suppose further that the prison had an echo which came from the other side, would they not be sure to fancy when one of the passers-by spoke that the voice which they heard came from the passing shadow?

No question, he replied.

To them, I said, the truth would be literally nothing but the shadows of the images.

That is certain.

And now look again, and see what will naturally follow if the prisoners are released and disabused of their error. At first, when any of them is liberated and compelled suddenly to stand up and turn his neck round and walk and look toward the light, he will suffer sharp pains; the glare will distress him, and he will be unable to see the realities of which in his former state he had seen the shadows; and then conceive someone saying to him, that what he saw before was an illusion, but that now, when he is approaching nearer to being and his eye is turned toward more real existence, he has a clearer vision—what will be his reply? And you may further imagine that his instructor is pointing to the objects as they pass and requiring him to name them—will he not be perplexed? Will he not fancy that the shadows which he formerly saw are truer than the objects which are now shown to him?

Far truer.

And if he is compelled to look straight at the light, will he not have a pain in his eyes which will make him turn away to take refuge in the objects of vision which he can see, and which he will conceive to be in reality clearer than the things which are now being shown to him?

True, he said.

And suppose once more, that he is reluctantly dragged up a steep and rugged ascent, and held fast until he is forced into the presence of the sun himself, is he not likely to be pained and irritated? When he approaches the light his eyes will be dazzled, and he will not be able to see anything at all of what are now called realities.

Not all in a moment, he said.

He will require to grow accustomed to the sight of the upper world. And first he will see the shadows best, next the reflections of men and other objects in the water, and then the objects themselves; then he will gaze upon the light of the moon and the stars and the spangled heaven; and he will see the sky and the stars by night better than the sun or the light of the sun by day?

Certainly.

Last of all he will be able to see the sun, and not mere reflections of him in the water, but he will see him in his own proper place, and not in another; and he will contemplate him as he is.

Certainly.

He will then proceed to argue that this is he who gives the season and the years, and is the guardian of all that is in the visible world, and in a certain way the cause of all things which he and his fellows have been accustomed to behold?

Clearly, he said, he would first see the sun and then reason about him.

And when he remembered his old habitation, and the wisdom of the den and his fellow-prisoners, do you not suppose that he would felicitate himself on the change, and pity him?

Certainly, he would.

And if they were in the habit of conferring honors among themselves on those who were quickest to observe the passing shadows and to remark which of them went before, and which followed after, and which were together; and who were therefore best able to draw conclusions as to the future, do you think that he would care for such honors and glories, or envy the possessors of them? Would he not say with Homer,

"Better to be the poor servant of a poor master,"

and to endure anything, rather than think as they do and live after their manner?

Yes, he said, I think that he would rather suffer anything than entertain these false notions and live in this miserable manner.

Imagine once more, I said, such a one coming suddenly out of the sun to be replaced in his old situation; would he not be certain to have his eyes full of darkness?

To be sure, he said.

And if there were a contest, and he had to compete in measuring the shadows with the prisoners who had never moved out of the den, while his sight was still weak, and before his eyes had become steady (and the time which would be needed to acquire this new habit of sight might be very considerable), would he not be ridiculous? Men would say of him that up he went and down he came without his eyes; and that it was better not even to think of ascending; and if anyone tried to loose another and lead him up to the light, let them only catch the offender, and they would put him to death.

No question, he said.

This entire allegory, I said, you may now append, dear Glaucon, to the previous argument; the prison-house is the world of sight, the light of the fire is the sun, and you will not misapprehend me if you interpret the journey upward to be the ascent of the soul into the intellectual world according to my poor belief, which, at your desire, I have expressed—whether rightly or wrongly, God knows. But, whether true or false, my opinion is that in the world of knowledge the idea of good appears last of all, and is seen only with an effort; and, when seen, is also inferred to be the universal author of all things beautiful and right, parent of light and of the lord of light in this visible world, and the immediate source of reason and truth in the intellectual; and that this is the power upon which he who would act rationally either in public or private life must have his eye fixed.

I agree, he said, as far as I am able to understand you.

Moreover, I said, you must not wonder that those who attain to this beatific vision are unwilling to descend to human affairs; for their souls are ever hastening into the upper world where they desire to dwell; which desire of theirs is very natural, if our allegory may be trusted.

Yes, very natural.

And is there anything surprising in one who passes from divine contemplations to the evil state of man, misbehaving himself in a ridiculous manner; if, while his eyes are blinking and before he has become accustomed to the surrounding darkness, he is compelled to fight in courts of law, or in other places, about the images or the shadows of images of justice, and is endeavoring to meet the conceptions of those who have never yet seen absolute justice?

Anything but surprising, he replied.

Anyone who has common-sense will remember that the bewilderments of the eyes are of two kinds, and arise from two causes, either from coming out of the light or from going into the light, which is true of the mind's eye, quite as much as of the bodily eye; and he who remembers this when he sees anyone whose vision is perplexed and weak, will not be too ready to laugh; he will first ask whether that soul of man has come out of the brighter life, and is unable to see because unaccustomed to the dark, or having turned from darkness to the day is dazzled by excess of light. And he will count the one happy in his condition and state of being, and he will pity the other; or, if he have a mind to laugh at the soul which comes from below into the light, there will be more reason in this than in the laugh which greets him who returns from above out of the light into the den.

That, he said, is a very just distinction.

But then, if I am right, certain professors of education must be wrong when they say that they can put a knowledge into the soul which was not there before, like sight into blind eyes.

They undoubtedly say this, he replied.

Whereas, our argument shows that the power and capacity of learning exists in the soul already; and that just as the eye was unable to turn from darkness to light without the whole body, so too the instrument of knowledge can only by the movement of the whole soul be turned from the world of becoming into that of being, and learn by degrees to endure the sight of being, and of the brightest and best of being, or, in other words, of the good.

Very true.

And must there not be some art which will effect conversion in the easiest and quickest manner; not implanting the faculty of sight, for that exists already, but has been turned in the wrong direction, and is looking away from the truth?

Yes, he said, such an art may be presumed.

And whereas the other so-called virtues of the soul seem to be akin to bodily qualities, for even when they are not originally innate they can be implanted later by habit and exercise, the virtue of wisdom more than anything else contains a divine element which always remains, and by this conversion is rendered useful and profitable; or, on the other hand, hurtful and useless. Did you never observe the narrow intelligence flashing from the keen eye of a clever rogue—how eager he is, how clearly his paltry soul sees the way to his end; he is the reverse of blind, but his keen eyesight is forced into the service of evil, and he is mischievous in proportion to his cleverness?

Very true, he said.

But what if there had been a circumcision of such natures in the days of their youth; and they had been severed from those sensual pleasures, such as eating and drinking, which, like leaden weights, were attached to them at their birth, and which drag them down and turn the vision of their souls upon the things that are below—if, I say, they had been released from these impediments and turned in the opposite direction, the very same faculty in them would have seen the truth as keenly as they see what their eyes are turned to now.

Very likely.

Yes, I said; and there is another thing which is likely, or rather a necessary inference from what has preceded, that neither the uneducated and uninformed of the truth, nor yet those who never make an end of their education, will be able ministers of the State; not the former, because they have no single aim of duty which is the rule of all their actions, private as well as public; nor the latter, because they will not act at all except upon compulsion, fancying that they are already dwelling apart in the islands of the blessed.

Very true, he replied.

Then, I said, the business of us who are the founders of the State will be to compel the best minds to attain that knowledge which we have already shown to be the greatest of all—they must continue to ascend until they arrive at the good; but when they have ascended and seen enough we must not allow them to do as they do now.

What do you mean?

I mean that they remain in the upper world: but this must not be allowed; they must be made to descend again among the prisoners in the den, and partake of their labors and honors, whether they are worth having or not.

But is not this unjust? he said; ought we to give them a worse life, when they might have a better?

You have again forgotten, my friend, I said, the intention of the legislator, who did not aim at making any one class in the State happy above the rest; the happiness was to be in the whole State, and he held the citizens together by persuasion and necessity, making them benefactors of the State, and therefore benefactors of one another; to this end he created them, not to please themselves, but to be his instruments in binding up the State.

True, he said, I had forgotten.

Observe, Glaucon, that there will be no injustice in compelling our philosophers to have a care and providence of others; we shall explain to them that in other States, men of their class are not obliged to share in the toils of politics: and this is reasonable, for they grow up at their own sweet will, and the government would rather not have them. Being self-taught, they cannot be expected to show any gratitude for a culture which they have never received. But we have brought you into the world to be rulers of the hive, kings of yourselves and of the other citizens, and have educated you far better and more perfectly than they have been educated, and you are better able to share in the double duty. Wherefore each of you, when his turn comes, must go down to the general underground abode, and get the habit of seeing in the dark. When you have acquired the habit, you will see ten thousand times better than the inhabitants of the den, and you will know what the several images are, and what they represent, because you have seen the beautiful and just and good in their truth. And thus our State, which is also yours, will be a reality, and not a dream only, and will be administered in a spirit unlike that of other States, in which men fight with one another about shadows only and are distracted in the struggle for power, which in their eyes is a great good. Whereas the truth is that the State in which the rulers are most reluctant to govern is always the best and most quietly governed, and the State in which they are most eager, the worst.

Quite true, he replied.

And will our pupils, when they hear this, refuse to take their turn at the toils of State, when they are allowed to spend the greater part of their time with one another in the heavenly light?

Impossible, he answered; for they are just men, and the commands which we impose upon them are just; there can be no doubt that every one of them will take office as a stern necessity, and not after the fashion of our present rulers of State.

Yes, my friend, I said; and there lies the point. You must contrive for your future rulers another and a better life than that of a ruler, and then you may have a well-ordered State; for only in the State which offers this, will they rule who are truly rich, not in silver and gold, but in virtue and wisdom, which are the true blessings of life. Whereas, if they go to the administration of public affairs, poor and hungering after their own private advantage, thinking that hence they are to snatch the chief good, order there can never be; for they will be fighting about office, and the civil and domestic broils which thus arise will be the ruin of the rulers themselves and of the whole State.

Most true, he replied.

And the only life which looks down upon the life of political ambition is that of true philosophy. Do you know of any other?

Indeed, I do not, he said.

And those who govern ought not to be lovers of the task? For, if they are, there will be rival lovers, and they will fight.

No question.

Who, then, are those whom we shall compel to be guardians? Surely they will be the men who are wisest about affairs of State, and by whom the State is best administered, and who at the same time have other honors and another and a better life than that of politics?

They are the men, and I will choose them, he replied.

G. J. WARNOCK

*Metaphysics as Vision**

G. J. Warnock (b. 1923) teaches philosophy at Oxford University where, since 1971, he has been Principal of Hertford College. He has written articles in the field of analytic philosophy and has been visiting professor at various American universities. His books include *English Philosophy Since 1900, Berkeley, Contemporary Moral Philosophy,* and *The Object of Morality.*

In the following selection we find Warnock rethinking the nature and function of metaphysics. While rejecting the claims of traditional metaphysicians who sought to determine the nature of "ultimate reality," he is equally incisive in discounting the contention of the logical positivists that metaphysics is "nonsense." Having explained his view of what metaphysics is all about, he examines the value of such philosophizing and suggests why there are today relatively few metaphysicians.

"Philosophy is many things and there is no formula to cover them all. But if I were asked to express in one single word what is its most essential feature I would unhesitatingly say: vision."—"There is something visionary about great metaphysicians as if they had the power to see beyond the horizons of their time."—"To say that metaphysics is nonsense *is* nonsense."

These three quotations are taken from a recent article by Dr. F. Waismann.[1] They certainly indicate no disposition to regard metaphysics with contempt, as a pure waste of time, or as the product of some fundamental misunderstanding. To do this, he observes, would be to fail to acknowledge "the enormous part played at least in the past by those systems." We ought now to consider what part they did play—and also, why Dr. Waismann should have been inclined to put in those qualifying words, "at least in the past."

What, roughly at any rate, are we to understand by the notion of metaphysical "vision"? Dr. Waismann writes that "what is decisive is a new way of seeing and, what goes with it, the will to transform the whole intellectual scene. This is the real thing and everything else is subservient to it." It is

*G. J. Warnock, from "Metaphysics," in *English Philosophy Since 1900,* pp. 136–145.

1. *Contemporary British Philosophy,* Third Series, 1956, pp. 447–90.

essential here, first of all, to distinguish carefully between a new way of seeing, and the seeing of something new. To see something new, to find out what was not known before, is not an exercise of *metaphysical* vision—even though the effect of this new knowledge may even be to "transform the whole intellectual scene." It may be, for example, that the theory of evolution has done as much as anything in the last hundred years to alter our ways of thinking, of seeing the world and our own place in it; but this of course was a scientific and not a metaphysical theory, supported not so much by arguments or would-be arguments as by an immense variety and range of empirical facts. It is by contrast characteristic of a metaphysical theory that facts should neither be cited in its support nor be brought in evidence against it; it was for this reason that the Positivists were able to object that metaphysical doctrines were "unverifiable"; such a theory consists not in an account of any new facts but in a new account of familiar facts, a new reading, so to speak, of what has already been agreed upon.

But do not some *scientific* theories still come within the scope of such a description? Certainly they do. For example, the heliocentric theory of the planetary system was of exactly this character. It offered a new "way of seeing" astronomical phenomena without, directly at any rate, adding to astronomical knowledge; and no doubt it was for this very reason that it was thought to be of far more than parochial significance—to be, in fact, a revolutionary and even a dangerous shift in the general intellectual landscape. However, though such theories may often be felt to be of very general, and therefore of some philosophical, importance, they themselves are certainly not metaphysical theories. Why not? Is it not because they are insufficiently general? The *direct* concern of the Copernican theory is solely with the movements of planets; its wider implications, if it really has any, are incidental. By contrast a metaphysical theory may be all-embracing, or immediately relevant at least to a very wide range of diverse phenomena. Such a theory as Spinoza's, for example, not only dictates a peculiar way of regarding facts in any field whatever; it was also at any rate intended to have precise moral and even religious consequences as well. It was intended to transform "the *whole* intellectual scene," and to do this *directly,* not merely by implication, or in virtue of some quirk of psychology or association of ideas. And Hegel notoriously had no doubt whatever that there was a Hegelian way of seeing *any* subject-matter, however little in certain cases he may have succeeded in conveying to others what that way was.

"Suppose that a man revolts against accepted opinion, that he feels 'cramped' in its categories; a time may come when he believes, rightly or wrongly, that he has freed himself of these notions; when he has that sense of sudden growth in looking back at the prejudices which held him captive; or a time when he believes, rightly or wrongly, that he has reached a vantage point from which things can be seen to be arranged in clean and orderly patterns while difficulties of long standing dissolve as though by magic." These words describe exactly the situation of, for example, Berkeley. "I wonder not," he wrote, "at my sagacity in discovering the obvious tho' amazing truth, I rather wonder at my stupid inadvertency in not finding it out before." He had the sense, as he freely asserted, of "a vast view of things soluble hereby." It is worth looking into his case a little further.

Berkeley was familiar, mainly through Locke, with a "way of seeing" the world that was chiefly derived from the thriving scientific inquiries of the seventeenth century. Material things were thought of as being atomic in structure, and in character predominantly mechanical. Our knowledge of them was supposed to be founded upon the occurrence in our minds of "ideas" caused ultimately by the mechanical operation of "corpuscles" upon our bodily organs; and it was thought to be at least an open question how far these ideas could be regarded as reliable indications of the actual character of the "external" world. Fundamentally the physical world was thought of as a mechanical system describable in quantitative laws, but known to us only "indirectly," through the mediation of sensory ideas which in some respects almost certainly misled us as to the real character of our physical environment. By this way of seeing things Berkeley felt most violently "cramped." It appeared to him that the interposition of "ideas" could end only in the sceptical overthrow of our claims to any actual knowledge of the physical world. He felt that the logical conclusion of the mechanistic view must be atheism, the idea that matter was God or that there was no god at all. He could not see (and neither could Locke) how on this view the existence and immortality of the soul could be established. And in countless lesser details he thought that he found insoluble difficulties or undesirable conclusions. But then—and as it appears, quite suddenly—he came to see the whole situation differently. He changed, so to speak, his angle of vision. And at once all the problems seemed to disappear, to be replaced by a strange but startlingly simple new picture. Suppose that matter did not exist at all! What would be the advantages of this supposition? It would simply eliminate the problems of scepticism—for then there would be no "external world" as to which we could wonder how far our "ideas" corresponded with it. It would utterly deflate the pretensions of physical science, the "corpuscular philosophy"—for there would be nothing for mechanistic hypotheses to be *true* of, they would have to be presented as, at best, convenient fictions to facilitate prediction. And what would be the disadvantages? None surely—for so long as we suppose "ideas" to occur, the course of our actual experience would be exactly the same. And does it matter that there are no longer objects to cause these ideas? On the contrary—the notion that matter could be a true cause was in any case a bad one; and now the way is clear to attribute the occurrence of ideas to their proper origin, the will of God. On this view, then, scepticism is impossible; materialism is impossible; atheism is actually self-contradictory; so far from its being questionable whether the soul exists, there in fact exists *nothing* but "spirits and ideas." It there not "a vast view of things soluble hereby"? And so far from worrying over the fact that his new view has no ordinary, gross, experimental and factual consequences, Berkeley is particularly pleased to observe that from it Common Sense "receives no manner of disturbance." He believed indeed that his doctrine was capable of proof; but he never for a moment supposed it to be "verifiable."

Here, then, is a fair example of a metaphysical theory. Almost every paragraph that Berkeley wrote was intended to amplify, to defend, to explain, to render more acceptable the "vision" of a theocentric, immaterial universe by which he had seemed able at one stroke to escape from the difficulties and horrors of Locke's scientific, "corpuscular," material world. "The arguments he will offer, the attacks he will make, the suggestions he will advance are all devised for one end: to win other people over to his own way of looking at things, to change the whole climate of opinion. . . . What is decisive is that he has seen things from a new angle of vision. Compared to that everything else is secondary." He is not like a man proving theorems or relating his discoveries; he is like a reformer endeavouring to propagate a cause.

Is there any value in such theories as these? Do such visionary projects of reform ever really succeed? It might be said that such theories may have, and often do have, the purely intrinsic value of admirable intellectual achievements; they speak well, as it were, for the capacities of the human mind; but do they ever make any actual difference? Sometimes they do—but seldom, it seems, quite the difference that their prophets intend. It appears to be most evidently true that, in its simple foundations, our ordinary "way of seeing" the world is absolutely stable and obstinately unshakeable. Such a project as Berkeley's, which really requires us to abandon our notion of things as solid, substantial, enduring, indifferent to the presence or absence of percipient organisms, seems to attack our conceptual habits at so deep a level that it can really have no serious chance of succeeding. It is doubtful how far even Berkeley was able to retain the full sense of his vision for more than an occasional moment; one cannot so easily shake off what is natural to one's species. But we may, in other cases, come to see things differently in certain restricted fields—and really come to do so *naturally,* not in visionary moments only or in abstract theory. Dr. Waismann suggests that in the work of Descartes there may be "a prophetic aspect of the comprehensibility of nature, a bold anticipation of what has been achieved in science at a much later date. The true successors of Descartes were those who translated the spirit of this philosophy into deeds, not Spinoza or Malebranche but Newton and the mathematical description of nature." (Here Berkeley can be seen to have been working *against* the main trend of thought in his time.) And similarly the "true successors" of Hegel might be said to be, not the philosophers who elaborated his doctrines into ever-deepening obscurity, but the historians whom he taught to find in the passage of time not merely a succession of independent episodes, but intelligible processes of change, of growth and decay, having certain analogies with the life-cycle of organic beings. Certainly there *may* be fields of inquiry, areas of knowledge, in which some metaphysician's new way of seeing may have the most fruitful and important results. But there may not be. His theory may stand as a mere eccentricity, with some interest perhaps, but no effect on anything whatever. Whether this will be so, he will doubtless be unable to foresee.

Why are there today few, if any, metaphysicians? The answer to this question, I believe, has at least three branches. First, there have never been many real metaphysicians at any time. To be, after all, sufficiently obsessed by a visionary project of intellectual reform to spend years upon its systematization and propagation is, fortunately no doubt, a very rare condition. There may well have been in earlier times a large number of *second-hand* metaphysicians, parasitic expositors of and elaborators on the theories of some truly original figure. But such secondary labours are surely as pointless as they are usually uninteresting. Of what interest would it be to patch up, to amend and expound, the doctrines of Bradley, if really one had no inclination whatever to share the queer view from which his own fervour was derived? It is reasonable enough to abstain from such work as this; for many vastly more interesting problems lie ready to hand. Is it really surprising that most philosophers should find in these other problems their best occupation? They are fortunate today in that so very many quite unmetaphysical problems have been brought into the light.

Second, it can, I think, be reasonably said that the condition of true metaphysical fervour is today more difficult to achieve than was formerly the case; for it depends in large part upon a kind of illusion which, for good or ill and almost certainly .for good, is now inevitably rare. Much admirable philosophical work has been done upon the notion of "ways of seeing," of angles of vision, of—to speak more ponderously—alternative conceptual systems. We have become familiar enough with the idea that phenomena may be viewed in more than one way, comprehended within more than one theory, interpreted by more than one set of explanatory concepts. It has thus become almost impossible to believe that some *one* way of seeing, some *one* sort of theory, has any exclusive claim to be the *right* way; the notion of "reality" itself, it would commonly be held, must be given its sense in terms of some particular theory or view, so that the claim that any such theory reveals or corresponds to "reality" can be given a circular justification which is also open, in just the same way, to quite other views as well. But the belief that some new sort of theory is merely *possible*—that some novel set of concepts or categories *could* be employed —is hardly a sufficiently dynamic incentive to engender the production of a true metaphysical theory. If one has not, and one scarcely can have, the initial conviction that a novel "way of seeing" has some *unique* claim to acceptance, one is unlikely to undertake the considerable labour of equipping it in a full metaphysical panoply. Such work is impossible perhaps, and certainly unattractive, to the disillusioned.

Finally, there are no doubt in our "climate of thought" many factors of a more general kind that are in some way unfriendly to the metaphysical temperament. One might perhaps hazard the idea that metaphysical speculation has often arisen from, and often too been a substitute for, religious or theological doctrine. If so, it could be expected to show some decline in a period when very many people neither have, nor appear to be much oppressed by the want of, any serious religious convictions. It is not obvious that, if this were so, it ought to be deplored. It is, on the other hand, quite clear how undesirable it would be for philosophers to *pretend* to suffer from cosmic anxieties by which they were in fact not seriously troubled at all. Metaphysics, like religion, ought not to be manufactured in deference to any supposed requirements of intellectual decorum, or in the pursuit of some once genuine fervour which, in present conditions, would be synthetic or simulated.

ALFRED NORTH WHITEHEAD

*Foresight and Adventure**

Alfred North Whitehead (1861–1947) was an English mathematician and philosopher. He attended and later taught at Cambridge University until 1910 when he moved to the University of London where he became dean of the faculty of science. In 1924 he joined the faculty of Harvard University where he remained as professor of philosophy until he retired in 1937. He was the recipient of many honors. With Bertrand Russell he wrote *Principia Mathematica.* His philosophical writings include *The Concept of Nature, Science and the Modern World, Religion in the Making, Process and Reality,* and *Aims of Education and Other Essays.*

In the following selection from *Adventures of Ideas,* Whitehead says that in

*Reprinted with permission of Macmillan Publishing Co., Inc. from *Adventures of Ideas* by Alfred North Whitehead. Copyright 1929 by Macmillan Publishing Co., Inc., renewed 1957 by Evelyn Whitehead. Chapters VI and XIX with omissions.

our preparation for the future, foresight, as well as science, is needed. This foresight requires understanding which to some degree can be taught and acquired by a conscious effort. One problem today in acquiring it, however, is a great shortening of the time span of significant change. This contraction comes at a time when mankind is shifting its outlook and the compulsion of tradition, which until now has guided mankind, is losing its force. Philosophy can help ease this transition by providing insight and foresight and a sense of the worth of life, as well as by clarifying fundamental beliefs that lie at the base of character.

By the phrase Historical Foresight, I mean something quite different from the accurate exercise of Scientific Induction. Science is concerned with generalities. The generalities apply, but they do not determine the course of history apart from some anchorage in fact. There might have been many alternative courses of history conditioned by the same laws. Perhaps, if we knew enough of the laws, then we should understand that the development of the future from the past is completely determined by the details of the past and by these scientific laws which condition all generation. Unfortunately our knowledge of scientific laws is woefully defective, and our knowledge of the relevant facts of the present and the past is scanty in the extreme....

This catalogue of ignorances at once reminds us that our state is not that of blank absence of knowledge. Our ignorance is suffused with Foresight. Also the basis of our defect in foresight is our scant knowledge of the relevant detailed facts in past and present which are required for the appliction of the scientific laws. Where the circumstances are comparatively simple, as in Astronomy, we know that the facts and the astronomical laws provide an apparatus of great accuracy in forecaste. The main difficulty in Historical Foresight is the power of collecting and selecting the facts relevant to the particular type of forecaste which we wish to make. Discussions on the method of science wander off onto the topic of experiment. But experiment is nothing else than a mode of cooking the facts for the sake of exemplifying the law. Unfortunately the facts of history, even those of private individual history, are on too large a scale. They surge forward beyond control.

It is thus evident that this topic of Historical Foresight is not to be exhausted by a neat description of some definite methods. It is faced with two sources of difficulty, where science has only one. Science seeks the laws only, but Foresight requires in addition due emphasis on the relevant facts from which the future is to emerge. Of the two tasks required for Foresight, this selection amid the welter is the more difficult. Probably a neat doctrine of Foresight is impossible. But what can be done is to confine attention to one field of human activity, and to describe the type of mentality which seems requisite for the attainment of Foresight within that field....

The recent shortening of the time-span between notable changes in social customs is very obvious, if we examine history. Originally it depended upon some slow development of physical causes. For example, a gradual change of physical configuration such as the elevation of mountains: the time-span for such a change is of the order of a million years. Again, a gradual change of climate: the time-span for such a change is of the order of five-thousand years. Again a gradual over-population of the region occupied by some community with its consequent swarming into new territories: having regard to the huge death-rate of pre-scientific ages, the time-span for such a change was of the order of five-hundred years. Again, the sporadic inventions of new technologies, such as the chipping of flints, the invention of fire, the taming of animals, the invention of metallurgy: in the pre-scientific ages, the average time-span for such changes was, at least, of the order of five-hundred years. If we compare the technologies of civilizations west of Mesopotamia at the epochs 100 A.D., the culmination of the Roman Empire, and 1400 A.D., the close of the Middle Ages, we find practically no advance in technology. There was some gain in metallurgy, some elaboration of clock-work, the recent invention of gun powder with its influence all in the future, some advance in the art of navigation, also with its influence in the future. If we compare 1400 A.D. with 1700 A.D., there is a great advance; gunpowder, and printing, and navigation, and the technique of commerce, had produced their effect. But even then, the analogy between life in the eighteenth century and life in the great period of ancient Rome was singularly close, so that the peculiar relevance of Latin literature was felt vividly. In the fifty years between 1780 and 1830, a number of inventions came with a rush into effective operation. The age of steam power and of machinery was introduced. But for two generations, from 1830 to 1890, there was a singular uniformity in the principles of technology which were regulating the structure of society and the usages of business.

The conclusion to be drawn from this survey is a momentous one. Our sociological theories, our political philosophy, our practical maxims of business, our political economy, and our doctrines of education, are derived from an unbroken tradition of great thinkers and of practical examples, from the age of Plato in the fifth century before Christ to the end of the last century. The whole of this tradition is warped by the vicious assumption that each generation will substantially live amid the conditions governing the lives of its fathers and will transmit those conditions to mould with equal force the lives of its children. We are living in the first period of human history for which this assumption is false.

Of course in the past, there were great catastrophes: for example, plagues, floods, barbarian invasions. But, if such catastrophes were warded off, there was a stable, well-known condition of civilized life. This assumption subtly pervades the premises of political economy, and has permitted it to confine attention to a simplified edition of human nature. It is at the basis of our conception of the reliable business man, who has mastered a technique and never looks beyond his contracted horizon. It colours our political philosophy and our educational theory, with their overwhelming emphasis on past experience. The note of recurrence dominates the wisdom of the past, and still persists in many forms even where explicitly the fallacy of its modern application is admitted. The point is that in the past the time-span of important change was considerably longer than that of a single human life. Thus mankind was trained to adapt itself to fixed conditions.

Today this time-span is considerably shorter than that of human life, and accordingly our training must prepare individuals to face a novelty of conditions. But there can be no preparation for the unknown. It is at this point that we recur to the immediate topic, Foresight. We require such an understanding of the present conditions, as may give us some grasp of the novelty which is about to produce a measurable influence on the immediate future. Yet the doctrine, that routine is dominant in any society that is not collapsing, must never be lost sight of. Thus the grounds, in human nature and in the successful satisfaction of purpose, these grounds for the current routine must be understood; and at the same time the sorts of novelty just entering into social effectiveness have got to be weighed against the old routine. In this way the type of modification and the type of persistence exhibited in the immediate future may be foreseen.

It is now time to give some illustrations of assertions already made. Consider our main conclusions that our traditional doctrines of sociology, of political philosophy, of the practical conduct of large business, and of political economy are largely warped and vitiated by the implicit assumption of a stable unchanging social system. With this assumption it is comparatively safe to base reasoning upon a simplified edition of human nature. For well-known stimuli working under well-known conditions produce well-known reactions. It is safe then to assume that human nature, for the purpose in hand, is adequately described in terms of some of the major reactions to some of the major stimuli. For example, we can all remember our old friend, the economic man.

The beauty of the economic man was that we knew exactly what he was after. Whatever his wants were, he knew them and his neighbours knew them. His wants were those developed in a well-defined social system. His father and grandfather had the same wants, and satisfied them in the same way. So whenever there was a shortage, everyone—including the economic man himself—knew what was short, and knew the way to satisfy the consumer. In fact, the consumer knew what he wanted to consume. This was the demand. The producer knew how to produce the required articles, hence the supply. The men who got the goods onto the spot first, at the cheapest price, made their fortunes; the other producers were eliminated. This was healthy competition. This is beautifully simple and with proper elaboration is obviously true. It expresses the dominant truth exactly so far as there are stable well-tried conditions. But when we are concerned with a social system which in important ways is changing, this simplified conception of human relations requires severe qualification.

It is, of course, common knowledge that the whole trend of political economy during the last thirty or forty years has been away from these artificial simplifications. Such sharp-cut notions as "the economic man," "supply and demand," "competition," are now in process of dilution by a close study of the actual re-actions of various populations to the stimuli which are relevant to modern commerce. This exactly illustrates the main thesis. The older political economy reigned supreme for about a hundred years from the time of Adam Smith, because in its main assumptions it did apply to the general circumstances of life as led, then and for innumerable centuries in the past. These circumstances were then already passing away. But it still remained a dominant truth that in commercial relations men were dominated by well-conditioned reactions to completely familiar stimuli.

In the present age, the element of novelty which life affords is too prominent to be omitted from our calculations. A deeper knowledge of the varieties of human nature is required to determine the reaction, in its character and its strength, to those elements of novelty which each decade of years introduces into social life. The possibility of this deeper knowledge constitutes the Foresight under discussion.

Another example which concerns sociological habits, and thence business relations and the shifting values of property, is to be seen in the history of cities. Throughout the whole span of civilization up to the present moment, the growth of condensed aggregates of humans, which we call cities, has been an inseparable accompaniment of the growth of civilization. There are many obvious reasons, the defence of accumulated wealth behind city walls, the concentration of materials requisite for manufacture, the concentration of power in the form of human muscles and, later, in the form of available heat energy, the ease of mutual intercourse required for business relations, the pleasure arising from a concentration of aesthetic and cultural opportunities, the advantages of a concentration of governmental and other directing agencies, administrative, legal, and military.

But there are disadvantages in cities. As yet no civilization has been self-supporting. Each civilization is born, it culminates, and it decays. There is a widespread testimony that this ominous fact is due to inherent biological defects in the crowded life of cities. Now, slowly and at first faintly, an opposite tendency is showing itself. Better roads and better vehicles at first induced the wealthier classes to live on the outskirts of the cities. The urgent need for defence had also vanished. This tendency is now spreading rapidly downwards. But a new set of conditions is just showing itself. Up to the present time, throughout the eighteenth and nineteenth centuries, this new tendency placed the homes in the immediate suburbs, but concentrated manufacturing activity, business relations, government, and pleasure, in the centres of the cities. Apart from the care of children, and periods of sheer rest, the active lives were spent in the cities. In some ways, the concentration of such activities was even more emphasized, and the homes were pushed outwards even at the cost of the discomfort of commuting. But, if we examine the trend of technology during the past generation, the reasons for this concentration are largely disappearing. Still more, the reasons for the choice of sites for cities are also altering. Mechanical power can be transmitted for hundreds of miles, men can communicate almost instantaneously by telephone, the chiefs of great organizations can be transported by airplanes, the cinemas can produce plays in every village, music, speeches, and sermons can be broadcast. Almost every reason for the growth of cities, concurrently with the growth of civilization, has been profoundly modified.

What then is to be the future of cities, three hundred years hence, a hundred years hence, or even thirty years hence? I do not know. But I venture a guess:—that those who are reasonably fortunate in this foresight will make their fortunes, and that others will be ruined by mistakes in calculation....

...We are faced with a fluid, shifting situation in the immediate future. Rigid maxims, a rule-of-thumb routine, and caste-iron particular doctrines will spell ruin. The business of the future must be controlled by a somewhat different type of men to that of previous centuries. The type is already changing, and has already changed so far as the leaders are concerned. The Business Schools of Universities are concerned with spreading this newer type throughout the nations by aiming at the production of the requisite mentality.

I will conclude this chapter by a sketch of the Business Mind of the future. In the first place it is fundamental that there be a power of conforming to routine, of supervising routine, of constructing routine, and of understanding routine both as to its internal structure and as to its external purposes. Such a power is the bedrock of all practical efficiency. But for the production of the requisite Foresight, something more is wanted. This extra endowment can only be described as a philosophic power of understanding the complex flux of the varieties of human societies: for instance, the habit of noting varieties of demands on life, of serious purposes, of frivolous amusements. Such instinctive grasp of the relevant features of social currents is of supreme importance. For example, the time-span of various types of social behaviour is of the essence of their effect on policy. A widespread type of religious interest, with its consequent modes of behaviour, has a dominant life of about a hundred years, while a fashion of dress survives any time between three months and three years. Methods of agriculture change slowly. But the scientific world seems to be on the verge of far-reaching biological discoveries. The assumption of slow changes in agriculture must therefore be scanned vigilantly. This example of time-spans can be generalized. The quantitative aspect of social changes is of the essence of business relations. Thus the habit of transforming observation of qualitative changes into quantitative estimates should be characteristic of business mentality.

I have said enough to show that the modern commercial mentality requires many elements of discipline, scientific and sociological. But the great fact remains that details of relevant knowledge cannot be foreseen. Thus even for mere success, and apart from any question of intrinsic quality of life, an unspecialized aptitude for eliciting generalizations from particulars and for seeing the divergent illustration of generalities in diverse circumstances is required. Such a reflective power is essentially a philosophic habit: it is the survey of society from the standpoint of generality. This habit of general thought, undaunted by novelty, is the gift of philosophy, in the widest sense of that term.

But the motive of success is not enough. It produces a short-sighted world which destroys the sources of its own prosperity. The cycles of trade depression which afflict the world warn us that business relations are infected through and through with the disease of short-sighted motives. The robber barons did not conduce to the prosperity of Europe in the Middle Ages, though some of them died prosperously in their beds. Their example is a warning to our civilization. Also we must not fall into the fallacy of thinking of the business world in abstraction from the rest of the community. The business world is one main part of the very community which is the subject-matter of our study. The behaviour of the community is largely dominated by the business mind. A great society is a society in which its men of business think greatly of their functions. Low thoughts mean low behaviour, and after a brief orgy of exploitation low behaviour means a descending standard of life. The general greatness of the community, qualitatively as well as quantitatively, is the first condition for steady prosperity, buoyant, self-sustained, and commanding credit. The Greek philosopher who laid the foundation of all our finer thoughts ended his most marvellous dialogue with the reflection that the ideal state could never arrive till philosophers are kings. Today, in an age of democracy, the kings are the plain citizens pursuing their various avocations. There can be no successful democratic society till general education conveys a philosophic outlook.

Philosophy is not a mere collection of noble sentiments. A deluge of such sentiments does more harm than good. Philosophy is at once general and concrete, critical and appreciative of direct intuition. It is not—or, at least, should not be—a ferocious debate between irritable professors. It is a survey of possibilities and their comparison with actualities. In philosophy, the fact, the theory, the alternatives, and the ideal, are weighed together. Its gifts are insight and foresight, and a sense of the worth of life, in short, that sense of importance which nerves all civilized effort. Mankind can flourish in the lower stages of life with merely barbaric flashes of thought. But when civilization culminates, the absence of a coordinating philosophy of life, spread throughout the community, spells decadence, boredom, and the slackening of effort.

Every epoch has its character determined by the way its populations re-act to the material events which they encounter. This reason is determined by their basic beliefs—by their hopes, their fears, their judgments of what is worthwhile. They may rise to the greatness of an opportunity, seizing its drama, perfecting its art, exploiting its adventure, mastering intellectually and physically the network of relations that constitutes the very being of the epoch. On the other hand, they may collapse before the perplexities confronting them. How they act depends partly on their courage, partly on their intellectual grasp. Philosophy is an attempt to clarify those fundamental beliefs which finally determine the emphasis of attention that lies at the base of character.

Mankind is now in one of its rare moods of shifting its outlook. The mere compulsion of tradition has lost its force. It is our business—philosophers, students, and practical men—to re-create and reenact a vision of the world, including those elements of reverence and order without which society lapses into riot, and penetrated through and through with unflinching rationality. Such a vision is the knowledge which Plato identified with virtue. Epochs for which, within the limits of their development, this vision has been widespread are the epochs unfading in the memory of mankind. . . .

. . . The prolongation of outworn forms of life means a slow decadence in which there is repetition without any fruit in the reaping of value. There may be high survival power. For decadence, undisturbed by originality or by external forces, is a slow process. But the values of life are slowly ebbing. There remains the show of civilization, without any of its realities.

There is an alternative to this slow decline. A race may exhaust a form of civilization without having exhausted its own creative springs of originality. In that case, a quick period of transition may set in, which may or may not be accompanied by dislocations involving widespread unhappiness. Such periods are Europe at the close of the Middle Ages, Europe during the comparatively long Reformation Period, Europe at the end of the eighteenth century. Also let us hope that our present epoch is to be viewed as a period of change to a new direction of civilization, involving in its dislocations a minimum of human misery. And yet surely the misery of the Great War was sufficient for any change of epoch.

These quick transitions to new types of civilization are only possible when thought has run ahead of realization. The vigour of the race has then pushed forward into the adventure of imagination, so as to anticipate the physical adventures of exploration. The world dreams of things to come, and then in due season arouses itself to their realization. Indeed all physical adventure which is entered upon of set purpose involves an adventure of thought regarding things as yet unrealized. Before Columbus set sail for America, he had dreamt of the far East, and of the round world, and of the trackless ocean. Adventure rarely reaches its predetermined end. Columbus never reached China. But he discovered America.

Sometimes adventure is acting within limits. It can then calculate its end, and reach it. Such adventures are the ripples of change within one type of civilization, by which an epoch of given type preserves its freshness. But, given the vigour of adventure, sooner or later the leap of imagination reaches beyond the safe limits of the epoch, and beyond the safe limits of learned rules of taste. It then produces the dislocations and confusions marking the advent of new ideals for civilized effort.

A race preserves its vigour so long as it harbours a real contrast between what has been and what may be; and so long as it is nerved by the vigour to adventure beyond the safeties of the past. Without adventure civilization is in full decay.

Index